T0301829

The Character of Petroleum Licences

NEW HORIZONS IN ENVIRONMENTAL AND ENERGY LAW

Series Editors: Kurt Deketelaere, *Professor of Law, University of Leuven, Belgium and University of Dundee, Scotland* and Zen Makuch, *Reader in Law, Barrister, Imperial College, London, UK*

Environmental law – including the pressing considerations of energy law and climate change – is an increasingly important area of legal research and practice. Given the growing interdependence of global society and the significant steps being made towards environmental protection and energy efficiency, there are few people untouched by environmental and energy lawmaking processes.

At the same time, environmental and energy law is at a crossroads. The command and control methodology that evolved in the 1960s and 1970s for air, land and water protection may have reached the limit of its environmental protection achievements. New life needs to be injected into our environmental protection regimes – perhaps through the concept of sustainability in its environmental, economic and social forms. The same goes for energy policy and law, where liberalization, environmental protection and security of supply are at the centre of attention. This important series seeks to press forward the boundaries of environmental and energy law through innovative research into environmental and energy law, doctrine and case law. Adopting a wide interpretation of environmental and energy law, it includes contributions from both leading and emerging international scholars.

Titles in the series include:

Managing Facts and Feelings in Environmental Governance
Edited by Lorenzo Squintani, Jan Darpö, Luc Lavrysen and Peter-Tobias Stoll

Managing the Risk of Offshore Oil and Gas Accidents
The International Legal Dimension
Edited by Günther Handl and Kristoffer Svendsen

Governing Marine Living Resources in the Polar Regions
Edited by Nengye Liu, Cassandra M. Brooks and Tianbo Qin

Tax Expenditures and Environmental Policy
Hope Ashiabor

The Character of Petroleum Licences
A Legal Culture Analysis
Edited by Tina Soliman Hunter, Jørn Øyrehagen Sunde and Ernst Nordtveit

The Character of Petroleum Licences

A Legal Culture Analysis

Edited by

Tina Soliman Hunter

*Professor of Energy, Environment and Resources Law,
Macquarie Law School, Macquarie University, Australia*

Jørn Øyrehagen Sunde

*Professor, Department for Public and International Law,
University of Oslo, Norway*

Ernst Nordtveit

Professor, Faculty of Law, University of Bergen, Norway

NEW HORIZONS IN ENVIRONMENTAL AND ENERGY
LAW

 Edward Elgar
PUBLISHING

Cheltenham, UK • Northampton, MA, USA

Published by
Edward Elgar Publishing Limited
The Lypiatts
15 Lansdown Road
Cheltenham
Glos GL50 2JA
UK

Edward Elgar Publishing, Inc.
William Pratt House
9 Dewey Court
Northampton
Massachusetts 01060
USA

A catalogue record for this book
is available from the British Library

Library of Congress Control Number: 2020944715

This book is available electronically in the **Elgar**online
Law subject collection
http://dx.doi.org/10.4337/9781788976206

ISBN 978 1 78897 619 0 (cased)
ISBN 978 1 78897 620 6 (eBook)

Printed and bound in Great Britain by TJ Books Limited, Padstow, Cornwall

Contents

List of contributors   vii
Acknowledgements   viii

1   Introduction   1
    Jørn Øyrehagen Sunde and Tina Soliman Hunter

2   Characterisation of Australia's petroleum licences:
    property capable of acquisition on 'just terms'?   16
    Tina Soliman Hunter

3   The legal character of petroleum licences in the United
    States of America   51
    John S. Lowe

4   The legal character of petroleum licences in Canada   72
    Nigel Bankes

5   The legal character of petroleum licences in Uganda   95
    Emmanuel B. Kasimbazi

6   Petroleum licences – a legal culture perspective: the United
    Kingdom   119
    Greg Gordon and John Paterson

7   Oil and gas licences – a legal nature perspective: the Netherlands   139
    Martha M. Roggenkamp

8   Legal character of petroleum licences under Norwegian law   159
    Ernst Nordtveit

9   Russia: legal culture and character of Russian petroleum licences   186
    Irina Fodchenko

10 The Mexican petroleum licence of 2013   207
    Guillermo J. Garcia Sanchez

11   The legal character of petroleum licences in the People's
     Republic of China   234
     Yong Li

12   Afterword: Licence rights – what's left?   253
     Terence Daintith

Index   262

Contributors

Nigel Bankes, Professor and Chair of Natural Resources Law, University of Calgary, Canada

Terence Daintith, Honorary Professor and sometime Director, Centre for Energy, Petroleum and Mineral Law and Policy, University of Dundee, UK

Irina Fodchenko, PhD Research Fellow, Faculty of Law, University of Oslo, Norway

Guillermo J. Garcia Sanchez, Associate Professor of Law, Texas A&M University School of Law, USA

Greg Gordon, Professor of Law, School of Law, University of Aberdeen, UK

Tina Soliman Hunter, Professor of Energy, Environment and Resources Law, Macquarie Law School, Macquarie University, Australia

Emmanuel B. Kasimbazi, Professor of Law, School of Law, Makerere University, Kampala, Uganda

Yong Li, Ph.D, Attorney at law, Sequoia Smith LLP, Beijing, China

John S. Lowe, George W. Hutchison Chair of Energy Law and Professor of Law, Southern Methodist University, Dallas, Texas, USA

Ernst Nordtveit, Professor dr. juris, Faculty of Law, University of Bergen, Norway

Jørn Øyrehagen Sunde, Department for Public and International Law, University of Oslo, Norway

John Paterson, Professor of Law, School of Law, University of Aberdeen, UK

Martha M. Roggenkamp, Professor in Energy Law and Director of the Groningen Centre of Energy Law and Sustainability, University of Groningen, The Netherlands

Acknowledgements

The editors would like to express their deepest gratitude to Professor Terence Daintith, who not only took the time to read all the chapters, but also, in writing the Afterword, brought together the 1981 study and this study.

This book would not have been possible without funding under the SPIRE-Program (Strategic Program for International Research Collaboration) at the University of Bergen. The editors wish to extend a warm thanks to the University of Bergen for providing the funding for the research group which initially explored this topic, and without which the book would not have been possible. Likewise, the editors also wish to thank the University of Aberdeen, and the Aberdeen University Centre for Energy Law (AUCEL) in particular, for hosting the research group, which enabled the authors to gather together.

Finally, thanks are extended to Edward Elgar, and especially our editor Amber Watts, for her infinite patience during delays, and her rapid response in a period of pandemic.

The book is dedicated to Associate Professor Anita Rønne from the University of Copenhagen who participated in the research group and should have contributed to the book, but tragically passed away before that could happen.

Tina Soliman Hunter, Jørn Øyrehagen Sunde, and Ernst Nordtveit.

1. Introduction

Jørn Øyrehagen Sunde and Tina Soliman Hunter

1. INTRODUCTION

Forty years ago, at the height of the dominance of the Organization of Petroleum Exporting Countries (OPEC) and the approaching peak of the importance of oil, scholars from a number of western legal traditions gathered to consider the legal character of the primary vehicle governing the relationship between oil companies and host states – the petroleum licence.[1] The resulting papers, collected together in the monograph *The Legal Character of Petroleum Licences: A Comparative Study* (the 1981 study) and edited by Terence Daintith, considered the legal nature and the legal context of the licence 'in the sense of several legal and constitutional rules of the relevant system within which it operates.'[2] Encompassing a variety of legal cultures and experiences, the 1981 study links the diverging jurisdictions through legal traditions – Australian, UK and Canada law through its common law heritage, and Denmark and Norway with its shared (until the 19th century) legal tradition based on *Dansk Lov* 1683, and the Norwegian equivalent of 1687.[3] In each of the countries examined in the 1981 study, the licences examined had broadly the same content and effect.[4] Collectively identified as an access licence, the licences examined grant the licence holder exclusive rights for exploration and/or production, and transfers to the licensee title in any petroleum extracted.[5] In receiving

---

[1]   Various terms in various jurisdictions are used to describe the document through which petroleum exploration rights are obtained. Like in the 1981 study, the term licence will be used inclusively here to collectively refer to these documents in a general sense. In the study of a particular jurisdiction the terms of art that used in that jurisdiction will be employed.

[2]   Terence Daintith (ed), *The Legal Character of Petroleum Licences: A Comparative Study* (IBA, 1981), 3.

[3]   Ibid, 9.

[4]   Ibid, 9.

[5]   Ibid, 9.

these rights from the state to explore for and take petroleum, the licence holder also has a corresponding duty to pay the host state certain fees, together with a royalty on production or a special taxation. In addition, the licence holder agrees to accept a range of obligations and powers of state supervision and/or intervention in the way he carries out operations under the licence. Therefore, as noted by Daintith, the licence contains elements of both consensus and bargain, particularly in relation to the financial terms on which the licensee undertakes the risky venture of petroleum exploration,[6] and the imposition by the state of a host of obligations 'designed to protect the public interest in the proper exploitation of the state's petroleum wealth.'[7]

Thus, the licence is essentially the vehicle upon which the state grants access to its petroleum resources and exerts control over the licensee exploiting that petroleum through varying levels of intervention. The question of the legal character of a petroleum licence is necessary in order to ascertain and understand the rights accrued by the licensee, and the way the host state can deal with the licence. Such dealings include the alteration of the conditions of the licence, the revocation, suspension or cancellation of a licence, or an alteration to the regulation of the operation of petroleum recovery. It is these first two elements upon which we primarily turn our attention to in this book. The unilateral alteration of the conditions for a licence has long been the subject of discussion and even disagreement between the licensee and the host state. Generally, such disagreement focuses on the fiscal terms relating to taxation or the payment of fees and royalties. However, in the modern age there are other reasons for the alteration of the terms of the licences.

Such alterations are exemplified by the UK jurisdiction where rapidly declining production in the North Sea has prompted the UK government to require licensees to work both individually and together in order to maximize the recovery of petroleum from the North Sea. Such 'working together' includes the requirement to allow third party access to facilities and infrastructure. Such an alteration, hitherto unheard of in the UK, challenges the very notion of the legal character of the petroleum licence in the UK. Similarly, public response to exploration drilling by Equinor in the frontier Great Australian Bight region raised the possibility of cancellation or revocation of exploration licences, or a failure to grant permission to undertake drilling activities, both prior to and after petroleum was discovered. It is within this modern context that the need to revisit the legal character of petroleum licences arose.

This book revisits the 1981 original study into the concept of the legal character of petroleum licences. It incorporates most of the original jurisdictions

---

6   Ibid, 9.
7   Ibid, 9.

studied, as well as encompassing some new jurisdictions, not all from the western legal tradition.[8] Aside from the incorporation of a study of Australia, Canada, Norway and the UK which were considered in the original study, this book has extended the study to include the USA, the Netherlands, Uganda, Russia, Mexico and China. The USA and the Netherlands were incorporated to reflect their longevity as petroleum jurisdictions and to demonstrate how the legal character of petroleum licences both exist and have evolved in those jurisdictions. Uganda, as an emerging petroleum jurisdiction operating within a former colonial common law jurisdiction, has been incorporated as it provides an excellent study of emerging post-colonial African states, and the challenges in establishing a licensing system. This book also incorporates three non-western legal traditions: Russia, Mexico and China. For Russia and Mexico, petroleum has been a longstanding resource that has been exploited in each state. However, due to political and ideological factors, production has been, until recently, the purview of the state only. Similarly, China, although without a long petroleum exploration and production history, also exerts strong state control over petroleum production. Given the prominence of these states in global petroleum, it is necessary to include such states that are prominent within the petroleum system but differ considerably to the previously studied western legal traditions. In doing so, it is possible to gain a different perspective on the legal character of petroleum licences by examining states where the control exerted is strong and the government seeks to not merely be a bystander but also participate in petroleum activities.

An important reason for considering the legal character of a petroleum licence is that of security for the licensee. As owner of the petroleum (except for the US in some circumstances), the state has the capacity to control access to, and conditions of, access to petroleum. A licence that grants access to petroleum differs to one that grants operational authority. Therefore, this study, like the 1981 study, focuses on petroleum exploration and production licences. However, in emerging jurisdictions such as Uganda and China, there is also a consideration of operational licences given the need to discern between the access and operational licences, and how they interact in these states. The rights conferred by access licences differ greatly to operational licences. By their very nature operational licences infer a mere administrative right to undertake an activity, such as the placing of an installation of a pipeline. Operational licences are therefore required for permission to use the area. Such use is part of the access licence but requires separate operational

---

[8]   Originally this study was to include an analysis of Denmark, in line with the original study. However, this chapter is not included due to the untimely death of Professor Anita Ronne, who participated in the workshop that preceded this book.

licences granted in some jurisdictions. An operational licence is administrative in nature, akin to other administrative rights that grant a right to use that can be withdrawn if the licence holder does not comply with the conditions. This is because under an operational licence nothing is taken from the land, but rather makes use of the land. What sets apart petroleum access licences from operational licences is that a petroleum access licence confers upon the licence holder the right to look for and ultimately take petroleum that belongs to the state (or the state has sovereign right over), which can then be sold for profit by the licence holder. Given the proprietary nature of a petroleum access title, the legal character of this title is of upmost importance and deserving of further study. Therefore, it is the petroleum access title that is the focus of this book in a similar manner to the focus of the original 1981 study.

2.   THE CONCEPT OF LEGAL CHARACTER

As a concept, 'legal character' has no set definition. If one were to look up the concept in a legal dictionary, it would not be possible to find legal character defined in a readily accessible manner. Yet, the concept of legal character first used by Daintith in *The Legal Character of Petroleum Licences* is not defined. [9] In the original 1981 study on the legal character of petroleum licences, Daintith discusses the notion, particularly in the context of clashing legal values specific to different cultures. However, the term itself is not defined even though it is clearly an integral part of the study and gives its name to the title of the book. This book, in continuing the work of Daintith, also utilises the concept of 'legal character.' Indeed, a search in legal databases finds many articles written on the 'legal character' of all manner of legal areas, including international agreements,[10] joint ventures[11] and agricultural enterprises.[12] Although utilising legal character in analysing a legal area, in all of these articles the term legal character is not defined. Yet in order to use 'legal character' as a handy taxonomy in analysing petroleum licences, it is necessary to define what 'legal character' is.

In this context, the term legal character refers to the attributes and qualities that a petroleum licence possesses. In broad terms, such a character may be

---

[9]   Terence Daintith (ed), *The Legal Character of Petroleum Licences: A Comparative Study* (IBA, 1981).
[10]   L E S Fawcett, 'The Legal Character of International Agreements' (1953) 30 *British Year Book of International Law* 381–400.
[11]   Ozel Hukuk, 'Legal Character of Joint Venture' (2017) 2017(2) *Yildirim Beyazit Hukuk Dergisi* 97–126.
[12]   Jean Schmidt and Akar Ocal, 'Legal Character of Agricultural Enterprises' (1980) 10(3) *Banka ve Ticaret Hukuku Dergisi* 769–72.

contractual in terms of the contractual relationship between the host state and the oil company or it may be administrative in nature, such as a grant of a petroleum licence as an administrative right. It may also be proprietary in nature, even though this may not be specified, since the grant of a right to recover petroleum necessarily imbue property rights, given that the oil company is granted permission to take petroleum from the land upon severance.[13]

The legal character also pertains to what category we place a legal phenomenon in, and this will influence the evaluation and which rules, principles and values influence the solution. In contract law the important value is to secure foreseeability by making the parties bound to the contract, while in constitutional and administrative law, the importance of the state maintaining its ability to secure public interests by new legislation is important. Licences are influenced by both considerations, thus presenting the legal classification conundrum. There is a clear difference between states as resource owners and private resource owners, as the latter do not have any responsibility for public interests and no possibility to change the legislation.

3. THE LEGAL CULTURE APPROACH

Legal culture is, like legal character, an unquestionable fact that is still hard to define. We can observe that law is experienced and practices differently at different times and in different places. However, it is difficult to analyse and precisely understand the reasons for the differences. Hence, too often legal character and legal culture just become labels put on a phenomenon when we know what matters, but do not know exactly how and why.

Still, we have chosen to ask the contributors to this book to use legal culture as a backdrop when exploring the petroleum licence regime of their country. In doing so, we wanted to obtain a more contextual and system-oriented approach, teasing out not only the facts of the petroleum licence regime, but its preconditions and inner coherence.

This is an ambitious goal. First, because a context and a system are endlessly far-reaching, and any delineation will be artificial. Second, because the context and system relations of each country is different, and hence where you draw the line differs. However, this is taking legal culture in its purity. However, legal culture varies, and hence studies with a legal cultural backdrop can and will be different. Importantly, a legal cultural approach can be used to bring out structures and patterns. We have found that despite all their differences, we can still group the petroleum licensing regimes investigated in this book

---

[13] The term severance refers to when the petroleum reaches the surface at the top of the wellhead.

into three categories, based on their distinct characteristics attributed to the relationship between state and industry: minimal, regulatory and participatory intervention regimes. On an abstract level, what determines the categorization are political, legal and economic factors. On a more fundamental level, the regimes are characterized by the role of courts in developing the law and securing rights, the character of the licences and how they are obtained, and the role of the industry in the economy.

Can legal culture explain the petroleum licensing regimes in different countries? To a large extent, a petroleum licensing regime is also a question of politics and economy, and not law alone. This we will deal with later. It is the character of a legal culture, that such factors are intertwined and hard to detect. In the following, we will use the legal cultural approach to detect and display what we find are the characteristics and the internal relationships of the petroleum regimes investigated in this book.

However, first we must start with an essential acknowledgement: the essence in the notion of legal culture is that one size does not fit all, also in a legal context. When it comes to petroleum licensing regimes, this means that one regime will not be exactly like another, even if efforts are made to achieve parallelism. This has two implications.

The first implication is that universal law can never be more than an ideal that serves as inspiration for local law. The existence of universal law can be debated endlessly. However, in European legal history the rule has been the existence of law with universal aspirations. That is law that at one point in history is experienced as and claimed to have universal validity. Such law is typically natural law, Roman law, Canon law, human rights, UN-law and – in a much narrower context – EU-law. EU-law does apply to some extent to petroleum licensing through the Hydrocarbons Licensing Directive of 1994. It is hence of importance to the United Kingdom, the Netherlands and Norway, whose petroleum regimes are explored in this book. However, EU-law has a limited effect on the regimes in these countries, and despite some similarities they are in general quite different. In general, law with universal aspirations does not shape petroleum regimes. The similarities and differences of different petroleum regimes can hence not be explained by their relation to law with universal aspirations, and this topic will not be any further explored. Instead, similarities and differences stem from the extent you build a petroleum licence regime on 1) existing national law, 2) the petroleum law of other countries, and 3) to what extent you alter and adjust the law you borrow from others to fit with existing national law.

This brings us to the second implication, which is that a legal idea, principle or rule cannot be transplanted from one legal context to another without an alteration of content and function. This is of large relevance to petroleum regimes. Historically, a country has looked to the legal regimes of other countries when making their own. The reason is that law is an instrument to create stability in society. To alter existing law and produce new law, we can rely on experience or experiment. Legal experiment is not unknown in legal history. When the Norwegian Parliament in 2002 enacted new legislation stating that 40% of board members must be women,[14] it was a globally unprecedented rule. The Norwegian legal experiment was later adopted in several countries based on the Norwegian experience.[15] However, even this legal experiment was not entirely cut loose from experience, since women from the middle of the 19th century had gradually been granted more and more rights and responsibilities without the anticipated catastrophe occurring.

In general, experience is the main source for legal change. Legal experience is, very generally speaking, of two kinds: historical and comparative. Historical experience can be of relevance when changing the law. For instance, the French mining legislation from 1810, *Loi conçernant les mines, les minières, et les carrières*, was adopted in the Netherlands during the French occupation during the Napoleonic wars becoming a pillar in Dutch petroleum legislation until it was replaced in 2003. In general, mining law has been of importance in the first phase when developing petroleum law. However, in general it is limiting to be guided by history when making something new. Rather you want to build on the more recent experience of others instead of your own history. It is in this transplanting process when looking to comparative experience that a notion of legal culture appears.

4.   LEGAL CULTURE AND PETROLEUM LICENSING REGIMES

A major acknowledgement made by Alan Watson in his classic *Legal Transplants: An Approach to Comparative Law* from 1974, is that legal transplanting is historically a major source of legal development. It can be debated how well the term 'legal transplant' describe the actual process.[16] We will instead turn our attention to history, since the notion of legal culture is as old as the idea of universal law and of legal transplanting. In the 7th century Isidor of Sevilla, a bishop on the Iberian Peninsula, noted that good laws were those adjusted to local conditions and customs: 'A law should be honourable,

---

[14]   Morten Huse, *Boards, Governance and Value Creation: The Human Side of Corporate Governance* (Cambridge, 1997) 94–95.

[15]   See for instance *New York Times*, 6 March 2015, 'Germany Sets Gender Quota in Boardrooms'; www.nytimes.com/2015/03/07/world/europe/german-law-requires -more-women-on-corporate-boards.html, accessed 14 April 2020.

[16]   See for instance Esin Örücü, 'Law as Transposition' (2002) 51(2) *The International and Comparative Law Quarterly* 205–23.

just, feasible, in agreement with nature, in agreement with the custom of the country, appropriate to the time and place.'[17] The need for local adjustment of law, as expressed by Isidor of Sevilla, became a central tenet within the Church in the Middle Ages. Hence, throughout the Middle Ages Canon Law was to a large degree generously adjusted to the local culture, including the legal culture, in which it was applied. The same idea was later expressed in 1748 by Charles Montesquieu in the publication *De l'esprit des lois*, where, like Isidor of Sevilla, Montesquieu advised the lawmaker to make law in accordance with the local natural and cultural conditions:

> They [the laws] should be in relation to the climate of each country, to the quality of its soil, to its situation and extent, to the principal occupation of the natives ... they should have relation to the degree of liberty which the constitution will bear; to the religion of the inhabitants, to the inclinations, riches, numbers, commerce, manners, and customs. In fine, they have relations to each other, as also to their origin, to the intent of the legislator, and to the order of things on which they are established; in all of which different lights they ought to be consider.[18]

In the aftermath it can be claimed that legal culture for Montesquieu was a factor to take into consideration when legislating. These ideas were of great importance to the emergence of the idea of a close relationship between nation and law.[19] Thus, the notion of legal culture was there, but not the term. This is because until recently, the notion of legal culture was based on observation of actual practice and not a theoretical exercise and label.

The American professor in law and legal historian Lawrence M. Friedman was a pioneer in taking the notion of legal culture and turning it into an analytical tool to understand law and – and not at least in – society. In his 1975 book *Legal Systems* he defined legal culture as 'ideas, values, attitudes and beliefs of a specific group of people towards law.'[20] In a 1990 article he refined the definition to be 'ideas, attitudes, values, and opinions about law, the legal system, and legal institutions in some given population.'[21] This definition can be taken as representative of a whole tradition within legal cultural research

---

[17]   Bishop of Seville, *The Etymologies of Isidor of Sevilla* (Cambridge, 2006) 121 no. xxi.

[18]   Charles Montesquieu, *The Spirit of the Laws* (Batoche Books, 2001) 23.

[19]   See Roger Cotterrell, 'Comparative Law and Legal Culture', in *The Oxford Handbook of Comparative Law*, Mathias Reimann and Reinhard Zimmermann (eds) (Oxford, 2019) 714–15.

[20]   Lawrence Friedman, *The Legal System: A Social Science Perspective* (Russell Sage Foundation, 1977) 223.

[21]   Lawrence M Friedman, 'Some Thoughts on Comparative Legal Culture', in *Comparative and Private International Law – essays in Honor of John Henry Merryman on his Seventieth Birthday* (Duncker & Humblot, 1990) 53.

where the emphasis is on mentality rather than on institutions.[22] There is also another tradition, and the English professor in law and comparatist John Bell claims that '[T]he law is something more than simply a system of rules or legal standards. Those rules operate in a context of institutions, professions and values that form together a "legal culture".'[23] Legal culture therefore is not merely a question of ideas and of law, but also the institutional practices that constitute law.[24] With this work we place ourselves more in the latter tradition, and define legal culture as ideas and expectations of law made operational through institutional(-like) factors.[25] We find that a legal culture is created in the interplay between ideas, expectations and practice.

The dominant practice shaping legal culture is conflict resolution. A society can do, and has historically done, without for instance legislation and professional lawyers. However, it cannot do without conflict resolution without collapsing in violence and chaos. When wanting to detect the character of law, starting by looking at conflict resolution will most of the time give the best result. Not because conflict resolution will always give you the answers you are seeking, but it will always direct you to the answers.

This acknowledgement is an important part of the backdrop for our classification of petroleum licence regimes in three categories: minimal, regulatory and participatory intervention regimes.[26] Viewing a petroleum licence as a contract becomes more natural in countries with the judiciary as a branch of government to be reckoned with in politics and society. This is because contract law is then mainly developed through court practice, which again assures that the courts, based on the actual arguments of the parties, will not restrain from reviewing the law in a petroleum licence dispute and act to secure rights. In countries where the judiciary (the courts) is a weak branch of government, the development of contract law will be done through legislation, and security for rights is hence secured by acts of the legislature rather than courts. Hence, petroleum licences tend to be more of an administrative right than a contract.

We find that the judiciary is a branch of government to be reckoned with in countries like Australia, USA and Canada. This is because the courts operate

---

[22]   See the discussion in Cotterrell 2019: 720–4.

[23]   John Bell, *Judiciaries within Europe* (Cambridge University Press, 2006) 6, a definition he also uses in John Bell, *French legal cultures* (Butterworths, 2001).

[24]   Jørn Øyrehagen Sunde, 'Managing the Unmanageable – an Essay Concerning Legal Cultural Understanding', in *Comparing Legal Cultures*, Knut Einar Skodvin, Søren Koch, Jørn Øyrehagen Sunde (eds), (Fagbokforlaget, 2017) 15 (13–25).

[25]   Jørn Øyrehagen Sunde, 'Champagne at the Funeral – An Introduction to Legal Culture', in *Rendezvous of European Legal Cultures*, Knut Einar Skodvin, Jørn Øyrehagen Sunde (eds), (Fagbokforlaget, 2010) 20 (11–28).

[26]   Brent F Nelsen, *The State Offshore: Petroleum, Politics and State Intervention on the British and Norwegian Continental Shelves* (Praeger, 1991) 8–9.

according to a *stare decisis* principle and are interpreters of the constitution. The petroleum licensing regimes in these countries also have much in common, and we have classified them as having a minimal intervention regime, where each jurisdiction is characterised by the State engaging in setting the laws and regulations for petroleum activities, and control over important aspects of petroleum development that have lasting effects, such as production levels and field priorities are largely left in the hands of the oil companies.[27] That means firstly that the petroleum licences, at least for the USA and Canada, are as much a contract as an administrative grant by government. This is again linked to petroleum being a part of a property rights regime instead of purely attributable to state sovereignty. In all these countries the federalist system of government means that the regulation of petroleum is a matter of constitutional interpretation, as well as often a negotiation between states/provinces and the federal government. Nowhere is this clearer than in Australia where the Offshore Constitutional Settlement sees the sharing of regulation of petroleum activities between the Commonwealth and states, with states regulating the first three nautical miles seaward from baseline, and the Commonwealth government the remainder. In these countries petroleum licences are granted according to a bidding system where the largest bid wins, and they have no national oil company that is both a petroleum industry and government actor at one and the same time. All together, these factors reflect that petroleum is an industry, and like any other industry is regulated legally and not politically.

Countries with a judiciary to be reckoned with to some extent, like the United Kingdom and the Netherlands,[28] we have classified as having a regulatory intervention regime. In this regime, the state assumes the role of overseer of activities, with the state not content to merely referee from the sidelines. Rather, they play an active role in every aspect of petroleum development, with the state involved as deeply as possible in the day-to-day operations without actually engaging in the activity itself.[29] Although the United Kingdom is the cradle of the *stare decisis* principle, due to the Parliament sovereignty principle the courts are no major interpreter of the constitution.[30] Dutch courts formally stand in the French tradition with a weak judiciary. However, they write

---

[27] Ibid, 8.
[28] Since the Uganda petroleum licence regime is still in an initial phase, we do not yet have the information we need to display the character of the Ugandan regime on the same level and the UK and Dutch regimes.
[29] Nelsen 1991: 8–9.
[30] See Neil Andrews, 'The Supreme Court of the United Kingdom: A Selective Tribunal with the Final Say in Most Matters', in *Supreme Courts in Transition in China and the West*, Cornelis Ehndrik (Remco) van Rhee and Yulin Fu (eds) (Springer, 2017) 39 (37–51).

lengthy decisions and take former decisions into account when passing new ones.[31] In both jurisdictions, Parliament sovereignty has been on the losing end for a couple of decades, as seen for instance by the Dutch *Urgenda* case and the English *Heathrow Third Runway* case, both dating from 2020.[32] In both the UK and the Netherlands, petroleum licences are partly contractual and partly grants. Licences are awarded according to an objective discretionary system. Here, there is no bid system, but rather a system where several considerations are also taken into account. The considerations to be taken into account have, since 1994, been stipulated in Articles 4 and 5 of the Hydrocarbon Directive.[33] There are no state-owned oil companies, but each has a major international oil company – British Petroleum in the United Kingdom and Shell in the Netherlands – that serves as a receiver of political signals to the industry. In these countries the petroleum industry is an industry, but more than just one industry among others. Here, the dominance of the petroleum activity and company is typical, as is the role of the state in actively managing both petroleum activities and the industry. Uganda appears to be an apparent outlier in this classification, given its weak judiciary. However, it must be remembered that the Ugandan legal system is based on the English legal system, dominated by residual British law. Hence, Uganda can be readily classified in a similar vein to UK common law.

Countries where the judiciary is a weak branch of government, that is where the courts do not operate according to a *stare decisis* principle and are no major interpreter of the constitution, often have a more participatory intervention regime. In these countries we find that petroleum licences are government grants based on state sovereignty, the highest bid is not the sole consideration if there is a bidding system, and state oil companies are both a petroleum industry and state interests influence petroleum governance. These countries in our study are Norway, Russia, Mexico and China. In Norway, Russia and Mexico, the petroleum industry is an industry of great national importance, while it in China is an industry of national priority.

---

[31]   See CR van Rhee and RR Verkerk, 'The Supreme Cassation Court of the Netherlands: Efficient Engineer for the Unity and Development of the Law', in *Supreme Courts in Transition in China and the West*, Cornelis Ehndrik (Remco) van Rhee and Yulin Fu (eds) (Springer, 2017) 95 (77–96).

[32]   The Urgenda-case in the Hoge Raad 13 January 2020; https://uitspraken .rechtspraak.nl/inziendocument?id=ECLI:NL:HR:2019:2007, accessed 14 April 2020, and the Heathrow third runway-case in the Court of Appeal (Civil Division) 27 February 2020; www.judiciary.uk/judgments/r-friends-of-the-earth-v-secretary-of -state-for-transport-and-others/, accessed 14 April 2020.

[33]   Directive 94/22/EC of the European Parliament and of the Council of 30 May 1994 on the conditions for granting and using authorisations for the prospection, explo-ration and production of hydrocarbons.

Table 1.1 Overview of petroleum licensing regimes

Country	The role of courts		Character petroleum licences	Bidding system	National petroleum company	The character of the petroleum industry
	Stare decisis	Constitutional interpreter				
Australia	Yes	Yes	Grant	Work Program and Cash Bid	No	Industry
USA	Yes	Yes	Contract	Cash Bid	No	Industry
Canada	Yes	Yes	Contract	Cash Bid	No	Industry
United Kingdom	Yes	Some	Contract and grant	Objective Discretionary	One large petroleum company in the nation	Industry of importance
The Netherlands	Some	Some	Contract and grant	Objective Discretionary	One large petroleum company in the nation	Industry of importance
Uganda	Yes, although rely on UK cases	Some	Contract and grant	To be decided/ cash	Contemplated but not to date	Not yet determined
Norway	Yes	Yes	Grant	Objective Discretionary	Yes	Industry of large national importance
Russia	No	No	Grant	Dysfunctional	Yes	Industry of large national importance
Mexico	No	No	Grant	Dysfunctional	Yes	Industry of large national importance
China	No	No	Grant	Dysfunctional	Yes	Industry of large national importance

This leaves us with the overview of the three different categories of petroleum licensing regimes we have identified in Table 1.1.

However, it is not quite as simple as this. If we first look at the category participatory intervention, Norway has a judiciary to be reckoned with, operating according to a *stare decisis* principle, with a major role in interpreting the constitution, having performed constitutional review since 1821,[34] yet is still a participatory intervention petroleum regime. Norway has no bidding system, not even a dysfunctional one like in Mexico, but grant licences according to an objective discretionary system. Norway has a tradition – though modified over the last two decades – of one single national oil company, like Mexico, and not two or three like Russia and China, that for decades was a dominant actor in the Norwegian sector. In addition, in Norway the state determines the joint venture parties within a licence and also selects the licence operator, which is a system you do not find in China for instance.

Perhaps one reason for this outlier nature of Norway is the type of state participation. Whereas once Norway had a state oil company that was a vehicle for state entrepreneurship and control, similar to Mexico, Russia and China, the partial privatisation of Statoil through an IPO on the Oslo and New York stock exchanges means that although Statoil – now Equinor – participates as a state oil company, it no longer acts on behalf of the state's interest. Rather it is now a state-owned entity used as a vehicle for commercial activities. This is because the company must meet the demands of the stock exchange and the shareholders rather than merely the state. Today Norwegian state participation is wielded through the *State Direct Financial Interest* where the state, when determining the joint venturers in a licence, inserts itself into a licence through the management company Petoro, thereby undertaking entrepreneurship activities through direct investment. Thus, today the 'participatory intervention' exhibited by Norway is less of a technical participation like Russia, Mexico and China, and more an economic participation.

Perhaps another reason for the poor fit of Norway into the participatory intervention category is the political ideology of Norway compared to that of Russia, Mexico and China. Dealing first with China, it is clearly a country that is communist with a market economy. Similarly, Russia arose from the ashes of the breakup of the communist former Soviet Union. Although not a communist state, Mexico nonetheless has communist influences on its government when seeking to exert control over its resources in the 1930s, particularly through Leon Trotsky and other left-leaning thinkers of the day. What is clear is that Mexico, Russia and China clearly value and promote strong state control

---

[34] Jørn Øyrehagen Sunde, 'Dissenting Votes in the Norwegian Supreme Court 1965–2009: A Legal Cultural Analysis' (2012) 1 *Rechtskultur – Zeitschrift für Europäische Rechtsgeschichte* 60–3 (59–73).

over the commanding heights of the economy,[35] a concept coined by Lenin in 1922 to refer to the critical parts of the economy, including electricity generation, heavy manufacturing, mining and transportation.[36] Although Norway does not share this history or style of leadership, it has, since gaining independence from Sweden and Denmark, forged a social-democratic state where the interests of the people, including access to the commanding heights of the economy, have been the forefront of government policy. Thus, the tie binding Russia, Mexico, China and Norway in such participatory intervention is strong state control over the economy's commanding heights.

With Norway we see that the basic structural elements – a judiciary not to be reckoned with – is different, and therefore Norway sits awkwardly in the category of participatory intervention petroleum regimes. This demonstrates that any kind of classification is only an instrument to create an unnatural order in a field that is multifaceted. If we take perhaps the most homogeneous category, minimal intervention regime, we also find differences. Australia has a far more constrained contractual and property right-based petroleum regime than, for instance, the USA. To some extent, Australia is in this aspect as close to the United Kingdom or Norway as the USA. If we then turn to the category regulatory intervention petroleum regimes, we find that in the Netherlands there is a tradition of state participation in the production of petroleum, similar to what we find in Norway, and different from what we find in the United Kingdom.

To understand these differences, we must turn to the starting point of this excursion – legal culture as an experience and not as a theoretical exercise. We can use legal culture to systematise and understand. However, what we label legal culture are ideas and expectations that are operationalised by institutions. These ideas, expectations and practices are linked to the interaction between law and context. Different context means difference in petroleum licensing regimes. Even though we can make and apply the categories minimal, regulatory and participatory interventions to petroleum regimes, they are only a theoretical instrument to order a complex reality. In reality, the variations will always overcome such theoretical tools. Hence, each petroleum licensing regime is unique, because they are fitted to a specific context. One size does not fit all where petroleum licensing regimes are concerned.

---

[35] See Daniel Yergin and Joseph Stanislaw, *The Commanding Heights: The Battle Between Government and the Marketplace that is Remaking the Modern World* (Simon and Schuster, 1998).
[36] Arnold Klingg, 'The New Commanding Heights' (2011) *Cato Institute*, www .cato.org/publications/commentary/new-commanding-heights. Accessed on 4th March 2020.

This is true for all legal fields. However, it is truer for petroleum law than for most fields of law. This is because petroleum is of great importance to the national economy. It can be important because of the revenues through sale and taxes, as in Mexico, for national industrial production, as is the case in China, or as an industry, as in the US. The development of the petroleum licensing regime will hence not only be a product of historical and comparative experience. It will also be a product of politics. For instance, Russia is placed in the category participatory intervention regime with China, Mexico and Norway. Russia has a communist past, China has a communist present, Mexico has a petroleum regime inspired by socialist ideas, and Norway had social democratic governments for most of the post-war period. This still does not explain why Russia is a part of the category. In the 1990s, Russia turned its back on its communist past, and was heading in a US direction in many policy fields. To make a turn from the way things were heading, was a political choice. However, the importance of the petroleum industry and experience with weak courts and instead the role of the legislator in developing law and ensuring rights made the political choice easier.

Isidor of Sevilla claimed in the 7th century that '[A] law should be honourable, just, feasible, in agreement with nature, in agreement with the custom of the country, appropriate to the time and place.' When reading this statement, we can imagine that it was made by a Prime Minister or Minister of Petroleum in almost any government in the world today instead of a Spanish bishop more than 1500 years ago. When it comes to the petroleum licensing regime, this is ensured by fitting it to the rest of the system, and by making political decisions. It is hence a question of a large dose of experience and a dash of experiment.

2. Characterisation of Australia's petroleum licences: property capable of acquisition on 'just terms'?

Tina Soliman Hunter

1. INTRODUCTION

The exploitation[1] of non-renewable resources such as petroleum creates risk for those undertaking the activity. A large part of the risk arises as a result of the long lead-time from the decision to develop the resource to first production. Such a period is usually several years, with further delays occurring if there are substantial changes to legislation.[2] Coupled with this is the immense level of capital required, making non-renewable resource development one of the most financially risky activities undertaken. In order to get access to resources, a company is usually beholden to the host state, who owns the resource and provides access to the resource. Such access is generally though either a contractual framework, such as a production sharing contract, or a licensing and concession system.

As a result of Australia's legal culture, the grant of a petroleum licence is complex, as there are multiple jurisdictions. As a federation, similar to Canada and the United States, Australia's states and territories have interests in both onshore and offshore petroleum licences. This differs to other States, such as

---

[1]   In this context exploitation means the exploration for, and production of, the resource. It does not mean negative connotations for the activity, rather a useful term for both exploration and production.

[2]   Such a delay occurred in 2009–12 when Arrow Energy submitted the appropriate Environmental Plan for approval in relation to *the Environmental Protection and Biodiversity Conservation Act 1999* (Cth) (EPBCA). During the period of assessment, the legislation was altered to include Coal Seam Gas development as a *Matter of National Environmental Significance* (MNES). As a consequence, Arrow fell 'behind' the other producers (QGC, Santos and Origin) in constructing wells and infrastructure. Such delay led to the decision to not construct infrastructure, but instead to collaborate with other producers, using existing infrastructure to bring their gas to market.

the UK, Norway, the Netherlands and Denmark, which are all unitary states. Therefore, this chapter analyses the complex question of the legal character[3] of the petroleum licence.

A consideration of the legal character of the Australian petroleum licence is not new. Indeed, Crommelin first examined the issue in 1979 when he examined the nature and security of offshore titles under the Petroleum (Submerged Lands) Act 1967 (Cth).[4] He considered whether the statutory rights conferred to exploration and petroleum titles amounted to a proprietary interest and if so, where in the common law classification of property rights do they fall?[5] In this 1979 consideration of the interests acquired under petroleum titles, Crommelin warns against rigidity in classifying the rights acquired (such as the rigidity developing in the US), instead urging a more flexible approach.[6] Furthermore, he noted that authority on these questions is sparse and inconclusive,[7] with most existing case law (particularly in the US and Canada) concerning private petroleum titles rather than Crown petroleum leases.[8]

The 1981 edited volume by Terence Daintith[9] further considered this issue, bringing together papers presented at an International Bar Association's Committee on Energy and Resources Seminar at the University of Dundee. In the volume Crommelin undertook a comprehensive analysis of the legal source and status of Australian petroleum licences.[10] This consideration of Australian petroleum licences provides both a historical factual background and a fundamental basis for this chapter. Crommelin's chapter was written prior to the conclusion of the United Nations Convention on the Law of the Sea (UNCLOS) III, and at a time when exploration on Australia's North-West Shelf (NWS) was just commencing.

---

[3]   The term 'legal character' in this context refers to the attributes and qualities that a petroleum licence possesses. In broad terms such character may be contractual, administrative or proprietary in nature.

[4]   Michael Crommelin, 'Petroleum (Submerged Lands) Act: The Nature and Security of Offshore Titles' (1979) 2(1) *Australian Mining and Petroleum Law Journal* 135–59.

[5]   Ibid, 143.

[6]   Ibid.

[7]   Crommelin notes that the classification of rights by the court range from *profit à prendre* (incorporeal hereditament in gross) in California, to personal realty in Oklahoma. See Crommelin, ibid, 143.

[8]   Ibid, 143.

[9]   Terence Daintith (ed), *The Legal Character of Petroleum Licences: A Comparative Study* (University of Dundee and the International Bar Association, 1981).

[10]   Michael Crommelin, 'The Legal Character of Petroleum Production Licences in Australia' in Terence Daintith (ed) *The Legal Character of Petroleum Licences: A Comparative Study* (University of Dundee and the International Bar Association, 1981).

In the subsequent years, further consideration of the question of the legal character of Australian petroleum licences was undertaken by leading academics, particularly Crommelin in his seminal article 'The Legal Character of Resource Titles' in 1998,[11] as well as considered by the courts.[12] However, such scarcity of authority relating to Crown petroleum titles has continued, with little contemplation of the characterisation of the legal status of these titles undertaken, and the effect of the legal character on the extinguishment of the interest.

Since the initial consideration of legal character of petroleum titles there has been much growth in Australia's petroleum sector. Almost all of the growth has occurred on the NWS. However, new technologies,[13] players[14] and laws[15] have stimulated interest in the Great Australian Bight (GAB), particularly the Ceduna Sub-Basin (CSB). Interest in the GAB originally occurred in the late 1960s/early 1970s as majors including Shell, BP and Esso explored the region as part of their investigation of Bass Strait. The same companies returned to the region for further exploration in the 1990s, leaving empty handed. In 2000 a Woodside/Anadarko/PanCanadian Joint Venture explored in the GAB, subsequently abandoning[16] the Basin due to weather conditions. Attempts to revive interest in the basin led Geoscience Australia to undertake a geosci-

---

[11]   Michael Crommelin, 'The Legal Character of Resource Titles' (1998) 17 *Australian Mining and Petroleum Law Journal* 57–70.

[12]   *Commonwealth of Australia v WMC Resources* [1998] HCA 8 2 February 1998.

[13]   In particular deep-water drilling technologies, and the use of semi-submersible rigs utilising dynamic positioning and transponders to maintain their position in ultradeep water.

[14]   Norwegian Giant Equinor (formerly Statoil) entered Australian offshore petroleum activities in 2013, and holds titles in the Great Australian Bight, initially in joint venture with BP, but now also holds a 100% interest in EPP 39 and EPP 40.

[15]   A major reform of petroleum law in Australia (Commonwealth) occurred in 2006, with a rewrite of the existing legislation – the *Petroleum (Submerged Lands) Act 1967* (Cth). The new act, the *Offshore Petroleum Act 2006* was substantially altered in 2008 to incorporate carbon sequestration, although the petroleum aspects were not altered. It was renamed the *Offshore Petroleum and Greenhouse Gas Storage Act 2006* (Cth). After the Montara oil spill further amendments to the Act were made, particularly when the existing Joint Authority/Designated Authority (JA/DA) arrangements were altered in 2012.

To incentivise companies to explore for petroleum in frontier areas in offshore Commonwealth Waters, in 2004 the Australian Government introduced new tax measures, enabling explorers in designated frontier areas (including the GAB/CSB) to claim 150% of the costs associated with exploration expenditure for the purposes of determining Petroleum Resource Rent Tax Payable. See Part V Division 3 of the *Petroleum Resource Rent Tax Assessment Act 1987* (Cth).

[16]   This well was abandoned due to physical conditions and will be considered further in section 3 below.

entific study of the CSB, identifying world-class marine oil-prone potential source rocks,[17] with the CSB again offered for frontier exploration in the 2009 licensing round and four exploration permits (EPP 37–40) awarded to BP in 2011.[18] The criterion for the award of these licences was a guaranteed primary work program (three years)[19] of $605 million, and a secondary (further three years) work program in excess of $800 million (Geoscience Australia, 2017, 12). Two of these licences, EPP 39 and EPP 40, were subsequently 100% acquired by Equinor, with plans to drill an exploration well in 2,200m of water in the late 2020 or early 2021. However, after the Deepwater Horizon (DWH) blowout and oil spill, Australia appears to have lost its appetite for offshore drilling in sensitive marine areas, and major public campaigns and concerns, hitherto unheard of in Australia, have occurred, in an attempt to prevent exploration drilling or oil production in the GAB.

If the Australian government were to cede to the demands of the community and revoke the licences granted or a permanent refusal of an operational plan,[20] a number of legal questions arise: what is the legal nature of a petroleum licence – is it a property interest or mere contractual/administrative interest? What are the legal effects of the revoking of a petroleum title? Would such revocation amount to the acquisition of property? If it were the acquisition of property, would the Commonwealth be liable for just terms, as set out under section 51(xxxi) of the Australian Constitution. The answers to these questions lie in the legal character of the petroleum title, which varies according to the type of title held, and existing legal precedent which considers the grant of an onshore mining lease and an offshore (in Commonwealth Waters) exploration permit.

This chapter represents a new attempt to analyse the character of Australian petroleum titles, and in particular offshore petroleum titles, in light of the significant possibility of revocation of petroleum titles in the GAB amidst public consternation. In undertaking the analysis, it will not only consider

---

[17] Geosciences Australia, Submission to the Senate Committee on Oil or Gas Production in the Great Australian Bight (2017) Submission No. 70, p12.

[18] This was a most unusual licence application for two reasons. First, was the amount of money bid for the work program, over 1.4 billion dollars over six years. Second, was the exposure of BP, given that this was not a joint venture. This is exceptionally rare in any petroleum province, even where prospectivity is assured, and unheard of in a Frontier Basin.

[19] The award of a licence in Australia is made to the successful bidder of a work program, as required by ss 104–9 of the *Offshore Petroleum and Greenhouse Gas Storage Act 2006* (Cth).

[20] An operational plan includes a safety plan, environment plan or a well operations management plan (WOMP). A refusal of one of these means operations cannot commence or continue.

offshore exploration permits, through an analysis of the judicial decision in *Commonwealth v WMC Resources*, but also offshore production licences awarded in the Commonwealth jurisdiction. Such analysis represents a significant contribution to the literature on the legal character of offshore petroleum licences on the Australian Continental Shelf (ACS), considering whether petroleum titles, and the revocation of such a title would amount to acquisition of property, and whether the Commonwealth would be required to pay just terms, as stipulated by section 51(xxxi) of the Australian Constitution.

2.   AUSTRALIA'S LEGAL HISTORY AND CULTURE

2.1   Australia's Legal Culture

As a consequence of its colonial beginnings as an extraterritorial prison for England, Australia is a common law jurisdiction. Given the hunter-gather nature of the indigenous people at the time, Australia was declared *terra nullius* and therefore adopted English law upon colonisation in 1788, with its reception into the colonies as they emerged.[21] The status of *terra nullius* was reinforced in the late 19th century,[22] and maintained until almost one hundred years later when the concept was overturned in *Mabo No. 2* in 1992.[23]

Australia commenced life as six independent colonies, with the independent development of the laws of each jurisdiction. Commencing with the establishment of the colony of New South Wales (NSW) in 1788, there was rapid expansion of convict colonies both south and north. New colonies were established – Van Diemen's Land (Tasmania) in 1828, Victoria in 1851 and Queensland in 1859. South Australia was established with the planned colonisation of Adelaide with free settlers in 1836, and similar colonisation by free settlers (as opposed to colonisation as a convict prison which occurred in the eastern states) in Western Australia from 1829, although only fully established when the import of convict labour ceased in 1868.

The independence of the colonies, established by the *Colonial Laws Validity Act 1865* (Imp) drove a period of inward focus, with the colonies determined to explore their territories and establish and extend infrastructure. However, from the early 1880s there was a more outward shift, with trade between colonies becoming important, resulting in protectionism and varying tariff rates to

---

[21] For a history of the development of Australian colonies see Tina Soliman Hunter, 'Introduction to Australian Legal Culture' in Jørn Sunde and Soren Köch (eds) *Comparing Legal Cultures: Volume II* (Fagbokforlaget, 2020).

[22] *Cooper v Stuart* (1889) 14 App Cas 286.

[23] *Mabo and Others v Commonwealth* (No. 2) (1992) 175 CLR 1.

protect local industries.[24] As a consequence, the idea of federation became of interest, driven largely by not only trade and commerce issues, but also that of military protection and strength, heightened by British request for assistance in the Boer War.

Australia was federated on 1 January 1901. At the time of Federation there were six state jurisdictions, plus a federal (known as Commonwealth) jurisdiction. Since Federation there has been the addition of two jurisdictions: the Northern Territory, created in 1911 by dividing South Australia; and the Australian Capital Territory, established in 1911 for the purposes of creating a capital of Australia. An additional jurisdiction was established in 1979 by the *Norfolk Island Act 1979* (Cth), which granted self-government to Norfolk Island. Upon the rescinding of self-government in 2015, all Norfolk legislation passed during self-rule converted to New South Wales (NSW) legislation from 1 July 2016. In addition, the NSW court system also now applies to Norfolk Island. Therefore, although there were ten jurisdictions, there are currently nine: six states, two territories (which can be over-ridden by the Commonwealth by virtue of section 122 of the Australian Constitution), and the Commonwealth (federal) jurisdiction.

The concept of *Stare Decisis* (The Doctrine of Precedent) applies in the state jurisdictions and in the Commonwealth jurisdiction. Each state is only bound by the decisions in that State, and decisions of the High Court. Decisions in the Commonwealth Jurisdiction, with the exception of the High Court, do not bind the states. Under section 122 of the Australian Constitution, the Commonwealth may make laws for the territory. Therefore, Commonwealth jurisdiction decisions, but not state decisions, bind the territories, as well as those decisions of the territory supreme court.

The establishment of a Commonwealth judicial system is enunciated in Chapter III of the Australian Constitution. Therefore, federal courts are referred to as Chapter III bodies. Section 71 of the Australian Constitution establishes the supreme court of Australia, to be known as the High Court of Australia (HCA). It was formally constituted in 1903 with the appointment of the first three judges under the *Judiciary Act 1903* (Cth). It expanded to five justices in 1906, and to seven in 1913, which continues today. Normally a case is heard by the Full Bench of the HCA, unless a justice recuses due to conflict of interest.[25] The HCA holds original jurisdiction under section 75 of

---

[24]   It is important to note that colonies' industries differed. New South Wales and Western Australia were largely wheat/sheep producers, with gold mining beginning to play some part in the economy towards the end of the century. Meanwhile, Victoria had established a strong manufacturing base.

[25]   The decision to recuse lies with the judge. There have been a number of instances where a justice has recused himself, such as Justice Stephen Gaegler in the case

the Australian Constitution, hearing matters related to national issues such as interpretation of treaties and conflict between states and the Commonwealth.

The HCA also holds an appellate function, as set out by section 73 of the Australian Constitution, whereby any case from a federal, state or territory court can be heard by the HCA. However, a case cannot be heard as a matter of right. An appellant must seek leave to appeal for the case to be heard in the High Court. Leave to appeal will only be granted where hearing the appeal will be relevant to the public interest rather than the personal interest of the party. In accordance with section 73 of the constitution, the judgment of the HCA shall be final and conclusive. Under this appellate function, cases could be appealed to the UK's Privy Council. This practice ceased in 1988, 200 years after the establishment of the Colonisation of Australia, through the enactment of the *Australia Act 1986* (Cth), and the *Australia Act 1986* (UK). In addition, until 1963 the HCA regarded the decisions of the UK's House of Lords as binding, thus leading to substantial uniformity between Australian and English Common Law until this time. The federal judicial system sits alongside the state and territory court systems. It comprises the Federal Court of Australia, the Federal Circuit Court of Australia and the Family Court of Australia.

The doctrines of the Rule of Law and the Separation of Powers are the cornerstone of the Australian Constitution, which is very much a hybrid system, incorporating many of the nuances of the Westminster system, as brought to the Australian shores upon colonization. It also embraces features of the American constitutional system, primarily due the existence of numerous Australian colonies at the time of Federation, analogous to the system of United States of America. This system is often described as the 'Washminster' system of democracy, where the founding fathers of Federation clearly sought to retain the Rule of Law, and the separation of powers, thereby taking many aspects of the Westminster system but incorporating some features from the US system in order to preserve the Rule of Law.[26] This system of government has been preserved to this day, with the High Court playing an ever-increasing role in the interpretation of the constitution, in both the separation of powers,

---

Commonwealth v Australian Capital Territory (2013) 250 CLR 441. In addition, there have been arguments where a justice was accused of apprehension of bias and requested to recuse himself: after controversy and public debate, Justice Ian Callinan recused himself from the Hindmarsh Island Bridge Act Case (*Kartinyeri v The Commonwealth* (1998) 195 CLR 337).

[26] The founding fathers believed the non-elected life peerage upper house of the Westminster system was inappropriate, and sought to emulate the US Congress system, albeit within the Commonwealth system where the Queen or her representative is retained as nominal head of state.

such as in the case of *Re Wakim*,[27] but also in the exercise of Commonwealth and State power throughout the 20th century.

Similar to other British colonies such as Canada, Australia is a co-operative federation. Chapter 1 Part V sets out the powers of the Commonwealth parliament, and in particular sections 51 and section 52 of the Australian Constitution enumerate the power of the Commonwealth. Section 51 of the Australian Constitution outlines the legislative powers of the Commonwealth Parliament, which includes trade and commerce, taxation, postal and other services, military defence, quarantine, fisheries beyond territorial limits, currency, corporations,[28] social benefits, marriage and divorce, immigration, external affairs, indigenous peoples, matters referred to the Commonwealth by the states,[29] and any matters incidental to the execution of any power vested by the constitution in any House of Parliament, the Executive or the Judicature.[30] Section 52 of the Australian Constitution is reserved for the exclusive powers of the parliament, enabling the Commonwealth parliament to have 'exclusive power to make laws for the peace, order, and good government of the Commonwealth with respect to' the seat of government of the Commonwealth and Commonwealth public places; the public service; and other matters so declared by the Constitution to be within the exclusive power of the Parliament.

Any powers not enumerated for the Commonwealth are the jurisdiction of the states, and, if so delegated, the territories. Any powers that are not defined in the Australian Constitution are reserved for the states/territories as a plenary power, enabling them to make laws. Each state's Constitution enables that state to 'make laws for the peace welfare and good government' of that state.[31] Generally, if the area is not enunciated in section 51 or section 52 of the Commonwealth Constitution, it will fall to the state to regulate it. This includes matters such as schools, hospitals,[32] roads, public transport, utilities

---

[27] *Re Wakim; Ex parte McNally & Anor; Re Wakim; Ex parte Darvall; Re Brown & Ors; Ex parte Amann & Anor; Spinks & Ors v Prentice* (1999) 198 CLR 511.

[28] The case *New South Wales v Commonwealth* (1990) 169 CLR 482 confirmed that the 'Corporations Power' extends only to those corporations that have already been formed. Therefore, the regulation of the formation of Corporations fell to the States. The scope of the Corporations power has been considerably enlarged and today is seen as all-encompassing regarding corporations that have already been formed.

[29] Section 51(xxxviii) of the Constitution – for example the formation of Corporations was referred by each state to the Commonwealth, to be regulated alongside the 'corporation Power', and the *Corporations Act* was created in 2001.

[30] Section 51(xxxix) of the Australian constitution.

[31] For example, s 2 of the *Constitution of Queensland 2001* (Qld), and s 5 of the *Constitution Act 1902* (NSW).

[32] Although the provision of medical services is regulated by the state, there is a Commonwealth health system (Medicare) that was established under s 51(xxiiiA), an

community services, police, prisons, agriculture, forestry, ambulances and mining (including petroleum extraction).

3. AUSTRALIA'S ONSHORE PETROLEUM TITLES

According to UN Resolution 1803 *United Nations Resolution on the Permanent Sovereignty over Natural Resources*,[33] a state, in this instance the Commonwealth of Australia, has sovereignty over its natural resources. However, given that the regulation of mineral and petroleum resources is not an enumerated Commonwealth power, the regulation of onshore petroleum resources onshore and in state waters is a state plenary power and therefore regulated by the states.[34] The Commonwealth may exert indirect regulatory control over resource activities pursuant to constitutional commerce, taxation and corporations powers.[35] It has the ability to exert direct control over petroleum resources in the states through environmental regulation under the *Environmental Protection and Biodiversity Conservation Act 1999* (Cth) (EPBCA), which gives effect to the numerous environmental treaties and conventions to which Australia is a signatory, and was enacted under section 51(xxix) (the External Affairs Power) of the Australian constitution.[36]

This EPBCA provides for protection of the environment in a number of circumstances, as well as protection of biodiversity, including some habitats. While the EPBCA is Commonwealth legislation and has as its ambit environmental protection, it does not apply to all petroleum activities. Day-to-day environmental management falls under the ambit of state/Northern Territory law. The EPBCA only applies where the onshore activity falls into an area

---

alteration to the Commonwealth Constitution by referendum in 1946. This enables the Commonwealth to establish and operate the Medicare Scheme, but not the operation of health services throughout Australia. Rather, health services are delegated to the states/ territories on behalf of the Commonwealth.

[33] GA Res 1803/17, UNGAOR, 17th Sess, 1194th plen mtg, UN Doc A/RES/1803/17 (14 December 1962).

[34] State waters are defined and delineated in s 6 of the *Offshore Petroleum and Greenhouse Gas Storage Act 2006* (Cth). See also section 3.2 below. Note that although as self-governing territories have the right to make laws with respect to petroleum activities onshore and in state waters, by virtue of the operation of s 122 of the Australian constitution it is possible that the commonwealth can override these laws and establish their own.

[35] Australian Constitution, ss 51(1), 51(ii) and 51(xx).

[36] *Environment Protection and Conservation Act 1999* (Cth); For a discussion on the scope and applicability of the EPBCA see Australian Government Department of the Environment *Local Government and Australian Environmental Law*, www.environment.gov.au/resource/local-government-and-australian-environment-law (last visited Feb. 4, 2016).

where referral for assessment is required under the EPBCA.[37] While the EPBCA is not core environmental legislation, it is nonetheless important and needs to be considered when examining environmental regulation of petroleum activities. Under the EPBCA any 'action' (activity) will require approval from the Environment Minister if the action has, will have or is likely to have a significant impact[38] on a matter of national environmental significance (MNES).[39] Under section 523 of the EPBCA, an action is defined broadly to include a project, a development, an undertaking, an activity or a series of activities, or an alteration of any of these things.[40] In relation to onshore petroleum activities, MNES comprise listed threatened species and ecological communities, migratory species protected under international agreements, and world heritage properties. The Commonwealth environmental assessment under the EPBCA is undertaken by the state regulator alongside that state/territory's environmental assessment for the petroleum activity.[41] Given the minor role confined to environmental legislation that the Commonwealth plays, onshore petroleum licences will not be considered further in this chapter.

The regulation of resource titles in the two Australian territories (especially the resource rich Northern Territory) is important in relation to the legal characterisation of onshore petroleum licences. By virtue of section 122 of the Australian Constitution, '… the Parliament may make laws for the government of any territory surrendered by any State to and accepted by the Commonwealth ….'[42] It is important to recognise that given that there is no enumerated power for the Commonwealth to regulate petroleum activities, the regulation of petroleum activities onshore[43] in Australian states is the purview of individual states, falling under the ambit of each state government's consti-

---

[37]   *Environment Protection and Conservation Act 1999* (Cth) ch 2. For a discussion of the applicability of the Act and the definition of 'significant impact' see Parliament of the Commonwealth of Australia, House of Representatives Standing Committee On Industry & Resources, *Exploring: Australia's Future – Impediments to Increasing Investment in Minerals and Petroleum Exploration in Australia* 106–10 (2003).

[38]   A significant impact is defined as: '[A]n impact which is important, notable, or of consequence, having regard to its context or intensity. Whether or not an action is likely to have significant impact depends on the sensitivity, value and quality of the environment which is impacted, and on the intensity, duration, magnitude and geographic extent of the impacts.' For this definition see *Significant impact*, GLOSSARY, AUSTL. GOV'T, DEP'T OF THE ENV'T, www.environment.gov.au/epbc/about/glossary .html#significant (last visited on January 28, 2016).

[39]   *Environmental Protection and Biodiversity Conservation Act 1999* (Cth) ss 11, 130.

[40]   Ibid s 523.

[41]   *Environment Protection and Conservation Act 1999* (Cth) ch 2 (Austl.).

[42]   Australian Constitution, s 122.

[43]   This includes state waters.

tution, which grants the right to make laws to ensure 'peace, welfare and good government' in each state.[44]

The legal character of onshore petroleum titles was tested in the early 1990s as a result of the extension of the boundaries of Kakadu National Park (KNP) in the Northern Territory in 1989 and 1991 by the Commonwealth government. In extending the boundaries, the Commonwealth incorporated land into KNP that was held by Newcrest Mining and subject to 25 mining leases under the NT's *Mining Act 1980* (NT), and which granted the right to recover various minerals including gold and other minerals. As a consequence of the extension of the national park boundary to include Newcrest's mining leases, the *National Parks and Wildlife Conservation Act 1975* (Cth) (NPWCA) prohibited the recovery of minerals, and effectively revoked Newcrest's 25 mining titles, since it was no longer able to mine. Newcrest argued that the loss of right to mine amounted to the Commonwealth acquisition of property from Newcrest. Such acquisition, Newcrest argued, breached the guarantee of just terms set out in section 51(xxxi).

In a majority decision, the HCA held that the extension of boundaries of KNP to incorporate Newcrest's mining leases amounted to the acquisition of property without just terms.[45] As noted by Crommelin, the reasoning for the HCA decision rested upon the reasoning of Gummow J supporting the original reasoning of Kitto J,[46] that the common law recognises that a mineral extraction lease confers two rights, that of the right to use the land belonging to another, and also to appropriate the mineral at the moment of severance.[47] This link between statutory mining titles and common law was acknowledged by Windeyer J in *Wade v New South Wales Rutile Mining Co. Ltd*,[48] who noted that 'a mining lease of this land is really a sale by the Crown of minerals reserved to the crown to be taken by the lessee at a price payable over a period of years as royalties.'[49]

Adopting the reasoning of both Kitto and Windeyer JJ, Gummow J reasoned that rather than statutory mineral titles being pure creatures of statute unrelated to common law concepts, he endorsed the idea that mineral titles emanate from the crown's proprietorship of land.[50] Further, Gummow J reasoned that there was a sufficient derivation of identifiable and measurable advantage to satisfy the Constitutional requirement of acquisition of property (i.e., Newcrest's

---

[44]   For example s 5 of the *Constitution Act 1902 (NSW)*.
[45]   *Newcrest Mining (WA) v The Commonwealth* (1997) 147 ALR 42.
[46]   In *Commissioner of Stamp Duties v Henry* [SR] (NSW) 298.
[47]   Crommelin 1998, 60.
[48]   *Wade v New South Wales Rutile Mining Co. Ltd* (1969)129 CLR 177 at 192–3.
[49]   Ibid at 192.
[50]   *Newcrest Mining (WA) v the Commonwealth* (1997) 147 ALR 42 at 129.

property rights had been deprived) due to the sterilisation of Newcrest's interests. Toohey, Gaudron and Kirby JJ agreed with the decision of Gummow J, with Brennan CJ, Dawson and McHugh JJ dissenting. Thus, the characterisation of the onshore statutory mineral lease was found to be grounded in common law concepts.[51]

4.   DEVELOPMENT OF AUSTRALIAN OFFSHORE PETROLEUM LICENCES

Offshore, although natural resources are not enumerated as a Commonwealth power, it falls under section 51(xxix) (external affairs) power,[52] and the trade and commerce power.[53] As a result of Australia's colonial history, the states and territories[54] had long held that the first three nautical miles seaward from baseline[55] was the jurisdiction of the states.[56] This 'state jurisdiction' (in this instance for fishing rights) was upheld in the case of *Bonser v La Macchia.*[57]

Given the complexities of the state/Commonwealth relationship and its application to the offshore jurisdiction, there is a long history of prescriptive offshore legislation. To reduce the capacity of the states to 'go their own way' in regulating petroleum activities in their jurisdictions, the *Petroleum (Submerged Lands) Act 1967* (Cth) (PSLA) set out to clearly enumerate responsibilities and regulatory aspects/role of the Commonwealth, as was

---

[51]   Ibid at 42. See Crommelin 1998, 61.

[52]   Relevant decisions regarding the scope of the external affairs power include *NSW v Commonwealth* (1975) 135 CLR 337; *Koowarta v Bjelke-Petersen* (1982) 153 CLR 168; and the *Commonwealth v Tasmania* (1983) 158 CLR 1 (Tasmanian Dams Case).

[53]   In particular, the decision in *Murphyores v Commonwealth* [1976] HCA 20 establishes the ability for the Commonwealth to regulate materials mined for export under s 51(i) of the Australian Constitution.

[54]   Section 4 of the *Sea and Submerged Lands Act 1973* (Cth) extends jurisdiction to the territories.

[55]   The definition of Baseline is conferred in the *Sea and Submerged Lands Act 1973* (Cth) s 7 to be whatever the Governor General defines it as. It is defined in Article 5 of the United Nations Convention on the Law of the Sea as the low water line along the coast as marked on large-scale charts of the Coastal State.

[56]   Note that NSW claimed that it held the right over 3NM of the Territorial Sea, claiming that since its time as a colony NSW has claimed control over the territorial sea under the 17th century 'cannon shot' rule which was received into New South Wales from England. Under this rule, a State could control its coastal waters based upon the reach of a cannon from the sea to shore, which was approximately three nautical miles, as calculated by Cornelius van Bynkershoek.

[57]   *Bonser v La Macchia* (1969) 122 CLR 177.

decided under the 1967 Petroleum Agreement. [58] The Agreement set out not
to create legal relations, but rather to establish uniform legislation: Clause 26
states that 'the Governments acknowledge that this Agreement is not intended
to create legal relationships justiciable [sic] in a Court of Law but declare
that the Agreement shall be construed and given effect to by the parties in
all respects according to the true meaning and spirit thereof.' The resulting
legislation was in the style of 'command and control', [59] requiring over 1000
amendments and 30 separate compilations of the Act as petroleum activities
blossomed. [60] By 2000 the Act stood at over 850 pages, addressing in minutiae
the award and management of licences, titles, safety and the jurisdiction of
states and territories. So cumbersome was the act, Daintith described it as 'old,
fat, and ugly, and not likely to score highly in a legislative beauty contest, [61]
and in need of rewriting'. In 2006 the PSLA was reincarnated as the *Offshore
Petroleum and Greenhouse Gas Storage Act 2006* (Cth) (OPGGSA). The
new OPGGSA is 'fatter and uglier' than the PSLA, and today is over 1430
pages and three volumes, accompanied by substantive regulations (Safety,
Environment, and Resource Management Regs). Such voluminous legislation
is not confined to petroleum legislation: Australia's principal Taxation Act[62]
runs to 12 volumes and over 10,000 pages.

In relation to the offshore jurisdiction, the assumption by the states and territories was that they held jurisdiction over the first three nautical miles (under
the concept of the cannon-shot rule, the internationally accepted width of the
territorial sea prior to the *Convention on the Territorial Sea and Contiguous
Zone* concluded at the 1958 Geneva Convention on the Continental Shelf 1958
(UNCLOS I)). [63] The Commonwealth sought to implement the conventions of

---

[58]   1967 Agreement Relating to the Exploration for and the Exploitation of, the
Petroleum Resources, and Certain Other Resources, of the Continental Shelf of
Australia and of Certain Territories of the Commonwealth and of Certain Other
Submerged Land signed October 16, 1967 (the Petroleum Agreement).

[59]   *Newcrest Mining (WA) v The Commonwealth* (1997) 147 ALR 42 at 129.

[60]   The full legislative history of the *Petroleum (Submerged Lands) Act 1967* (Cth)
can be found at www.legislation.gov.au/Details/C1967A00118/Download. Accessed 7
March 2020.

[61]   Terence Daintith, 'A Critical Evaluation of the Petroleum (Submerged Lands)
Act as a Regulatory Regime' (2000) *AMPLA Yearbook* 2000 91, 92.

[62]   *Income Tax Assessment Act 1997* (Cth).

[63]   By 1960 only 26 states, of which Australia was one of them, claimed the limit
of their Territorial Sea as three nautical miles, while 66 nations claimed a wider
breadth, from four miles to over 12 miles. See Major Thomas E. Behuniak, 'The
Seizure and Recovery of the S.S. Mayaguez: Legal Analysis of United States
Claims, Part 1' (Fall 1978) 82 *Military Law Review*. Department of the Army
https://web.archive.org/web/20170111060430/https://www.jagcnet.army.mil/
DOCLIBS/MILITARYLAWREVIEW.NSF/20a66345129fe3d885256e5b00571830/

UNCLOS I through the *Sea and Submerged Lands Act 1973* (Cth) (SSLA), claiming sovereignty over the Territorial Sea from baseline[64] and sovereign rights in respect of the Continental Shelf.[65] The States took great umbrage at this claim, with New South Wales challenging the validity of the SSLA, which relied on the Commonwealth's scope under section 51(xxix) of the Australian Constitution (External Affairs Power). The validity of the Commonwealth's claim of sovereignty over the Territorial Sea under the scope of the external affairs power in relation to treaties was tested in the *Sea and Submerged Lands Case*,[66] where Australia sought to implement the 1958 Geneva Convention on the Continental Shelf through the *Sea and Submerged Lands Act 1973* (Cth). In contesting the validity of the Commonwealth's claim over the Territorial Sea under the SSLA, New South Wales argued that the Commonwealth had no right to claim the Territorial Sea under treaty provisions.[67] In *NSW v Commonwealth*[68] the Justices, with the exception of Gibbs and Stephen JJ in dissent, held that sovereignty in the territorial waters was vested in the Commonwealth.[69] Furthermore, the HCA held that sovereign rights in relation to the Continental Shelf vested in the Commonwealth.

As a consequence of this decision, the states were denied property rights in the seabed and subsea terrain of the territorial waters, since their territory ended at low-water mark.[70] This decision had a major impact on the states and territories' jurisdiction over, and income from offshore petroleum, and prompted negotiations between petroleum-producing states/territories and the Commonwealth. The States continued to argue that they held petroleum rights in the territorial waters from the baseline seaward three nautical miles, given

---

b3197adca4437e4d85256e5b0057ee6a/$FILE/MLR%2027-100-82%2019781001.pdf. 114–21. Accessed 20 February 2020.

    Note that several other treaties were concluded including the *Convention on the Continental Shelf, Convention on the High Seas,* and the *Convention on fishing and the Conservation of Living Resources on the High Seas.*

  [64] *Sea and Submerged Lands Act 1973* (Cth), s 7.

  [65] *Sea and Submerged Lands Act 1973* (Cth), s 11.

  [66] *New South Wales v Commonwealth* (1975) 135 CLR 337.

  [67] Note that NSW claimed that it held the right over 3NM of the Territorial Sea, claiming that since its time as a colony NSW has claimed control over the territorial sea under the 17th century 'cannon shot' rule which was received into New South Wales from England.

  [68] *NSW v Commonwealth* (1975) 8 ALR 1.

  [69] Ibid.

  [70] Pat Brazil, *Offshore Constitutional Settlement 1980: A Case Study in Federalism* (2001) Centre for International and Public Law, Faculty of Law, Australian National University, 2.

that the HCA had upheld fishing rights in the Territorial Sea in *Bonser v La Macchia* (*Bonser*)[71] less than a decade previously.

However, it is possible to distinguish the decision in *Bonser* and that in the *Sea and Submerged Lands Case*. *Bonser* granted rights to 'living resources' in the water column, with Barwick CJ stating, relying on the majority decision in *R v Keyn*,[72] that the common law did not extend to the bed of the sea.[73] Furthermore, Barwick CJ noted that legislative authority beyond the low water mark is extraterritorial, with the bed of the sea adjacent to the sea said to be the ownership of the Crown according to UK *Admiralty Court Act 1840* (UK) (3 & 4 Vic c 65).[74] Justice Barwick further stated that 'the colonies were never at any stage international personae nor sovereign and the States still are not.'[75] Therefore, Barwick CJ reasoned, any conventions made between nations as to the use of the bed of the sea applies only between nations, and therefore extended only to Great Britain and not to her colonies, dominions or their territories in their own right.[76]

Aside from confirming the validity of the scope of the external affairs power, in the *Sea and Submerged Land Case* the HCA also examined the dominion of the states, not surprising given Barwick CJ's reasoning in *Bonser*. Indeed, Barwick CJ and McTiernan, Mason, Jacobs and Murphy JJ held that the States do not have any international personality, and any rights derived from international law with respect to the territorial sea and continental shelf attach to Australia as a nation, with the boundaries of the colonies (and therefore states) ending at low water mark, meaning that no sovereign or proprietary rights were conferred with respect to the Territorial Sea or Continental Shelf. Such reasoning did not deter the states, who collectively continued to be vexed and disgruntled at the withdrawal of rights that had been assumed for over one hundred years prior to international law developments and endorsed under the 1967 Petroleum Agreement, which sought to avoid such constitutional issues in order to progress petroleum exploitation.[77]

Citing *Pearce v Florenca*,[78] which upheld state fisheries laws in the Territorial Sea, the Commonwealth saw the need for the 'reordering and read-

---

[71]   *Bonser v La Macchia* (1969) 122 CLR 177.
[72]   *R v Keyn (The Franconia)* (1876) 2 Ex. D 63.
[73]   *Bonser v La Macchia* (1969) 122 CLR 177, 184.
[74]   Ibid.
[75]   Ibid.
[76]   Ibid. Ultimately, Barwick CJ dealt with the question at hand regarding fishing rights, and left the issue of the dominion of the sea bed unanswered.
[77]   *Offshore Constitutional Settlement: A Milestone in Co-operative Federalism* (AGPS: 1980) 2.
[78]   *Pearce v Florenca* (1976) 135 CLR 507.

justment of powers and responsibilities-as between the Commonwealth and the States' was required.[79] The *Offshore Constitutional Settlement* (OCS), which was completed at the Premiers Conference in 1979 and forged within the spirit of 'co-operative federalism', was the agreed solution to states' rights over the territorial sea. Under section 51(xxxviii) of the Australian Constitution, the Commonwealth enacted Legislation to vest in each state or territory proprietary rights and title with respect to the adjacent territorial sea, including the seabed.[80] This agreement would be mirrored in both Commonwealth and State/territory legislation (Commonwealth and state *Petroleum (Submerged Lands) Acts*).[81] In addition, a plethora of other necessary legislation was enacted to enable the implementation of the OCS.[82] Today the offshore jurisdiction of the states/territories is defined in section 5 of the *Offshore Petroleum and Greenhouse Gas Storage Act 2006* (Cth) (OPGGSA) as agreed to by the states and the Commonwealth in the *Offshore Constitutional Agreement*, and the regulatory regime for Australia's offshore zones comprises the following:

1. *State Waters* (including *Internal Waters*), which is regulated by the state/Northern Territory, unless the state has conferred regulatory power to NOPSEMA/NOPTA. These waters are regulated by state onshore legislation.[83]

---

[79]   As noted in the *Offshore Constitutional Settlement,* Australia's experience in jurisdiction over the territorial sea has also been considered by the United States and Canada. in all jurisdictions, the courts held that 'the jurisdiction on the part of the central government extended to low-water mark.' It also observed that in each instance 'the constitutional ruling is not the end of the matter and that adjustment is necessary.' *Offshore Constitutional Settlement: A Milestone in Co-operative Federalism* (AGPS: 1980) 4–5.

[80]   Ibid, 6.

[81]   *Petroleum (Submerged Lands) Act 1967* (Cth), *Petroleum (Submerged Lands) Registration Fees Act 1990* (WA), *Petroleum (Submerged Lands) Act 1982* (Vic), *Petroleum (Submerged Lands) Act 1982* (Qld), *Petroleum (Submerged Lands) Act 1982* (SA), *Petroleum (Submerged Lands) Act 1982* (Tas), *Petroleum (Submerged Lands) Act 1982* (NSW), and *Petroleum (Submerged Lands) Taxation Act 1967* (NSW), as outlined in Crommelin 1981, 62.

[82]   Required Acts include *Coastal Waters (State Powers) Act 1980; Coastal Waters (Northern Territory Powers) Act 1980; Coastal Waters (State Title) Act 1980; Coastal Waters (Northern Territory Title) Act; and Offshore Minerals Act 1984* (Cth).

[83]   For example, Western Australia's State Waters are regulated under the *Petroleum and Geothermal Energy Resources Act 1967* (WA). See *Offshore Petroleum and Greenhouse Gas Storage Act 2006 (*Cth), s 5(2)d.

2. *Coastal Waters*, from baseline to the first three nautical miles of the territorial sea, are regulated by the state/territory under state/territory 'mirror'
   legislation as agreed under the *Offshore Constitutional Settlement*.[84]
3. *Commonwealth Waters*, seaward of three nautical miles to the outer
   limits of the Exclusive Economic Zone (EEZ) and Continental Shelf (CS)
   extension, where granted,[85] and the administration is shared in the manner
   provided by in the OPGGSA.[86]

An illustration of the jurisdictions established by the OCS and resultant legislation is found in Figure 2.1.

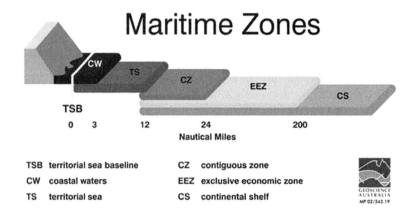

Note: Able to be released under creative commons licence.
Source: © Commonwealth of Australia (Geoscience Australia) 2013.

Figure 2.1   Australia's offshore petroleum zones

Thus, given the settled case law of *Newcrest* and the right of each state to
regulate petroleum activities onshore, the remainder of this chapter will focus
on offshore petroleum licences.

---

[84]   For example, petroleum activities in the Coastal Waters of Western Australia
are regulated under the *Petroleum (Submerged Lands) Act 1982* (WA). See *Offshore
Petroleum and Greenhouse Gas Storage Act 2006 (*Cth), s 5(2)b.
[85]   *Offshore Petroleum and Greenhouse Gas Storage Act 2006 (*Cth), s 5(2)a.
[86]   Ibid, s 5(2)c.

5.   COMMONWEALTH OFFSHORE PETROLEUM LICENCES: PROPERTY CAPABLE OF ACQUISITION?

To analyse the legal nature of the offshore petroleum licence, it is necessary to consider the rights granted to the licensee. Under OPGGSA, the grant of an access licence to petroleum is illustrated in Figure 2.2.

Analysis of the nature of the petroleum licence will encompass the conferral of an exploration licence for exploration, a production licence for the recovery of petroleum where the find is commercial, and the grant of a retention licence where a discovery is not yet commercially viable,[87] but is likely to be in the next 15 years.[88]

One may ask why the legal character of petroleum titles in Australian jurisdictions matter. An important power of the Australian Constitution, and vital to the characterisation and character of Australia's petroleum licences, is section 51(xxxi), which establishes that there will be *acquisition of property on just terms*. This means that if the Commonwealth acquires property, just compensation must be paid. Therefore, the issue of whether petroleum titles constitute property and are acquired by the Commonwealth are Commonwealth jurisdictions are important, since if they are property, then the Commonwealth will be required to pay just compensation if a title is acquired. In those areas where the state has jurisdiction, the characterisation of petroleum titles is not subject to just terms, since if a state or territory wishes to rescind a title, then they are bound only by the state constitution. This concept of 'acquisition of property on just terms' is imbued in the OPGGSA. Section 780(1) of OPGGSA states that 'if the operation of this Act or the Regulations would result in an acquisition of property from a person[89] otherwise than on just terms, the Commonwealth is liable to pay a reasonable amount of compensation to the person'.

In his seminal 1998 work on resource titles,[90] Crommelin rightly asserted a number of questions relating to the issue of the legal character of Australian petroleum titles including:

1. Do such titles confer contractual rights and obligations?

---

[87]   Although 'commercially viable' is not defined in OPGGSA, it is defined in National Offshore Petroleum Titles Authority, *Guideline - Grant and Administration of a Retention Lease and Other Related Matters in relation to the Offshore Petroleum and Greenhouse Gas Storage Act 2006* (2019) [3.5].
[88]   *Offshore Petroleum and Greenhouse Gas Storage Act 2006* (Commonwealth) ss 129–33.
[89]   Where a person can be either a 'natural person' or a 'legal person.'
[90]   Crommelin 1998, 57–70.

34 *The character of petroleum licences*

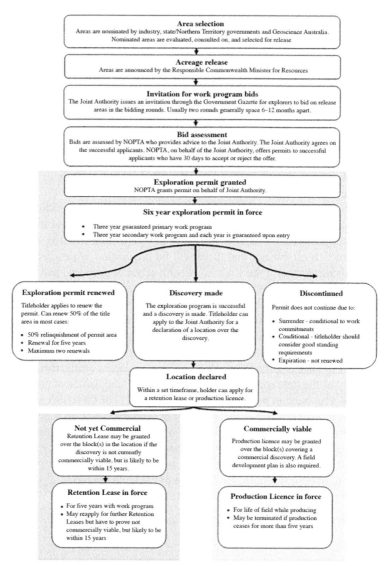

Source: Geoscience Australia, Overview of Australia's Offshore Petroleum Regime (2018) https://webarchive.nla.gov.au/awa/20181010050846/https://petroleum-acreage.gov.au/2018/ supporting-information/overview-australia%E2%80%99s-offshore-petroleum-regime. Accessed 22 February 2020.

Figure 2.2   Process for the allocation of access licences in Australia

2. Do such titles amount to proprietary interests?
3. If so, do these interests amount to an interest in land?
4. If they are an interest in land, can they be classified in terms of common law interests such as a leasehold interest, a profit à prendre or an easement?
5. Is there any significance attached to the statutory origin of these titles?[91]

In assessing the legal character of petroleum titles in Australia, this analysis will have due regard for the 'Crommelin criteria' outlined above.

In determining the legal character of such licences, Crommelin places importance on the role of the statute creating the title, where the characterisation of a licence is no more than one of statutory interpretation, assuming that the legislature expresses a statement of the legal character conferred.[92] Where such statement is lacking, as it is in the statute which has created many of Australia's petroleum titles (the PSLA), Crommelin suggests that context is critical for characterisation, placing an emphasis on registration and dealings with titles when interpreting the legal character of titles.[93] Due regard will also be had for such registration and dealings in the current act, the OPGGSA, when analysing the legal nature of Australian petroleum licences.

Prior to an analysis of whether offshore petroleum titles amount to real property interests, it is important to determine what the titles are *not*. Section 8 of the *Personal Property Securities Act 2009* (Cth) (PPSA) stipulates that a title granted by the Commonwealth is not personal property within the meaning of the PPSA, and therefore cannot be used as a personal property security. Therefore, the property interests conferred by a title must amount to a proprietary or real property interest rather than a personal interest if a property right is created.

It is important to note when examining the legal nature of Australia's petroleum titles what they are not. Unlike many jurisdictions, there is no standard form or document used, nor are there model contract provisions in the Act. No contract is formed when the Commonwealth grants a title (EL or PL) to a titleholder, rather a statutory right is granted. It is the legal nature of this 'right' that is the subject of this chapter – is the right merely administrative, or is a greater right conferred, perhaps that of a property right? Furthermore, if a property right is created, is that property right capable of being acquired by the Commonwealth, and is just compensation payable under the constitutional guarantee found in section 51(xxxi) of the Australian Constitution? It is these legal questions that are the focus of the following analysis of petroleum titles.

---

[91]   Ibid, 57.
[92]   Ibid.
[93]   Ibid, 57–8.

5.1   Exploration Permit

The initial access licence granted under the OPGGSA in accordance with the
process illustrated in Figure 2.2 above is that of the exploration permit (EP).
Section 97 OPGGSA makes it an offence to explore for petroleum in an offshore area unless otherwise authorised.[94] Such authorisation is given through
the grant of an exploration licence,[95] which confers the right to explore for
petroleum in the permit area, recover petroleum for appraisal use only, and
carry out operations and works necessary for the exploration and recovery (on
appraisal basis) of petroleum, in accordance with the conditions (if any) to
which the permit is subject.[96]

Aside from granting access to explore for petroleum, an EP also grants other
rights of a proprietary nature – the permit may be transferred,[97] and interests
may be created or assigned[98] subject to the approval of the relevant regulatory
authority. Thus, the interests of the permittee are susceptible of realisation by
sale or assignments.[99] Such qualities of an exploration permit are recognised
by the HCA as being indicative of the proprietary nature of the rights possessed by the holder of an exploration permit.[100] The Commonwealth itself
recognises that the rights attached to an offshore exploration permit amount
to property,[101] although it continues to assert that such property rights are
not capable of acquisition,[102] and cease to exist rather than being acquired by
the Commonwealth where the Commonwealth extinguishes the exploration
permit.[103]

Whereas the legal character of some resource titles are clearly characterised,
especially in light of the *Newcrest* mining case, there still remains questions
over the legal character of the Commonwealth offshore petroleum exploration,
production and retention titles. When analysing the nature and security of offshore titles in 1979, Crommelin noted that 'one can assert with confidence that
it is the substance of the transaction rather than its form that will determine its
legal character.'[104] Furthermore, Crommelin warned against a rigid approach

---

[94]   *Offshore Petroleum and Greenhouse Gas Storage Act 2006* (Cth), s 97.
[95]   Ibid, s 99.
[96]   Ibid, s 99 (1) and (2).
[97]   Ibid, Part 2.11.
[98]   Ibid.
[99]   *Commonwealth of Australia v WMC Resources* [1998] HCA 8 2 February 1998
[9].
[100]   Ibid.
[101]   Ibid, [43].
[102]   Ibid.
[103]   Ibid.
[104]   Crommelin 1979, 144.

in asserting title rights (such as those found in the US),[105] instead encouraging a flexible approach to characterisation, particularly given that authority with relation to questions of legal characterisation are sparse.

The question of the substance of an EP and the rights conferred was examined in *Commonwealth v WMC Resources* (*WMC Resources*).[106] Under the PSLA (the relevant Act at the time of the grant of exploration title) *WMC Resources* were granted a number of blocks under licence in an area of the Timor Sea, and the permit was issued at a time of competing claim for sovereign rights in the Timor Sea between Australia and Indonesia under the UNCLOS; but for the purposes of the judicial determination by the HCA, Australia was deemed to have possessed the sovereign rights pursuant to section 11 of the SSLA. In accordance with section 28 of the PSLA

> A permit, whilst it remains in force, authorises the permittee, subject to this Act and the regulations in accordance with the conditions to which this permit is subject, to explore for petroleum, and to carry on such operations and execute such works [as] necessary for that purpose, in the permit area.

The permit area (WA-74-P) was affected when the Commonwealth excised blocks or parts of blocks within WMC's permit area lying within Area A of the Petroleum Zone of Cooperation between Australia as a consequence of the *Petroleum (Australia-Indonesia Zone of Cooperation) (Consequential Provision) Act 1990* (Cth) (Consequential Provisions Act). WMC contested the excising of the blocks of which it held exploration title, contending that this amounted to acquisition of property, and sued the Commonwealth initially in the Federal Court of Australia, seeking a declaration that the excision from the permit area of the affected blocks would be an acquisition of property otherwise than on just terms.

In the federal court case, the Commonwealth maintained that the interest conferred in the exploration title did not amount to property.[107] However, in the High Court case of *Commonwealth v WMC Resources* it was not the Commonwealth's contention that there was no property in the title.[108] Rather, the Commonwealth abandoned the argument that there was no property in an exploration title, and acknowledged that some form of property rights existed in an offshore petroleum exploration licence.

---

[105] Ibid, 143.
[106] *Commonwealth of Australia v WMC Resources* [1998] HCA 8 2 February 1998.
[107] Ibid.
[108] Ibid.

In *WMC Resources* the justices considered and adjudicated on three questions:

1. Whether the rights afforded in an EP could be said to be property rights;
2. Whether the Commonwealth acquired these property rights; and
3. Whether the rights, if so acquired by the Commonwealth, were acquired in a manner other than on just terms.

The decision of the High Court in *WMC Resources* is distinctive for not only its consideration and treatment of the legal character of petroleum licences but also for the range of opinions of the justices. A summary of the justices' opinions and decisions is found in Table 2.1 below.

In the leading judgment, Brennan CJ at [13] noted that in the *Australian Tape Manufacturing Association Case*[109] the mere extinction or diminution of a property right residing in one does not necessarily result in the acquisition of property by another. Rather, he pointed out that there may be a mere extinguishment of a right. However, in *Mutual Pools*[110] Brennan CJ stated that where property rights against the Commonwealth are extinguished there is an acquisition of property by the Commonwealth.[111] Although WMC's exploration permit was recognised by Brennan CJ as a property right, he distinguished that right to be that of a creature of statute (the PSLA), where its continued existence depended on the continued existence of the statute that supported it. Further, he argued that if the statute diminishes the right, then acquisition of property is diminished.[112] This begs the question if the statute is amended to diminishing the rights granted, does this amount to an acquisition of property?[113]

In *WMC Resources*, Brennan CJ argued that the laws of the Commonwealth which extinguish purely statutory property rights can have an effect on acquisition of property within section 51(xxxi) where the statutory right impacts a third party.[114] He also argued that in this instance, the *Consequential Provisions Act*, which excises WMC's interest, does not have the effect of impacting a third party.[115] Utilising the reasoning from *Newcrest*, Brennan J noted that the law that sterilised the land with respect to the recovery of minerals on land vested in the Commonwealth was a law for the acquisition of property, since it extin-

---

[109] *Australian Tape Manufacturers Ltd v Commonwealth* (1993) 176 CLR 480.
[110] *Mutual Pools and Staff PTY v The Commonwealth* (1994) 179 CLR 115.
[111] *Commonwealth of Australia v WMC Resources* [1998] HCA 8 2 February 1998 [13].
[112] Ibid, [14].
[113] Ibid.
[114] Ibid, [16].
[115] Ibid.

guished liability of the Commonwealth to have minerals extracted from its land and therefore enhanced the property of the Commonwealth.[116] However it is important to note two distinguishing features of the *Newcrest* case. First, in the *Newcrest* case, the Commonwealth exerts *sovereignty* over the land (in line with the two-limb test of Crommelin). Second, the rights conferred by the mining leases to take minerals from the land confer an equivalent right of an offshore *production licence* and not an exploration permit, which *WMC Resources* considers. This then raises the question whether if petroleum were recovered from the seabed in Commonwealth areas under a production licence where the crown has sovereign right, would this amount to acquisition of property in the same way? Such an issue will be considered in section 5.2 below.

In considering the question of whether property rights were acquired by the Commonwealth through modification or extinguishment the majority of the justices Brennan CJ, Gaudron, McHugh and Gummow JJ concluded that the property rights were not acquired by the Commonwealth.[117] The reasoning varied between the justices for such a determination, with Brennan CJ concluding that such statutory modification did not amount to acquisition of property.[118] On the other hand, Gaudron J concluded that there was no proprietary estate in the Continental Shelf, and if there were it would effect an acquisition of property. However, under statute the Commonwealth did not create such an interest, rather merely conferring a right to explore.[119] In denying the acquisition of property rights by the Commonwealth, McHugh J reasoned that section 51(xxxi) did not withdraw from the parliament the power to enact legislation (in this instance the *Consequential Provisions Act*), which extinguished the property rights of WMC.[120] Gummow J's reasoning argued that the Commonwealth acquired no right since the scope created under the PSLA, and any property rights therein established, were liable to defeasance.[121] In the minority, Toohey J reasoned that proprietary rights had been acquired by the Commonwealth since the 'immunity lost here was identifiable, assignable, exclusive and valuable.' In contrast to Gummow J, who contended that the property rights were inherently unstable,[122] Kirby J reasoned that a stable title was created under the PSLA.[123] Furthermore, he asserted that the PSLA

---

[116] Ibid, [17].
[117] See Table 2.1 for the reasoning of the individual justices on this matter.
[118] *Commonwealth of Australia v WMC Resources* [1998] HCA 8 2 February 1998 [24].
[119] Ibid, [84].
[120] Ibid, [150].
[121] Ibid, [203].
[122] Ibid, [194].
[123] Ibid, [241].

went to great lengths to assure permit holders that their property rights were guaranteed against arbitrary or discretionary loss.[124] On the basis of this reasoning, Kirby J recognised that the Commonwealth, through modification and extinguishment, acquired property rights.

Turning our attention to the issue of acquisition of property, Brennan CJ reasoned that statutory modification or extinguishment of the interest granted by an exploration permit is not an acquisition of property by the Commonwealth, since the Commonwealth was under no liability reciprocal to the permit and acquired no benefit by the modification or extinguishment of the permit. This question of benefit was also considered by Toohey J[125] in his discussion of *Mutual Pools*,[126] where Dawson and Toohey JJ held that the extinguishment of a right to proceed against the Commonwealth was not an acquisition of property because 'when a chose in action is extinguished, the debtor receives merely a financial advantage not a proprietary interest in the choses in action.'[127]

Given the reasoning of Brennan, Gaudron, McHugh and Gummow JJ that property rights were not acquired by the Commonwealth, it is clear that since there was no acquisition of property the issue of just terms does not need to be considered. However, the reasoning of Toohey J asserted that the Commonwealth acquired property rights. Furthermore, his honour reasoned that the 'just terms' imposes a requirement of fairness rather than equivalence,[128] and where these terms depart from equivalence there is a strong indication that they are not fair or just.[129] Given that WMC received blocks in exchange that were less valuable than what they held in the original exploration permit, on its face WMC was disadvantaged and therefore the acquisition of the property was on terms other than on just terms.[130] In a similar vein, Kirby J reasoned that the Consequential Provisions Act failed to enact or provide for just terms for WMC Resources and therefore was not a law with respect to the acquisition of property on just terms. Thus, he concluded that section 24 of the *Consequential Provisions Act*, providing for the acquisition of such property, would be unconstitutional.

Taking the reasoning of all of the justices and the decision of the court, the High Court of Australia determined that WMC's EP in Commonwealth Waters

---

[124] Ibid.
[125] Ibid, [56].
[126] *Mutual Pools and Staff PTY v The Commonwealth* (1994) 179 CLR 115.
[127] Ibid at 195.
[128] *Commonwealth of Australia v WMC Resources* [1998] HCA 8 2 February 1998 [114].
[129] Ibid.
[130] Ibid, [66].

was a property interest. However, the majority of the justices (Brennan CJ, Gaudron, McHugh and Gummow JJ) found that the creation of those rights under statute (the PSLA), and the extinguishment of such property rights, was not enough to constitute an acquisition of property by the Commonwealth. Following this, the Court also found since there was no acquisition of property, there was no issue of whether the acquisition occurred under terms that were just or not.

5.2   Production Licences

As demonstrated in Figure 2.2 above, the transition from an EP to a production licence (PL) in offshore Commonwealth Waters occurs upon the discovery of petroleum. An EP holder is required to declare a discovery of petroleum to the titles regulator, the National Offshore Petroleum Titles Authority (NOPTA).[131] Where the discovery is deemed to be commercially viable, the EP holder is required to apply for a production licence (PL) in order to exploit the petro-leum. According to section 161(1) of OPGGSA, a PL authorises the licensee, in accordance with any conditions to which the licence is subject to:

(a) to recover petroleum in the licence area (for commercial purposes);
(b) to recover petroleum from the licence area in another area to which the licensee has lawful access for that purpose; and
(c) to explore for petroleum in the licence area; and
(d) to carry on such operations, and execute such works, in the licence area as are necessary for those purposes.

Given that the grant of a PL is subject to an assessment of the commerciality of the field, as made under the OPGGSA, and has conditions attached to it set by NOPTA, two characteristics of a property licence can be ascertained: the grant of a PL confers a statutory right to use an area to recover petroleum (akin to a profit-a-prendre),[132] having an element of discretion.

The OPGGSA confers a set of rights applicable to a PL. Perhaps the most important right conferred is the right to take petroleum upon severance.[133] This means that once petroleum is severed from the land on the Continental Shelf/EEZ, ownership of the petroleum is conferred upon the PL holder. It is important to note that title to petroleum does not pass from the State

---

[131] OPGGSA ss 129–33; National Offshore Petroleum Titles Authority, *Offshore Petroleum – Declaration of a Location Guideline in relation to the Offshore Petroleum and Greenhouse Gas Storage Act 2006* (2019).
[132] A *profit a prendre* is a right to enter the land to take natural resources.
[133] OPGGSA s 485.

Table 2.1   Summary of the legal character of WMC's exploration permit by Justices

Legal issues	Brennan CJ	Toohey J	Gaudron J	McHugh J	Gummow J	Kirby J
Do the proprietary rights granted by the Exploration licence amount to property?	YES: Exploration permit can be transferred and interests can be created, assigned and sold therefore proprietary and property @[9]	YES: rights granted by virtue of PSLA @[53]. Also: based on Cth disavowing submission to Full Federal Court that rights attributed to Exploration Permit were not property	YES, based on Cth disavowing submission to Full Federal Court that rights attributed to Exploration Permit were not property	YES, based on Cth accepting that Exploration Permit is property, and FN191, @ [150] contending that intangible property rights and 'innominate and anomalous interests' qualify as property for the purpose of s 51(xxxi)	YES, based on Cth disavowing submission to Full Federal Court that rights attributed to Exploration Permit were not property. Contended the property rights were 'inherently unstable' @[194]	YES, based on Cth disavowing submission to Full Federal Court that rights attributed to Exploration Permit were not property
Were the property rights acquired by the Commonwealth (through modification or extinguishment)	No @[24]: statutory modification or extinguishment of permit/interest in permit not an acquisition of property	Yes @[59], since the 'immunity lost here was identifiable, assignable, exclusive and valuable'[58]	NO: no proprietary estate in the continental shelf. If it was, it would effect an acquisition of property, but the Cth did not create an interest, merely conferred a right to explore [84]	No: @[150] as s 51(xxxi) did not withdraw from the parliament the power to enact legislation to extinguish property rights of WMC	NO: as scope of rights created under the PSLA and any property rights created under the EP were liable to defeasance @[203]	YES: Stable title created under the PSLA for investment purposes and assure permit holders that their property rights are guaranteed against arbitrary or discretionary loss @[241].

Legal issues	Brennan CJ	Toohey J	Gaudron J	McHugh J	Gummow J	Kirby J
Was the acquisition of the property on 'just terms'	No acquisition therefore not applicable	Yes, @[66]	No acquisition therefore not applicable	No acquisition therefore not applicable	No acquisition therefore not applicable	Yes, @[267]
Would the right to apply for a PL, or the granting of a PL, create property rights capable of acquisition	Yes where the acquisition of property by the Commonwealth must involve obtaining 'some identifiable benefit or advantage relating to the ownership or use of the property' @[13]	Yes, recognises property in the lesser right of an Exploration Permit.	Yes, creates a property right capable of acquisition where petroleum is capable of being recovered @ [81]	Yes, property rights created (as per reasoning at [144], FN 191), and capable of acquisition. But: argued the operation of 'Acquisition on just terms' extinguished where rights not recognised at common law (on continental shelf)	SILENT any proprietary rights created by the EP under the PSLA are liable to defeasance. Other interests not considered	Yes, as reasoned at [267] where EP is a property right capable of acquisition on just terms, therefore the greater right attached to a PL would also be capable.
Would the right to apply for a RL, or the granting of a RL, create property rights capable of acquisition	Yes, since the commonwealth would obtain 'some identifiable benefit or advantage relating to the ownership or use of the property' from an RL similar to that of a PL once commercial viability is established - @[13]	Yes, as it recognises property in the lesser right of an Exploration Permit	Yes, since a RL creates a property right capable of acquisition because petroleum is capable of being recovered once it becomes commercially viable@ [81]	Yes as analogous property rights are created to that where a PL can be acquired (as per reasoning at [144], FN 191),	SILENT – however any proprietary rights created by the EP under the PSLA are liable to defeasance	Yes, @ [267] – an EP is a property right capable of acquisition on just terms, therefore the equal or greater right attached to a RL would also be capable.

(Commonwealth) to the PL holder, but rather ownership of the petroleum is vested in the first instance in the PL holder. This is because the State does not 'own' the mineral resources contained in the EEZ and CS, but rather only has Sovereign Rights over them, which does not confer ownership of the resources.[134] However, the Commonwealth does have the right to confer ownership of the mineral rights once exploited under Article 56 (1)(a) of UNCLOS (and implemented into Australian law by section 6 (the Territorial Sea) and section 11 (Continental Shelf) of the *Sea and Submerged Lands Act 1973*), and does so under section 485 of OPGGSA.

The PL (like all petroleum titles) must be registered, and entered into the register by the Titles Administrator.[135] Registration is required since ownership of petroleum can only pass to the titleholder, and in order to be a titleholder the title must be registered. Titles can be transferred,[136] and this requires the approval of the Titles Administrator (NOPTA), but not the Authority regulating activities (NOPSEMA).[137] The Title Administrator can deny title transfer,[138] and a notation in the Register is required where refusal of a transfer occurs.[139] There is the capacity of devolution of rights that attach to a particular title,[140] as well as other dealings with existing titles, including the assignment of an interest or right (incorporating a carried interest),[141] which must all be approved by Title Administrator.[142] The sum effect of these dealings is the creation or assignment of rights, interests and options in the title.[143] However, OPGGSA specifically notes that the instrument of transfer does not create an interest in the title.[144] There is also a right to make an application for a future interest (i.e., a title that may come into existence in the future) under section 498 of the OPGGSA.

As explained in section 5.1 above, the High Court states, as accepted by the Commonwealth, that a EP confers 'property rights', although the strength of

---

[134] Crommelin 1998.
[135] *Offshore Petroleum and Greenhouse Gas Storage Act 2006* (Cth), Ch 4.
[136] Ibid, Part 4.3.
[137] Ibid, s 472.
[138] Ibid, s 478.
[139] Ibid, s 478(5).
[140] Ibid, s 482.
[141] Ibid, s 486.
[142] Ibid, s 487.
[143] National Offshore Petroleum Titles Authority, *Offshore Petroleum Guideline: Transfers and Dealings Relating to Petroleum Titles in relation to the Offshore Petroleum and Greenhouse Gas Storage Act 2006* (2018) [2.5].
[144] *Offshore Petroleum and Greenhouse Gas Storage Act 2006* (Cth), s 480.

those rights are considered 'weak' by some justices.[145] The rights conferred under a PL are considerably greater than that of an EP. Whereas the grant of an EP only grants the right to explore for petroleum, and for registration and transfer of title, the PL confers a right to take a natural resource (petroleum) from the 'land', in this instance the Continental Shelf.

Considering the reasoning of Brennan CJ in *WMC Resources*, particularly the consideration on property rights,[146] a question arises whether if a petroleum title recovered commercial quantities of petroleum (i.e., a PL from the seabed where the Commonwealth has sovereign rights were granted), would this amount to a property right, and would the property rights conferred under a PL be greater than those conferred under an EP? Furthermore, if the Commonwealth acquired the interest in the same manner as the acquisition of WMC Resources' interest, would this amount to acquisition of property? Or to put it simply, if the licence under consideration in *WMC Resources* were PL and not an EP, would the High Court have found that the legal character was that of stronger property rights that were capable of being acquired by the Commonwealth?

In *WMC Resources*, Brennan CJ noted that the rights conferred under the PSLA were not equivalent to those conferred on land where the Crown has the authority to alienate its interests. Whereas acts granted on land assume the existence of the Crown's radical title to land lying above the below water mark, and which is sufficient to support the alienation of interests in that land, the position in relation to interests in or over the continental shelf differs.[147] Further, Brennan CJ contended that although the Commonwealth has the power to legislate in respect of the exploration for and exploitation of the resources of the continental shelf, it has no property in the continental shelf at common law.[148] Rather, property rights are a creation of statute (section 11 of the SSLA), with diminished property rights. Brennan CJ further argued that 'acquisition of property' by the Commonwealth must involve the obtaining of 'some identifiable benefit or advantage relating to the ownership or use of the property.'[149] Such a benefit would be similar to the benefit identified

---

[145] In particular see the reasoning of Gummow, J in *Commonwealth of Australia v WMC Resources* [1998] HCA 8 2 February 1998, who described the rights of an EP as 'inherently unstable' [194], compared to the reasoning of Kirby J who sees the rights as inherently stable under a statutory title designed to create stability of reinvestment [241].

[146] *Commonwealth of Australia v WMC Resources* [1998] HCA 8 2 February 1998 [17].

[147] Ibid, [80].

[148] Ibid, [23].

[149] Ibid, [13] citing *Mutual Pools and Staff PTY v The Commonwealth* (1994) 179 CLR 155 at 223.

in *Newcrest*, where the High Court found that Commonwealth acquisition of titles for the production of minerals were acquired on just terms where the Commonwealth gained a benefit from the royalties associated with extraction. When petroleum is extracted from the continental shelf under a PL and title over the petroleum granted to the PL holder, the Commonwealth is entitled to recover PPRT from any petroleum produced thereby gaining a benefit for production of petroleum on the continental shelf.

Toohey J argued that although the EP was transient, finite and did not confer a property right in this instance, he reasoned that during a period of operation of a permit, it could confer rights capable of acquisition, including where the holder of an EP has the right to make an application for a PL.[150] Picking up on Brennan CJ's reasoning regarding the gaining of a benefit by the Commonwealth, Toohey J reasoned that, in light of *Georgiadis v Australian OTC*[151] and *Commonwealth v Mewet*[152] where the recovery of petroleum confers a distinct financial benefit upon the titleholder by the Commonwealth (such as under a PL), the extinguishment of the title will amount to an acquisition of property.[153] Given this reasoning, the extinguishment of a PL in Commonwealth waters will not only have property rights conferred but is likely to meet the criteria for acquisition of property by the Commonwealth, and as such it would be liable for acquisition on just terms in accordance with section 51(xxxi) of the Australian Constitution.

The issue of property rights, sovereignty and sovereign rights was considered by Gaudron J in *WMC Resources*, who noted that

> it may well be that if after the discovery of petroleum, an exploration permit were extinguished or modified with the consequence that the right to apply for a lease or production licence was destroyed or otherwise negated that would constitute an acquisition for the purposes of section 51(xxxi) of the Constitution.[154]

Such reasoning relating to the legal character of an EP *after* the discovery of petroleum differs from Gaudron's view of the rights accorded under an

---

[150] *Commonwealth of Australia v WMC Resources* [1998] HCA 8 2 February 1998 [54].
[151] *Georgiadis v Australian and Overseas Telecommunications Corporation* (1994) 179 CLR 297.
[152] *Commonwealth v Mewett* (1997) 146 ALR 299.
[153] *Commonwealth of Australia v WMC Resources* [1998] HCA 8 2 February 1998 [56], referring to *Commonwealth v Mewett* (1997) 146 ALR 299 at 310, 317, 332–3, 353.
[154] *Commonwealth of Australia v WMC Resources* [1998] HCA 8 2 February 1998 [81].

EP *prior* to the finding of petroleum,[155] which she concluded did not create an interest but merely conferred a right to explore. Furthermore, Gaudron J argued that acquisition of property would 'also be the case if an exploration permit were modified or extinguished with the consequence that the holder of the permit were denied a lease or production licence to which it was otherwise entitled.'[156] Essentially, Gaudron J found that although the existing WMC EP did not confer strong enough property rights for extinguishment, an EP where petroleum had been found and the right to apply for a PL or a retention lease arose, then property rights capable of acquisition would be conferred.

Justice McHugh recognised in *WMC Resources* that property rights were created, contending that intangible property rights and 'innominate and anomalous interests' that were created under the EP qualify as property for the purpose of section 51(xxxi) and capable of acquisition.[157] However, although McHugh J recognised that property rights that were capable of acquisition of property were established, he argued that operation of 'Acquisition on just terms' extinguished where rights not recognised at common law (on continental shelf). Thus, given McHugh J's unequivocal recognition of property rights in an EP, the property rights imbued by a PL would be capable of acquisition.

To answer this question, it is also necessary to examine whether the sovereign rights granted under UNCLOS and imported into domestic law under section 11 of the SSLA amount to a property right. According to the reasoning of Crommelin, there 'seems no reason in principle why qualified property rights should not flow from sovereign rights enjoyed by the Commonwealth over the continental shelf, just as radical title flowed from the sovereignty exercisable over the territorial sea and land territory.'[158] Although sovereignty (as expressed in section 6 of the SSLA) is a stronger term than sovereign rights (as declared in section 11 SSLA regarding the continental shelf) and observed by Gummow J in *WMC*,[159] a variety of property interests in land are recognised. Crommelin argues that such flexibility in property interest allows the derivation of a proprietary interest in natural resources from Australia's declared sovereign rights over the continental shelf, but remains an interest that is less than absolute title.[160]

---

[155] Ibid, [84].
[156] Ibid.
[157] See *Commonwealth of Australia v WMC Resources* [1998] HCA 8 2 February 1998 [144].
[158] Crommelin 1998, 68–9.
[159] *Commonwealth of Australia v WMC Resources* [1998] HCA 8 2 February 1998 [160].
[160] Crommelin 1998, 69.

5.3   Retention Licences

Whereas a PL will be granted where the declaration of a location is of a commercially viable petroleum discovery, an application for, and the granting of, a retention lease is made where the declaration of a location is made[161] for a discovery which is not yet commercially viable, but is likely to be so in the next 15 years.[162] The objective of a retention lease is 'to ensure a lessee actively seeks to address the barriers to commercial development of petroleum resources and, where it is commercially viable to do so, brings those resources to production in a timely manner.'[163] Under section 135(1)of the OPGGSA, the grant of a retention lease authorises the lessee, *in accordance with the conditions (if any) to which the lease is subject*:

(a) to explore for petroleum in the lease area; and
(b) to recover petroleum on an appraisal basis in the lease area; and
(c) to carry on such operations, and execute such works, in the lease area as are
    necessary for those purposes.

When comparing the rights granted by a RL with that of an EP, it is clear that a RL grants property rights that are, at a minimum, equal to that of the EP. Therefore, it is undisputed, according to the reasoning of the six justices in *WMC Resources*, that a RL grants property rights. Whether these property rights are more than the EP, and capable of acquisition, depends on the nature of the retention lease. As illustrated in Figure 2.2 above, a RL is granted where petroleum has been discovered and a declaration has been made. In essence, this means that petroleum has been found, and will be recovered by the licence holder once it is commercially viable to do so.[164] Examining Table 2.1, and the analysis of judicial reasoning in *WMC Resources*, it is clear that like a PL, the majority of the justices (5:1) recognise that where there is a discovery of petroleum which is likely to be recovered, real property rights exist which are capable of acquisition. In addition, similar to that of the PL, the operation of section 780 of the OPGGSA establishes a right that where a property interest is

---

[161] Under s 131 of the OPGGSA.

[162] *Guideline – Grant and Administration of a Retention Lease and Other Related Matters in relation to the Offshore Petroleum and Greenhouse Gas Storage Act 2006* (2019) [1.1].

[163] Ibid, [1.2].

[164] For a decision of commercially viable refer to *Guideline – Grant and Administration of a Retention Lease and Other Related Matters in relation to the Offshore Petroleum and Greenhouse Gas Storage Act 2006* (2019), [3.5].

established under the OPGGSA, any acquisition of that property must be made with just terms.[165]

6.   SO WHAT IS THE LEGAL CHARACTER OF PETROLEUM TITLES IN AUSTRALIA?

According to the reasoning in *WMC Resources*, a exploration permit granted under the PSLA is accepted as property, but the majority reasoned that the property rights were insufficient to be acquired by the Commonwealth, and therefore no just terms were payable. Applying such reasoning to the current OPGGSA, it is clear that the rights granted by an EP are property. It can also be reasoned that under section 780 of the OPGGSA that 'property' includes an EP. Under OPGGSA, the scope of section 780 appears wide, particularly given that property is not defined in the OPGGSA, and there is uncertainty as to whether the provisions would indeed apply to EPs. An examination of the provisions relating to acquisition of property in the original drafting of the *Offshore Petroleum Act 2006* (Cth) (OPA) (the act that preceded OPGGSA, which was created with the introduction of the Greenhouse gas storage provisions) demonstrates a narrower application of the term property. Section 249 (1) of the OPA states that if the operation of section 139(1) (duration of petroleum licences), section 140 (4) (termination of the life of a field), section 169 (4) termination of an Infrastructure licence), or section 229 (suspension of an EP or RL due to national interest), would result in acquisition of property, otherwise than on just terms, and compensation has not been paid, then the Commonwealth is liable for payment of compensation. Of particular interest here is section 229, which includes the acquisition of an EP due to national interest. In this section the 'acquisition of property on just terms' provision, even in its narrow construction, applied where interests conferred under an EP were affected. Given that in this narrow construction of the acquisition of property section in 2006 applied to EPs, it is reasonable to infer that the wider construction under section 780 (where the generic term property is used) is meant to include EPs.

Regarding PLs, the above reasoning demonstrates that PLs in the Territorial Sea would confer property rights capable of acquisition, since a PL confers on the title holder the right acquire petroleum upon severance from 'land' where the Commonwealth holds sovereignty. Furthermore, Crommelin's analysis of sovereign right and the conferring of ownership of petroleum to the PL holder

---

[165]   *Offshore Petroleum and Greenhouse Gas Storage Act 2006* (Cth) s 780 (1).

upon severance on the continental shelf[166] together recognize that real property rights, stronger than those conferred by an EP prior to the discovery of petroleum, exist on the continental shelf.

In addition, examining the reasoning of all six justices in *WMC Resources*, it is clear that the majority of the justices (5:1) recognise that the grant of a PL in Commonwealth Waters (whether the territorial sea or the continental shelf) would grant property rights sufficiently capable of acquisition.[167] Finally, the operation section 780 of OPGGSA, which establishes that 'if the operation of this Act or the Regulations' would result in an acquisition of property from a person otherwise than on just terms, the Commonwealth is liable to pay a reasonable amount of compensation to the person', creates a statutory right to just compensation for acquisition of property (including a PL) established by the OPGGSA. Clearly the hurdle in attaining just compensation upon acquisition is fourfold: Firstly, whether the petroleum title held is a property interest; secondly, whether the property interests created by the grant of a petroleum title are sufficient to be capable of acquisition; thirdly, whether the interest was acquired; and fourthly, whether such acquisition created a right for just compensation. The majority judicial position on property rights in *WMC Resources*, combined with a statutory guarantee of just terms upon the acquisition of property rights emanating from the OPGGSA, establishes a clear view that where a PL is acquired in Commonwealth Waters, compensation on just terms must be paid.

Finally, an analysis of the legal nature of the RL demonstrates that, similar to the PL, the right to recover petroleum and obtain title to the petroleum, as conferred under a RL and reasoned in *WMC Resources*, is sufficient to confer property rights. These property rights are also similarly protected from acquisition on anything other than just terms by the action of section 780 of the OPGGSA.

---

[166] By virtue of s 11 of the *Sea and Submerged Lands Act 1973* (Cth) and s 285 of the *Offshore Petroleum and Greenhouse Gas Storage Act 2006* (Cth).

[167] See summary of the position and reasoning of each justice in Table 2.1.

3. The legal character of petroleum licences in the United States of America

John S. Lowe[1]

1. LEGAL CHARACTER OF THE JURISDICTION

Private property ownership is a "driver" of the legal system of the United States of America, including the legal character of oil and gas licences, both private and public. The United States of America is a democratic republic, a federal nation with 50 states and five inhabited territories. Its Constitution, adopted in 1787, includes a Bill of Rights that protects individual freedoms including private property rights; the Fifth Amendment states that "nor shall private property be taken for public use without just compensation".[2] The concept of the sanctity of private ownership is extended to the states, many of which have provisions protecting private property rights in their own constitutions, by the Fourteenth Amendment[3] to the United States Constitution.

The United States is committed to the rule of law at both the federal and state levels, though there is often raucous disagreement about what the law is or should be. By design, the United States Constitution is structured to provide checks and balances on the powers of government. The United States Constitution grants the federal government limited enumerated powers reserving the remaining powers to the states, but the breadth of the federal government's authority to regulate commerce, to protect property, to spend and tax,

[1] Portions of this chapter are based on materials that the author has written or edited with others, including JOHN S. LOWE, OWEN L. ANDERSON, ERNEST E. SMITH, DAVID E. PIERCE, CHRISTOPHER S. KULANDER AND MONIKA U. EHRMAN, CASES AND MATERIALS ON OIL AND GAS LAW (West 7th ed. 2018) and JOHN S. LOWE, OIL AND GAS LAW IN A NUTSHELL (West 7th ed. 2019). I thank my administrative assistant, Donna Gaubert, for her technical support in this project, and the Peter S. Chantillis, Esq., Class of 1957, Memorial Faculty Research Fund for its financial support.
[2] U.S.CONST. amend. V.
[3] U.S.CONST. amend. IV.

and to make treaties has over time made the federal government preeminent over the states. Further, the federal government has the ability to preempt state action because of the Supremacy Clause of the Constitution[4] which bars state and local governments from "regulating" the federal government. But the United States is committed to "co-operative federalism"; the federal government and the states often share powers. Many federal laws, including environmental laws that affect petroleum licences, are administered by the states. The federal government also shares with the states some of the production revenues from federal leases: for example, under the Mineral Leasing Act the state where a lease is located receives 50 percent (90 percent in Alaska) of the bonus, rental, and royalty revenues generated.[5]

Government powers in the United States are separated both at the federal and state levels. There are three "branches" of government in the United States – the executive, the legislative and the judicial. The legislative branch enacts laws, the executive interprets the laws through regulations and administers them, often with the help of administrative agencies, and the judiciary interprets them. The United States is primarily a common law jurisdiction,[6] but much of the common law has been codified.

The diffusion of powers is enhanced by the electoral system. At the national level, each state regardless of population has two senators elected on a statewide basis for staggered six-year terms. Members of the 435-seat House of Representatives, however, are allocated on the basis of population and elected every two years from districts within each state with redistricting based upon censuses conducted every ten years. Judges of the Supreme Court, the 13 courts of appeal, and 92 judicial districts are appointed for life by the President, with the advice and consent of the Senate.

The federal structure of separation of power is mirrored in the 50 states. But each state has its own constitution, and there are significant differences in how powers are allocated among the executive, legislative and judicial branches at the state level. For example, the former members of the Confederate States of America, which were subject to military occupation and "carpetbagger" administration for several years after the end of the Civil War in 1865, tend to have weak executive branches and to elect judges periodically.

Though administrative agencies are not directly addressed in the United States Constitution, both the federal government and the states rely on inde-

---

[4]   U.S.CONST. art. VI, cl.2.
[5]   30 U.S.C. § 191.
[6]   The sole civil law jurisdiction among the states is Louisiana, which is a major player in the oil and gas sector. The principles of Louisiana's oil and gas law – embodied in the Louisiana Mineral Code, Title 31 of the Louisiana Revised Statutes – are much the same as those of the common law jurisdictions.

pendent and expert administrative and regulatory agencies that often exercise combined executive, legislative and judicial authority. Courts generally show deference to the actions of administrative agencies because of their expertise if agencies follow strictly the terms of the statutes that authorize them.

International law plays only a limited role in the United States legal system, though United States courts consider treaties and other international agreements "the law of the land" and large quantities of both oil and gas are produced from federal leases in the exclusive economic zone. The United States has signed but not ratified the United Nations Convention on the Law of the Sea. The North American Free Trade Agreement restricted regulation of Mexican and Canadian investors in the United States. The United States-Mexico-Canada Agreement, adopted in 2020, modified but largely continued those restrictions.

2.   PROCESS FOR OBTAINING A PETROLEUM LICENCE

A petroleum licence, known as an oil or gas *lease* in the United States, may be obtained from a private mineral owner, from a state, from an Indian Tribe or from the federal government.

2.1   Oil and Gas Leases on Privately Owned Mineral Rights

The United States is an "outlier" by international standards in that more than 70 percent of onshore mineral rights are privately owned, legally a part of the "bundle of sticks" of land ownership, by individuals or business entities rather than by governments. Most Americans who own real estate own the mineral rights to valuable substances including oil and gas under their property, though mineral rights are often "severed" from real estate and sold separately. Private mineral rights are governed by state law, and generally treated as interests in real estate.

Private ownership of minerals in the United States appears to be largely an historical accident. It is not clear why the British Crown did not retain valuable minerals when it made land grants to the colonists in what became the United States. Once the United States was established the federal government intended to retain lands of known "mineral" character beyond the 13 original colonies and Texas, but did not realize the extent of mineral deposits as it sold or opened lands to settlement. Consequently, much land containing valuable minerals passed from the federal government into private hands.[7] Very

---

[7]   In the early years of the nation, the focus of the government of the United States was on acquisition of lands to enhance national security; public land was sold to

quickly, land owners expected that when they acquired land they also acquired ownership of minerals in the land.[8]

A fundamental legal principle of oil and gas law in the United States is the Rule of Capture – a legal rule of non-liability that the owner of mineral rights in a tract of land acquires title to the oil and gas produced from wells drilled on that land though part of the oil and gas may have migrated from adjoining property. The Rule of Capture is limited by the correlative-rights doctrine, the principle that the right to capture oil and gas from potentially producing formations is subject to the concomitant duty to exercise the right without negligence or waste, and extensive and diverse state petroleum conservation laws and regulations, but it provides private mineral owners with a powerful incentive to explore and develop sooner rather than later. If they do not use their right to try to capture oil and gas from their property, they may lose it.

There is no standard process to obtain an oil and gas lease on privately owned mineral rights. Generally, however, leasing is initiated and controlled by the oil and gas industry rather than by the mineral-rights owners. The United States was settled, mostly for the purpose of agriculture development, by small land grants or sales of a few hundred acres or so made by the federal and state governments to private individuals. None of the American states adopted the feudal rule of primogeniture, the rule that the first-born surviving male heir took all, rather than sharing with other heirs, so over time privately owned mineral-interest ownership in land has become highly fractionalized. A single well spacing unit may have hundreds of owners.[9]

Leasing of private mineral rights in the United States is often highly speculative and competitive. Oil-company-employed or independent geologists and engineers identify "prospects" for drilling. "Landmen" – acting either for themselves or as agents for oil companies – identify mineral owners from

---

finance additional acquisition and pay debt. After the Louisiana Purchase in 1803, the focus turned to settlement and agricultural development through land sales and land grants. Beginning in the early 1900s, the United States reserved minerals when it issued patents to settlers, but it was not until the Stock Raising and Homestead Act of 1916 that the federal government started retaining all minerals, including oil, gas and geothermal resources from its grants. Since the Federal Land Policy and Management Act of 1976 (FLPMA), retention of mineral rights has been the official policy of the federal government.

[8]   See Terence Daintith, Finders Keepers? How the Law of Capture Shaped the World Oil Industry (RFF Press 2010).

[9]   For example, the Oklahoma pooling order example shown at John S. Lowe, Owen L. Anderson, Ernest E. Smith, David E. Pierce, Christopher S. Kulander and Monika U. Ehrman, Forms Manual to Cases and Materials on Oil and Gas Law 218–37 (West 7th ed. 2018), hereinafter cited as "Forms Manual", lists 208 potential owners in a 640-acre drilling and spacing unit.

county property records and approach them asking for leases. The parties may negotiate lease terms but usually negotiations begin with the offer of a printed-form lessee-oriented lease to the mineral owner. The lessee pays the lessor a bonus to grant the lease; the bonus may run thousands of dollars per acre. Often bonus is paid by a bank draft conditioned on the lessee's acceptance of title.

Leases are generally executed by lessors alone and recorded by lessees in the real property records of the county where the land is located. What those records are called and how they work differs from state to state and sometimes even within a state. Generally, however, the records provide constructive notice to the public and permit title examiners to construct "chains" of title ownership.

Oil and gas leases of privately owned mineral rights may generally be freely transferred. In most states, lease restrictions on transferability are likely to be ruled by courts to be unenforceable restraints against alienation. Indeed, the speculative and competitive nature of leasing, combined with the fractionalization of mineral rights, means that leases are often transferred many times before they are drilled.

2.2   Oil and Gas Leases from Governments

Oil and gas leases in the United States may also be obtained from state governments, Indian tribes or from the federal government. The process of government leasing is much more structured than that for leasing of privately owned minerals. Leases are generally awarded to the highest qualified bidder after an open and transparent bidding process.

2.2.1   State leases

The states of the United States own substantial public lands including oil and gas rights, both onshore and off the coast. For example, Texas owns approximately 21 million acres of oil and gas rights. Upon Alaska assuming Statehood in 1959 the federal government granted it more than 100 million acres of land including mineral rights.[10] Further, the federal government ceded, as part of a historical political compromise, to the coastal states submerged lands within three miles from their shorelines.[11] The structures by which the various states grant leases vary substantially from state to state and from agency to agency

---

[10]   Act of July 7, 1958, Pub.L.No. 85–508, 72 Stat. 339.

[11]   The Submerged Lands Act of 1953, 43 U.S.C. §§ 1301–15. Texas and Florida have even larger boundaries – three marine leagues, or a little more than ten standard miles.

within states, but generally leases are sold by agencies acting in a fiduciary capacity for fair market value either at public auction or by a transparent application process.

2.2.2   Indian leases

The United States Department of the Interior's Bureau of Land Management (BLM) grants leases and regulates development of oil and gas on American Indian Lands in conjunction with the Bureau of Indian Affairs.

American Indian Tribes, which are considered "domestic, dependent sovereigns", own approximately 138 million acres of land and mineral rights within reservations, communities, or pueblos in the United States that include an estimated four percent of United States onshore oil and gas resources. Further, individual members of Indian tribes may own "allotted" or "restricted fee" lands. The federal government recognizes a fiduciary relationship between the United States and Indian tribes and their individual members. The federal government is the guardian of tribes and their members, bound to meet the strictest fiduciary standards by what is called the Trust Doctrine.[12] Generally, all leases and mineral-related agreements entered into by a tribe or individual Indians must be examined and approved by the Secretary of the Interior.[13]

The primary mechanism for obtaining a lease on Indian-owned mineral rights is the Indian Mineral Leasing Act of 1938.[14] Indian leases must be advertised before they are granted. The process may be initiated either by the Indian mineral owner or by a prospective lessee. Tracts are leased to responsible bidders who offer the highest bonus; usually, bidding is by sealed bids. Indian oil and gas leases must be contained within a single governmental survey section and may not exceed 640 acres. Leases are granted for a primary term of ten years and as long thereafter as minerals specified are produced in paying quantities.

2.3   Federal Leases

The federal government is the largest single land and mineral owner in the United States. Federal public lands comprise almost 655 million acres, or

---

[12] For discussion *see* 2 Law of Federal Oil and Gas Leases, ROCKY MTN. MIN. L. FOUND. at § 26.02[b].

[13] *Id.*

[14] A later statute, the Indian Mineral Development Act of 1982· 25 U.S.C. §§ 2101–08. allows qualifying tribes to attract, negotiate and manage their own mineral development, subject to final approval by the Bureau of Indian Affairs, an agency within the Department of Interior.

about 29 percent of the total land area of the 50 states.[15] In addition, the United States has reserved minerals in more than 57 million acres of lands that it has turned over to private ownership.[16] The United States government also claims the exclusive right to control the exploitation of oil and gas resources on most of the Outer Continental Shelf (OCS) and other submerged lands bordering the United States seaward at least 200 nautical miles. The federal OCS includes all submerged lands that lie seaward of state-owned submerged lands ceded to the states by the Submerged Lands Act of 1953[17] to the extent of the Exclusive Economic Zone (EEZ).[18] The EEZ of the United States is one of the largest in the world spanning over 13,000 miles of coastline and containing 3.4 million square nautical miles of ocean – as large as the combined land area of all 50 states. Policy barriers to the development of federal minerals have limited production from the OCS. Approximately 90 percent of federal offshore acreage is off limits to development as a result of Executive, Congressional or regulatory action.[19]

2.3.1 Federal leases onshore

The Mineral Leasing Act of 1920[20] as amended by the Federal Onshore Oil and Gas Leasing Reform Act of 1987 governs onshore leasing of federal lands in the United States. The BLM, an agency of the United States Department of the Interior, grants leases and regulates development of oil and gas on federally owned onshore mineral rights. The Mineral Leasing Act authorizes the Interior Department to lease available lands that are "known or believed to contain

---

[15] Department of the Interior, Public Land Statistics, 2017 available at www.blm.gov/sites/blm.gov/files/PublicLandStatistics2017.pdf (last visited May 25, 2019).

[16] *Id.* at 7.

[17] 43 U.S.C. §§ 1301–15. Under the Submerged Lands Act, all coastal states except Texas and Florida hold title to the inlets and offshore lands within three miles of their respective shore lines. Florida, on its Gulf coast, and Texas hold title to offshore lands within three marine leagues of their shore lines, about 10.5 miles.

[18] Under Presidential Proclamation No. 5030, the United States claims the sovereign rights to the Exclusive Economic Zone (the "EEZ"), an area extending seaward for a distance of 200 miles from the coast of the United States and its territories and possessions. 48 Fed.Reg. 10,605 (1983). The 1982 U.N. Convention on the Law of the Sea, 21 I.L.M. 1261 (1982), recognizes a sovereign nation's right to develop natural resources from the adjacent seabed. Although the United States has not ratified the Convention, the EEZ claimed by the United States is consistent with arts. 55–75.

[19] In fact, offshore leases have been issued only off the coasts of Texas, Louisiana, Mississippi, Alabama, and the western portion of Florida. The Trump Administration seeks to expand offshore leasing in areas of Alaska and the Atlantic coast that President Obama withdrew from leasing "without specific expiration" under 43 U.S.C. § 1341(a), by a Presidential Memoranda dated Dec. 20, 2016.

[20] Act of Feb. 25, 1920, ch. 85, § 1, 41 Stat. 437, 30 U.S.C. § 181 et seq.

oil or gas deposits",[21] but rather than affirmatively identifying and classifying lands available for leasing, the Act and other federal statutes and regulations classify lands that cannot be leased. For example, other federal agencies, such as the National Park Service, the Fish and Wildlife Service and the Forest Service, manage the surface of federal lands and decide whether the lands that they manage may be leased for oil and gas exploration and development, and the extent to which a lessee will have access to and use of the surface.[22]

There is a four-step process to identify federal onshore lands available for leasing of which the first two are largely environmentally focused. The BLM first prepares a Resource Management Plan, setting long-term goals for management of mineral, timber, grazing, recreational and other resources on BLM-administered lands.[23] The Resource Management Plan identifies the public land available for each use, often calling for multiple use management. For mineral-development activities such as oil and gas leasing, the Resource Management Plan also sets the conditions under which development should occur.[24] Second, the Bureau of Land Management prepares a Master Leasing Plan that analyzes the type and extent of disruption that the proposed development might cause, considering the impact that oil and gas development may have on air quality, recreation, flora and fauna, cultural properties of American Indian communities or paleontological resources, watersheds and aquifers, erosion and soils, and health and safety. Third, BLM selects tracts nominated by the Secretary of Interior for lease and gives public notice. Fourth, lease sales are held quarterly at the Bureau's state offices.

Competitive leasing is the norm. Lessees do not negotiate terms of leases, which are set in advance by the BLM. The highest qualified bidder gets the lease, and bidding, which is oral or internet based, is on the basis of bonus alone.[25] To own, hold or control an interest in a federal lease a person must

---

[21]   30 U.S.C. § 226(a).

[22]   BLM's authority comes from the Federal Land Policy and Management Act ("FLPMA"), 43 U.S.C. §§ 1701–85 and the Mineral Leasing Act of 1920, Act of Feb. 25, 1920, ch. 85, § 1, 41 Stat. 437. A brief history of the development of U.S. law relating to federal lands onshore leasing is at JOHN S. LOWE, OWEN L. ANDERSON, ERNEST E. SMITH, DAVID E. PIERCE, CHRISTOPHER S. KULANDER AND MONIKA U. EHRMAN, CASES AND MATERIALS ON OIL AND GAS LAW 1219–28 (West 7th ed. 2018) [hereinafter cited as "Cases and Materials"].

[23]   43 U.S.C. § 1712(a).

[24]   43 C.F.R. § 1601.0–5(k).

[25]   The bid must equal or exceed the "national minimum acceptable bid", 30 U.S.C. § 226(b)(1)(B), which as this chapter is written in 2019 was $2.00 per acre, but the Secretary of the Interior has the discretion to increase the amount. 43 C.F.R. § 3120.1–2(c).

meet citizenship requirements[26] as well as financial security standards.[27] Aliens may hold federal leases whether onshore or offshore only through stock ownership, holding or control of corporations, and only if the laws, customs or regulations of the alien's home country do not deny similar privileges to citizens or corporations of the United States.[28] Subject to a few exceptions, "[n]o person or entity shall take, hold, own or control more than 246,080 acres[29] of federal oil and gas leases in any one State [except Alaska] at any one time".[30] If a tract offered does not attract any bids, it may be leased non-competitively for a period of two years following the lease sale.[31]

Federal leases onshore are registered with the Bureau of Land Management office in the state where the property is located. Once issued the Secretary may cancel a lease only after the lessee is given notice of noncompliance and an opportunity to cure. If the leasehold contains a well capable of production in paying quantities and the lessee has failed to comply with a law, regulation, or lease provision, a judicial proceeding is required for cancellation. Improperly issued leases are also subject to cancellation either by a judicial proceeding or by the Secretary, depending on whether the leasehold contains a well capable of production in paying quantities.[32] In addition, for noncompliance with regulations or directives the BLM may assess civil penalties, may order remedial work, and may even order the immediate shut down of operations.[33]

2.3.2 Federal offshore leasing[34]

Offshore federal petroleum rights of the United States are managed by the Department of the Interior's Bureau of Ocean Energy Management (BOEM),

---

[26] The citizenship requirement is not difficult; a person qualifies if he is a citizen of the United States or an alien stockholder in a corporation organized under state or federal law.

[27] 43 C.F.R. § 3102.5–1.

[28] 43 C.F.R. §§ 3472.1–2(d), 3502.13. Qualification Stipulations for alien ownership of mineral rights are described in 43 C.F.R. § 3502.10.

[29] Section 352 of the Energy Policy Act of 2005, Pub. L. No. 109–58, amended section 27(d)(1) of the MLA, 30 U.S.C. 184(d)(1), by excluding from the acreage limitation all acreage committed to a federally approved unit or communitization agreement or for which royalty was paid in the preceding calendar year.

[30] *Id.* § 3101.2–1(a). Alaska is divided into two leasing districts. A person or entity is limited to 300,000 acres of federal leases in each district. Id. §§ 3102.5–1(b) and 3101.2–1(b).

[31] 30 U.S.C. § 226(b)(1)(A).

[32] 43 C.F.R. § 3108.3(a).

[33] *Id.* Subpart 3163.

[34] Portions of this abbreviated analysis of the offshore oil and gas leasing system of the United States are drawn from Owen L. Anderson and Christopher S. Kulander, *United States Offshore Licensing and Concession System*, in Tina Hunter (ed),

while the Department's Bureau of Safety and Environmental Enforcement (BSEE) administers related environmental protection and safety regulations. Before the 2010 Deepwater Horizon disaster, an agency called the Minerals Management Service administered both onshore and offshore leasing. After the accident, MMS was criticized for conflicts of interest that arose from the breadth of its duties and BOEM and BSEE were created.

Federal offshore leasing is governed by the Outer Continental Shelf Lands Act of 1953.[35] As is the case with onshore leasing, offshore leasing is heavily focused upon planning. The Department of the Interior first prepares a five-year leasing plan that indicates the size, timing, and location of the leasing activity that the Secretary determines will best meet the United States' energy needs for the following five years, taking into account economic, social, and environmental impacts, including equitable sharing of developmental benefits and environmental risks.[36] The Secretary then solicits comments from other federal agencies and the governors of states that could be affected by offshore operations, particularly the states onshore near the leases that would be granted.[37] The Secretary of the Interior submits the proposed final program and any comments to the President and Congress, and the President must then give final approval to the plan.[38] The process of developing and approving a leasing plan may take as long as two years.

After the plan has been approved, BOEM asks the industry to nominate areas identified in the plan for leasing, identifies areas that likely contain hydrocarbons,[39] and then almost always orders an environmental impact statement and allows time for public comments before giving public notice of the sale.[40] The Secretary of the Interior must solicit bids, set the timing of lease sales and the location of leased tracts to strike a proper balance among the potential for environmental damage, the potential for the discovery of oil and gas, and the potential for any adverse impact on the coastal zone.[41]

REGULATION OF THE UPSTREAM PETROLEUM SECTOR: A COMPARATIVE STUDY OF LICENSING AND CONCESSION SYSTEMS (Edward Elgar, 2014).

[35]   43 U.S.C. §§ 1331–1356b.

[36]   43 U.S.C. § 1344(a).

[37]   *Id.* § 1344(c)(1). Under the Coastal Zone Management Act of 1972, 16 U.S.C. §§ 1451–66, federal offshore leasing activities "directly affecting the coastal zone" must be consistent with each coastal state's approved coastal zone management plan.

[38]   *Id.* § 1344(d)(2).

[39]   30 C.F.R. §§ 556.301–302.

[40]   Information about the offshore leasing plan and planned lease sales as this is written is available at www.boem.gov/National-OCS-Program-for-2017-2022/.

[41]   Presidential Memoranda dated Dec. 20, 2016.

Bidding is competitive, by sealed bids.[42] Often companies submit joint bids. The "highest responsible qualified" bid wins the lease, subject to review for anti-trust violations and to assure that the government has realized fair market value.[43] The government need not accept any bid and makes public the terms of a winning bid.[44]

The Secretary has broad authority to use alternative forms of bidding systems and leases, including cash bonuses, fixed or variable royalties, work commitments or net profits,[45] but almost all federal offshore leases are granted to the highest qualified bidder on the basis of bonus alone for five-year primary terms with a fixed royalty of 12.5 percent or more. Federal leases may also be transferred to those who would have qualified to purchase them. Federal leases offshore are registered with the BOEM.

3.   RIGHTS CREATED BY LICENCES

Oil and gas leases in the United States are almost always structured as concessions – the lessee pays all of the costs of exploration and development and owns the production it obtains from operations. The lessee compensates the lessor with a royalty and recovers its costs and (hopefully) generates a profit by selling production. The legal instrument creating the concession arrangement is generally structured as a contract.

3.1   Oil and Gas Leases on Privately Owned Mineral Rights

A private mineral owner can drill for and produce oil or gas without a lease. There are many millions of private mineral-rights owners in the United States, many of whom own tiny fractional interests in small tracts of land[46] and few have either the capital or expertise to develop their own mineral rights. Therefore, in the United States, oil companies usually control exploration and development transactions. There are thousands of privately owned oil companies, both large and small.[47] The United States has no "national" oil

---

[42]   43 U.S.C. § 1337(a)(1).

[43]   43 U.S.C. § 1337(c).

[44]   30 C.F.R. § 556.516(b).

[45]   43 U.S.C. § 1337(a)(1)(A)–(H).

[46]   For example, the author once owned .000762 percent interest in a 160-acre well drilling and spacing unit in Oklahoma.

[47]   The U.S. Internal Revenue Code section 613A(d) defines an independent producer as a producer who does not have more than $5 million in retail sales of oil and gas in a year or who does not refine more than an average of 75,000 barrels per day of crude oil during a given year. According to the Independent Petroleum Association of America, there are about 9000 independent oil and natural gas producers in the United

company, leaving petroleum exploration, development, and infrastructure to private companies.

Oil companies generally acquire leases on privately owned minerals on contract forms the oil companies select or draft, as noted above. Usually the lease imposes no legal obligation to drill on the lessee. The typical oil and gas lease grants the lessee an option to drill during a "primary term", which usually runs for two to five years. The primary term permits the lessee to evaluate the property and to plan to trade or develop it. If the lessee exercises its option to drill and finds oil or gas, the lease moves to its "secondary term" for "as long thereafter as oil or gas is produced" in paying quantities, which simply means that operating revenues must be greater than operating costs over a reasonable period of time. Theoretically "paying quantities" may be forever, and practically it may well mean that the lease will extend 30 or 40 years. Most leases also modify the "production in paying quantities requirement" by including clauses that extend the lease term without actual production in stated circumstances that advantage lessees. Such clauses provide for constructive production in the context of the lease, permitting lessees to extend the lease without actual production. This group of savings clauses includes: (1) operations clauses, (2) pooling and unitization clauses, (3) force-majeure clauses, (4) shut-in royalty clauses and (5) cessation-of-production clauses.

Leases of private mineral rights are subject to implied covenants – to test, to protect against drainage, to reasonably develop, to market, to operate diligently and prudently, and in some states, to further explore. Effectively, lease implied covenants amount to a promise by the lessee to act as a reasonable prudent operator, taking into account the interests of the lessor as well as itself. Increasingly, sophisticated lessors protect themselves with complicated express provisions addressing the issues raised by implied covenants, restricting land use and detailing how royalty payments are to be made. Furthermore, leases generally establish a right over the entire subsoil (to infinity), unless otherwise specified in the lease.

A lessor is paid a "royalty" – a percentage of gross production or production revenue. Historically, royalty percentages were one-eighth or one-sixth. Currently lease royalty percentages range from one-eighth to 30 percent or even more depending upon demand in the area at the time of the grant. Large mineral owners, particularly, have the economic power to bargain effectively, and the ease of communication in the 21st century tends to make today's "best deal" tomorrow's norm.

States operating in 33 states and the offshore and employing an average of just 12 people. *See* www.ipaa.org/independent-producers/.

Disputes over oil and gas leases are common, particularly about how royalty is to be calculated and paid. A current issue with gas royalty is whether a lessee who chooses to transport production away from the lease to a pipeline or to a market center for sale, or even to an end user, can charge its lessor with its proportionate share of costs beyond the wellhead. Courts in most states have distinguished between costs of production and costs subsequent to production, requiring a lessee to pay all costs of producing and saving production, but permitting the lessee to charge the lessor proportionately for costs subsequent to production since they are incurred after production and ordinarily increase the value of production. What the court has called the "marketable-product rule", adopted in somewhat different terms by courts or statutes in several states, requires a lessee to pay all costs of producing and of making the production marketable.

Courts almost never cancel private leases for failure to pay royalties or any other reason. Courts do not lack the power to terminate leases; they merely refrain from exercising it. If, for example, a lessee knowingly withheld lessor's royalties for speculative purposes, a court might properly decide to exercise its power. Two states – Louisiana and North Dakota – have statutes that expressly permit courts to terminate leases for egregious failure to pay. And while it is unusual for private oil and gas leases to provide for cancelation for breach, appropriate drafting may provide for it.[48]

Courts generally have classified the lessee's interest in an oil and gas lease covering privately owned minerals as a form of real property ownership. Some states, including Texas, have described the leasehold interest as an *estate* in fee-simple determinable in the oil and gas in place. Others, including Oklahoma, Kansas, California, Montana and Wyoming, have classified the lessee's interest as a *profit a prendre*, the right to use the land to look for and take away something of value. Some Appalachian states have classified the lessee's interest under a lease as an inchoate right that becomes a vested tenancy only after production begins.

Whatever the classification of the lessee's interest, the lessee's lease rights are subject to the Rule of Capture, the legal rule that the owner of the mineral interest in the land where oil and gas are captured owns the produced mineral. Regardless of the classification of the lessee's interest, the lessee's right under and oil and gas lease on privately owned mineral rights is akin to

---

[48] In Hitzelberger v. Samedan Oil Corp., 948 S.W.2d 497 (Tex.App.1997), for example, the court held that a lessee's failure to pay royalty timely caused a lease to terminate where the lease habendum clause provided for a secondary term for "as long thereafter as oil and gas, or either of them, is produced in paying quantities from said land or lands with which said land is pooled hereunder *and the royalties are paid as provided*". (Italics added.)

a common-law *profit a prendre* in real estate; the surface owner's right to use the surface is servient to the lessee's right to use the leased property to search for, develop, produce and market oil and gas.

3.1.1   Oil and gas leases on state, Indian and federally owned mineral rights

Private ownership has set the legal culture and the legal character for petroleum rights in the United States. The system relies on private enterprise even for publicly owned rights; as noted previously, there is no national or state-owned oil company. At the federal and state levels, there is significant diversity in the design of oil and gas leasing systems, but the result of those systems is the grant by a government of a "lease" that looks and works much like an oil and gas lease granted by a private owner. State, Indian, and federal leases are concession-style contracts.

State, Indian, and federal leases are typically relatively short – the current federal onshore form is just four pages, for example[49] – but they incorporate by reference other statutes and regulations, often including future changes. Like leases of privately owned minerals, there is no work obligation during the evaluation period, called the primary term, leases are potentially perpetual in their secondary term – as long thereafter as there is production in paying quantities, and the rule of capture applies, though governments may require protective measures such as protective drilling, compensatory royalty or unitization. And state, Indian, and federal leases generally provide for royalty rather than some form of profit sharing. United States courts recognize implied covenants in state, Indian, and federal leases, but they are rarely the basis of claims.

As noted by Professor George Coggins, the similarities between oil and gas leases on privately owned mineral and state, Indian and federal leases are more apparent than real:

> [t]he government as mineral lessor is still the government, with all of the procedural trappings and substantive subtleties that inevitably accompany activities of the sovereign. Prospective lessees are not free to negotiate lease terms and covenants because most requirements are set by law ... Federal lessees by statute acquire interests and procedural remedies unknown to the common law. But, unlike private leases, federal oil and gas leases do not necessarily convey a "dominant estate" with all appurtenant rights and easements. Other areas of difference between federal and private leases include acreage limitations, diligence requirements that affect other leaseholds, and minimum bonus systems ... All in all, practitioners will seldom be

---

[49]   A copy of a federal onshore lease in use at the time this is written is at FORMS MANUAL 514–17 (West 7th ed. 2018).

able to transpose their expertise in private oil and gas law bodily into federal oil and gas leasing.[50]

Further, while the rights given by state, Indian, and federal leases are constitutionally and statutorily protected, both at the federal and state levels, they create contract rights to the leased property,[51] not ownership rights in the real property itself, as do most leases on privately owned land.[52]

So though state, Indian, and federal leases look like and share many features with private-lands leases, they are different in important ways. They often are bigger; for example, a maximum of 2560 acres for federal onshore leases.[53] They are often for longer primary terms; lease terms for both competitive and non-competitive federal onshore leases are a ten-year primary term. They often require lower royalty payments; federal onshore leases provide for just a 12.5 percent royalty. Rentals for federal onshore leases are $1.50 per acre for the first five years, then $2 per acre thereafter – again less than many private leases.

Like private leases, state, Indian, and federal leases are potentially infinite in duration; if the lessee produces oil or gas "in paying quantities" by the end of the primary or extended term, then the lease extends into the secondary term as long as the lessee continues to produce oil or gas marginally profitably. But state, Indian, and federal leases have provisions that favor the lessor that private leases usually do not have. Under federal leases for example, after a discovery a minimum royalty of not less than the annual rental is due, and leases do not contain savings clauses found in typical private leases such as force majeure, shut-in royalty and pooling or unitization clauses that the lessee may invoke to hold the land without drilling or producing; rather the United States may require the lessee to pool or unitize on terms approved by the Secretary of the Interior.[54]

---

[50] 2 GEORGE C. COGGINS, PUBLIC NATURAL RESOURCES LAW § 23.01[1] (1992).

[51] So for example, the current onshore federal competitive form grants the lessee the exclusive right to drill, not the land itself. A copy of a federal onshore lease in use at the time this is written is at FORMS MANUAL 514–17 (West 7th ed. 2018).

[52] Federal oil and gas leases grant the lessee the exclusive right to "drill for, mine, extract, remove, and dispose of all the oil and gas deposits, except helium gas, in the lands leased …" For discussion *see* 1 Law of Federal Oil and Gas Leases, ROCKY MTN. MIN. L. FOUND., at § 9.04[1].

[53] The primary term may be extended for two years if the lessee begins drilling before the end of the primary term. Many onshore federal leases are smaller, conforming to the "standard" 640-acre land description system, but Leases in Alaska may be as large as 5760 acres. 30 U.S.C. § 226(b)(1); 43 C.F.R. § 3120.2–3.

[54] 1 Law of Federal Oil and Gas Leases, ROCKY MTN. MIN. L. FOUND., at § 9.04[2].

Federal offshore leases[55] tend to be of a larger area, reflecting the economics necessary to explore and develop them. They typically cover a compact area not exceeding 5,760 acres[56] and provide for a lease primary term of five years – still probably longer than most leases on private mineral rights – and for a secondary term for so long as oil or gas is produced in paying quantities or approved drilling or well-reworking operations are being conducted.[57] They require payment of the amounts or values specified by the bidding system including a minimum 12.5 percent royalty,[58] annual rentals,[59] and royalties.[60] Lease rights are conditioned upon due diligence requirements and upon approval of a plan of development;[61] offers of production to small or independent refiners under the Emergency Petroleum Allocation Act of 1973,[62] rights of first refusal to the United States to buy production in the event of war or at the President's discretion,[63] and leases provide for suspension or cancellation of the lease if the lessee defaults.[64]

Perhaps the biggest difference between leases on private mineral rights in the United States and Indian and federal leases is the flexibility that the latter give the federal government as lessor to change the rules, including how royalty is calculated. Indian and federal lessees agree to subject themselves to reasonable rules and regulations, both those in force when the lease is granted, and those thereafter issued, including those that establish the reasonable value of production for royalty purposes. So while the percentage of royalty due is established when the lease is granted, the methodology of calculating it may change. Though the Secretary's determinations are subject to judicial review under the Administrative Procedure Act,[65] courts have given them deference.[66] The government has used its authority to promulgate complicated and elab-

---

[55] A copy of a federal offshore lease in use at the time this is written is at FORMS MANUAL 519–26 (West 7th ed. 2018).

[56] 43 U.S.C. § 1337(b)(1).

[57] *Id.* § 1337(b)(2). The primary term in deep water or under adverse conditions may be up to ten years.

[58] 43 U.S.C. § 1337(a)(1). But many newer offshore leases have a royalty rate as high as 18.75 percent.

[59] *Id.* § 1337(b)(6).

[60] The royalty rate is commonly one-sixth.

[61] *Id.* § 1337(b)(4).

[62] *Id.* § 1337(b)(7).

[63] 43 U.S.C. 1341(c).

[64] *Id.* § 1337(b)(6).

[65] 5 U.S.C. §§ 701–06.

[66] *See, e.g.*, Independent Petroleum Association of America v. DeWitt, 279 F.3d 1036 (D.C. Cir. 2002); Marathon Oil Co. v. United States, 604 F. Supp. 1375 (D.Alaska 1985), *aff'd*, 807 F.2d 759 (9th Cir. 1986); United States v. Ohio Oil Co., 163 F.2d 633 (10th Cir. Wyo. 1947); Shoshone Indian Tribe v. Hodel, 903 F.2d 784 (10th Cir. 1990);

orate regulations to try to ensure that royalty under Indian and federal leases is based on the higher of what the lessee actually receives or the fair market value.[67]

Moreover, government lessors may have cudgels to use in disputes that arise under leases that they grant that private lessors do not. Several statutes, including the Federal Oil and Gas Royalty Management Act of 1982[68] and the False Claims Act,[69] empower the federal government as lessor to recover penalty-interest rates, civil penalties, treble damages and even criminal penalties, for disagreements that begin as lease disputes, usually over royalty calculation or payment.[70]

4.   THE LEGAL CHARACTER OF LEASE RIGHTS AND THE LEASING REGIME

There are recurring problems both with leases on private lands and with leases from governments. First, private interest owners may not adequately protect themselves. Some private mineral interest owners are extremely creative in structuring and drafting leases; "landowners' leases" or lease addenda are often extensive and complicated, often focused on restricting lessees' surface uses and ensuring payments due under the leases are made. But since most private mineral owners own only small fractions of the mineral rights in relatively small tracts of land, they may not actively or adequately protect their rights. For example, the author once owned .000761 percent of the mineral rights in a 160-acre production unit. Often the "game is not worth the candle" for a private owner of minerals to act to protect small interests.

Government-owned or regulated leases too may be inadequate to protect the public interest, either because they are poorly drafted or poorly administered. The failure of the Minerals Management Service in the late 1990s to set "price thresholds" for leases issued subject to the Deepwater Royalty Relief Act of

---

Continental Oil Co. v. United States, 184 F.2d 802 (9th Cir. 1950); California Co. v. Udall, 296 F.2d 384 (D.C. Cir. 1961).

[67]   There is a more complete explanation at CASES AND MATERIALS 1359–68. The Federal government also has the right to take royalty in kind. The Mineral Leasing Act's authority to take royalty in kind is found in 30 U.S.C. § 192, and the OCSLA authority is 43 U.S.C. § 1353(a)(1). Leases issued also expressly reserve the in-kind right.

[68]   30 U.S.C. §§ 1701 *et seq.*

[69]   31 U.S.C. § 3729 *et seq.*

[70]   See the more complete discussion at CASES AND MATERIALS 1429–32. Penalties may be hefty. For example, in Quinex Energy Corp., 192 IBLA 88 (2017), a $120,242 royalty underpayment led to a penalty of $3,217,250, 26 times the amount of the underpayment.

1995,[71] which was intended to lower royalty rates when oil prices were low to encourage drilling and production from the Outer Continental Shelf, reputedly cost the United States government $10 billion dollars in royalty payments as prices rose in the 2000s.[72] Government leasing and administrative procedures are often both complicated and opaque leading both lessors and lessees to costly mistakes.

Second, there are simply too many different leases subject to too many possible interpretations; the law of oil and gas leases is often unclear. The administrative burden of millions of leases on privately owned minerals negotiated and executed over time by more than ten million lessors and thousands of lessees is overwhelming. For example, natural gas production from the privately owned mineral rights of Texas's Barnett shale ramped up in the early 2000s and peaked in 2012,[73] but lawyers are still struggling to clear titles. Litigation is constant in the United States, and litigation in multiple legal jurisdictions results in torrents of case law, often with disparate results. Since private mineral rights are generally considered real estate, disputes arising from privately owned mineral leases usually go to state courts, often with elected judges and juries drawn from local residents who sometimes "home town" oil companies; this happens less in federal courts, where judges are generally better qualified and juries are drawn from larger areas, but federal leases too result in complicated litigation that discourages investment and drains money that could have been directed to increasing production.

Third, Indian and federal leases are often granted too cheaply. Royalty rates are often too low when compared with private and state leases, primary terms are too long, and there is no "work program" as is the norm internationally. As noted above, the Secretary of Interior has broad authority to use alternative forms of bidding systems and leases, but almost all Indian and federal leases, onshore or offshore, are granted to the highest bonus bidder for five-year or ten-year primary terms with a fixed royalty of 12.5 percent, 16 2/3 percent, or 18.75 percent, well below the "normal" primary term lengths and royalty rates for private and state lands in many areas.[74] Some have argued that the federal

---

[71]   Pub. L. 104–58, Title III, §§ 301 *et seq.*, 109 Stat. 563–66.

[72]   Without the price thresholds, deepwater producers continued to benefit from royalty relief even as oil prices hit record levels. See Marc Humphries, Royalty Relief for U.S. Deepwater Oil and Gas Leases, www.everycrsreport.com/files/20071207 _RS22567_f4d02b9d92a63553b6ca50c0b807beb99bd7cd8c.pdf.

[73]   www.rrc.state.tx.us/media/51506/barnett-gas.pdf.

[74]   In 2017 the Government Accountability Office conducted studies that concluded that raising federal lease royalty rates would likely have a small or negligible effect on production but over time significantly increase royalty revenues. See Raising Federal Rates Could Decrease Production on Federal Lands but Increase Federal Revenue, GAO-17-540.

leasing system encourages oil companies to "pad" their balance sheet reserves to support their stock prices.[75]

Fourth, structuring leases to pay lessors royalty is economically inefficient. Royalty is a burden on the lease working interest because it does not share in costs. Royalty is simple to administer, but discourages investment, because to break even the lessee must produce enough oil or gas to cover the costs of the investment, plus the royalty on what is produced. A fixed royalty also makes leases more quickly unprofitable when production prices are low, and under-compensates lessors when prices are high. Variable royalty or a net profits interest is better though much harder to administer.

Finally, both private leases and government leases last too long. The potentially infinite "as long thereafter as there is production in paying quantities" duration is bad policy. Production peaks early, but because oil and gas production is capital intensive and because the paying-quantities test requires merely marginal profitability, oil companies are able to speculate on future technological development. Shale development is a good example. Much of the Utica and Marcellus gas production in Ohio, Pennsylvania and West Virginia and the Haynesville/Bossier shale in East Texas is from old low-royalty leases. So is much of the oil production in Texas's and New Mexico's Permian Basin.

Some have argued that leases for both the privately owned minerals and those granted by governments in the United States should be rethought and revised.[76] That is not likely to happen in my opinion. In general the system of leasing and developing both privately owned and public mineral rights in the United States has served the country well. Rapid exploration and development of oil and gas resources spurred by short-term self-interest of private owners has made energy generally cheap and readily available for more than a century and a half, which has in turn sustained economic development. Further, for most of the 150-year history of the petroleum industry, the United States has been a significant energy exporter. United States production largely fueled the Western Allies in World War II, for example, though beginning in the 1970s, United States oil and gas production stalled and then fell, while demand continued to rise, resulting in the United States becoming a major importer of both oil and gas. That changed near the beginning of the 21st century when technological developments focused on private mineral rights – horizontal

---

[75] www.americanprogress.org/issues/green/reports/2018/08/29/455226/oil-gas
-companies-gain-stockpiling-americas-federal-land/.
[76] One is my colleague at SMU, Professor James Coleman. See James W. Coleman, The Third Age of Oil and Gas Law, 95 IND. L.J. 389 (2020) https://ssrn.com/abstract
=3367921. See also https://naturalresources.house.gov/imo/media/doc/Testimony
%20Attachment%20-%20Dan%20Bucks%20-%20EMR%20Leg%20Hrg%2009.24
.19.pdf.

drilling and hydraulic fracturing – turned the tide.[77] In 2019 the United States is one of the top producers of both oil and gas in the world, mostly from privately owned mineral rights.[78] Indeed, the Trump Administration is now talking about "energy dominance" rather than "energy independence".[79]

Leases on privately owned mineral rights generate huge economic benefits for the mineral owners. The National Association of Royalty Owners estimates that some 12 million American mineral-rights owners receive royalties for the exploitation of oil, gas and other mineral resources under their property.[80] One estimate put the share of total oil and natural gas production attributable to privately owned minerals at approximately 75 percent in 2011–12 which generated approximately \$21–22 billion in royalties.[81]

The picture is much the same for federal and Indian owned oil and gas rights. Production from federally owned mineral rights is huge except when compared to production from private mineral rights. In 2016 there were more than 94,000 producible or service well bores located on nearly 24,000 onshore federal leases out of more than 40,000 leases in effect. In 2017 there were more than 54,000 oil and gas wells on 875 offshore leases out of nearly 3000 in effect. In fiscal year 2016 federal onshore leases produced more than 157 million barrels of oil and 3.1 billion MCF of natural gas, while federal offshore leases produced nearly 554 million barrels of oil and more than 1.25 billion MCF of natural gas.[82] Oil production from Indian leases is about a third as much as that from onshore federal leases, totaling nearly 58 million barrels of oil in fiscal year 2016, and gas production is about a tenth that from onshore federal leases, totaling about 317 million MCF in fiscal year 2016.[83]

And federal leases generate large amounts of money for the United States Treasury and the tribes. In fiscal year 2018, the federal government generated

---

[77] Illustrative historical data visualizations prepared by Professor James Coleman are at www.energylawprof.com/?p=993.

[78] *See* www.bloomberg.com/news/articles/2018-12-06/u-s-becomes-a-net-oil -exporter-for-the-first-time-in-75-years.

[79] *See* www.whitehouse.gov/briefings-statements/president-donald-j-trump-paving -way-energy-infrastructure-development/.

[80] www.npr.org/2018/03/15/592890524/millions-own-gas-and-oil-under-their -land-heres-why-only-some-strike-it-rich (last visited May 23, 2019).

[81] Timothy Fitzgerald and Randal R Rucker, US private oil and natural gas royalties: estimates and policy relevance, OPEC Energy Review March 2016.

[82] United States Government Accountability Office Report to Congressional Committees, Oil, Gas, and Coal Royalties, Appendix 1, Table 6, GAO-17-540, June 2017.

[83] United States Government Accountability Office Report to Congressional Committees, Oil, Gas, and Coal Royalties, Appendix 1, Table 6, GAO-17-540, June 2017.

slightly more than $8 billion in bonuses, rents, royalties, and other revenues from mineral leasing activities. Federal royalties are the third largest source of revenue for the United States Treasury.[84] In Fiscal Year 2013, the Office of Natural Resources Revenue within the Department of the Interior collected and disbursed more than $932.9 million to 34 American Indian Tribes and approximately 30,000 individual Indian mineral owners.[85]

There is an adage that the perfect should not be the enemy of the good. That philosophy applies to petroleum licences in the United States, both private and public. The U.S. system of leasing for petroleum development is not theoretically pristine; it is what it is in large part because of historical accident. But it works relatively well and there is little sentiment to change it radically.

---

[84]   Department of the Interior, Office of Natural Resources Revenue available at https://revenuedata.doi.gov/ (last visited May 23, 2019). Federal onshore leases generated just over $3.5 billion and offshore leases more than $4.75 billion and in bonuses, rents and royalties. Onshore figures include revenues generated by federally owned minerals other than oil and gas, but most were derived from oil, gas and coal leasing activities. Revenue amounts rise and fall with the price of oil and natural gas; these numbers are a little more than half of what the Federal Government collected when prices for oil and gas were at their peak in fiscal year 2013.

[85]   www.onrr.gov/about/faqs.htm (last visited Dec. 30, 2018).

4. The legal character of petroleum licences in Canada

Nigel Bankes

This chapter begins with some general observations on Canada's legal system before moving to consider the more specific rules relating to petroleum licences. Following some brief comments on private petroleum and natural gas leases the balance of the chapter focuses on the petroleum licensing regime for offshore Newfoundland. The chapter canvasses the elements of the licensing scheme, licence cancellation issues, changes to the licensing regime over time and the legal character of the licence within this regime.

1. CANADA'S LEGAL SYSTEM AND CHARACTER

Canada is a federal state with ten provinces and three territories. While the province of Quebec follows the civil law tradition, all other jurisdictions are part of the common law tradition. Each jurisdiction has a Westminster style of government. The provinces and territories each have a unicameral legislature with the power to make laws in relation to all local matters and property and civil rights within the geographical bounds of the province or territory.[1] Executive power is exercised by the government of the day headed by a premier and made up of the party that commands the confidence of the legislature. Hence the executive branch is typically able to control the legislative branch of government. The premier appoints ministers for the various departments of government and collectively these ministers, along with the premier, form the cabinet. The formal head of state is still the English monarch (the Crown) represented in each of the provinces by the Lieutenant Governor and at the federal level by the Governor General. All laws passed by the legislative branch require the consent of the representative of the Crown but this is a formality. The federal legislature (parliament) is a bicameral institution with

---

[1] *Constitution Act, 1867*, ss. 92 and 92A.

both an elected house of commons and an appointed senate. The head of the federal government is known as the prime minister.[2]

Canada has a decentralized form of federalism within which the provinces exercise significant legislative and executive authority. This is particularly evident in the oil and gas sector. All publicly owned resources within a province are vested in the Crown in right of that province rather than in the federal Crown,[3] and each provincial legislature has the exclusive authority to make laws with respect to the development of energy resources within the province.[4] The same is true for two (Yukon and Northwest Territories) of the three territories; in the case of the third (Nunavut) the federal government has yet to transfer ownership (administration and control) of the publicly owned resources of Nunavut to the Nunavut government.

Generally, the boundaries of the coastal provinces and territories are delimited by the ordinary low water mark with some exceptions for historic internal waters and to accommodate the particular constitutional history of the individual provinces and territories.[5] The Supreme Court of Canada has confirmed the exclusive authority of parliament with respect to petroleum activities in marine areas beyond the province[6] but as a matter of practice the federal government has agreed to co-operative arrangements with the coastal provinces for the shared management of offshore petroleum resources. This has been achieved through intergovernmental agreements or accords,[7] which have then been

---

[2]   For further details on all of the issues summarily canvassed in this paragraph see P Hogg, *Constitutional Law of Canada* (2019, Student Edition).

[3]   *Constitution Act, 1867*, s. 109 and *Constitution Act, 1930* and the scheduled Natural Resources Transfer Agreements. There are limited exceptions for some federal property such as national parks.

[4]   *Constitution Act, 1867*, ss. 92 and 92A. See GV Laforest, *Natural Resources and Public Property under the Canadian Constitution* (1969).

[5]   For example, the waters between the mainland of British Columbia and Vancouver Island are considered to fall within the province of British Columbia: *Reference re: Ownership of the Bed of the Strait of Georgia and Related Areas*, [1984] 1 SCR 388.

[6]   *Reference Re: Offshore Mineral Rights*, [1967] SCR 792; *Reference re Newfoundland Continental Shelf*, [1984] 1 SCR 86.

[7]   There are three such accords: (1) Memorandum of Agreement between the Government of Canada and the Government of the Province on offshore petroleum resource management and revenue sharing, February 11, 1985 (the Atlantic Accord), www.servicenl.gov.nl.ca/printer/publications/aa_mou.pdf; (2) Canada-Nova Scotia Offshore Petroleum Resources Accord, August 26, 1986 (Nova Scotia Accord), www.cnsopb.ns.ca/sites/default/files/pdfs/Accord.pdf; (3) Accord between the Government of Canada and the Government of Quebec for the Shared Management of Petroleum Resources in the Gulf of St. Lawrence, March 24, 2011, https://mern.gouv.qc.ca/presse/pdf/Canada-Quebec-Accord-EN.pdf.

implemented by mirror (i.e., identical) legislation of the federal parliament[8] and the respective provincial legislature ("Accord Acts").[9]

Shared management occurs through a "petroleum board" for each offshore area. In each case this legislation (the offshore accords legislation) is based on the federal oil and gas licensing and conservation statutes that apply in Nunavut (and historically in all three territories).[10] Under the offshore accords legislation certain decisions are denominated as "fundamental decisions" which require the concurrence of both the federal and provincial governments.[11]

The judicial branch in Canada comprises a system of provincial superior courts for each province plus a federal court system that has jurisdiction with respect to actions against the federal Crown and with respect to the judicial supervision of executive authority by federal ministers, officials and administrative tribunals.[12] Judicial supervision of the offshore boards is exercised by the relevant provincial superior court.[13] Judicial review of administrative action is premised on the idea of the rule of law, which aims to ensure that all executive decision-making can be justified under a grant of authority from the legislative branch. In some cases judicial review demands a standard of correctness from the administrative decision maker (i.e., the court must agree that the administrative decision maker made the correct decision) whereas in other cases the standard of review is the more deferential standard of reasonableness (i.e., the court need not agree with the conclusion of the administrative deci-

---

[8]   *Canada–Newfoundland and Labrador Atlantic Accord Implementation Act*, SC 1987, c. 3 (*CNLA*) and *Canada-Nova Scotia Offshore Petroleum Resources Accord Implementation Act*, SC 1988, c. 28. There is as yet no implementing legislation for the Quebec, Bill C-75, 41st Parliament 2nd Session, An Act to implement the accord between the Government of Canada and the Government of Quebec for the joint management of petroleum resources in the Gulf of St. Lawrence and to make consequential amendments to other Act was given first reading on June 18, 2015 in the House of Commons but it did not proceed further.

[9]   *Canada-Newfoundland and Labrador Atlantic Accord Implementation Newfoundland and Labrador Act* SNL 1986, c.37 and *Canada-Nova Scotia Offshore Petroleum Resources Accord Implementation (Nova Scotia) Act*, SNS 1987, c. 3.

[10] *Canada Petroleum Resources Act*, RSC 1985 c. 36 (2nd supp) and *Canada Oil and Gas Operations Act*, RSC 1985, c. O-7.

[11] *CNLA*, ss. 31–40. In *Mobil Oil Canada Ltd v. Canada-Newfoundland Offshore Petroleum Board* [1994] 1 SCR 202, 221 the Supreme Court of Canada characterized this as "A form of control over Board decisions retained by the executive branch of government …". Fundamental decisions include a decision to issue a call for bids (CNLA, s. 58(2)), additional terms and conditions to be included in a licence (s. 67(1) and s. 73(4)), or the amendment of a licence (s. 68(1)).

[12] *Federal Courts Act*, RSC 1985, c. F-7.

[13] *CNLA*, s. 124(10) and s. 215.

sion maker but must be of the view that the decision represents a reasonable interpretation and application of the relevant statutory power).[14]

There is now a presumption that a statutory decision maker is generally entitled to a degree of deference and accordingly a standard of review of reasonableness unless the decision engages questions of constitutional law, general questions of law of central importance to the legal system as a whole or questions related to the jurisdictional boundaries between two or more administrative bodies.[15]

As a consequence of the above division of legislative authority there is not one but many petroleum licensing schemes in Canada. Each province has its own licensing scheme, as do Yukon and Northwest Territories. Canada maintains a petroleum licensing scheme for Nunavut as well as the shared schemes for the offshore areas mentioned above. In addition, individual jurisdictions may maintain more than one petroleum licensing scheme to account for the different forms of hydrocarbon resources – in particular to make provision for oil sands resources. This is the case for example in Alberta. Alberta maintains a framework licensing statute for all mines and minerals[16] but under the auspices of that legislation maintains two distinct licensing schemes for hydrocarbons, one for conventional oil and gas resources (the Petroleum and Natural Gas Tenure Regulation)[17] and one for the oil sands resource.[18] In addition, not all petroleum resources are owned by the Crown. Rather, some are privately

---

[14] See generally *Canada (Minister of Citizenship and Immigration) v. Vavilov*, 2019 SCC 65 (*Vavilov*) and most recently applied in *David Suzuki Foundation v. Canada-Newfoundland and Labrador Offshore Petroleum Board*, 2020 NLSC 94 (*David Suzuki* (2020)).

[15] Ibid at para 53. In the context of decision making by the CNLOPB see *Hibernia Management and Development Company Ltd v. Canada-Newfoundland and Labrador Petroleum Board*, 2008 NLCA 456 [44]–[58] (dealing with the authority of the Board to apply new Guidelines pertaining to research expenditures to existing projects) and *Shin Han F & P Inc v. Canada-Nova Scotia Offshore Petroleum Board*, 2014 NSCA 108 (dealing with the Board's decision to cancel a licence and applying identical provisions in the Nova Scotia legislation). By contrast, in the earlier decision of the Supreme Court of Canada in *Mobil Oil* (n 11) at 215, the Court indicated that it was "unnecessary to consider the standard of review applicable in this case" but seems to have proceeded on the basis of correctness. See also another earlier decision, *Petro-Canada et al. v. Canada-Newfoundland Offshore Petroleum Board*, 1995 CanLII 10613 (NL SC) ruling [37] that "The standard of review, therefore, in this case is correctness for questions of law and reasonableness for issues involving the weighing of factors contemplated by the legislation".

[16] *Mines and Mineral Act*, RSA 2000, c. M-17.

[17] Alta Reg 263/1997.

[18] Oil Sands Tenure Regulation, Alta Reg 196/2010. The oil sands regime has more in common with a hard rock mining regime than a conventional oil and gas regime insofar as it emphasizes the importance of investing in gaining knowledge as to the

owned, since in the early days of settlement Crown grants included mines and minerals.[19] By the end of the 19th century the Crown typically reserved the mines and minerals from any grants. There is no private ownership of land or minerals in the offshore.

Given the multiplicity of licensing schemes in Canada it is not possible to cover all of these schemes here. The balance of this chapter therefore provides a brief discussion of private oil and gas leases and then focuses on the petroleum licensing scheme for the offshore area of Newfoundland and Labrador as administered by the Canada Newfoundland Offshore Petroleum Board (CNLOPB or Board).[20]

2.   THE PROCESS FOR OBTAINING A PETROLEUM LICENCE

2.1   Privately Owned Minerals

Rights to privately owned minerals are typically acquired by means of a document known as a petroleum and natural gas lease. There is no standard form lease,[21] but the lease usually takes the form of a short "primary term" (three to five years), during which time the lessee must establish production. This can be considered as the exploration phase. If production is established the lease continues into its secondary term and continues for so long as the property is capable of production. The lease grants the lessee the right to win, work and remove the leased substances subject to the payment of a royalty. The lease does not grant ownership of the hydrocarbons in place but title to produced hydrocarbons passes to the lessee as personal property on severance. Given the rights that the lease conveys, the Courts have consistently held that while termed a lease the instrument is more correctly characterized as an incorporeal hereditament in the form of a *profit à prendre* for a term of uncertain duration.[22] In addition to its petroleum and natural gas lease the lessee will also require a well licence from the relevant regulator before it can commence

---

extent, quality and recoverability of the resource rather than the importance of the discovery well.

[19]   In Alberta for example about 20% of minerals (including hydrocarbons) are privately owned.

[20]   The Board's website provides information on the Board, links to its constituent legislation and regulations, guidance documents and bidding documents etc, www .cnlopb.ca/.

[21]   Perhaps the most frequently used forms are those developed by CAPL, the Canadian Association of Petroleum Landmen http://landman.ca/resources/forms-store/.

[22]   *Berkheiser v. Berkheiser*, [1957] SCR 387 and more recently see *Orphan Well Association v. Grant Thornton Ltd.*, 2019 SCC 5 [11].

operations.[23] The rule of capture is part of the law of Canada.[24] The necessary consequence of this is that a well drilled on B's land may drain resources from under C's neighbouring land. This is not per se unlawful although conservation rules may restrict B from drilling close to the boundary of B's lands or the rate at which B produces. C's principal remedy is to drill its own well.[25]

2.2 Petroleum Licensing Scheme for the Offshore Area of Newfoundland and Labrador

The Accord Acts establish a three-step tenure system consisting of an exploration licence (EL), a significant discovery licence (SDL) and a production licence (PL). While a licensee will ordinarily progress through each stage of licence there are circumstances (discussed below) where there may be direct issuance of either a SDL or a PL.

2.2.1 Calls for nominations and calls for bids

Licences are issued through a nomination and bidding process that the CNLOPB describes as a "scheduled land tenure system".[26] The Board adopted this system in 2013 "to improve transparency, predictability and input".[27] The scheme involves a regular cycle of nominating and bidding rounds, which allows industry to engage in the acquisition of seismic data in advance of bidding. Under this scheme the Board has divided the offshore area into three categories based on the level of oil and gas activity. Low activity areas are areas where there is limited seismic data and where few wells have been drilled. High activity areas are characterized by increased seismic data acquisition and exploratory wells. A mature region is characterized by substantial seismic coverage, extensive drilling (exploration and delineation), and production activities. In low activity regions the Board has adopted a four-year cycle in which a call for nominations will be initiated in the fall with the call for bids scheduled to close four years later. The Board has indicated that expenditures made by a party from the time of the call for nominations could be counted as qualifying expenditures in the subsequent work bid. The cycle is shorter for other regions. High activity regions follow a two-year cycle and mature regions a one-year cycle.

---

[23] *Grant Thornton*, ibid [12]; *Oil and Gas Conservation Act*, RSA 2000, c. O-6, s. 11 (*OGCA*).

[24] *Borys v. Canadian Pacific Railway*, [1953] AC 217 (JCPC).

[25] *Borys*, ibid; and for the conservation rules see *OGCA* (n 23).

[26] CNLOPB News Release, December 19, 2013, at www.cnlopb.ca/news/ nr20131219/.

[27] ibid.

In response to a call for nominations a party may identify blocks or parcels that it would like to see opened for bidding.[28] The call may specify maximum and minimum parcel sizes. Recent calls have emphasized that parties responding should consider providing information or data on the prospectivity of the lands nominated and consider meeting with Board staff to provide a technical geoscientific briefing before submitting a nomination.[29] The *Canada–Newfoundland and Labrador Atlantic Accord Implementation Act* (*CNLA*) does not mention a "call for nominations" but section 58(3) provides that "Any request received by the Board to make a call for bids in relation to particular portions of the offshore area shall be considered by the Board in selecting the portions of the offshore area to be specified in a call for bids".

The *CNLA* is more prescriptive in relation to the call for bids. Section 58 prescribes that the call for bids must specify the form of the licence and "the sole criterion that the Board will apply in assessing bids submitted in response to the call".[30] This is known as a single bidding variable. The Board cannot, for example, assess both a work commitment and a cash bonus. The most common bidding variable is a work expenditure bid.[31] The bidding documents require the bidder to post a bid deposit (in the amount of the minimum bid, currently $10 million) to be followed or replaced by a security deposit provided by the successful bidder in the amount of 25% of the total work bid. The call for bids includes the form of the licence that will be issued to the successful bidder.

Some of the most active exploration areas on the Newfoundland and Labrador shelf are in the area beyond 200 nautical miles (nm) where Canada claims an extended shelf. Canada has now made its full submission to the Commission on the Limits of the Continental Shelf under the Law of the Sea Convention (LOSC)[32] but the Commission is not expected to provide its advice

---

[28] For an example of a call for nominations by the CNLOPB, August 31, 2018 see Call for Nominations No. NL18-CFNO3 (Parcels – Jeanne d'Arc Region), www.cnlopb.ca/wp-content/uploads/landissuance/cfn02legal.pdf.

[29] ibid.

[30] *CNLA* s. 58(4)(g).

[31] See for example the calls for bids issued by the CNLOPB in the Jeanne d'Arc and Eastern Newfoundland Areas in 2018, www.cnlopb.ca/exploration/issuance/#bids-active. The Board has also used a similar "drilling deposit" bid variable in the case of direct issuance of a PL where the area of the licence includes lands that are covered by a declaration of commercial discovery. See, for example a call for bids issued by the CNLOPB in 2018 for a PL in the Jeanne d'Arc region in an area covered by the Terra Nova K-08 Commercial Discovery Area, www.cnlopb.ca/wp-content/uploads/landissuance/nl1803legal.pdf.

[32] United Nations Convention on the Law of the Sea, (LOSC) adopted 10 December 1982, 1833 UNTS 3 (entered into force 28 July 1996), Article 76.

to Canada for a number of years.[33] As a result, calls for nominations and calls for bids include a caveat which addresses two issues, first the possible need to reconfigure the area covered by the licence, and second, a warning that production in the extended shelf may be subject to revenue or production sharing with the world community under the terms of Article 82 of the LOSC.[34]

2.2.2 Exploration licence

An exploration licence grants: the right to explore for, and the exclusive right to drill and test for, petroleum; the exclusive right to develop those portions of the offshore area in order to produce petroleum; and the exclusive right, subject to compliance with the other provisions of this Part to obtain a PL.[35] The maximum duration of an EL (subject to exceptions discussed below) is nine years and "shall not be extended or renewed".[36] However, it is the practice of the CNLOPB to divide the duration of the licence into Periods I and II; the licensee is only able to move to Period II if it commences the drilling of a validation well during Period I.[37] The validation well "must adequately test a valid geological target to be declared to the Board by the [licensee] prior to the commencement of the well".[38] Period I is consistently for a six-year period but a licensee can extend Period I by posting an escalating drilling deposit. The deposit is forfeited if the validation well is not drilled.[39] Upon the expiration

---

[33] Submissions are available on the Commission's web page, www.un.org/Depts/los/clcs_new/commission_submissions.htm (Canada's submissions are #70 and #84).

[34] For example, part of the caveat included in the CNLOPB August 2018 call for nominations provides as follows (n 22) "The boundaries of sectors, parcels or licences in areas beyond 200 nautical miles may be revised to reflect the limits of the Outer Continental Shelf established by Canada. All interest holders of production licences containing areas beyond 200 nautical miles may be required, through legislation, regulation, licence terms and conditions, or otherwise, to make payments or contributions in order for Canada to satisfy obligations under Article 82 of the United Nations Convention on the Law of the Sea".

[35] *CNLA*, s. 65.

[36] *CNLA*, s. 69. For a recent decision confirming that this is ordinarily a hard limit see *David Suzuki* (2020) (n 14).

[37] "Failure to fulfil this drilling requirement will result in the termination of this Licence at the end of Period I". Section 5(4) of the EL attached to the Jeanne d'Arc (2018) call for bids (n 31).

[38] ibid s. 5(5).

[39] News Release December 19, 2013. This degree of flexibility has not always been available. Under earlier forms of the licence the Board could only extend Period I if the Board was satisfied that the failure to drill was beyond the licensee's reasonable control. *See Polaris Resources et al v. Canada NL Offshore Petroleum Board et al*, 2006 NLTD 143. In that case the Court concluded that the Board had failed to give proper reasons for declining to extend Polaris' Period I on the basis of Polaris' claim that it was unable to finance the drilling of a well because the province had failed to put

of the EL the lands revert to the Crown except to the extent that the lands have been included within an SDL or a PL.[40]

As noted above there are some limited exceptions to the nine-year duration rule for ELs. Section 56 of the *CNLA* contemplates that the Board (and in some cases the federal minister) may make an order prohibiting a licensee from undertaking work on the licensed block, in particular where there is "an environmental or social problem of a serious nature" or "dangerous or extreme weather conditions affecting the health or safety of people or the safety of equipment".[41]

As a corollary to this, section 56(5) extends the period of the licence for the period of the prohibition order. In at least one case a licensee has tried to take advantage of this provision to gain additional time to address what it perceived to be unusually onerous environmental assessment requirements which had to be met before it could commence the drilling of a well.

Corridor Resources held an EL for a prospect known as Old Harry in the Gulf of St Lawrence with a nine-year term effective January 15, 2008 and a five-year Period I. Its proposal (February 2011) to drill a well on the prospect triggered an environmental assessment (EA). The federal Minister responsible for the EA (Minister Kent) concluded (August 2011) on the basis of public comments that it would be appropriate to adopt a two-pronged approach to the EA. One track would involve having the Board update its strategic environmental assessment (SEA) for this area of the offshore; the second track was to continue with the screening of Corridor's application. In response to this, Corridor applied under s.68 *CNLA* to have the Board amend its EL to extend Period I to seven years. The Board, having gone through the fundamental

---

in place its royalty regime. However, having reached that conclusion Justice Hall went on to say that the Board could have given good and convincing reasons for refusing to accede to Polaris' request. In particular he expressed the view [22] that "the failure to drill an exploration well for reasons beyond the reasonable control of the interest owner are confined to physical or technical matters which would have prevented or delayed the drilling of the well and that this section of the Licences is not intended to deal with the financial capacity of a licence holder to fund its exploration. If financial or royalty regimes' requirements were allowed to creep into the bidding process, this would allow bidders into the process who had no capacity whatsoever to undertake the drilling program requisite in order to promote discovery of significant quantities of petroleum. The end result would be a delay in exploration and development, rather than the encouragement of exploration and development".

[40]   *CNLA*, s. 69(4). *Mobil Oil* (n 11) 224.
[41]   *CNLA*, s. 56.

decision process, acceded to this request (November 2011) and also permitted Period I to be extended by a further one year on payment of a drilling deposit.[42]

However, in addition to this, Corridor also applied to the Board (January 2012) to have it make a Prohibition Order under section 56 on the basis that Minister Kent's recommendation that the Board update its regional SEA identified "an environmental or social problem of a serious nature", or alternatively that this criterion was met by the "unprecedented public interest and concern" that its drilling proposal had triggered. The Board gave three reasons for rejecting Corridor's application for a prohibition order, all on the general grounds that the application was premature. First, Corridor was not currently engaged in any "work or activity" on its EL (it has only proposed a drilling operation for which it had yet to obtain a drilling authorization). Second, the ongoing SEA might provide the Board with information as to whether or not there is "an environmental or social problem of a serious nature" but that had yet to be clarified. And third, the amendment to Corridor's EL already afforded it additional flexibility.[43]

But that was not the end of the matter. Notwithstanding the extensions Corridor was unable to drill a well within the term of its EL.[44] Shortly before the EL was due to expire (January 14, 2018) the Board, with the approval of Ministers as required for a "fundamental decision", resolved to issue Corridor a new EL for the same lands without going through a call for bids.[45] The Board purported to rely on section 61 of *CNLA* that allows the Board to issue a licence without a call for bids where it does so in return for the surrender, at the request of the Board, of an existing licence. The David Suzuki Foundation and others challenged this decision on the basis that the power to exchange interests cannot be used to circumvent the nine-year limit on the life of a licence. The Court agreed with the Foundation and quashed the decision authorizing the new licence.[46]

---

[42] These details are discussed in CNLOPB, Reasons for Decision, Corridor Resources, Application for Prohibition Order in respect of EL 1105, February 2012, on line, www.cnlopb.ca/news/nr2012feb28/. It bears noting that under the current rules for ELs Corridor would have been entitled to extend Period I of its own motion by paying additional deposits. See discussion of the Board's "scheduled land tenure system" above. It seems likely that the Board introduced this flexibility to avoid requiring licensees to go through the amendment procedure that also triggers the fundamental decision process.

[43] ibid.

[44] *David Suzuki Foundation v. Canada-Newfoundland Offshore Petroleum Board*, 2018 NLSC 146 [6].

[45] ibid [8].

[46] ibid. This decision was an interlocutory decision dealing with the standing of the non-governmental organization to bring its application to quash the decision author-

2.2.3 The significant discovery licence

An SDL grants the licensee exactly the same rights as the EL but for an unlimited term. The SDL is thus best thought of as a form of holding licence issued to a licensee that has made a discovery but has yet to establish that that discovery is commercial. The ordinary procedure for issuing an SDL commences when the licensee drills a well that it considers to have made a "significant discovery". The *CNLA* defines a significant discovery as "a discovery indicated by the first well on a geological feature that demonstrates by flow testing the existence of hydrocarbons in that feature and, having regard to geological and engineering factors, suggests the existence of an accumulation of hydrocarbons that has potential for sustained production".[47] The next step is for the licensee to apply to the Board to have it make a declaration of significant discovery (DSD) and delineate the area covered by the discovery.[48] The courts have emphasized that the threshold established by the definition is not high and in one case concluded that the Board erred when it required an applicant "to prove the likelihood of sustained production, instead of just the possibility of this".[49] If the Board finds that the licensee has met the onus it will make a DSD and delineate the areal extent of that discovery.[50] To the extent that

---

izing the EL as well as various applications by others to intervene. The Court granted the applicant public interest standing and denied the applications to intervene. The evidence before the court suggested that other industry players supported the Board's approach [42]–[43] notwithstanding that it denied them the opportunity to bid on the property. This was perhaps not surprising given the public opposition to drilling in this area. In other circumstances one might anticipate that competitors in the industry might not be so supportive. The decision on the merits is *David Suzuki* (2020) (n 14).

[47]   *CNLA*, s. 47. A discovery requires a well and there can be only one discovery per geological structure: *Mobil Oil* (n 11) 218. A licensee may apply to expand the DSD area but such an application requires a new well, ibid and CNLA, s. 71(4) "the results of further drilling". If there is no "new well" on the structure the Board is entitled (*Mobil Oil*, at 223) to dismiss the application summarily without triggering the involvement of the Oil and Gas Committee (the role of this Committee is discussed below). The Committee would however have to be involved if there was some doubt as to whether a well was on the same structure as the initial discovery well (ibid).

[48]   *CNLA*, s. 71. The Board together with the Canada/Nova Scotia Board has issued a set of Joint Guidelines for Applications for Significant and Commercial Discoveries (2003) available at www.cnlopb.ca/wp-content/uploads/guidelines/sda_0503.pdf. In *Mobil Oil* (n 11) 221, the Supreme Court of Canada emphasized that by contrast with the executive control associated with "fundamental decisions" this is intended to be a process that is "technical in nature" and not subject to political interference. This intent was consistent with the objective of the Atlantic Accord (n 7) which was to produce and stable and fair regime "for industry".

[49]   *Petro-Canada* (n 15) [54].

[50]   More precisely, the Board must provide notice in advance of its proposed decision to the licensee who can then request that the proposed decision be referred to the

DSD areas fall within the applicant's licence area the Board must issue an SDL to the licensee for that part of the SDL.[51] To the extent that the DSD extends to Crown reserve lands outside the area of an EL the Board may elect to issue a call for bids for those lands (an example of the direct issuance of an SDL).[52]

Unlike the EL, the SDL is issued without term in the sense that it continues in force so long as there is a valid DSD in effect for the area covered by the licence.[53]

2.2.4　The production licence

A PL grants the licensee: the right to explore for, and the exclusive right to drill and test for, petroleum; the exclusive right to develop those portions of the offshore area in order to produce petroleum; the exclusive right to produce petroleum from those portions of the offshore area; and title to the petroleum so produced.[54] The ordinary procedure for issuing a PL commences when a licensee of an EL or, more likely, an SDL reaches the conclusion that its discovery is commercial. The *CNLA* defines a commercial discovery as "a discovery of petroleum that has been demonstrated to contain petroleum reserves that justify the investment of capital and effort to bring the discovery to production". This time the licensee applies to the Board to have it issue a declaration of commercial discovery (DCD) whereupon the licensee will be entitled to have the Board issue it a PL for the area of the DCD contained within its existing licence.[55] Any part of the DCD that extends to Crown reserve lands may be offered for direct issuance of a PL by the Board following a call for bids.[56] A PL is issued for a 25-year term which is extended automatically for so long as petroleum is commercially produced from the licence.[57]

Oil and Gas Committee for its review. The role of the Oil and Gas Committee is discussed in more detail below in the context of licence cancellations. The Supreme Court of Canada in *Mobil Oil* (n 11) 222 emphasized that it was not helpful to distinguish between the existence of a discovery and the area of a discovery. Both issues were related and thus the Oil and Gas Committee (discussed below) might have input into both aspects of this decision.

[51]　*CNLA*, s. 73(1).
[52]　*CNLA*, s. 73(2).
[53]　*CNLA*, s. 75. *Mobil Oil* (n 11) 208.
[54]　*CNLA*, s. 80. The licensee is however subject to escalating rentals. For example, the SDL appended to the Jeanne d'Arc (2018) call for bids (n 31) contemplates (s. 6) zero rental for the SDL for its first five years but by year 16 the rental payable is $800 per hectare, Section 6(b) confirms that the licensee may relinquish lands to reduce future rental payments.
[55]　*CNLA*, s. 81(1).
[56]　For an example see the call for bids for a PL in the Jeanne d'Arc area (n 31).
[57]　*CNLA*, s. 84. The Board also has discretionary authority (subject to the fundamental decision procedure) to extend a PL where commercial production has ceased

3.   GENERAL RULES IN RELATION TO LICENCES

Licences may be held (and invariably are) by multiple parties. The Board plays no role in the appointment of the operator.[58] Neither does the Board prescribe the terms of the operating agreement between the working interest parties other than to require that the parties acknowledge in writing that they have entered into a joint operating agreement (JOA) "which addresses voting procedures and a procedure to allow less than all participants to proceed with a program which is not approved pursuant to the voting procedures with provisions for maintenance of participant ownership and sharing of results within [*sic*] non-participant Interest Holders where a program proceeds and is successful".[59]

Licences are freely assignable under the *CNLA* and under the terms of the individual licences. However, where a licensee or the holder of a working interest in the licence enters into "an agreement or arrangement that is or may result in a transfer, assignment or other disposition" then the party shall provide the Board with notice of that agreement or arrangement and a summary of its terms or conditions, and, upon the request of the Board a copy of the agreement or arrangement.[60] The *CNLA* establishes a system for registering licences and transfers of licences as well as security interests in those licences.[61]

4.   LICENCE CANCELLATION

Sections 123 and 124 of the *CNLA* deal with the cancellation of licences. Section 123 provides that if the Board has reason to believe that a party is failing or has failed to comply with Part II of the Act (dealing with the granting of petroleum rights), Part III of the Act (dealing with petroleum operations and conservation issues) or Part III.I of the Act (dealing with occupational health and safety issues) then the Board may give notice to that party requiring compliance within a prescribed time. Where the party fails to comply the Board

---

but where the Board has reasonable grounds to believe that commercial production will recommence.

[58]   The EL merely requires that the working interest owners appoint a representative who "may be changed from time to time during the term of the Licence", Jeanne d'Arc (2018) call for bids (n 31) s. 18. In the event that the parties fail to appoint a representative s. 53 of the *CNLA* permits the Board to designate one of the working interest owners as the representative.

[59]   ibid, s. 12.

[60]   *CNLA*, s. 103.

[61]   *CNLA*, ss. 102–18.

may, if it considers that the failure to comply warrants cancellation, cancel that licence.

The decision to cancel is however subject (as with some other important listed decisions that the Board can take)[62] to the important procedural safeguard offered by section 124 of the Act. Section 124 provides that where the Board proposes to make a listed decision (including a decision to cancel a licence or to issue a DSD or DCD) the Board must first provide notice of its intention to do so to the licensee whereupon the licensee may request a hearing before a committee known as the Oil and Gas Committee.[63] The Committee has all the powers of a superior court, and, on conclusion of the hearing the Committee must provide its recommendations to the Board whereupon the Board, having considered those recommendations, can make a decision. The licensee is entitled to reasons for that decision and furthermore the statute expressly provides that the licensee is entitled to seek judicial review of that decision.

This complicated procedure was the subject of judicial comment in *Shin Han F & P Inc v. Canada-Nova Scotia Offshore Petroleum Board*.[64] That case involved the efforts of the Nova Scotia Board to cancel Shin Han's EL by reason of the failure of the licensee to provide a work deposit as required by the terms of the EL. The EL provided for the payment of licence deposit of $50,000 but also required payment of a work deposit of 25% of the work bid by the third anniversary of the licence. The clause warned that failure to make the deposit "will result in cancellation of this Licence and forfeiture of the Licence deposit".

Shin Han had made a work bid of $129 million and accordingly a deposit of $32,250,000 was due by January 1, 2012. In January 2011 the Nova Scotia Board adopted a Work Deposit Deferral policy which it posted on its website.[65] In that document the Board held out the possibility that a licensee might be able to defer posting the work deposit for up to two years if it could meet certain conditions. Any application for relief had to be made 120 days before

---

[62]   These decisions are decisions in relation to a DSD (s. 71), decisions with respect to a DCD (s. 78), decisions with respect to drilling orders issued to the holder of an SDL (s. 76) and cancellation decisions (s. 123(2)). The Committee process has already been referenced above with respect to the DSD.

[63]   The Supreme Court of Canada emphasized the importance of these procedural protections in *Mobil Oil* (n 11) 222. In the context of a DSD these provisions "go some distance towards ensuring that [licensees] have ample opportunity to prove an entitlement objectively before the Committee". The Committee is established by s. 141 of the *CNLA*.

[64]   2014 NSCA 108. The case deals with the similar provisions of the Nova Scotia offshore legislation.

[65]   www.cnsopb.ns.ca/sites/default/files/pdfs/Work_Deposit_Deferal_Policy _Website_Notice_January_2011.pdf.

the due date for payment of the deposit. No application was forthcoming but on December 15, 2011 Shin Han requested an extension of its EL. The Board responded to the effect that it was treating the requested extension as an application for relief from posting the deposit but that the request did not meet the terms established by the deferral policy and was accordingly denied.

When Shin Han did not make the deposit on January 1 the Board served notice under section 126 of the Nova Scotia Accord Act (the equivalent of section 123 of the CNLA) that the EL would be terminated if the deposit were not made within 90 days. On April 25 the Board gave Shin Han a "Notice of Proposed Decision" under section 127 of the Nova Scotia Accord Act (the equivalent of section 124 of the CNLA) proposing to cancel its EL. Shin Han thereupon requested a hearing before the Committee. Following a hearing the Committee recommended cancellation on the grounds that acceding to the request would:[66]

- Lead to similar requests from other licence holders, to which, on the basis of consistency, the Board would have to accede;
- Undermine confidence in the land tenure system; and
- Impede the exploration of petroleum in the Nova Scotia Offshore Area.

The Board reviewed the Committee's recommendations, concurred with its reasons and decided to cancel Shin Han's EL. Shin Han sought judicial review of the Board's decision. The hearing judge concluded that the standard of review was reasonableness and that the Board's reasoning was "transparent and justifiable on the facts and the law" and fell within the range of reasonable outcomes.[67] The Court of Appeal agreed and offered useful comments as to the jurisdiction of the Committee and as to the relationship between the Committee and the Board.

As to the first, counsel for Shin Han argued that the Committee had erred in confining its analysis to the proposed cancellation decision and that it should also have considered the Board's decision not to grant the application for a work deposit deferral. The Court was not convinced; it reasoned that the legislation was clear:

> committee review does not apply to every order of the Petroleum Board. The ... *Act* specifies that it only applies to actions "in respect of which it is expressly stated in this Part to be subject to this section". The language used is unambiguous. The

---

[66]   *Shin Han* (n 64) [24].
[67]   2013 NSSC 341 [77].

committee review process is not available as a general review of all Petroleum Board actions but instead is only activated for certain decisions.[68]

The Court emphasized that the Committee's only role was to conduct a hearing and make recommendations. "The Committee was not the decision-maker. It exercised no discretion of its own. The focus of the judicial review is on the decision of the Board, not on the recommendations of the Committee".[69] It was therefore appropriate in the judicial review application to focus on the Board's decision, but, since the Board considered and adopted the Committee's recommendation, it was also "necessary to review the Committee's recommendations to determine whether the Board's adoption of them was reasonable".[70] That led the Court to a detailed review of the Committee's legal and policy reasons (outlined above) for recommending that the Board cancel Shin Han's licence. The Court concluded that "The Board's consideration of the Committee's recommendation and its adoption of that determination that the Exploration Licence should be cancelled fall within the range of reasonable outcomes based on the facts and the law".[71]

5.   CHANGES TO THE LICENSING REGIME OVER TIME

One of the implications of implementing a petroleum licensing scheme based on an intergovernmental agreement is that the agreement and its implementing legislation may confer an element of stability on the licensing scheme simply by making it more difficult to amend. There is some evidence of this in the terms of the Accord and the implementing legislation as well as in practice. While there have been some important amendments to the health and safety regime of the Accord legislation there have been no significant amendments to the petroleum licensing provisions of the *CNLA*. That said, the Board itself (as discussed above) has made some adjustments over time, particularly with respect to its approach to licensing rounds and with respect to the distinction between Phase I and II of the EL. These changes seem to have been made to provide clarity to licensees as to the terms on which they can postpone drilling and to reduce administrative costs (by avoiding the need to apply for a licence amendment) while at the same time preserving the incentive to drill in a timely manner (through escalating deposits).

---

[68]   2014 NSCA 108 [50] leave to appeal to the Supreme Court of Canada denied 2015 CanLII 38343 (SCC).

[69]   ibid [68].

[70]   ibid [70].

[71]   ibid [78].

The text of the Accord provides for "joint management" of offshore oil and gas resources and recognizes "the equality of both governments in the management of the resource".[72] It also emphasizes the need to "provide for a stable and fair offshore management regime for industry" and "a stable and permanent arrangement for the management of the offshore".[73] As previously noted the Accord called for these arrangements to be implemented through mirror legislation and to that end the Accord provides that "neither government will introduce amendments to the legislation or regulations implementing the Accord" except by mutual consent.[74] Furthermore, the Government of Canada even committed to pursue constitutional entrenchment of the Accord, should the Government of Newfoundland and Labrador be able to secure the support of other provinces.[75]

The legislation itself maintains these commitments. Thus, the single preambular provision in the *CNLA* records the commitment not to introduce amendments to the legislation and regulations absent mutual consent.[76] Furthermore, section 9, which establishes the Board by the joint operation of the federal and provincial statutes, goes on to provide that "The Board may be dissolved only by the joint operation of an Act of Parliament and an Act of the Legislature of the Province".[77] While the doctrine of the supremacy of parliament suggests that there may be reason to doubt whether these provisions would actually prevent Parliament from proceeding unilaterally to change the terms of the legislation,[78] they do represent a strong political commitment to proceeding by agreement which in turn makes it harder and more time-consuming to effect change.

While there have been only minor changes to the petroleum licensing scheme under the Atlantic Accord, one set of changes introduced by the Board has attracted a lot of attention and litigation, both in the Newfoundland courts and within the context of investment treaty arbitration. These changes dealt

---

[72]   Atlantic Accord (n 7), s. 1 and s. 2(d).
[73]   Atlantic Accord, s. 2(f) and (g).
[74]   Atlantic Accord, s. 60.
[75]   Atlantic Accord, s. 63. This never happened but the mere inclusion of this clause does suggest a degree of political commitment to the permanence of the arrangement.
[76]   *CNLA*, Preamble.
[77]   *CNLA*, s. 9(4).
[78]   See *Reference re Pan-Canadian Securities Regulation*, 2018 SCC 48 (CanLII), [2018] 3 SCR 189. Perhaps the strongest argument with respect to the need to observe consensus is that s. 9 pertaining to the creation and dissolution of the Board has created a "manner and form" requirement that must be observed. Canadian courts have generally been prepared to enforce manner and form requirements. See, most recently, *Mikisew Cree First Nation v. Canada (Governor General in Council)*, 2018 SCC 40.

with required investments in research and development within Newfoundland and Labrador rather than with changes to the petroleum licences themselves.

The Board first developed research and development (R & D) guidelines in 1986 revising them successively in 1987, 1988 and 2004. The early versions of the guidelines focused on the exploration phase rather than the development phase of project activities. The 2004 Guidelines introduced the idea of an industry wide benchmark against which to measure R & D investments. The Board made this change because it was concerned that R & D investments were falling as the projects moved into the production phase.[79] The next few paragraphs discuss the evolution of the Guidelines and related benefit plans and the ensuing litigation.

The Board established and approved Benefit Plans for two early projects: Hibernia (1985) and Terra Nova (1997). These plans were heavy on principles rather than detailed commitments. The 2004 R & D Guidelines are considerably more prescriptive and require operators to make certain levels of expenditure on R & D matters for each of the exploration, development and production phases of the project. The required expenditure is determined by reference to Statistics Canada data for average R & D expenditures in the upstream oil and gas industry. In default of required expenditures, operators were required to contribute any shortfall to a Board administered R & D Fund. The Guidelines were made enforceable by making them a condition of the operator's Production Operations Authorization (POA), which is renewed annually.[80] When the Board sought to apply these new Guidelines not only to new projects but also to the existing Hibernia and Terra Nova projects, the working interest owners sought to contest the Guidelines in both the domestic courts and ultimately before an international investment tribunal.

In the domestic judicial review application the working interest owners sought to question not only the application of the Guidelines to these two pre-existing projects but also the Board's authority to issue the Guidelines at all. The applicants were unsuccessful both at first instance and in the Court of Appeal.

The majority of the Court of Appeal concluded that it was reasonable for the Board to apply the new Guidelines to existing projects. The Court noted that section 45 of the Act requires that a benefits plan "contain provisions intended to ensure" R & D expenditures within the province, and the operator knew that

---

[79] This section draws on two previous publications Nigel Bankes, "From Regulatory Chill to Regulatory Concussion", May 6, 2013, http://ablawg.ca/wp-content/uploads/2013/05/Blog_NB_Mobil_Investments_May20131.pdf and Nigel Bankes, "Canada" in Eduardo Pereira and Tonje Gormley (eds), *Local Content for the International Petroleum Industry* (Pennwell, 2018) 102–24.

[80] *CNLA*, s. 138.

its POA was subject to annual renewal depending on its performance[81] and knew that its performance would be monitored.[82] The Court also concluded that the Guidelines themselves were reasonable and that it was reasonable for the Board to base the level of required expenditures on the standard in the industry.[83] Finally, the Court concluded that it was reasonable for the Board to require payments into a fund as an alternative means of securing compliance with the R & D objectives[84] and reasonable as well for it to tie compliance to the POA.[85]

Justice Rowe in dissent saw the matter very differently and emphasized the "colossal" sums of money involved[86] and the need for stability in the offshore investment climate[87] and concluded, in language that reflects the idea of the obsolescing bargain, as follows:[88]

> ... it is to me inconceivable that the Parliament of Canada intended to confer on the Board authority of a nature that would allow the Board to approve a project for development and, then, when billions of dollars had been invested to put the project into production, to say to the operators that they will no longer be permitted to operate the project unless they spend phenomenally large sums on matters un-related to the project because the Board has decided that *it* (and not a government) wishes to create for the province a "legacy", as the Board conceives this from time to time.

Some of the working interest owners were more successful in their arbitration under the Investment chapter of the North American Free Trade Agreement (NAFTA).[89] While the unanimous tribunal concluded that Canada had not breached the fair and equitable treatment standard under NAFTA a majority of the tribunal concluded that the 2004 R & D guidelines did breach the domestic performance provisions of NAFTA (Article 1106) and were not grandparented

---

[81]   *Hibernia Management* (n 15) [65]. References are to the leading judgement given by Justice Welsh. Justice Barry gave separate concurring reasons and Justice Rowe dissented.

[82]   ibid [67]–[69].

[83]   ibid [83]–[92].

[84]   ibid [93]–[99].

[85]   ibid [99]–[109].

[86]   ibid [163] and suggesting that the Board's approach would only be supportable to the extent that there was a close connection between R & D expenditures and the needs of the particular project.

[87]   ibid [170]–[173] and referring to the terms of the underlying political Accord that should inform the interpretation of the legislation: *Mobil Oil Canada Ltd v. Canada-Newfoundland Offshore Petroleum Board*, [1994] 1 SCR 202.

[88]   ibid *Hibernia Management* [181]. Emphasis in original.

[89]   NAFTA cannot be used to protect those working interest owners that are domestic investors or foreign investor beyond the United States or Mexico.

by the exceptions provisions (Article 1108 and Annex I) of that Agreement.[90] As a result, the operators/investors were entitled to damages. The Tribunal issued its Final Award on February 25, 2015 awarding Mobil damages of C$13,893,000 and Murphy Oil C$3,401,000 (Mobil I decision).[91]

The Award in Mobil I confirms that in some circumstances the provisions of international investment agreements may be used to provide the stability and certainty that a licensee desires and which may not be obtainable from the domestic courts.

Shortly after the Mobil I Award Mobil sought the assurance of the Board that it would not apply the 2004 Guidelines to ExxonMobil.[92] The Board categorically declined to give that assurance:[93]

> In response to your correspondence of July 5, 2012, the validity of the Board's guidelines has been affirmed by the Courts and we will continue to verify an Operator's obligation to ensure that research and development and education and training projects, initiatives and expenditures are aligned with the eligibility criteria and benchmarks established by these guidelines.
>
> There is no intention to "waive" in whole or in part any of the Operator's obligations respecting research and development or education and training for any of the projects that fall under the Board's jurisdiction.

Mobil launched a second arbitration two and half years later in January 2015 seeking damages arising from the continued application of the Guidelines between 2012 and 2015. In a decision on jurisdiction and admissibility in July 2018 the arbitration panel confirmed that Mobil had commenced the arbitration in a timely way and that was not precluded from proceeding by the

---

[90]   In addition, the tribunal unanimously concluded that the application of the R & D guidelines to the existing projects of the investors was not a breach of the fair and equitable treatment standard.

[91]   See synopsis available here: Mobil and Murphy v. Canada, www.international.gc.ca/trade-agreements-accords-commerciaux/topics-domaines/disp-diff/mobil.aspx?lang=eng; Les Whittington, "Oil giants win $17M from Ottawa under NAFTA", Toronto Star, 13 March 2015, www.thestar.com/news/canada/2015/03/13/oil-giants-win-17m-from-ottawa-under-nafta.html.

[92]   See *Mobil Investments Canada Inc. v. Canada (ICSID Case No. ARB/15/6), Decision on Jurisdiction and Admissibility*, July 13, 2018 (Mobil II), [78]. http://icsidfiles.worldbank.org/icsid/ICSIDBLOBS/OnlineAwards/C4205/DS11312_En.pdf.

[93]   ibid [79].

doctrine of res judicata.[94] This second arbitration was ultimately settled at the beginning of 2020.[95]

6.   THE LEGAL CHARACTER OF THE LICENCES

There is little direct judicial authority on the legal character of licences under the accord legislation.[96] In *Mobil Oil* Justice Iacobucci opened his remarks with the somewhat offhand comment that "a group of resource companies sought a kind of statutory interest in respect of an offshore area".[97]

Analysis of the terms of the standard form licences suggests elements of administrative law, contract and property. As for administrative law characteristics, the licence is "issued" by the Board to the licensee and the licence is

---

[94]   The Tribunal also noted that while an Article 11 tribunal can only award damages for breach of Article 11 (NAFTA Article 1135 and [163]) this did not mean that the continued application of the Guidelines was lawful as a matter of international law, at least as against Mexico and the United States if not as against Mobil [170]. On the contrary [165], references omitted:

> NAFTA Article 1106(1) prohibits Canada from imposing or enforcing measures which are contrary to its terms. That obligation is a continuing one and, like any treaty obligation, must be performed in good faith. Once a Chapter Eleven tribunal found that the imposition and enforcement of the 2004 Guidelines was contrary to Article 1106, it is difficult to see how Canada could discharge its duty to perform its obligations under Article 1106 in good faith while still enforcing the Guidelines. That conclusion is reinforced by the ILC Articles on State Responsibility, Article 30 of which provides that a State which is responsible for an internationally wrongful act is under an obligation to cease that act if it is a continuing one.

[95]   See *Mobil Investments Canada Inc. v. Canada (ICSID Case No. ARB/15/6), Consent Award*, February 4, 2020 www.italaw.com/sites/default/files/case-documents/italaw11182.pdf.

[96]   There is a more extensive jurisprudence dealing with the characterization of petroleum interests under both private leases and provincial leasing regimes. See *Berkheiser* (n 22) and *Orphan Well Association* (n 23). As noted in Part 2.1 of the chapter Canadian courts generally characterize such interests (whatever the label or name attached to the statutory interest) as a *profit à prendre*. This is a logical characterization of a *production* interest and the reasoning in those cases would support characterizing a PL under the *CNLA* as a *profit*. ELs and SDLs do not lend themselves to a similar characterization since neither affords the right to produce but only the right to acquire a PL (and thence the right to produce) provided that certain pre-conditions can be satisfied.

[97]   [1994] 1 SCR 202, 206. There are further references to Mobil's interest as a statutory interest at 224 and thus perhaps not entitled to protection as "vested rights" but nevertheless still entitled to some degree of procedural fairness particularly in relation to "final" decisions such as whether or not lands should be included in a DSD or just expire (i.e., revert to the Crown).

executed by the Chair on behalf of the Board but not by the licensee. Similarly, the EL form contains complex provisions relating to allowable expenditures, which have a distinctly administrative law flavor in which the licensee is an applicant and the Board the ultimate decision-maker.[98] The licensee must make annual filings with the Board,[99] pay a levy to support environmental studies,[100] and the EL expressly contemplates that decisions of the Board may be subject to judicial review.[101]

But there are also contractual and property elements to the documents and indeed the dominant impression is that these documents are more private law than public law in their nature. As a matter of contract the recitals to the Board's standard form EL indicate that the licensee in submitting its bid "has agreed to the terms and conditions of this Licence" while the operative clauses reinforce this with a statement to the effect that the response to the call for bids and selection by the Board as the winning bid "constitutes an agreement between the Interest Owner and the Board as to the terms and conditions contained herein".[102] Similarly the EL contains liability and indemnity provisions which would look very familiar in any commercial contract[103] and at various points the EL is careful to stipulate that the undertakings of the licensee shall survive the EL and be incorporated into any subsequent SDL or PL.[104]

The licences also carry elements of a property relationship between the Board and the licensee. First and most obviously the licence applies to specific offshore lands (delineated in the schedule).[105] Second, the licence grants a set of exclusive rights "pursuant to the Act". Third, the licence form provides for the payment of rent, and finally the licence contains an enurement clause indicating that the licence "enures to the benefit of and is binding on the Board and the Interest Owner and their respective heirs, administrators, successors and assigns".[106]

In sum, licences under the *CNLA* are something of a hybrid bearing some of the trappings of both public and private law. While it may be difficult to characterize either the EL or an SDL as a form of property right in the nature of a *profit à prendre* (since neither affords the licensee the right to win, work

---

[98]　EL appended to the Jeanne d'Arc (2018) call for bids (n 31).
[99]　ibid, s. 11 (exploration plan).
[100]　ibid, s. 10.
[101]　ibid, s. 15(2).
[102]　ibid, quotations from the preamble and s. 3 "Agreement".
[103]　ibid, ss. 13 and 14.
[104]　ibid, ss. 13(2) and 14(4).
[105]　ibid, s. 2 (rights).
[106]　ibid, s. 16.

and remove hydrocarbons) there seems little doubt that a production licence deserves this classification.[107]

7.   CONCLUSIONS

As a federal State in which the provinces play a dominant role in relation to natural resources and where there exist both private and public ownership of natural resources including hydrocarbons, there is considerable diversity in petroleum licensing schemes in Canada. Furthermore, some forms of hydrocarbons (especially oil sands) lend themselves to different forms of licensing schemes. This contribution has offered some preliminary comments with respect to private leasing arrangements but has focused on Canada's offshore petroleum licensing regime using as an example the licensing regime applicable in the Newfoundland/Labrador offshore under the terms of the *CNLA* and the mirror provincial legislation.

The regime presents a three-step licensing scheme consisting of the EL, SDL and PL. A licensee that fails to drill, or that drills and fails to make a discovery, will not proceed beyond the EL phase. But a licensee that makes a discovery can expect to proceed to the SDL phase and on to the PL phase if its discovery is economic. Taken as a whole, the regime offers its licensees significant stability and security. Once a discovery has been established a licensee enjoys important procedural safeguards. The decision-making in relation to the declaration of significant discovery and the declaration of commercial discovery is objective and expert in nature rather than political, and the licensee may access both the expert Oil and Gas Committee review process as well as judicial review before the ordinary courts if it believes that the Board has not treated it fairly. Furthermore, the joint federal/provincial nature of the offshore scheme makes it hard to amend the basic structure of the legislation, thus affording licensees additional security from changes in the law. And where changes have been made at the margins in a way that affects a licensee's profitability, licensees have met some success in obtaining compensation through the international investment arbitration process – although the availability of such a remedy will be contingent upon the existence of a relevant international investment treaty.

---

[107]   *Orphan Well Association* (n 23).

5. The legal character of petroleum licences in Uganda

Emmanuel B. Kasimbazi

1. INTRODUCTION

Oil and Gas exploration and production in Uganda is currently taking place in the Albertine Graben region.[1] This region is part of the East African Rift System and runs along Uganda's western border with the Democratic Republic of Congo (DRC). The region is approximately 500 kilometres long, averaging 45 kilometres in width and 23,000 square kilometres in Uganda.[2]

The occurrence of petroleum was first recorded in the Uganda's Albertine Graben during the colonial days in the early 1920s. The first Production Sharing Agreement (PSA) between Petrofina Exploration Uganda and the Government signed over the entire Albertine Graben in 1991, and in 2006 the first commercial discovery was declared. Since then, Uganda has progressed from the exploration and appraisal to the development and production phases in the petroleum upstream value chain. The tenure of Exploration Licences (EL) are now maturing into the development phase of the petroleum value chain and progressing towards production. The first production licence issued over the Kingfisher field in 2013 was granted to the Chinese company CNOOC and other licences have been issued to Tullow and Total Oil Companies.

This chapter considers the legal character of the petroleum licensing regime in Uganda. The chapter is divided into four parts. Subsequent to this introduction, the second section provides an overview of Uganda's legal system and structure of government. The third section defines petroleum according to the Ugandan law, explains the nature of public ownership of petroleum and individual rights to the land where such land has petroleum deposits and the rights of the licensees. The fourth section describes the process for obtaining petroleum licences, based on the structure of the petroleum industry in

---

[1]   Petroleum Authority of Uganda, 'Frequently Asked Questions', https://pau.go
.ug/about-us/resources/faqs/, accessed 18 April 2019.
[2]   Ibid.

Uganda, which is classified into upstream, midstream and downstream and the final section is the conclusion.

2.   LEGAL CHARACTER OF THE JURISDICTION

Uganda is located in East Africa and lies across the equator, about 800 kilometers inland from the Indian Ocean.[3] It lies between 10° 29' South and 40° 12' North latitude, 290° 34' East and 350° 0' East longitude.[4] The country is land-locked, bordered by Kenya in the East; South Sudan in the North; Democratic Republic of Congo in the West; Tanzania in the South; and Rwanda in South West.[5] It has a total area of 241,551 square kilometers, of which the land area covers 200,523 square kilometers.[6] The total population of Uganda was estimated to be 44.3 million in March 2020.[7]

Uganda is a former British colony that gained its independence in October 1962. As a British colony, Uganda's legal system draws its origins from English Common Law, which was introduced in the late 1800s. Prior to its introduction, Ugandan indigenous communities were organised according to their customs. The law applicable today in Uganda derives from various sources. Common law, with the concomitant doctrine of equity, pursuant to the Judicature Act, Cap.13 is applicable. Customary law is also recognised by the courts of Uganda by virtue of section 14 (2) (b) (ii) of the Judicature Act, that provides for the application of "any established and current custom or usage". Statutory law and judicial precedents emanating from superior courts in Uganda are key sources of law. Finally, international law, consisting of treaties and principles of customary international law incorporated into domestic law through the parliament, are also sources of law in Uganda.

Uganda has adopted three Constitutions since independence in 1962. The first was the 1962 Constitution, which was replaced by the 1967 Constitution. In 1995, a new Constitution was adopted and promulgated on October 8, 1995. It is the 1995 Constitution and its amendments that are applied in Uganda today. Thus, the laws applicable in Uganda today are constitutional law, statutory law, common law, the doctrine of equity and customary law.

---

[3]   Republic of Uganda, 'National Population and Housing Census Report' (2014) at p. 8.

[4]   Ibid.

[5]   Ibid.

[6]   Worldometer,   *Uganda*,   www.worldometers.info/world-population/uganda-population/ (accessed 30 March 2020).

[7]   Republic of Uganda, 'National Population and Housing Census Report' (2014) at p. 8.

The 1995 Constitution provides for and upholds the doctrine of separation of powers. This it does by establishing the three arms of government that are the executive,[8] legislature and the judiciary,[9] the legislature is provided for under chapter six of the Constitution, and the Parliament established under Article 77. The Parliament is constituted for a term of five years from the date of its first sitting after a general election. The functions of Parliament are set out under Article 79 of the Constitution, granting the parliament authority to make laws on any matter for the peace, order, development and good governance of Uganda.[10] It is further required to protect the Constitution and promote democratic governance of Uganda.[11] Parliament is mandated to make laws, which commence as bills tabled before Parliament (either as private member's bill or a bill presented by the government through the relevant line ministry).[12] Bills are then passed by Parliament[13] into Acts of Parliament, which form statutory law. A Bill is read three times prior to passing by Parliament.[14] A bill once passed by parliament has to be sent to the President for assent, which the President may do with or without suggesting any changes to the said Bill. The President may also refuse assenting to a bill until certain changes are made, such Bill is then sent back to Parliament to effect the changes and once the said bill is rejected by the President twice, on the third time, it is automatically passed into law with the support of at least two-thirds of all members of Parliament without being assented to by the President.[15]

The executive is established under chapter seven of the Constitution, which details the President as Head of State, Head of Government and

---

[8]   Chapter Seven of the Constitution 1995 as amended makes provisions for the Executive arm of government. Under Article 99, the executive authority of Uganda is vested in the President of Uganda and shall be exercised in accordance with the Constitution and the laws of Uganda.

[9]   Article 126 of the Constitution makes provisions for the judiciary. Under the Article, judicial power is derived from the people and shall be exercised by the courts established under the Constitution in the name of the people and in conformity with law and with the values, norms and aspirations of the people.

[10]   Ibid, Article 79.

[11]   Ibid, Article 79 (3).

[12]   Section 1 (c) of the Parliament Act Cap.2 defines a bill to mean the draft of an Act of Parliament and includes both a private member's bill and a Government bill.

[13]   Article 77 (1) of the Constitution of Uganda 1995 as amended.

[14]   The first reading is the formal introduction of the Bill in Parliament and the Bill is then committed to the relevant sessional committee of Parliament for consideration. At the second reading, the sessional committee submits a report on the Bill to the plenary of Parliament that debates on the principles and policies of the Bill. At the third reading, the bill is not debated and it is passed as a formality upon a motion. Rule 126 of the Rules of Procedure of Parliament, 2012.

[15]   Ibid, Article 91 (5).

Commander-in-Chief of the Uganda People's Defence Forces, and the Fountain of Honour,[16] meaning that the President holds sovereignty and has the exclusive right of conferring legitimate titles of nobility and orders of chivalry on other persons and he or she is protected against court proceedings while he or she is in office. The Constitution vests executive authority of Uganda in the President, who shall exercise the same in accordance with the Constitution and the laws of Uganda.[17] Like the parliament, the position of President is held for a period of five years and a person may be elected for one or more terms. Provision is also made for the Vice President, the Prime Minister, the Attorney General, deputy Attorney General and the cabinet. The cabinet consists of the President, the Vice President, the Prime Minister and such number of ministers as the president deems reasonably necessary for the efficient running of the state. The cabinet functions are to determine, formulate and implement the policies of government and perform such other functions as may be conferred by the Constitution.

The third arm of government is the judiciary, established under chapter eight of the Ugandan Constitution. Article 126 of the Constitution provides for the exercise of judicial power, which is derived from the people and exercised by the courts in the name of the people and in conformity with the law and with the values, norms and aspirations of the people. The judiciary is independent in the exercise of judicial power, not subject to the control or direction of any person or authority.[18] The hierarchy of the courts is provided for under Article 129 as the Supreme Court, the Court of Appeal, the High Court and such subordinate courts as Parliament may by law establish. The Court of Appeal also sits as the constitutional court in questions that require the interpretation of the constitution under Article 137.

In principle, all the three arms of government are not only independent of each other but also supplement each other. To ensure this, the Constitution establishes the Inspectorate of Government as the Ombudsman to provide checks and balances amongst the three arms of government. It is specifically mandated to promote and foster strict adherence to the rule of law and the principles of natural justice in administration, promote fair, efficient and good governance in public offices. All this is intended to ensure that the three arms of government operate efficiently without interference from any one thereby ensuring each arm's independence.

---

[16]   Constitution of Uganda, Article 98.
[17]   Constitution of Uganda, Article 99 (1).
[18]   Ibid, Article 128.

3.   OVERVIEW OF THE LEGAL CHARACTER OF THE PETROLEUM INDUSTRY

The Constitution and the Petroleum (Exploration, Development and Production) Act 2013 (EDP Act) define petroleum to mean the following:

(a) any naturally occurring hydrocarbons, whether in gaseous, liquid or solid state;
(b) any naturally occurring mixture of hydrocarbons, whether in a gaseous, liquid or solid state; or
(c) any naturally occurring mixture of one or more hydrocarbons and any other substances, and includes any petroleum as defined by paragraph (a)(b) or this paragraph that has been returned to a natural reservoir, but does not include coal, shale, or any substance that may be extracted from coal or shale.[19]

Uganda applies English Common Law, which presumes that the owner of the land is entitled to all that is located above and below the land "*cujus est solum ejus est usque ad colum et usque ad inferos*". Under common law, mineral and petroleum resources naturally occurring form part of the land on which they are situated unless these resources are specifically severed from the state land grant, which is the case in Uganda.

Uganda's natural resources laws adopted the practice of reserving a title to mineral and petroleum *in situ* exclusively to the State.[20] Ownership in such resources *in situ* therefore rests with the State. The vesting of ownership of mineral and petroleum resources *in situ* together with the vesting of the prerogative to licence the exploration and production of these resources, and the prerogative to manage the exploration and development of same, provides the foundation of resources law. It underpins the legal arrangement under which the resources are developed. The Constitution of Uganda and the Petroleum (Exploration, Development and Production) Act 2013 (EDP Act) vest ownership and control of all minerals and petroleum resources in the Government on behalf of the people of Uganda. Under Article 244 the Constitution provides that, subject to Article 26 (the right to property and its protection), the entire property in, and the control of, all minerals and petroleum in, on or under, any land or waters in Uganda are vested in the Government on behalf of the Republic of Uganda. The same wording is repeated in Section 4 of EDP Act. The EDP Act prohibits petroleum activities without authorisation, licence,

---

[19]   Ibid, Article 244(4).
[20]   Ibid, Article 237 (2) (b) 2.

permit or approval, as required under the law.[21] This implies that oil and gas as underground resources, is exclusive State property and therefore it is not possible to engage in any petroleum activities without first obtaining relevant permits and licences.

The licensing system governing petroleum exploration and production is therefore the ultimate exercise of the State's ownership of these resources and the exercise of the management prerogative is the ultimate exercise of sovereignty over the exploration and production of the resources. It is important to note that despite State ownership of the petroleum naturally occurring, the resources are developed by private enterprises and hence the petroleum legal regime is geared towards encouraging private sector investment in petroleum development.

The Constitution provides that minerals, mineral ores and petroleum shall be exploited taking into account the interests of the individual landowners, local governments and the government.[22] The legal regime therefore provides for the protection of individual rights to the land where such land has petroleum deposits. It has to be acquired in accordance with the law, which provides for:

a. where the taking of possession or acquisition is necessary for public use or in the interest of defence, public safety, public order, public morality or public health; and

b. The compulsory taking of possession or acquisition of property is made under a law which provides for-

    i.   prompt payment of fair and adequate compensation, prior to the taking of possession or acquisition of the property; and

    ii. A right of access to a court of law by any person who has an interest or right over the property.[23]

The law that provides for compulsory acquisition of land in Uganda is the Land Acquisition Act (LAA), Cap 226. It regulates the compulsory acquisition of land by the government for public purposes. Section 2 of the LAA empowers any person authorised by the Minister to enter upon the land and survey the land; dig or bore into the subsoil and remove samples; and do any other thing necessary for ascertaining its suitability for that purpose. The land to be compulsorily acquired shall be assessed and valued so as the owner is adequately compensated before the land can be taken over. A person who is aggrieved by such an award under Section 13 can appeal against an award under Section 6. It is the LAA and the Guidelines for Compensation assessment under the Land

---

21   EDP Act, s 5.
22   Constitution of Uganda, Article 244 (3).
23   Ibid, Article 26 (2).

Acquisition Act (GCALA) 2017 that apply when the government intends to compulsorily acquire land for petroleum exploration and production activities.

Section 6 of EDP Act allows the Government of Uganda to enter into an agreement relating to petroleum activities and consistent with this Act, with any person with respect to the following matters the grant of a licence, the conditions for granting or renewing a licence, the conduct by a person, of petroleum activities on behalf of any person to whom a licence is granted; and any other matter incidental or connected to the matters in above. The responsible Minister is further required to develop or cause to be developed a model Production Sharing Agreement or any other model agreement as may be entered into by Government of Uganda, which shall be submitted to Cabinet then Parliament for approval.

Under Section 135 of the EDP Act, a provision is made for restrictions and the rights of others. A licensee shall *not* exercise any right under a licence:

a. without the written consent of the relevant authority, upon any land dedicated or set apart for a public purpose or for a place of burial, or upon land over which a mining lease, an exploration licence or a right to cultural site has been granted;
b. without the written consent of the land owner—
    i. upon any land which is the site of or which is within two hundred meters of any inhabited, occupied or temporarily unoccupied house or building;
    ii. within fifty metres of any land which has been cleared or ploughed or otherwise *bona fide* prepared for the growing of agricultural crops or on which agricultural crops arc growing;
    iii. upon any land from which, during the year immediately preceding, agricultural crops have been reaped; or
    iv. upon any land which is the site of or which is within one hundred metres of a cattle dip-tank, dam or water used by human beings or cattle.
c. in a national park or wildlife reserve without the written authority of the Uganda Wildlife Authority;
d. in a forest reserve without the written consent of the National Forestry Authority;
e. upon any land reserved for the purposes of a railway track or within fifty meters of any railway track, without the written consent of the railway administration concerned;
f. upon any land within two hundred metres of, the boundaries of any township, without the written consent of the local council concerned;

g. upon any street, road, public place or aerodrome without the written
    consent of the Minister or other authority having control of the street, road,
    public place or aerodrome; or
h. in a fish breeding area without the written consent of the department
    responsible for fisheries.

The above provisions clearly indicate that a licence does not confer *absolute*
rights on the licensee to do anything they wish to do, but rather can only
carry out activities as specified in the licence in accordance to relevant laws
(and associated consents) of the government of Uganda, and to recognise the
rights of the people, animals and environment which may be affected by such
a licensee's activities.

Under section 136 of the EDP Act, a land owner in an exploration or
development area shall retain the right to graze stock upon or to cultivate the
surface of the land insofar as the grazing or cultivation does not interfere with
petroleum activities or safety zones in the area. In the case of a development
area, the landowner within the area shall not erect any building or structure
on the land without the written consent of the licensee or, if the consent is
unreasonably withheld the written consent of the Minister in consultation with
the Authority. The rights conferred by a licence are therefore to be exercised
reasonably so as to affect as few of the interests of any landowner of the land
on which the rights are exercised. Thus, petroleum activities shall be carried
out in a proper manner.[24]

A landowner or licensee with a different licence other than one under the
EDP Act shall, with regard to an exploration or development area, retain the
right to movement and other activities where the subsurface activities do not
interfere with an exclusive right, or with petroleum activities in the area.[25]

The EDP Act also provides for situations where a licensee may acquire
exclusive rights and this is subject to Section 135 and any law relating to acquisition of land.[26] Section 138 (1) further provides that a holder of a petroleum
production licence may, if he or she requires the exclusive use of the whole or
any part of a block in a development area, obtain a lease of the land or other
rights to use it upon such terms as to the rent to be paid for the land, the duration and extent or area of the land to which the lease or other right of the lease
shall relate as may be agreed upon between the holder of a licence and the land
owner.[27] This means that consideration has to be paid to the landowner for such
exclusion from his land and where the holder of a licence and the land owner

---

24   EDP Act, s 136(3).
25   EDP Act, s 137.
26   EDP Act, s 138.
27   EDP Act, s 138 (1).

fail to agree on the consideration, the matter shall be referred to the Chief Government Valuer for determination.

A licensee is enjoined to pay, on demand by a land owner, fair and reasonable compensation for any disturbance of his rights and for any damage done to the surface of the land due to petroleum activities, and shall, at the demand of the owner of any crops, trees, buildings or works damaged during the course of the activities, pay compensation for the damage.[28] The law provides for the qualification of this in that the licensee and other persons engaged in petroleum activities shall be persons who possess the necessary qualifications to perform the work in a prudent manner. In the same vein, the licensee shall ensure that any person carrying out work for the licensee possesses the necessary qualifications.[29] Thus, this section creates obligations for the licensee, or any person carrying out work on behalf of the licensee, to possess the necessary qualifications for carrying out petroleum activities.

4.   PROCESS FOR OBTAINING PETROLEUM LICENCES

A Petroleum Exploration Licence is granted in accordance with section 58 of the EDP Act and a Petroleum Production Licence is granted in accordance with Section 75 of the Act. Under section 8 of the EDP Act the Minister of Energy and Mineral Development (the "Minister") is responsible for, inter alia, granting and revoking petroleum licences. The Minister must also seek the approval of the Cabinet before (i) opening an area for petroleum exploration; (ii) granting an exploration licence; or (iii) granting a production licence.[30]

Under section 10 the Petroleum Authority of Uganda (PAU) will advise the Minister in the granting and revocation of licences.

Licensing in Uganda is based on the structure of the petroleum industry in Uganda which is classified into Upstream, Midstream and Downstream. Upstream involves promotion and licensing, exploration, development, production and decommissioning. Midstream involves transportation, refining, gas processing and conversion. Downstream involves distribution, marketing and sales.

---

[28]   Ibid, s 139.
[29]   Ibid, s 146.
[30]   Ibid, s 52.

4.1   Upstream Sector

The upstream sector involves exploration, development and production. It is
the first stage of the extractive industry. The sector is governed by the EDP Act
2013, the EDP Regulations 2016 and the EDP Metering Regulations, 2016.

4.1.1   Exploration and appraisal
This stage requires an application for a Reconnaissance Permit and a Production
Exploration Licence (PEL).

4.1.2   Reconnaissance permit
The reconnaissance permit is granted to a person intending to carry out reconnaissance surveys. These permits are non-exclusive since they may be issued
to different persons in respect of different reconnaissance activities in the same
area or areas,[31] and therefore do not confer property rights to the holder. The
reconnaissance permit allows the undertaking of preliminary petroleum activities for the purpose of acquiring geoscientific data and includes geological,
geophysical geochemical surveys and drilling of shallow boreholes for calibra-
tion. Under the EDP Act,[32] applications for reconnaissance permits are made to
the minister as prescribed in Form 2 under Schedule 1 of EDP Regulations.[33]

The application must be specific and state the geographically delineated
area. The permit may be issued to different persons in respect to the same
area since it is wholly for seismic survey and shallow drilling for data cali-
bration purposes.[34] The minister may issue the permit within 90 days from
the date of receipt of the application and after the applicant has met all the
necessary requirements.[35] The reconnaissance permit application fee is USD
10,000.[36] This permit cannot be granted to a body corporate incorporated
outside Uganda unless it has established a place of business in Uganda and is
registered in accordance with the Companies Act, 2012.[37] This permit expires
within 18 months from the date of issue.[38]

---

[31] EDP Act, s 48 (4)
[32] EDP Act 2013, s 48.
[33] Petroleum (Exploration, Development and Production) Regulations, 2016 SI 47
reg 8.
[34] EDP Act, s 51.
[35] Ibid, s 49.
[36] EDP Regulations Schedule 1.
[37] Ibid reg 9(3).
[38] EDP Act , s 51.

4.1.3   Petroleum exploration licence

The minister is required by section 52 of the EDP Act to announce areas open for bidding for an exploration licence by notice published in the Gazette and a newspaper of national and international circulation.[39] The petroleum exploration licence (PEL) is issued through a competitive bidding process, which must be carried out in a fair, open and competitive (bidding) manner in accordance with EDP Act,[40] take into account the following principles: promotion of competition; non-discrimination; transparency, accountability and fairness; protection of confidential information; promotion of national content; and zero tolerance to corrupt practices.[41] The bidding process undertakes the following stages: (a) announcement of areas open for bidding; (b) pre-qualification; (c) request for proposals; (d) evaluation and the award process.

Uganda's first competitive bidding round was finalized in 2016; Oranto from Nigeria and Armour Group from Australia got licences to explore two blocks in the Albertine Graben. Oranto has a licence to explore in the Ngassa block while Armour Energy has a licence for the Kanywataba area. The PEL is for four years and activities commenced in 2017.[42] Uganda is set to announce a second competitive exploration bidding round that will see new fields developed.[43]

In exceptional circumstances, the Minister is permitted to receive direct applications for an exploration licence including: (i) where there are no applications received in response to an invitation for bids for an area; (ii) applications in respect of areas that are adjacent to an existing licensed reservoir; and (iii) promotion of national interests.[44]

An application for an exploration licence is made to the Minister and must be submitted in writing and must: (i) contain the name of the body corporate, place of incorporation, the names and nationality of the directors, its share capital, and the names of holders of more than five percent of the issued share capital; (ii) identify the block or blocks in respect to which it is made (it should be in respect of not more than ten blocks); (iii) be accompanied by a statement giving particulars of work and the minimum expenditure proposed for the blocks over which the licence is sought; (iv) give information on the

---

[39]   EDP Regulations, reg 11.
[40]   Section 56 (6). This implies the bidding process for a petroleum licence is not under the Public Procurement and Disposal of Public Assets Act, 2003 as is the case for other goods and services.
[41]   EDP Regulations 2016 SI 47, reg12.
[42]   Edner Mubiru, 'Uganda gears up for second oil exploration bidding' (*New Vision*) Kampala 8 November 2018.
[43]   Ibid.
[44]   EDP Act, s 53(2) (a–c).

financial status and the technical and industrial competence and experience of the applicant; and (v) be accompanied by a statement giving particulars of the applicant's proposals with respect to the employment and training of citizens of Uganda.[45] PEL applications shall be as prescribed in Form 4 under Schedule 2 of the Regulations.[46] A PEL application is subject to bond execution, other form of security for performance of the PEL conditions and the necessary insurance policies to protect against liabilities.[47] The PEL application fee is USD 20,000.[48] [49]

The PEL confers a licensee with the *exclusive right* to explore for petroleum, and to carry on such petroleum activities and execute such works as may be necessary for that purpose, in the exploration area.[50] The licensee is required to notify the minister of the discoveries whether they are of commercial quantity or not. The holder of an exploration licence who has made a discovery of petroleum in an exploration area shall have exclusive right to apply for the grant of a production licence over any block or blocks in that area which, following appraisal, have been shown to contain a petroleum reservoir or part of a petroleum reservoir.[51] The licensee can apply for a petroleum production licence within two years from the date on which the technical evaluation of test results was submitted to the Minister or other period as may be stipulated in the PSA. Any party affected by the proposed exploration activity is given an opportunity to lodge, with the Minister, an objection to the grant of the exploration licence, setting out the grounds of the objection.[52] Where the Minister dismisses the objection, the Minister may grant the petroleum exploration licence. An aggrieved party by the Minister's decision may appeal to the High Court.

Provision is made for the renewal of an exploration licence where an application for the same has to be made not later than 90 days before the day on which the licence is due to expire; but the Minister may, where he or she deems fit, accept an application for the renewal of a petroleum exploration licence made later than 90 days before, but not in any case after, the date of expiry of the licence.[53] The Minister may in consultation with the Authority grant a renewal of the licence. However, under Section 64(2) of the EDP Act,

---

[45]   Ibid, s 56.
[46]   EDP Regulations, reg 13.
[47]   EDP Act, s 56.
[48]   EDP Regulations, Schedule 1.
[49]   Ibid.
[50]   Ibid, s 60.
[51]   Ibid, s 67.
[52]   EDP Act, s 55.
[53]   Ibid, s 63.

the Minister shall in consultation with the Authority not renew a petroleum exploration licence where the licensee has violated the provisions of this Act or a condition of the licence. Further, the Minister shall not grant a renewal of a petroleum exploration licence if the licensee is in default unless the Minister considers that special circumstances exist which justify the granting of the renewal, notwithstanding the default.[54] The Act does not require the licence holder to sign a contract with the government for this licence but where the licence holder violates the provisions of the Act, the Minister may refuse to renew the licence.

4.1.4 Permit to drill

Licensees can only operate a drilling rig with a permit obtained from the Petroleum Authority of Uganda (PAU) and in accordance with the terms and conditions so specified.[55] The operator is required before drilling a well to submit a detailed report on the technique to be employed, duration it will take, material to be used and the safety measures to be undertaken. The licensee is also required before drilling any well, to submit to PAU an application for consent to drill, which is accompanied by a well proposal and drilling programme.[56] Drilling rigs imported into Uganda are required to be certified by an internationally recognised entity for technical capacity and health, safety and environment before it is brought into Uganda.[57]

4.1.5 Development and construction

This phase involves planning, placement, construction and installation of facilities needed for petroleum production. A facility licence is required under this stage.

4.1.5.1 A facility licence

A facility licence is required to install, operate or use a facility to carry out a petroleum activity. The application is made to the minister who may in consultation with PAU grant a facility licence,[58] and the format of application is prescribed in Form 11 set out in Schedule 2 to the Regulations.[59] The application fee for a facility licence is USD 30,000.[60] The facility licence is granted on the basis of: the technical competence, capacity, experience and

---

[54] Ibid, s 64 (4).
[55] EDP Act, ss 93 and 94.
[56] EDP Regulations, reg 42.
[57] Ibid, reg 51.
[58] Ibid, s 81.
[59] Ibid, reg 25.
[60] Ibid, Schedule 1.

financial strength of the applicant; the licensee's safety measures; and the applicant's plan for construction and operation of the facility.[61] The licensee is also required to obtain other permissions for a licensed facility under other applicable laws. The duration for the licence is specified in the licence and can be renewed as the Minister may determine.[62] For the period the facility licence remains in force, it confers on the licensee the right to install, place, operate or use a facility.[63] However no alterations can be made to that facility without approval of the Minister.[64] This provision of the regulations confers an administrative right of the Minister to require that the holder of the licence goes through a process and get an approval before they can make any alterations to the facility or use the facility.

4.1.6   Production
The production stage involves activities relating to recovering oil and gas from a reservoir and preparing it for evacuation from the field area. It requires a petroleum production licence (PPL) and an annual production permit (APP). These licences are akin to property in that the EDP Act provides for rights conferred by the PPL to include to sell or otherwise dispose of the licensee's share of petroleum recovered (severed from the land) in accordance with the field development plan.[65] In essence, this establishes a *profit a prendre* for the licence holder to take from the land something which it does not own, and once ascertained, to own the acquired petroleum, and dispose of it.

4.1.7   Petroleum production licence (PPL)
The holder of a PEL who has made discovery in an exploration area or any other person who does not have a PEL may make an application for a PPL. The application for a PPL is made to the minister in accordance with Form 8 set out in Schedule 2 to the Regulations.[66]

A holder of a PEL has an exclusive right to apply for a PPL over any block in that area which has been shown to contain a petroleum reservoir. This area is shown by the holder of a PEL who has discovered petroleum in his exploration area under section 69 of the EDP Act. The holder of PEL licence is required under section 66 of the Act to notify the Minister immediately upon discovery of petroleum. The PEL holder should make the application within two years

---

[61] Ibid, reg 26.
[62] Ibid, reg. 27.
[63] EDP Act, s 83.
[64] EDP Regulations, reg 28.
[65] EDP Act, s 78.
[66] Ibid, s 69; Petroleum (Exploration, Development and Production) Regulations 2016 SI 47, reg 19.

after the date of submitting the technical evaluation for the test results to the minister. The application shall be accompanied by a report on the petroleum reservoir, a field development plan and other information as the minister may require. The licensed oil companies use the data and information acquired during appraisal to prepare Field Development Plans (FDPs) and Petroleum Reservoir Reports (PRRs) that are submitted to Government as part of the application for production licences. The fee for the PPL application is USD 40,000.[67]

In case of interested individual without a PEL, an application is made to the minister after an announcement published that areas are open for bidding for a PPL. The duration for processing applications or bids for PPL is 180 days from the date of receipt of the application.[68] The minister, with approval of cabinet, grants the PPL.[69] The PPL may be granted jointly to the applicant and National Oil Company (UNOC). The duration of a PPL is a period not exceeding 20 years and renewal for five years upon an application for renewal.[70] Licences issued under the EDP Act shall not be transferred without the written consent of the Minister in consultation with the Authority.[71] This implies that the licence can be transferred, which is a characteristic of property and under section 92 of the EDP Act, the Minister shall cause to be kept, a register of all licences issued under this Act called the Petroleum Register, in accordance with regulations made under this Act. Therefore, the PPL can be registered, sold, transferred and registered under the Act.

4.1.8   Annual production permit (APP)

The Annual Production Permit (APP) concerns approval of the licensee's production schedule for the year and the Minister may, in consultation with the Authority, upon application from the licensee, approve for a fixed period of time, the quantity of the petroleum which may be produced or injected at all times. The Minister, in consultation with PAU before or concurrently with the grant of a PPL, approves the production schedule contained in the Field Development Plan (FDP) and issues an APP to the licensee.[72] The application for the APP is made to the Minister as in Form 13 set out in Schedule 2 of the Regulations.[73] The application is accompanied by a report on field related

---

[67]   Ibid, Petroleum (Exploration, Development and Production) Regulations 2016 SI 47, Schedule 1.
[68]   EDP Act , s 72.
[69]   Ibid, s 75.
[70]   Ibid, s 77.
[71]   Ibid, s 87 (1).
[72]   Ibid, s 96.
[73]   EDP Regulations, reg 69.

matters, including alternative schemes for production.[74] The minister also approves test production of a reservoir, the duration, quantity and other conditions for the test production.[75]

4.1.9   Decommissioning and rehabilitation

This stage involves removal of all process plant equipment, decontamination and demolition of structures and restoration of the environment. The licensee must submit a decommissioning plan to PAU before a PPL or a specific licence to install and operate facilities expires or is surrendered.[76] PAU charges the licensee every calendar quarter a portion of the estimated future cost for decommissioning of facilities to be deposited in the decommissioning fund.[77] Therefore, the licensee pays for decommissioning. The amount deposited in the fund shall be charged as operating costs subject to the cost of recovery limitations stipulated in the petroleum agreements. Management of the fund shall be done by a Committee consisting of government representatives and the licensee as prescribed by the regulations.[78]

The Authority may issue directions relating to the disposal of decommissioned facilities and shall stipulate a time limit for the implementation of the directions.[79] The Government may take over the facilities of the licensee when a licence expires; a licence is surrendered or cancelled; the licensee's costs have been fully recovered; or the use of the facility has been terminated permanently. In the event of takeover of a facility subject to private property rights, compensation shall be paid where required by law and in accordance with the procedure prescribed by regulations.[80]

4.1.10   Dealings with licences

All licences issued under the Petroleum (Exploration, Development and Production) Act are able to be transferred with the written consent of the Minister in consultation with the Authority.[81] A licensee may apply to the Minister, in the prescribed form and manner, for the transfer of a licence and shall fulfil any other financial obligations under the laws of Uganda. The Minister shall satisfy himself or herself of the legal and technical capacity, competence and financial strength of the person to whom the licence is to be

---

[74]   Ibid, reg 69 (4).
[75]   EDP Act, s 96 (5).
[76]   Ibid, s 112.
[77]   Ibid, s 113 (4).
[78]   Ibid, s 113 (8).
[79]   Ibid, s 115.
[80]   Ibid, s 120.
[81]   Ibid, s 87.

transferred. The Minister shall not unreasonably withhold consent to an application to transfer a licence unless he or she has reason to believe that the public
interest or safety is likely to be prejudiced by the transfer. Given this capacity
to transfer the drilling permit, it is clear that the rights granted are more than
administrative, and more akin to property in nature.

All licensees are enjoined to carry out petroleum activities in the licence
area in a proper and safe manner and in accordance with the requirements of
the applicable law, regulations and conditions stipulated by lawful authorities
and best petroleum industry practices.[82] A licensee who fails or neglects to
comply with any requirement under section 88 commits an offence and is
liable on conviction to a fine not exceeding 200,000 currency points. The
licence can be revoked under section 91 of the EDP Act and there are consequences of the cancellation in that the licensee shall not be discharged from the
financial obligations under the Act hence being more administrative in nature.

The Act provides for surrender of licence and a licensee who wishes to surrender all or any of the blocks subject to the licence shall apply to the Minister
for a certificate of surrender in the case of a petroleum exploration licence, not
less than 90 days before the date on which he or she wishes the surrender to
have effect; and in the case of a petroleum production licence, not less than one
year before the date on which he or she wishes the surrender to have effect.[83]

A licence issued may be suspended or cancelled where a licensee is in
default, because of violations of the Ugandan law. Before such suspension or
cancellation can be done, the Minister is required to consult with the Authority
and get the approval of Cabinet, by notice in writing served on the licensee.[84]
The Minister may further cancel a licence under the following circumstances:

a. if the licensee is adjudged bankrupt or enters into any agreement or scheme
    of composition with his or her creditors or takes advantage of any law for
    the benefit of debtors; or
b. where the licensee is a body corporate, and an order is made or a resolution
    is passed winding up the affairs of the body corporate; except where the
    winding up is for the purpose of-
    i.   amalgamation and the Minister has consented to the amalgamation; or
    ii. reconstruction and the Minister has been given notice of the
         reconstruction.[85]

---

[82] Ibid, s 88.
[83] Ibid, s 89.
[84] Ibid, s 90.
[85] Ibid, s 90 (3) (a), b, (i) and (ii).

It suffices to note that under Section 91 revocation of a licence, surrender of rights or lapse of rights for other reasons do not discharge the licensee from the financial obligations under this Act, regulations issued under this Act or specific conditions attached to the licence. Under the same Section, where a work obligation or other obligation including decommissioning has not been fulfilled, the licensee shall pay the amount which fulfilment of the obligation would have cost the licensee if the work had been completed.

The Act imposes the following obligations where a licence has been surrendered or has expired, or has by reason of relinquishment ceased to comprise any area subject to the licence:[86]

- to remove property or cause to be removed from the area which was, but no longer is, subject to the licence all property brought into that area by any person engaged or concerned in the petroleum activities authorised by the licence, or to make arrangements that are satisfactory to the Authority with respect to that property;
- to plug or close off, to the satisfaction of the Authority, all wells drilled in that area by any person engaged or concerned in those operations; and
- To make provision, to the satisfaction of the Authority, for the conservation and protection of the natural resources in that area.

Where a person who has been directed to remove any property does not do so, the Authority may remove or cause to be removed such property and sell any property by public auction from which proceeds it is to recover the costs and expenses incurred in respect to the said property.[87] Under the Act, where the licensee or owner abandons a facility, the licensee or owner is liable for damage caused in connection with the abandoned facility.

The Act imposes strict liability on a licensee for pollution damage under Section 130, except where it is demonstrated that an inevitable event of nature, act of war, exercise of public authority or a similar force majeure event has contributed to a considerable degree to the damage or its extent under circumstances which are beyond the control of the licensee, in which case the liability may be reduced to the extent it is reasonable taking into consideration the following:

- the scope of the activity;
- the situation of the party that has sustained the damage; and
- the opportunity for taking out insurance on both sides.

---

[86]   Ibid, s 116.
[87]   Ibid, s 117.

In situations where the pollution damage occurs during a petroleum activity and the activity has been conducted without a licence, the party that conducted the petroleum activity is liable for the damage, regardless of fault.[88]

Where a licence is terminated, revoked or expires, the person who was the licensee immediately before the termination, revocation or expiration of the licence is required to immediately deliver to the Authority in a format acceptable to the Authority:

- all records with respect to the licence;
- all plans or maps of the licence area which were prepared by or on the instructions of the licensee;
- all tapes, diagrams, profiles and charts which were prepared by the licensee; and
- other documents as the Authority, may, by notice given to the licensee, require him or her to deliver.[89]

The law also imposes a continuing obligation on a holder of a petroleum exploration or production licence to pay annual fees in respect of the licence as may be prescribed by regulations. The annual fees include: acreage rental, including for strati graphically delineated acreage where applicable; training and research fees. These fees shall be payable on the grant of a licence and thereafter annually on the anniversary of the grant until the termination of the licence.[90] Failure to pay the said annual fees leads to the cancellation of the licence.

The EDP Act provides for security for fulfilment of obligations. The Minister is under an obligation to require an applicant to make arrangements as may be satisfactory to the Minister for the execution of a bond or other form of security for the performance and observance of the conditions to which the licence may be subject; and to require the applicant to take the necessary insurance policies to protect against liabilities that may arise as a result of petroleum. This is intended to guard against the misuse of the licence and reduce the risk of incompetence among the applicants for the respective licences under the EDP Act.[91]

Provision is also made for force majeure under section 188 of the EDP Act. It specifically provides that any failure on the part of the licensee or Government to fulfil any of the conditions of a licence or to meet any requirement of this Act or of a petroleum agreement shall not constitute a breach of the licence

---

[88] Ibid, s 131.
[89] Ibid, s 150.
[90] Ibid, s 155.
[91] Ibid, s 173.

or of this Act or the Agreement, in so far as the failure results from an act of war, hostility, insurrection, storm, flood, earthquake or such other natural phenomenon beyond the reasonable control of the licensee or Government as constituting force majeure. In such a situation, the licensee is required to immediately notify the Minister, giving particulars of the failure and its cause.

4.2   Midstream Sector

The midstream sector deals with the movement of crude oil from the location of discovery to the refinery, the refining and storage of the refined products. This sector is mainly regulated by the Petroleum (Refining, Conversion, Transmission, and Midstream Storage) Act 2013 and the Petroleum (Refining, Conversion, Transmission and Midstream Storage) Regulations, 2016. Licensing within this sector is confined to "operational licences" (i.e., those licences necessary for petroleum operations to occur), and is a function of the minister empowered by the Act to grant and revoke licences.[92] The PAU has a mandate to monitor and regulate midstream operations and activities and administer petroleum agreements and contracts related to midstream operations.[93]

The Act requires licences in respect of the following operations: to construct a refinery, conversion plant or other petroleum process plant,[94] to commence operations of refinery, conversion plant or other petroleum process plant,[95] a facility for refining crude oil, facility for conversion of natural gas, transmission pipeline, midstream storage facility and any other facility for the purpose of midstream operations subject to the Act and regulations.[96]

Applications are made to the Minister by two or more persons jointly.[97] The application is accompanied by copies of company details, the feasibility and justification of the project, a description of the proposed facility, list of process technologies, a planned production and operation schedule and project duration inter alia. The applicant must also show the ability to comply

---

[92]   Petroleum (Refining, Conversion, Transmission and Midstream Storage) Act 2013, s 4.

[93]   Ibid, s 6.

[94]   The Petroleum (Refining, Conversion, Transmission and Midstream Storage) Regulations, 2016, reg 4.

[95]   Ibid, reg 16.

[96]   RCTMS Act s 9 (a–e).

[97]   Ibid, s 10 (2). Section 24 of RCTMS 24 provides that two or more applicants enter into a co-operation agreement with a view to apply for a licence under the Act. Such cooperation agreement has to be submitted to the Minister and the Minister may require alterations to be made in the agreement as a condition for granting of the licence in accordance with the Act.

with all applicable labour, health, safety and environmental legislation plus proposals for employment and training of Ugandan citizens. The applicant is also required to execute a performance bond or other form of security for observance of the conditions of the licence and take out necessary insurance policies. The application is published in the gazette for public inspection and affected persons if any may lodge a complaint on either personal or environmental grounds within 30 days after the notice.[98] An appeal can be made to the High Court against the decision of the minister.

The law under section 18 of the Petroleum (Refining, Conversion, Transmission and Midstream Storage) (RCTMS) Act 2013 provides for conditions of a licence to be stipulated by the Minister with regard to the main configurations and related capacities, the regularity and availability of capacities, the access to a facility used for midstream operations by third parties other than licensees, including terms and conditions in contractual arrangements that regulate access, pricing and tariffs, the construction and operation of a facility for which the licence was granted, payment of annual fees, levies or charges, access by third parties on commercially reasonable terms to uncommitted capacity in a facility, except that on application for the use of a facility, the licensee may elect to give users access to the facility on the basis that the capacity is shared among all users in proportion to their needs among others. These licences hereunder do confer a right of operation and therefore are administrative in nature.

Where the applicant satisfies the requirements, the minister in consultation with PAU processes the application within 180 days. A licence for construction of a midstream operations facility is granted for an initial period of five years and upon satisfactory completion of the construction, a licence to operate the facility will be in force for 20 years renewable for another period of five years.[99] Licences under the Midstream are not freely transferable and any such transfer must obtain the approval of the Minister.[100]

4.3   Downstream Sector

The downstream sector involves the selling and distribution of natural and oil based products (gasoline, petrol, diesel, lubricants, natural gas etc.) to final consumers. The sector is governed by the Petroleum Supply Act 2003, the Petroleum (Marking and Quality Control) Regulations 2009, the Petroleum

---

[98]   Ibid, s 12.

[99]   Ibid, s 20.

[100]   Ibid, s 25; Petroleum (Refining, Conversion, Transmission and Midstream Storage) Regulations, reg 166.

(Spirit) (Licencing, Testing and Possession) Rules (149 – 1) and the Petroleum (Spirit) (Conveyance by Road) Rules (149 – 3).

The Commissioner of the Department of Petroleum in the Ministry of Energy and Mineral Development has administrative functions of receiving, evaluating and processing of all applications for permits and licences under the Act.[101] Several permits/licences are required under the Act.

4.3.1   Petroleum construction permit
The petroleum construction permit is required for any construction or modification of an installation or facility of the supply chain.[102] Applications of permits are made in writing to the commissioner and are administrative in nature.

4.3.2   Petroleum operating licence
The petroleum operating licence is required for petroleum supply operations, that is, all operations and activities for or in connection with the import, landing, loading, processing, transport, storage, distribution, wholesale or retail of petroleum products including the operations of industrial consumers who buy their products directly from importers or wholesalers. Applications for licences are made in writing to the commissioner,[103] and a licence if granted is valid for a period not exceeding 25 years but renewable in accordance with the regulation. Permits or licences are not transferable without the written approval of the commissioner.

4.3.3   Container, underground tank and bulk storage licences
A container licence is issued for storage of petroleum spirit in containers of an individual capacity not exceeding 50 gallons.[104] An underground tank licence is issued for storage of petroleum spirit in underground tanks.[105] A bulk storage licence is issued for bulk storage of petroleum spirit.[106] The licensing authorities for container licence, underground tank licence, and bulk storage licence are the municipal council, town council or district administration. These licences if not revoked last for one year. Considering the rules, there are opportunities for amalgamation in the case of container, underground tank

---

[101]   The Petroleum Supply Act 2003, s 7 (2)(a),(c) and (d).
[102]   Ibid, s 17(1).
[103]   Ibid, s 18 (1) and (7).
[104]   The Petroleum (spirit) (licencing, testing and possession) Rules 149 – 1, rule 5 and 7.
[105]   Ibid.
[106]   Ibid.

and bulk storage licences since these variations in licensed activities are not significantly different as to warrant separate licences.[107]

4.3.4 Rights in operational licences

It suffices to note that each and every licence issued under the respective Acts and Regulations thereunder is unique. It is subject to and limited to the purpose and conditions of its grant. The licence does not confer ownership rights in the land or the said petroleum but rather grants an administrative right to carry out the permitted activity.

Once a licence is granted, it can be revoked where the issuing authority is of the view that the licensee is not carrying out the permitted activity in accordance with the terms of the said licence or in total violation of environmental principles. Such a right of revocation is consistent with an administrative right granted. However, unlike administrative rights granted in other sectors, an operational licence issued under the requisite law can be used by the licensee as security in financing the operation prescribed by the licence, commensurate upon the Minister's consent which is granted after consulting with the Authority. It is this right of revocation that makes such licences administrative in nature, yet the right to use a licence issued under the law as security for financing implies that a licence is more than a mere administrative right, instead imbuing a proprietary right of some nature. However, whether such a proprietary right is akin to a property right is unlikely, given that no property attaches to the licence, no right to take from the land, or other hallmarks of a real property interest.

5.   CONCLUSION

Uganda's petroleum sector is progressive and still at the upstream level. It has developed a legal, regulatory regime and institutional framework for licensing based on the structure of the petroleum industry, which is classified into downstream, midstream and upstream. The petroleum licensing regime provides several rights. In the upstream sector, the property in and the control of petroleum in its natural condition in or upon any land or waters in Uganda is vested in the Government on behalf of the Republic of Uganda and the rights to explore and produce oil are granted through a PSA after which the relevant licence is granted to the contractor which is issued in accordance with the terms provided in the PSA. In terms of proprietary interests, a licensee is

---

[107] The Business Licensing Reform Committee Appointed by Minister of Finance, Planning and Economic Development, 'Report on sector analysis business licenses in Uganda' (Volume II, March 2012) p.96.

granted an exclusive right to explore for petroleum and execute petroleum operations within a defined contract area under an exploration licence. Once a commercial discovery is made, the licensee may apply for a production licence. The petroleum exploration licence confers a licensee with the exclusive right to explore for petroleum, and to carry on such petroleum activities and execute such works as may be necessary for that purpose, in the exploration area. The EDP Act further establishes the right for the government to participate in petroleum activities through a specified participating interest of a licence or contract granted under the EDP Act and in the joint venture established by a joint operating agreement in accordance with the licence and the Upstream Act.

There are also administrative aspects of the licensing regime. The Minister may revoke a licence of the licensee who fails or neglects to comply with requirements stipulated under the licence. Under the Midstream Act, the Minister may grant licensing of midstream operations such as establishing facilities for refining crude oil, conversion of natural gas, midstream storage and establishment of transmission pipeline. The administrative aspects of the licensing regime include the Minister providing some conditions for the licences and varying them. Further, the Commissioner of the Department of Petroleum may receive, evaluate process permits and licences and no permit or licence can be transferred without the prior approval of the Commissioner and payment of the prescribed fees.

Overall, the licensing system regime provided in the legal framework exhibits a reasonable level of transparency since it promotes a competitive bidding process, gives an aggrieved party the right of appeal, provides for the publication of certain applications and enables the affected people to lodge their complaints with the Minister before the grant of the said licences. However, there are some challenges related to petroleum licensing in Uganda. These include imbalance in the negotiation powers due to lack of technical capacity to negotiation and award of contracts, enforcing high standards of corporate responsibility and compliance on the part of the investing petroleum companies and limited enforcement of high standards of transparency and accountability in licensing.

6. Petroleum licences – a legal culture perspective: the United Kingdom

Greg Gordon and John Paterson

1. LEGAL CULTURE OF THE JURISDICTION

The United Kingdom (UK) is a Parliamentary Constitutional Monarchy.[1] As such, whilst power is nominally in the hands of the monarch, it must be exercised in accordance with the constitution and, more particularly, through Parliament. Much that has been taken for granted regarding the UK constitution has been tested to the extreme by the "Brexit" referendum of 2016 and its aftermath.[2] At the time of writing (in the summer of 2019), the UK remains part of the European Union. Following the referendum vote to leave, however, Article 50 of the Treaty on European Union has been triggered, and a withdrawal agreement[3] has been negotiated along with a political declaration[4] setting out the intentions of the parties for a further agreement on the future relationship. It has so far proved impossible to achieve ratification of

[1] UK Parliament, "Parliament and Crown", available online at: www.parliament.uk/about/how/role/relations-with-other-institutions/parliament-crown/ (visited 22 July 2019).

[2] European Union Referendum Act 2015.

[3] Agreement on the withdrawal of the United Kingdom of Great Britain and Northern Ireland from the European Union and the European Atomic Energy Community, as endorsed by leaders at a special meeting of the European Council on 25 November 2018, available online at: https://assets.publishing.service.gov.uk/government/uploads/system/uploads/attachment_data/file/759019/25_November_Agreement_on_the_withdrawal_of_the_United_Kingdom_of_Great_Britain_and_Northern_Ireland_from_the_European_Union_and_the_European_Atomic_Energy_Community.pdf (visited 22 July 2019).

[4] Political Declaration Setting Out the Framework for the Future Relationship Between the European Union and the United Kingdom, available online at: https://assets.publishing.service.gov.uk/government/uploads/system/uploads/attachment_data/file/759021/25_November_Political_Declaration_setting_out_the_framework_for_the_future_relationship_between_the_European_Union_and_the_United_Kingdom_.pdf (visited 22 July 2019).

the withdrawal agreement in Parliament, meaning that two extensions of the initial two-year withdrawal period have granted.[5] The inability to achieve parliamentary approval hints strongly at the divisive nature of the referendum and at the differential attitude to the EU that exists between and within the constituent parts of the UK: Scotland, Northern Ireland and London were among the most Europhile and the North of England and Wales were among the most Eurosceptic.[6] The various issues mentioned in this opening paragraph equally point to some of the idiosyncrasies of the UK's constitutional order which will be discussed in the following paragraphs.

In international law terms, the UK is a unitary state. However, that unitary state is made up of four different nations and three different legal systems (England and Wales, Scotland and Northern Ireland).[7] The Supreme Court of the UK (as successor to the Judicial Committee of the House of Lords)[8] serves as the highest court for all three jurisdictions (save in relation to Scottish criminal matters, where the highest court is the High Court of Justiciary on Appeal).[9] England and Wales is a common law jurisdiction;[10] so too is Northern Ireland.[11] Scotland is a mixed jurisdiction. Primarily the mix is as between common law and civilian influences, although there are also some customary law and Celtic law survivals.[12] As is common with mixed legal

---

[5]   Given the fast-moving nature of this issue, the "Leaving the European Union" page on the website of the UK Parliament provides a useful one-stop-shop for key events and documents: https://assets.publishing.service.gov.uk/government/uploads/system/uploads/attachment_data/file/759021/25_November_Political_Declaration_setting_out_the_framework_for_the_future_relationship_between_the_European_Union_and_the_United_Kingdom___.pdf (visited 22 July 2019).

[6]   The Electoral Commission, EU Referendum Results, available online at: www.electoralcommission.org.uk/find-information-by-subject/elections-and-referendums/past-elections-and-referendums/eu-referendum/electorate-and-count-information (visited 22 July 2019).

[7]   For a discussion see Matthew Graves, "The United Kingdom between Unitary State and Union State: a geopolitical analysis", in Isabelle Bour and Antoine Mioche (eds), *Bonds of Union: Practices and Representations of Political Union in the United Kingdom (18th–20th centuries)*, Tours: Presses universitaires François-Rabelais, 2005, pp. 179–90.

[8]   Constitutional Reform Act 2005, s. 23.

[9]   A useful infographic is available from the Supreme Court website at: www.supremecourt.uk/docs/UKSC_StoryPanel_9_1100hx800w_v6.pdf (visited 22 July 2019).

[10]   See John Baker, *English Legal History* (5th ed.), Oxford: Oxford University Press, 2019.

[11]   Brice Dickson, *Law in Northern Ireland: An Introduction*, SLS Legal Publications, 2011.

[12]   See Andrew Simpson and Adelyn Wilson, *Scottish Legal History, Volume 1: 1000–1707*, Edinburgh: Edinburgh University Press, 2017.

systems, the degree of mixedness is not consistent throughout the system. Instead, civilian influence is highly prominent in certain areas of law (e.g., property) while in others (e.g., the law of negligence) the influence of English law is much more apparent.

The UK Parliament sits in Westminster and is bi-cameral. The lower chamber, the House of Commons, is comprised of 650 MPs elected on a first-past-the-post system to represent geographically-based constituencies.[13] The voting system has traditionally been justified on the grounds that it produces clear electoral results and thus strong governments, even if this generally meant that whatever the actual number of votes cast for other parties nationally, their failure to achieve concentrations of support favoured an effective two-party system with power alternating between the Conservative and Labour Parties. A hung Parliament in the 2010 general election produced a rare coalition between the Conservatives and Liberal Democrats, with the price of the latter's support including a promise to hold a referendum on the voting system. This was duly held in 2011 and asked voters whether they wanted to shift to an Alternative Vote system. The result was an overwhelming rejection of any change from first-past-the-post.[14]

The upper chamber of the UK Parliament, the House of Lords, is unelected and comprises a mix of Lords Spiritual (Bishops) and Temporal (a mix of hereditary and life peers).[15] Reforms during the first term of the New Labour Government coming to power in 1997 saw a reduction in the number of hereditary peers sitting in the Lords,[16] but more thoroughgoing reform efforts, despite extensive debate and legislative proposals, have largely come to naught.[17] The role of the Lords is to scrutinise legislation, through participation in the legislative process, and also the Executive, by way of questions and debates.[18]

The New Labour Government coming to power in 1997 also followed through swiftly on electoral promises to devolve power to (most of) the constituent parts of the UK, the outlier being England, which has no national or regional assembly. There are three devolved assemblies, each with accom-

---

[13]   See House of Commons, www.parliament.uk/business/commons/ (visited 22 July 2019).

[14]   John Curtice, "Politicians, voters and democracy: the 2011 UK referendum on the Alternative Vote", 2013, Electoral Studies, 32:2, 215–23.

[15]   See House of Lords, www.parliament.uk/business/lords/ (visited 22 July 2019).

[16]   Alexandra Kelso, *Parliamentary Reform at Westminster*, Manchester: Manchester University Press, 2009, pp. 155ff.

[17]   The exception is the House of Lords Reform Act 2014. For a chronology of reform efforts, see www.parliament.uk/business/lords/lords-history/lords-reform/ (visited 22 July 2019).

[18]   See www.parliament.uk/business/lords/work-of-the-house-of-lords/ (visited 22 July 2019).

panying executive arms and possessing varying degrees of legislative power. In contrast to the Westminster Parliament, each is unicameral and elected using proportional representation (although the precise system used varies as between the different assemblies). The Northern Irish Assembly sits at Stormont near Belfast; the Scottish Parliament at Holyrood in Edinburgh; and the Welsh Assembly in Cardiff.[19]

The UK Parliament is supreme, in the sense that its law-making power is unfettered by the existence of the devolved assemblies. There is, however, a Constitutional Convention – the Sewell Convention – to the effect that the UK Parliament will not normally legislate on matters which have been devolved to a regional assembly without that assembly's consent.[20] (If the Parliament were to do so, the legislation passed would still be law, but a constitutional crisis would be precipitated.)[21] The UK Parliament is not supreme, however, in the sense that in the event of a clash between domestic legislation and EU legislation having direct effect, the EU legislation has primacy[22] – albeit that this situation will, depending upon the precise terms of the UK's departure, change following the UK's exit from the EU.

Legislation passed by the devolved assemblies is law only if it lies within the legislative competence of the assembly in question and if it complies with other criteria. For instance, unlike the UK Parliament, the Scottish Parliament has no power to pass a measure which contravenes the European Convention on Human Rights. The different devolved assemblies have different areas of legislative competence.[23] At the time of its establishment, the Northern Irish Assembly had the strongest competence relative to energy matters.[24] Initially the Scottish Parliament's competences were restricted to matters such as fuel poverty and the encouragement of renewables. However, with the entry into force of section 47 of the Scotland Act 2016, the Scottish Government became the licensing authority for oil and gas operations within the "Scottish onshore area" – a new power granted as part of the process of "further devolution"

---

[19]   For a useful introduction, see James Mitchell, *Devolution in the UK*, Manchester: Manchester University Press, 2009.
[20]   This now has a legislative foundation: Scotland Act 1998, s. 28(8) (inserted by the Scotland Act 2016, s. 2).
[21]   Peter Leyland, "The multifaceted constitutional dynamics of UK devolution", 2011, International Journal of Constitutional Law, 9(1), 251–73, 269.
[22]   Mark Elliot, "Constitutional Legislation, European Union Law and the Nature of the UK's Contemporary Constitution", 2014, European Constitutional Law Review, 10, 379–92.
[23]   CMG Himsworth, "Devolution and its jurisdictional asymmetries", 2007, Modern Law Review, 70(1), 31–58.
[24]   Northern Ireland Act 1998, schd. 2, paras 9 and 18.

following Scotland's decision to remain part of the UK in the independence referendum in 2014.[25]

The UK is committed to the rule of law and generally adheres to the doctrine of the separation of powers (executive, legislative, judicial);[26] arguably this adherence is becoming more scrupulous than before with, for example, independent bodies now involved in judicial appointments that were previously within the gift of the Executive.[27] Courts were historically deferential to the Executive in judicial review matters with judges emphasising that they were not concerned with the outcome of the decision-making process so much as with the process itself. Accordingly, the grounds for judicial review historically comprised illegality or exceeding the powers delegated; irrationality or a lack of proportionality; and procedural unfairness. Since the incorporation (in 1998) of the European Convention on Human Rights, this has changed such that courts may now also consider whether executive action is compatible with the ECHR.[28] A disproportionate volume of the Supreme Court's business is administrative or constitutional in nature.[29]

The discussion so far gives a sense of the extent to which constitutional arrangements in the UK have not been the subject of a foundational legal document in the same way as practically every other jurisdiction in the world. It is not unusual to hear this situation being described as the UK having an "unwritten constitution".[30] It is, however, more accurate to describe it as an

---

[25]   Scotland Act 2016, ss47–49. See also HM Government, The Parties' Published Proposals on Further Devolution for Scotland, Cm 8946, October 2014. For further discussion, see Tina Hunter, Steven Latta and Greg Gordon, "Current Practice and Emerging Trends in Regulating Onshore Exploration and Production in Great Britain", in Greg Gordon, John Paterson and Emre Usenmez, *UK Oil and Gas Law: Current Practice and Emerging Trends: Volume 1: Resource Management and Regulatory Law*, Edinburgh: Edinburgh University Press, 2018, pp. 272–82.

[26]   For a recent discussion in the context of devolution, see The Rt Hon Lord Keen of Elie QC, "The Rule of Law and the Role of the Law Officers", Address to the SPLG Conference, 11 June 2018, available online at: www.gov.uk/government/news/the-rule -of-law-and-the-role-of-the-law-officers (visited 22 July 2019).

[27]   See Erin Delaney, "Searching for constitutional meaning in institutional design: The debate over judicial appointments in the United Kingdom", 2016, International Journal of Constitutional Law, 14(3), 752–68.

[28]   For an indication of the relatively rapid impact of the Human Rights Act 1998 on judicial review, see Varda Bondy, "The impact of the Human Rights Act on judicial review", 2002, Judicial Review, 8(3), 149–56.

[29]   For an excellent recent discussion, see Jo Eric Khushal Murkens, "Judicious review: the constitutional practice of the UK Supreme Court", 2018, Cambridge Law Journal, 77(2), 349–74.

[30]   See, for example, Robert Blackburn, "Magna Carta Today", The British Library, available online at: www.bl.uk/magna-carta/articles/britains-unwritten-constitution (visited 22 July 2019).

uncodified constitution, because there are, as has already been seen, constitutional documents (such as the Human Rights Act 1998 and the Scotland Act
1998) which are supplemented by constitutional conventions.

The UK respects property rights.[31] Historically, property rights have not been
given special constitutional protection, but this situation has been changed as
a consequence of Article 1 Protocol 1 of the ECHR. International law in the
UK plays only a limited role; as treaties must be transposed into domestic law
in order to have substantive (rather than interpretive) effect. Unlike many other
countries in the EU, the UK is thus a dualist as opposed to a monist state.

It is rather difficult to identify a single national character. Significant differences in attitude exist as between the different regional assemblies and within
the communities those assemblies represent (most obviously, in Northern
Ireland). The free-market economics and small-state mode of government so
popular in the South-East of England was markedly less popular in the North
of England and even less popular in Scotland, where communitarian values
persist to a greater extent and attitudes to the role of the state are somewhat different. Many in Scotland would assert that Scotland has more in common with
Scandinavian attitudes than with those in England. That said, there is significant national pride in the National Health Service, a broadly liberal approach
to LGBTQ rights including same-sex marriage, and a general willingness to
accept regulation of matters such as ownership of firearms.[32]

The UK is no longer a net exporter of energy, but it is interesting to note that
the steadily rising trend of net import dependency evident from the early 2000s
has begun to reverse in the last few years,[33] to a great extent attributable to the
increasing importance of renewables in the overall energy mix.[34] With regard
to oil and gas, the ongoing long-term trend of declining production from the
United Kingdom Continental Shelf (UKCS) makes the UK a considerable net
importer of these commodities.[35] A significant effort has been made in recent
years to reverse this latter trend by means of the establishment of a dedicated
regulator, the Oil and Gas Authority, tasked with implementing a strategy
dedicated to maximising economic recovery of hydrocarbons.

---

[31] The country scores relatively highly in the International Property Rights
Index 2018. For details, see: www.internationalpropertyrightsindex.org/country/united
-kingdom (visited 22 July 2019).
[32] The annual British Social Attitudes reports published by the National Centre
for Social Research provide a rich source of data in these regards. These are available
online at: www.bsa.natcen.ac.uk (visited 22 July 2019).
[33] Department of Business, Energy and Industrial Strategy, Digest of United
Kingdom Energy Statistics 2018, p. 17.
[34] Ibid., p. 11.
[35] Ibid., p. 77; pp. 89–90.

Marked differences exist between the energy policies of the UK government and those of the regional assemblies and executives. This is evident in renewables (where the Scottish Government's targets are more ambitious than the UK Government's);[36] nuclear (which the UK government wishes to encourage whereas the Scottish Government has articulated a policy of "no to new nuclear");[37] and in relation to the development of shale gas (which the UK government strongly supports, perceiving a contribution to energy security as well as direct and indirect economic benefits, whilst the Scottish and Northern Irish governments have imposed precautionary moratoria).[38]

2.   GRANT OF PETROLEUM LICENCES (EXPLORATION AND PRODUCTION) IN THE UK

2.1   Offshore

The great majority (in excess of 95%) of current hydrocarbon production comes from offshore areas.[39] The devolved assemblies have no competence in relation to the offshore area and the licensing authority for offshore oil and gas is the Oil and Gas Authority (OGA), a relatively new resource management authority created in 2015 and which – subject to some limits – enjoys operational independence from the relevant government department (formerly the Department for Energy and Climate Change or DECC; now the Department for Business Energy and Industrial Strategy or BEIS).[40] BEIS continues to

---

[36] Scottish Government, Scottish Energy Strategy: The Future of Energy in Scotland, December 2017, available online at: www.gov.scot/binaries/content/ documents/govscot/publications/strategy-plan/2017/12/scottish-energy-strategy-future -energy-scotland-9781788515276/documents/00529523-pdf/00529523-pdf/govscot %3Adocument/00529523.pdf (visited 22 July 2019).

[37] Although the door is not as firmly shut as may at first appear; the Scottish Energy Strategy indicates a willingness to keep new nuclear technologies under review. Ibid., p. 60.

[38] See further Tina Hunter, Steven Latta and Greg Gordon, n.25, above. A useful overview of the Scottish position is available on the Scottish Government website at: www.gov.scot/policies/oil-and-gas/unconventional-oil-and-gas/ (visited 22 July 2019). The presumption against the development of shale gas in Northern Ireland is contained in Department for the Environment Northern Ireland, Strategic Planning Policy for Northern Ireland: Planning for Sustainable Development, September 2015, para. 6.157.

[39] Full details of UK production are available at: https://data-ogauthority.opendata .arcgis.com/pages/production (visited 22 July 2019).

[40] For a discussion, see Greg Gordon, John Paterson and Uisdean Vass, "The Wood Review and Maximising Economic Recovery upon the UKCS", in Greg Gordon, John Paterson and Emre Usenmez, *UK Oil and Gas Law: Current Practice and Emerging*

have responsibility for the development of policy but in practice it seems that much of that function is effectively outsourced to the OGA.[41]

The grant of petroleum licences in the UK, whether onshore or offshore, depends ultimately on the *Petroleum Act 1998* (UK), section 3 which, as amended, provides that the OGA "may grant to such persons as the appropriate authority thinks fit licences to search and bore for and get petroleum".[42] The breadth of the discretion thus afforded becomes even more evident when the section continues: "Any such licence shall be granted for such consideration ... as the appropriate authority with the consent of the Treasury may determine, and upon such other terms and conditions as the appropriate authority thinks fit".[43] Thereafter, the statute requires the Minister to make regulations setting out the details for a licensing regime,[44] but little further detail is offered in the primary legislation and thus its development has been a matter for the Secretary of State and now for the OGA.[45]

Whilst primary legislation does not specify what sorts of licences the Secretary of State (and now the OGA) may grant, it allows that "[d]ifferent regulations may be made for different kinds of licence".[46] In practice, off-shore petroleum licences fall into two principal categories – exploration and production. Exploration licences[47] are non-exclusive[48] and last three years.[49] They allow the undertaking of seismic and other surveying activities within the UKCS as a whole (save for any areas already subject to a production licence). Despite their name, they do not allow for serious exploratory drilling.[50]

Production licences are necessary to carry out any meaningful drilling operations. They are generally granted in rounds, although out-of-round applications are possible on cause shown. There have been 31 offshore rounds and in the recent past they have occurred every 18 months to two years; the 32nd round

---

Trends: Volume 1: Resource Management and Regulatory Law, Edinburgh: Edinburgh University Press, 2018, pp. 132–69.

[41]   For a discussion, see Terence Daintith, "Government Companies as Regulators", 2019, Modern Law Review, 82(3), 397–424.

[42]   Subs. (1).

[43]   Subs. (3).

[44]   S. 4(1).

[45]   The Petroleum (Transfer of Functions) Regulations 2016, SI 2016/898.

[46]   Petroleum Act 1998, s. 4(2).

[47]   The Offshore Exploration (Petroleum, and Gas Storage and Unloading) (Model Clauses) Regulations 2009 (SI 2009/2814).

[48]   The licence and liberty is granted "in common with all other persons to whom the like right may have been granted or may hereafter be granted". See Model Cl. 2.

[49]   Renewable for a further three years upon three months' notice. See Model Cl. 4.

[50]   Model Cl. 3.

was launched on 11 July 2019 with applications due by 12 November 2019.[51] Earlier rounds offered specific areas for licence; over the last two decades, the practice has generally been to offer the whole unlicensed area (save for those being retained for use for another purpose or deemed to be off-limits following Environmental Assessment). As the province matures, many of the areas now on offer are being recycled, having been previously held under licence and relinquished.[52]

Cash bidding is theoretically possible and has been used on rare occasions, with only very limited success.[53] The predominant method of licence allocation – the only method used within the last 30 years – is essentially to bid by exploration programme ("work programme", in the terminology of the system), with the licence group offering to undertake the greatest amount of exploration being scored more highly than other licence groups. The practice has been for the marking scheme against which applications will be measured to be published in advance of each licensing round, and for the licensing authority to base its assessment upon the technical understanding demonstrated by the applicant at interview; the generation of valid prospectivity derived from evaluation of available data; the quality of the work that it has already done; and the proposed work programme.[54] There is no requirement to obtain a separate land right from the Crown in addition to the licence.[55] This position can be distinguished from that in the case of obtaining offshore renewables or carbon

---

[51]   Details are available online at: www.ogauthority.co.uk/licensing-consents/licensing-rounds/offshore-licensing-rounds/#tabs (visited 22 July 2019).

[52]   For a discussion of the genesis of this approach, see Greg Gordon and John Paterson, "Mature Province Initiatives", in Greg Gordon, John Paterson and Emre Usenmez, *UK Oil and Gas Law: Current Practice and Emerging Trends: Volume 1: Resource Management and Regulatory Law*, Edinburgh: Edinburgh University Press, 2018, 450–75.

[53]   The UK experimented in the 4th, 8th and 9th Licensing Rounds with a two-tier system whereby cash premium bidding – effectively an auction – was utilised in relation to a relatively small number of fields alongside the usual discretionary arrangements. A variant upon this system was in addition utilised in the 7th Licensing Round. For a fuller account, see Daintith, Willoughby and Hill, *United Kingdom Oil and Gas Law*, Sweet and Maxwell at paras 1-317 to 1-322.

[54]   OGA, *Applications Guidance* at para 41. The OGA's *Technical Guidance* and *Financial Guidance* is available online at: www.ogauthority.co.uk/licensing-consents/licensing-rounds/ (visited 8 May 2017).

[55]   The OGA does now explicitly point applicants for petroleum licences to the potential for conflict with Crown Estate interests. See www.ogauthority.co.uk/licensing-consents/overview/the-crown-estate-interests/ (visited 22 July 2019).

sequestration, where a lease must be obtained from the Crown Estate, even for areas located upon the continental shelf.[56]

2.2   Onshore

At present, much less oil and gas are produced from the onshore area than offshore.[57] The onshore licensing system in England and Wales is broadly similar to the offshore system. The onshore production licence is the PEDL (Production, Exploration and Development Licence).[58] It is offered in rounds (14 so far) in a system administered by the OGA. In the event of competition for acreage, the licence group with the more ambitious work programme will again prevail, all else equal. As mentioned previously, the Scottish Government is to become the licensing authority in the Scottish onshore area, following the devolution of further powers under the *Scotland Act 2016* (Scot). It had already enjoyed devolved competence relative to planning matters and, also as mentioned previously, had used this to impose a precautionary moratorium relative to shale gas and underground gasification activities.

3.   SPECIAL CONDITIONS ATTACHED TO THE LICENCE

Conditions are comprised of a mix of standard terms ("the Model Clauses") which are set out in delegated legislation and incorporated into all licences granted while that set of Model Clauses is extant,[59] and individually-negotiated

---

[56]   Under the Energy Act 2004, s 84 in relation to renewable energy infrastructure and the Energy Act 2008, s. 1 in relation to carbon sequestration.

[57]   See Ruth Hayhurst, "2018 onshore oil production down – under 2% of UK total" Drill or Drop, 18 April 2019, for a very useful and accessible analysis based on OGA data. Available online at: https://drillordrop.com/2019/04/18/2018-onshore-oil -production-down-under-2-of-uk-total/ (visited 22 July 2019).

[58]   The Petroleum Licensing (Exploration and Production) (Landward Areas) Regulations 2014 (SI 2014/1686) Sch. 2. The Petroleum Licensing (Exploration and Production) (Landward Areas) (Amendment) (England and Wales) Regulations 2016 (SI 2016/1029) amend the 2014 Regulations by introducing (at Reg 2) a prohibition on hydraulic fracturing from a location within a protected area; a definition which includes Conservation Sites protected under European Law and Sites of Special Scientific Interest. The previous set of model clauses (which will continue to govern the majority of PEDLs for some time) were to be found in the Petroleum Licensing (Exploration and Production) (Seaward and Landward Areas) Regulations 2004, at Sch. 6, as the same has been amended by the Petroleum Licensing (Exploration and Production) (Seaward and Landward Areas) (Amendment) Regulations 2006.

[59]   The licence does not incorporate the model clauses "as they are or may come to be"; it incorporates the relevant set of model clauses in force at the time of the licence's

terms which are appended to the licence in a series of schedules. There is an increasing trend towards flexibility and individualised negotiation. Among other things, these conditions stipulate the term structure of the licence, impose relinquishment obligations, provide the state with certain (limited) rights to influence the manner and pace of operations, allow the state to demand unitisation; impose an obligation to request permission before undertaking certain obligations, and require the retention of samples and data.

The term structure of the licence has changed over the years and continues to evolve. Licences granted in the first four rounds had a relatively simple term structure of an initial term of six years (which provided exclusivity while exploratory drilling was undertaken) followed by a second term of 40 years. This was regularly changed until the 20th round, when (following a joint industry and government review) a 4-4-18 model was alighted upon for the standard licence. The initial term was for exploration; the second term for development; and the final term for production. This remained in place until the 29th round, where a more flexible model was introduced. From the 22nd round onwards, variant licences (the frontier and promote) were granted to encourage the opening up of frontier areas of the province and the entry of smaller players respectively.[60] As of the 29th round, these licence variants are no longer offered; however the flexibility of the new licence type, the "Innovate" licence,[61] carries forward the essential purpose and some features of these variants.[62]

The licence was previously the principal means of regulating health and safety and environmental matters, but it now sits alongside a relatively mature body of regulatory law[63] which – following the implementation of the Wood

---

grant. Thus, a large number of different sets of model clauses, each to a greater or lesser extent different in their terms, will be in force at any given time.

[60]   For a discussion, see Greg Gordon, "Petroleum Licensing", in Greg Gordon, John Paterson and Emre Usenmez, *UK Oil and Gas Law: Current Practice and Emerging Trends: Volume 1: Resource Management and Regulatory Law*, Edinburgh: Edinburgh University Press, 2018, pp. 119–24.

[61]   See the Petroleum and Offshore Gas Storage and Unloading Licensing (Amendment) Regulations 2017, reg. 2.

[62]   For a discussion, see Greg Gordon, "Petroleum Licensing", n. 60 above, pp. 125–27.

[63]   See especially the Offshore Installations (Offshore Safety Directive) (Safety Case etc.) Regulations (SI 2015/398). For a discussion, see John Paterson, "Health and Safety at Work Offshore", in Greg Gordon, John Paterson and Emre Usenmez, *UK Oil and Gas Law: Current Practice and Emerging Trends: Volume 1: Resource Management and Regulatory Law*, Edinburgh: Edinburgh University Press, 2018, pp. 284–338.

Review – must be taken to include the obligation to maximise economic recovery upon the UKCS (MER UK).[64]

4.   SUPRANATIONAL LAWS AFFECTING THE GRANT OF THE LICENCE

EU law presently applies to petroleum-related activities both on- and offshore. Assuming Brexit goes ahead, it is likely that some EU provisions will fall out of UK law over time; however as the legislative approach of the *European Union (Withdrawal) Act 2018* is to translate EU law into national law,[65] it will be presumed that the relevant provisions of EU law will remain in effect for some considerable time.

For present purposes, the provision of most obvious relevance is the Hydrocarbons Licensing Directive,[66] discussed further below; however other provisions are also important. Much of the UK's offshore environmental law (including that which relates to Environmental Impact Assessment[67] and Strategic Environmental Assessment,[68] both of which are germane to which areas may be licensed) stems from European law. Provisions relative to state aid and competition law are also relevant.[69] In addition, the sector previously had to have regard to EU public procurement law but, a block exemption having been obtained, this is no longer relevant.[70]

The Hydrocarbons Licensing Directive is relevant both to the issue of licence allocation and to the question of which terms and conditions may be imposed in the licence.

---

[64]   See Greg Gordon, John Paterson and Uisdean Vass, "The Wood Review and Maximising Economic Recovery Upon the UKCS", n. 40 above.

[65]   For an accessible explanation of the approach of the Act, see: www.legislation .gov.uk/ukpga/2018/16/notes/division/4/index.htm (visited 22 July 2019).

[66]   Directive 94/22/EC of the European Parliament and of the Council of 30 May 1994 on the conditions for granting and using authorizations for the prospection, exploration and production of hydrocarbons.

[67]   Council Directive 85/337/EEC of 27 June 1985 on the assessment of the effects of certain public and private projects on the environment as amended by Directives 97/11/EC, 2003/35/EC and 2009/31/EC.

[68]   Directive 2001/42/EC of the European Parliament and of the Council of 27 June 2001 on the assessment of the effects of certain plans and programmes on the environment.

[69]   See Arts 101 to 109 of the Treaty on the Functioning of the European Union.

[70]   Commission Decision 2010/192/EU of 29 March 2010 exempting exploration for and exploitation of oil and gas in England, Scotland and Wales from the application of Directive 2004/17/EC of the European Parliament and of the Council coordinating the procurement procedures of entities operating in the water, energy, transport and postal services sectors, OJ 31/3/2010, L 84/52.

On licence allocation, implementing regulations[71] provide that every application for a licence shall be determined on the basis of the following criteria:

(a)   the technical and financial capability of the applicant;
(b)   the way in which the applicant proposes to carry out the activities that would be permitted by the licence;
(c)   in a case where tenders are invited, the price the applicant is prepared to pay in order to obtain the licence;[72]
(d)   where the applicant holds, or has held, a petroleum licence, any lack of efficiency and responsibility displayed by the applicant.[73]

The licensing authority is specifically empowered to refuse an application for a licence, even where there is no competition.[74] In the event that two or more applications for a licence have equal merit when assessed according to the principal criteria, "other relevant criteria" may be applied.[75] Neither the principal criteria nor any such "tie-break" criteria may be applied in a discriminatory manner.[76] The OGA is empowered to refuse to grant a licence on the basis of national security where the applicant is effectively controlled by a foreign state other than a Member State of the EU (or by nationals of such a state).[77]

The Hydrocarbons Licensing Directive also places restrictions upon the types of terms that the OGA is entitled to include in a licence. The only terms and conditions permissible are those justified exclusively for the purpose of:

(a)   ensuring the proper performance of the activities permitted by the licence;
(b)   providing for the payment of consideration for the grant of the licence; and
(c)   for certain other purposes set out in regulations (national security, public health, safety, etc).[78]

International investment law (in the form of, for example, the Energy Charter Treaty and Bilateral Investment Treaties) can also have a bearing upon licensing and other resource management activities. There is current speculation that the MER UK obligation could – depending on how aggressively it is implemented by the OGA – lead to challenge under such instruments. This is considered further in the following section, after consideration is given to the legal character of the UK petroleum licence.

---

[71]   Hydrocarbon Licensing Directive Regulations (SI 1995/1434).
[72]   As noted above, in practice, this does not arise in the UK.
[73]   Reg. 3(1).
[74]   Reg. 3(1).
[75]   Reg. 3(2).
[76]   Reg. 3(4).
[77]   Reg. 3(4).
[78]   Reg. 4(1).

5.   THE LEGAL CHARACTER OF THE UK PETROLEUM LICENCE

The licence is silent on the question of its legal character. The production licence is generally considered to be hybrid in nature.[79] It is contractual in form, narrating that it is "between" the parties and being careful to state that it has been granted in exchange for valuable consideration. As noted above, it incorporates the model clauses extant at the time of its grant and there is no mechanism for adjusting these provisions throughout the life of the licence. The contractual nature raises the possibility of the availability of contractual remedies in the event of breach, although these have not, to date, been sought either by the Government or the licensee. However, there is also plainly a regulatory dimension and the discretionary decision-making of the OGA would seem to be subject to judicial review.[80]

Whilst there has been no judicial consideration in the UK of the legal nature of an offshore licence, a recent English case has considered this question in relation to an onshore one. It is instructive to look at this in a little more detail with a view to determining what the implications might be for the offshore. In the case of *Dean v Secretary of State for Energy and Climate Change*,[81] the plaintiff challenged the propriety of the Secretary of State agreeing to vary an onshore petroleum licence by means of a deed. The claim was that insofar as the licence is a creature of statute the Secretary of State has no right to purport to vary it by way of a contractual agreement following its grant. The request from the licensee in this case to vary the original licence arose because protesters were occupying the site from which exploratory drilling operations were to be undertaken, meaning that there was a risk that the licensee would be unable to complete the work programme within the initial term of the licence. The Secretary of State, therefore, agreed to extend that initial term by way of a deed of variation. What might appear to be a relatively minor issue, perhaps with significance only in the context of the ongoing tension between oil companies and protesters regarding the development of shale gas in the UK, takes on broader importance when it is realised that a similar approach has been

---

[79]   See Daintith, Willoughby and Hill, n. 53 above, at para 1-323. Greg Gordon, "Petroleum Licensing", n. 60 above, pp. 90–91.

[80]   See Stephen Dow, "Energy" in *The Laws of Scotland: Stair Memorial Encyclopaedia*, Reissue, (2000) at para. 19; Terence Daintith, "Contractual Discretion and Administrative Discretion: A Unified Analysis", 2005, MLR, 68, 554 at 592: "Courts in…the United Kingdom will not however accept even [unfettered] discretions … as simply unreviewable".

[81]   [2017] EWHC 1998 (Admin).

taken offshore for decades when requests have been made to extend the period allowed for completion of a work programme.

Thus, were there to be a finding in favour of the plaintiff in the present case, there could be significant knock-on effects for many offshore licences which would thereby turn out to have been improperly amended, perhaps requiring statutory intervention to correct the defect. In the event, however, the judge's decision was that the licence is contractual and concerned with the grant of property rights. Mr Justice Holgate stated that "In my judgment, the grant of a licence under section 3 is essentially a property transaction"[82] and that "a licence under section 3 of the 1998 Act is more than simply a contractual agreement between two parties, it is a grant of an interest in land".[83] It might be objected, however, that since the case dealt with an onshore rather than an offshore licence it is, therefore, not possible to draw firm conclusions in relation to the latter. This argument may be fortified by the fact that when the onshore licensing regime (under which the state expressly claimed ownership of petroleum *in strata*[84]) was extended offshore by the *Continental Shelf Act 1964* (UK), Parliament chose not to apply the proprietary claim offshore, but to claim only the "sovereign rights" recognised by international law.[85] Thus, there would seem to be a material difference between the underlying legal right extended to the licensee in the onshore and offshore licence. Be that as it may, lawyers representing the industry have been quick to claim that the case removes doubts about variations agreed between the parties in both onshore *and* offshore licences[86] and there has certainly been no indication from the OGA that it takes a contrary view. On that evidence, the contractual dimension of the offshore licence appears uncontroversial to industry lawyers and the regulator.

As hinted at above in the context of the reference to international investment law, however, the case of *Dean* may have broader significance. In implementing the MER UK Strategy, the Oil and Gas Authority must now, for example, balance decisions on decommissioning redundant offshore installations with the current and potential future needs of other licensees who may be unable to develop new discoveries in the absence of existing nearby infrastructure. It is

---

[82]   *Dean v SoS for BEIS* [2017], para. 92.
[83]   Ibid., para. 102.
[84]   Petroleum (Production) Act 1934 s. 1(1).
[85]   Although the majority of the provisions of the Petroleum (Production) Act 1934 were extended offshore by the 1964 Act, s. 1(1) was not. See the Continental Shelf Act 1964 s. 1(3).
[86]   See, for example, www.eversheds-sutherland.com/global/en/what/articles/index.page?ArticleID=en/Energy/UK_Petroleum_Licence_Judicial_Review_Landmark_judgment_of_14_August_2017_stands (visited 12 July 2020).

not difficult to identify situations where what would once have been a straight-forward approval of a decommissioning plan would now lead to a more complex range of considerations which may ultimately mean that, in terms of the MER UK Strategy, the plan must be rejected. Indeed, the licensee seeking to decommission could even be asked instead to maintain the infrastructure in place. Safeguards in the Strategy offer reassurance that "No obligation imposed by or under this Strategy requires any person to make an investment or fund activity (including existing activities) where they will not make a sat-isfactory expected commercial return on that investment or activity",[87] though it is a question whether industry and OGA will always (or ever) have a similar view of what constitutes a "satisfactory expected commercial return". In fact, the Strategy is clear that situations may well arise where although the overall value of a mandated arrangement between different industry actors must be greater than would otherwise be the case, individual actors may receive less.[88] Furthermore, an additional "safeguard" perhaps leaves industry more uncertain than reassured insofar as it states that where a licensee is required to make such an investment under the Strategy but either intends to delay or not to make it at all, precisely "because it will not produce a return which they consider to be sufficiently high", "the OGA must discuss the situation with that relevant person before taking any enforcement action in relation to that decision".[89]

What happens if after such discussion the OGA takes enforcement action that the licensee is still not happy with? The licensee has various powers of appeal against the enforcement action, most notably for present purposes in relation to "the measures that are required to be taken for the purposes of compliance with the petroleum-related requirement".[90] The possible grounds for such an appeal are listed as either that it was "unreasonable" or that it "was not within the powers of the OGA".[91] The Tribunal in such a case has the power either to confirm or quash the decision, but not to vary it.[92] Albeit that the Strategy itself is rather unusual, in that while it is made in the same way as a piece of secondary legislation it does not have the same form, it is nevertheless expressed in mandatory terms and has a clear and unequivocal statutory foundation. As such, it appears difficult to imagine a Tribunal inter-fering with the OGA's decision in relation to enforcement unless something fairly unusual had occurred. Does that mean that the disgruntled licensee is left

---

[87] MER UK Strategy, para. 3.
[88] MER UK Strategy, para. c.
[89] MER UK Strategy, para. 4.
[90] Energy Act 2016, s. 52(3)(a)(i).
[91] Energy Act 2016, s. 52(4).
[92] Energy Act 2016, s. 52(5)(a).

without a remedy in a situation where he or she is being compelled to make an investment that would otherwise not be made?

Here is where the case of *Dean* reappears. Whereas the UK petroleum licence proceeded for years without there ever being a clear enunciation of its character (permit, regulation, contract or a hybrid) and whereas a variety of unusual interventions were made to make up for perceived shortcomings (including retrospective amendment by way of statute[93] and the development of mysterious hybrid arrangements described as voluntary, but backed by unspecified ministerial powers),[94] Mr Justice Holgate has now clarified that the licence is essentially *contractual*. As a consequence, although there are limitations in terms of the relevance of the Model Clause as to what sort of disputes under a licence may be taken to arbitration, one could well imagine a foreign investor referring instead to the Energy Charter Treaty or a Bilateral Investment Treaty and considering whether international arbitration would be appropriate. Depending on the precise circumstances, a licensee might argue that legitimate expectations have been disappointed, that the effect of the Strategy is to effect a unilateral change to the contract – perhaps to produce a material change that adversely affects the economic balance – or even, in the extreme, that there has been a de facto uncompensated expropriation. One could argue conversely that a tribunal could find plenty of reasons to deny any such claim. For example, investors in the UK have always known that there is no stabilisation.[95] Equally, even if the Strategy did have the effect of retrospectively changing licences, which must now be understood as contracts, this is not the first time this has happened (albeit that the last time substantively was 1975[96] and there have been various indications since then that it is recognised that this is not an optimal way to proceed). Then again, in a world where petroleum contracts now routinely include economic balancing arrangements, the Strategy could appear to an arbitral tribunal to be at odds with contemporary practice internationally. Might there be sympathy, therefore, for a disgruntled licensee? It is not possible to be definitive, but if nothing else, this is yet another indication of the way in which even as the UK enters its sixth decade

---

[93]   The Petroleum and Submarine Pipelines Act 1975, s. 18.

[94]   See Greg Gordon and John Paterson, "Mature Province Initiatives", n. 53 above.

[95]   Albeit that the advent of the Decommissioning Relief Deed marks a change in approach by the UK in that regard in the specific context of tax treatment of decommissioning tax relief. For a discussion, see Judith Aldersey-Williams, "Decommissioning Security", in Greg Gordon, John Paterson and Emre Usenmez, *UK Oil and Gas Law: Current Practice and Emerging Trends: Volume 1: Resource Management and Regulatory Law*, Edinburgh: Edinburgh University Press, 2018, p. 435 at pp. 447–49.

[96]   Op cit n. 93, above.

of experience with offshore petroleum licences, the scope and scale of legal
and regulatory issues appears only to grow rather than to diminish.

6.   RIGHTS CONFERRED BY THE UK PETROLEUM LICENCE

As noted previously, the petroleum licence confers the right "to search and
bore for and get" petroleum. To what extent, however, can that right be transferred? In answering that question, it is first of all instructive to note that there
is no formal registration scheme for such licences.[97] Thus – while some licence
data are displayed on the OGA's website – there is no formal system of licence
registration, meaning that in the event of a sale of assets all novations, assignments and links in title need to be checked – a sometimes laborious process.
Be that as it may, it is the case that licence interests are commonly traded,
with major oil companies re-aligning their asset-base and selling licences
on to smaller companies. However, this is subject to certain state rights of
control, the details of which vary depending on whether the commercial deal
is an asset sale or a share sale. In an asset sale, Model Clause 40(1) provides
that OGA approval is required for any transaction involving the assignment
or other transfer of benefit under a licence. The OGA looks at the financial
and technical capability of a licensee in considering whether or not to allow
such a transfer. In the case of a share sale, MC 41(3) provides that the OGA
may revoke a licence if a licensee undergoes a change of control which is not
followed by such further change of control as the OGA requests, and within
such period of time as the OGA specifies by written notice. This provision has
rarely been used but was invoked when the LetterOne group purchased the
assets of DEA. DECC (OGA's predecessor as licensing authority) had concerns that LetterOne or its major shareholder could potentially become subject
to sanctions following the annexation of Crimea by Russia and insisted upon
a change of control.[98] It would also be possible, then, for the licence to be used
as a corporate asset, subject to these controls and restrictions.

---

[97]   It is understood that proposals to introduce such arrangements were made by
the United Kingdom Offshore Operators Association in the mid-2000s, but came to
nothing.
[98]   See further Norman Wisely, "Acquisitions and Disposals of Upstream Oil and
Gas Assets", in Greg Gordon, John Paterson and Emre Usenmez, *UK Oil and Gas Law:
Current Practice and Emerging Trends Volume II: Commercial and Contract Law
Issues*, Edinburgh: Edinburgh University Press, 2018, pp. 297–330 at p. 310.

7.   CONCLUSION

Whatever clarity exists, however, in relation to the rights conferred by the UK petroleum licence, however, must ultimately be set against what the foregoing discussion reveals about that which is less fixed in the surrounding context within which the licence operates. In these concluding remarks, three key issues are highlighted in this regard: (1) the indirect effect on the licence of the MER UK Strategy; (2) the flexible approach of the OGA; and (3) the ongoing significant transition in the constitutional order of the UK. It is difficult to predict with any certainty how these will play out in practice because, if there is a common factor among these issues, it is that they are each characterised by change rather than stasis.

If one were to consider only the model clauses that constitute the terms and conditions of the petroleum licence, one would conclude that the outcome of the process which resulted in the establishment of the MER UK Strategy and the Oil and Gas Authority had had little effect on the licence. Given what has been said above about the contractual dimension of the document, however, this should come as no surprise. Containing no provision that would allow the state to make retrospective amendments to its terms, any desire to adjust the behaviour of the industry has to rely on changing the context within which the licence operates. What this means, of course, is that the significance of the licence is thereby diminished, with the action taking place at the level of the MER UK Strategy. It is still important to have a licence – and to understand how one maximises one's chances of obtaining one – but, once held, the state's ability to regulate depends to a lesser extent on the terms and conditions of the licence and much more on the Strategy and its statutory foundation. Much, therefore, now depends upon how the new regulator, the OGA, makes use of the powers it has had conferred upon it by that Strategy and that statutory foundation.

At the time of writing, the OGA has been in operation for a comparatively short period of time in the context of the overall history of the petroleum licensing regime. It is already clear, however, that its overall approach to licensing is characterised by flexibility. To some extent, of course, this was already present insofar as even in the pre-OGA era new forms of licence were produced to meet particular challenges. The introduction of the Innovate Licence as the new standard, however, allows for significantly greater flexibility. The fact that this approach will require additional regulatory effort indicates that licensees are likely to find themselves in a much less *laissez-faire* world than they had become used to under DECC and its predecessors. Whether consistency and transparency can be maintained in such a setting remains to be seen, but there is no doubting the confidence on the part of the state that the new approach signals.

But if the foregoing two points indicate an unusual degree of uncertainty for the industry in the UK, this is perhaps less surprising when one considers the extent to which the broader constitutional, legal and political order has been upended in recent years. As the opening section of this chapter demonstrated, much that would be taken for granted in a country that has a traditional con- stitution has undergone significant reform in the UK in the last two decades, and there is no sense that the transformation is complete. Whether the ultimate destination is not dissimilar to what obtains at the time of writing or one that is radically different is not easy to determine – and as a concluding statement in a chapter about the UK, that surely speaks volumes.

7. Oil and gas licences – a legal nature perspective: the Netherlands

Martha M. Roggenkamp

1. INTRODUCTION

This chapter presents an overview of the legal perspective of oil and gas licences in the Netherlands. For this purpose the chapter first outlines some key elements relating to the Dutch legal culture and some of the main elements that have influenced the current licensing regime. Thereafter it will discuss the transition from a traditional concession regime to the current licensing regime as elements of the former concession regime still have an impact on the current system of licensing. Thereafter the licensing regime will be analyzed in more detail. This will be followed by a conclusion. Please note that the focus is on licences governing the exploration for and exploitation of oil and gas. Other licences governing, for example, storage of substances or production of other substances have not been taken into account.

2. LEGAL CULTURE OF THE NETHERLANDS

2.1 Overview

The Kingdom of the Netherlands dates from 1813 and was established in the aftermath of the Napoleonic reign (1795–1815).[1] Currently it consists of the territory of the Netherlands (including the Dutch part of the continental shelf of the North Sea) and six West-Indian Islands in the Caribbean Sea: St Maarten, Curacao, Aruba, Bonaire, Saba and St Eustatius. Whereas the latter three (small) islands are special municipalities of the Netherlands, St Maarten, Curacao and Aruba are together with the Netherlands constituent countries of the Kingdom and subject to the Charter of the Kingdom of the Netherlands.

---

[1]   The Kingdom of the Netherlands consisted of the present-day Netherlands and Belgium, which were officially unified by the Treaty of Vienna of 1815.

The Netherlands legal regime is based on the civil law system and influenced by the *trias politica* model that aims at separating the legislature, executive and judiciary branches of the State. However, as more often in parliamentary systems, the legislature and executive branches to some extent overlap as the government has both an executive and legislative task. The tasks and powers of each of them is defined in the Constitution.

The first Constitution of the Netherlands of 1814 established a decentralized unitary state, which remained in force after the constitutional reforms in 1848 and 1983.[2] Sovereignty is vested jointly in the central institutions of the State, consisting of Government and the two Houses of Parliament, i.e., the House of Representatives and the Senate. The Constitution also gives considerable powers to the 12 provinces and the local authorities (decentralized authorities). The Constitution does not contain provisions regarding energy, but has a strong focus on the need to protect property rights.[3]

The relationship between the central Government and the decentralized authorities is not hierarchical. The provinces and local authorities (municipalities) are autonomous public institutions, subject to various types of central control. Government and Parliament have statutory powers. The Acts of Parliament may provide for further delegation of law-making at both central and decentralized levels. On the central level, further delegated legislation can be issued by Orders of Council (*Algemene Maatregelen van Bestuur*), which are made by the Government alone.[4] In addition, individual Ministers can issue sub-delegated legislation as Ministerial regulations.

The Minister of Economic Affairs and Climate is responsible for the energy sector. In the case of economic regulation, it is customary for an Act to consist only of outlines while the larger part of the material is left to the 'lower' (delegated) lawmakers. Regarding petroleum licensing, it should be noted that the lower governments have few decision-making powers. This is currently one of the major issues of debate in relation to developments onshore.

---

[2]   When Belgium and the Netherlands separated in 1848 this led to the new Constitution of 1848. In 1983 the Constitution was almost entirely rewritten and as a result many articles were abolished but new provisions regarding social rights and the environment were included.

[3]   Article 14 para 1 of the Constitution states that 'Expropriation may take place only in the public interest and on prior assurance of full compensation, in accordance with regulations laid down by or pursuant to Act of Parliament'. This provision needs to be read in conjunction with Article 5.1 Civil Code that provides in paragraph 1 that 'ownership is the most comprehensive property right that a person, the "owner", can have to (in) a thing'.

[4]   Orders of Council are considered and decided upon by the Council of Ministers (after consultation with the Council of State). They are signed by the Sovereign and one or more of the Ministers involved and are therefore also referred to as Royal Decrees.

Judicial power belongs to the Courts, which is largely based on the French system and follows the hierarchical pattern, with a case commencing at one of the 11 District Courts, followed by a procedure at one of the four Courts of Appeal and subsequently the Supreme Court. The Council of State (*Raad van State*), founded in 1531, acts as the highest administrative appeal court. In addition the Council of State must be consulted by the government on all proposed legislation before a law is submitted to parliament. The administrative court has been 'active' over the last few years in relation to disputes on gas production in Groningen.

2.2 Legislation Governing Exploration and Production of Oil and Gas

The exploration and production of oil and gas is heavily affected by some non-Dutch, EU and international influences.

First, account needs to be taken of the fact that during the Napoleonic reign (1795–1815) French laws were applied to the Netherlands and that these laws remained in place until they were gradually replaced by national law. Hence, the Dutch legal system is heavily influenced by the French legal tradition and examples of this can be found in the Civil Code and Criminal Code[5] but in particular in the French Mining Code, the *Loi concernant les mines, les minières, et les carrières* (hereafter, Mining Act 1810) enacted during the French occupancy of the Netherlands and which remained in place 'provisionally' until 2003.[6] This French law has been used to govern the production of subsoil resources like coal and salt but also to produce oil and gas until the entry into force of the new Mining Act in 2003. By then the initial division between an onshore and offshore licensing regime also disappeared.

Secondly, we can note the influence of EU law. The Netherlands is also one of the founding members of the European Economic Community and signed the Treaty of Rome in 1957. Although European law ranks higher than national law, European law has had limited impact on the energy sector until the early 1990s. This has changes as a result of the policy to establish an internal energy market as confirmed by article 194 Treaty on the Functioning of the European

---

[5]   Whereas the French Civil Code was replaced by a Dutch Civil Code in 1838, it took several decades to draft a Dutch Penal Code. The latter entered into force in 1881.

[6]   Bulletin des Lois, No 285. This Act was introduced during the French reign by Napoleon Bonaparte. When the Netherlands regained its independence in 1813 it was decided that this Act would be retained 'provisionally, until further measures are taken'. See *Staatsblad* (Stb) 1813, 3.

Union (TFEU).[7] Of special importance for this chapter is Directive 94/22/EC on the conditions for granting and using authorizations for the prospecting, exploration and production of hydrocarbons (Hydrocarbon Directive).[8] The need to implement this Directive has led to major changes in the Dutch licensing regime, culminating in the entry into force of a new Mining Act in 2003 which replaced the 'provisional' French Mining Code. Other relevant pieces of EU law are the Gas Directive (governing upstream pipelines) and the Offshore Safety Regulation (offshore health and safety regime) but neither of them has a direct impact on the award of oil and gas licences.

Thirdly, account needs to be made of the influence of international law, and in particular in relation to developments offshore. Whereas the total surface of the Netherlands onshore is 41,785 square kilometers, the Dutch Continental Shelf of the North Sea comprises 56,814 square kilometers. Approximately 50% of the offshore territory is utilized in the exploration and production of oil and gas. Although the Netherlands as a seafaring country for many decades applied the principle of 'Mare Liberum' by the Dutch lawyer Hugo Grotius,[9] the Netherlands recognized the desire to extend national claims to waters beyond the national boundaries and signed and ratified the 1958 Geneva Conventions as well as the subsequent 1982 UN Convention on the Law of the Sea.[10] Following the entry into force of the Convention on the Continental Shelf in 1964, the Netherlands could exercise its functional jurisdiction with regard to the exploration and production of oil and gas offshore, and issued the Continental Shelf Mining Act in 1965.[11] Like other North Sea states, the Netherlands is also a party to the Convention for the Protection of the Marine Environment of the North-East Atlantic (the 'OSPAR Convention')[12] and the London Convention for the Prevention of Marine Pollution by Dumping of Wastes and Other Matters as amended by the Protocol to the Convention on

---

[7]   'In the context of the establishment and functioning of the internal market and with regard for the need to preserve and improve the environment, Union policy on energy shall aim, in a spirit of solidarity between Member States, to' develop new and renewable forms of energy, among other aims. It adds that: 'Such measures shall not affect a Member State's right to determine the conditions for exploiting its energy resources, its choice between different energy sources and the general structure of its energy supply'.

[8]   OJ, 30 June 1994, L 164/3.

[9]   Hugo Grotius, *Mare Liberum*, 1609, Elzevir, p. 68.

[10]   Trb. 1984, 55.

[11]   CS Mining Act of 23 September 1965, Staatsblad 428.

[12]   Convention for the Protection of the Marine Environment of the North-East Atlantic (Paris) 22 September 1992 (in force 25 March 1998), 2354 U.N.T.S. 67.

the Prevention of Marine Pollution by Dumping of Wastes and Other Matter (London Protocol).[13]

Finally, mention needs to be made of the increasing importance of the European Convention on Human Rights (ECHR), which was signed by the Netherlands on 4 November 1950 and entered into force on 3 September 1953. Within the jurisdiction of the signatory parties, the convention aims at protecting fundamental rights such as the right to life, privacy and the peaceful enjoyment of one's possessions. In several procedures relating to the volumes of gas production in the Groningen concession area, recourse was made to the ECHR as gas production led to a situation where house owners are deprived of a peaceful enjoyment of their property.[14]

3. FROM CONCESSIONS TO LICENCES

As mentioned above, historically a distinction was made between the legal regimes governing oil and gas exploration and production onshore and those offshore. This distinction is primarily the result of the pragmatic approach taken by the Dutch legislature. Although it recognized the need to replace the 'provisional' Mining Act of 1810 with a new (Dutch) law, such revision did not take place in the interest of, for example, coal mining activities in the province of Limburg or the urgent need to start exploration activities on the Dutch continental shelf, which could not be postponed pending the development of one single statute covering onshore and offshore developments.[15] Ultimately, such an integrated approach was achieved in 2003 and primarily as a result of the complex legal structure that had arisen following the transposition of the Hydrocarbons Directive. In 1995 the Minister of Economic Affairs therefore initiated a legislative process resulting in the entry force of a new Mining Act in 2003, which applies to the exploration, production and storage of minerals such as oil and gas onshore as well as offshore. As a general rule, the 2003 Mining Act applies to all new and existing exploration and production activities but some exemptions were made with regard to concessions awarded

---

[13] Convention on the Prevention of Marine Pollution by Dumping of Wastes and Other Matter (London), 13 November 1972 (in force 30 August 1975), 26 U.S.T. 2403, TIAS 8165; U.K.T.S. 43 (1976), Cmnd. 6486; 11 I.L.M. 1294 (1972); Protocol to the Convention on the Prevention of Marine Pollution by Dumping of Wastes and Other Matter, 24 March 2006, 36 ILM 1 (1997).

[14] M.M.E. Hesselman, J.G. Brouwer, 'De gaswinning en het recht op veiligheid', in *Juridische Aspecten van Gaswinning,* Wolters Kluwer, 2019, p. 23–p. 50.

[15] Martha Roggenkamp, *Oil & Gas: Netherlands Law and Practice,* Chancery Law Publishing, 1991, p. 7–p.8.

prior to 2003. Hence, there is a need to discuss the Mining Act of 1810 and the concession regime related thereto.

3.1   Concessions

Following the discovery of an oil field in Winterswijk in 1924, oil and gas production started after World War II following the award of several conces-sions,[16] culminating in the discovery of the Groningen gas field in 1959[17] and other onshore gas fields primarily in the Northern and Western parts of the Netherlands.[18] The concessions that allow for the production from these fields are based on the earlier mentioned *Loi conçernant les mines, les minières, et les carrières* (hereafter, Mining Act 1810).[19] This act provides for a concession regime for resources that are classified as 'mines',[20] i.e., important resources like silver, gold, salt and coal.[21] Obviously oil and gas were unknown resources when the act was drafted and thus not categorized as 'mines'. The award of a concession therefore required a legal 'trick' and subsequently the conces-sions provided that concessionaires were entitled to produce bitumen such as oil and/or gas. Apart from this it should be noted that the Mining Act 1810 did not contain any explicit provisions regarding the ownership of subsoil minerals *in situ*. It could be argued that the general rule in Article 525 of the (French) Civil Code that 'the ownership of the land carries with it ownership of what is on and in the land' would also apply to subsoil minerals. However, such reading would be too straightforward given the disagreement between the French legislators of the Mining Act 1810 and Napoleon about the application of either the rule of accession (ownership of the minerals run with the own-ership of the land) or the dominial system (according to which all important minerals are owned by the State).[22] By contrast, the Mining Act 1810 explicitly provided that the ownership of the subsoil minerals (mines) was transferred to

---

[16]   See, the 'Schoonebeek' concession of 1948 (Stc. 3-5-1948, no 110), the 'Tubbergen' concession of 1953 (Stc 11-3-1953, no 80), the 'Rijswijk' concession of 1955 (Stc. 3-1-1955, no 21), and the 'Rossum de Lutte' concession of 1961 (Stc 12-5-1961, no 116).

[17]   Concession was awarded on 30-5-1963, Stc no. 126.

[18]   See for a complete overview the annual reports of the Ministry of Economic Affairs and Climate on www.nlog.nl.

[19]   As the Act is in French, changes to the Act were included in the Mining Act 1903.

[20]   Article 5 Mining Act 1810.

[21]   See article 2 Mining Act 1810. Articles 3 and 4 provide definitions of 'minières' and 'carrières'.

[22]   B.F. Boekhold, *Mijnrecht*, University of Leiden, unpublished dissertation, 1912, p. 93–p. 121.

the concessionaire by means of the award of the concession.[23] In other words, after a concession had been awarded the concessionaire holds full ownership of all unproduced subsoil minerals. Moreover, these minerals were considered by law as immovable property.[24] Apart from these rules on ownership, the Act governed the application (on the basis of 'first come, first served') and subsequent award of concessions as well as the relationship with landowners affected by exploration and production. However, all other relevant issues such as the duration of the concession, the area to which it applies, payments to government and landowners and reporting obligations are included in the deed of concession. Most importantly, all concessions issued before 1988 have been awarded in perpetuity. With the discovery of natural gas, the deeds of concession also required that the Minister of Economic Affairs and the concessionaire conclude an agreement based on a model agreement attached to the concession. This agreement sets out in detail the financial obligations of the concessionaire and the way in which the State participates in gas production and/or supply.

Following the discovery of the Groningen gas field in 1959 some important changes were introduced to the concession regime, which also has impacted the offshore licensing regime (see below). These changes were based on the need to develop a gas policy that take into account and coordinate the interests of private parties (the oil companies) and public interests (the State) in future gas production and supply.[25] Consequently, the Groningen concession of 1963 included, inter alia, the condition that 'the extraction of natural gas shall take place according to a cooperation agreement, approved by the Minister of Economic Affairs, between the concessionaires and the state participant'.[26] The *Staatsmijnen* (State Coal Mines) was then appointed as the State participant, but since 1989 the company *BV Energiebeheer Nederland* (or EBN) has been acting as the state participant.[27] Pursuant to this cooperation agreement the parties established a partnership (*Maatschap*) in which the state participant and the concessionaire (the company NAM) hold a 40%:60% interest but act in accordance with a voting proportion of 50%:50%. The concessionaire exploits

---

[23]   Article 7 Mining Act 1810, which was removed from the Act in 1988.

[24]   Article 8 Mining Act 1810.

[25]   This was based on the gas policy note of Minister 'De Pous' that introduced a regime of close cooperation between production and supply. See M.M. Roggenkamp, 'Energy Law in the Netherlands', *Energy Law in Europe – National, EU and International Regulation*, Oxford University Press, 3d ed., 2016, p. 755–p. 756.

[26]   Art 11, para 1, concession 'Groningen'.

[27]   The *Staatsmijnen* was initially a branch of the Dutch government, in 1973 it was reorganised and turned into a limited liability company NV DSM in which the State held all shares. Following the privatization of NV DSM in 1989, its shares transferred to EBN, which is a public limited company in which the State holds all shares.

the reservoir for the account of the *Maatschap*. This means that the partnership decides on the actual extraction and disposal of the minerals. Although the state does not participate in the concession, it can directly influence gas production through its share in the *Maatschap*. Similar provisions have been included in subsequent gas concessions, which usually were awarded to one single company.

As the discovery of the Groningen gas field led to great interest in further exploring the Dutch subsoil, the Dutch government decided to issue a separate law to regulate exploratory drilling. The Minerals Exploration Act of 1967[28] required a licence for exploratory drilling onshore, except for exploratory drillings in concession areas for scientific purposes. Such a drilling licence was awarded on a 'first come, first served' basis and in exclusivity. One of the questions raised during the parliamentary debate of the Minerals Exploration Bill was the relationship between the drilling licence and the concession, as neither the Minerals Exploration Act or the Mining Act provided any certainty that the holder of the drilling licence would be awarded a concession if an exploitable quantity of minerals would be discovered. Regarding the Zuidwal concession, the Council of State ruled that although the Crown has the freedom to refuse an application for a concession, even if the applicants meet the conditions of the Mining Act 1810, the Crown needs to take all interests concerned and take into account the basic principles of administrative law.[29] Hence, the concession was awarded to the holder of the drilling licence.

The above shows that the entire legal framework governing exploration and production of oil and gas resulted from ad hoc decisions, and led to a regime without any elements of competition.

3.2   Licences

Exploration and production of oil and gas offshore has taken place since the mid-1960s. Despite high expectations, the offshore fields are smaller in size than most onshore fields. In order to regulate exploration and production of oil and gas offshore, the Dutch government issued the Continental Shelf Mining Act of 1965.[30] It is a framework Act and has been supplemented with several Royal Decrees organizing in greater detail exploration and production of oil and gas.[31] Similar to the situation onshore, the offshore regime provides for two

---

[28]   Act of 3-5-1967, Stb 258.
[29]   See Royal Decree of 28-8-1984, Stc 190, and Martha Roggenkamp, *Oil and Gas: Netherlands Law and Practice*, p. 123.
[30]   CS Mining Act of 23 September 1965, Stb 428.
[31]   The most important Royal Decrees dated from 1967 (Stb 24), 1976 (Stb 102) and 1996 (Stb 212, 213, 214).

separate licences – an exploration licence and a production licence – awarded for a specific period of time and the rule of financial participation of the Dutch state via a State participant in the production of oil and/or gas. However, by contrast to the situation onshore, an exploration licence is awarded in competition to a joint venture of companies; all interested parties could apply for a licence in a specific period of time (usually three months) for all parts of the Dutch continental shelf that was not used for other purposes.

As a result of the need to implement the Hydrocarbons Directive, the Netherlands decided to replace the onshore and offshore regimes with a new Mining Act in 2003. This Act replaces previous (mining) laws, integrates the onshore and offshore regimes, as well as implements the key elements of the EU Hydrocarbon Directive. Although the previous concessions have turned into production licences, the 2003 Mining Act leaves prior arrangements governed by the concessions in place. In other words, the provisions that provided a concessionaire with an eternal concessions and full ownership of the subsoil minerals *in situ* remain place. Any intervention in these key provisions would have led to discussions about breach of ownership rights and potential financial claims, as such a change could be considered as expropriation.[32]

3.3 Legal Character of the Licence

The above also shows that a distinction has to be made between the regime governing onshore and offshore mining activities. Although the Mining Act of 2003 provides for one common regime, some traces of the previous regimes still remain.

Although all concessions have been converted into production licences, the key requirements of the previous concession regime (the deed of concession and the concession agreement) are still in place. Although not clear whether the provisions in the deeds of concession were based on prior negotiations between the government (initially the Crown) and the concessionaire, the deeds of concession are considered as some sort of contract, combining elements of public and private law.[33] Given the fact that concessions provided the concessionaire with full ownership of the subsoil resources, it also grants a property right to the concession holder over the resource in situ.

Licences, however, are considered as an administrative decision as a result of which the Minister can award an exclusive right to explore and/or exploit

---

[32] See also Explanatory Memorandum presented with the Mining Bill, TK 1998–1999, 26219n, no. 3.

[33] See also D.L.M.T. Dankers-Hagenaars, *Op het spoor van de concessie – Een onderzoek naar het rechtskarakter van de concessie in Nederland en in Frankrijk*, Boom Juridische Uitgevers, 2000, p. 421.

the subsoil for specific resources if the applicant meets some minimum requirements. The award of such a right is subject to the procedures of the General Act on Administrative Law.[34] Noteworthy is also the increasing role of a range of plans such as the need for a production plan and a measurement plan without which oil and gas production cannot take place. These plans are based on the Mining Act and also considered as administrative decisions pursuant to the General Act on Administrative Law.[35]

In addition to these licences use is made of several private law instruments. This involves first and foremost the requirements to conclude an agreement of cooperation with the State participant (now EBN). This agreement of cooperation is a contract under private law (and confidential). In addition, most offshore licences and increasingly also onshore licences are awarded to joint ventures. These joint ventures operate on the basis of a joint operating agreement (JOA) which is also a private law agreement and in the Netherlands not subject to any supervision control by the Government.

Given the above, it can be concluded that exploration and production in the Netherlands is based on a hybrid system consisting of administrative decisions as well as contractual and property rights.

4.   LICENSING REGIME

4.1   The 2003 Mining Act

Currently licensing is governed by the 2003 Mining Act and rules, which have been included in secondary legislation such as the Mining Decree and the Mining Regulations.[36] Onshore, some additional licensing requirements may apply based on, for example, the Environmental Protection Act and the Physical Planning Act. Given the more limited (functional) jurisdiction of the Netherlands offshore, the Environmental Protection Act does not apply on the Dutch continental shelf and therefore environmental protection at sea is governed on the basis of a specific permit granted under the 2003 Mining Act.[37] Moreover, the 2003 Mining Act provides for a range of licences. In addition to an exploration licence and a production licence, it also requires a storage licence and a licence to produce geothermal heat. The latter two licences were included as both activities have a direct impact on the use of the subsoil.

---

[34]   Art. 6a Mining Act.
[35]   Arts. 34 and 41 Mining Act.
[36]   Mining Act of 31 October 2002, Stb 542, Mining Decree of 6 December 2002, Stb 604 and Mining Regulations of 16 December 2002, Stc 245, which entered into force on 1 January 2003.
[37]   Art. 40 para 2 Mining Act.

Subsequently the procedures for granting these licences are similar to the ones that are applied for exploration and production licences. Moreover, by contrast to many other North Sea states, the 2003 Mining Act does not provide for the award of a pipeline licence, i.e., a licence to develop and operate a pipeline connecting a production installation and the transmission system. The governance of such a pipeline is limited to a construction permit on the basis of the 2003 Mining Regulation.[38]

4.2   Award of Licences

Under the 2003 Mining Act all licences are awarded on the basis of the key principles of the Hydrocarbons Directive, which requires that procedures for granting authorizations must be transparent and based on objective, non-discriminatory criteria and be open to all interested entities.[39,40] This entails that the licensing requirements are included in the Mining Act and/ or Mining Decree and Mining Regulations. As provided for by the Directive, licence applications can only be assessed on the basis of (i) the technical or financial capability of the applicant, (ii) the way in which applicants have operated under previous and other licences, and (iii) how the applicant intends to carry out the activities for which the licence is sought. Such an appraisal is made on the basis of a work submitted together with the application. If a choice has to be made between two or more applicants of equal quality and standing, the Minister's decision will be made in the interests of efficient and dynamic exploration or production.[41]

The Dutch licensing regime has some specific features. One of them is the existence of two separate licences: an exclusive exploration licence and an exclusive production licence. Each licence is awarded for a specific period of time, which may differ per licence (see next paragraph). The first licence, an exploration licence, involves the right to search for the presence of minerals like oil and gas by means of drilling.[42] The holder of an exploration licence may apply for a production licence if an 'economically viable quantity' of oil/ gas has been found. The 2003 Mining Act does not define when a discovery is considered 'economically viable', but in practice it depends on a range of

---

[38]   Art. 94 Mining Decree.
[39]   Art. 5 Hydrocarbons Directive.
[40]   Art. 5 Hydrocarbons Directive.
[41]   Arts. 9 and 15 Mining Act and ch 1, Mining Regulations.
[42]   Seismic surveying and other exploratory investigations not involving drill holes are thus not considered an 'exploration activity' within the meaning of the Mining Act and do not require a licence. Further rules regarding such activities are included in chapter 2 Mining Decree.

elements such as the price of oil, the dollar exchange rate, and the distance to existing pipeline infrastructure. As indicated in the Hydrocarbons Directive,[43] it is possible to directly apply for a 'spontaneous' production licence if, for example, a field straddles outside the licensed area.

Licences are basically awarded using a system of competitive bidding based on the assessment of work plans submitted. This usually starts with an application for an exploration licence. Use is made of an 'open door' regime as provided for by Article 3 paragraph 2b of the Hydrocarbons Directive, where any (legal or natural) person can apply for an exploration licence at any time for any 'unused' area, but as soon as the competent authority has received a notice of application, it is required to invite other parties to file a competitive application within a period of 13 weeks.[44] The licence has to be awarded within six months of the expiry of the application period.[45] The Minister of Economic Affairs and Climate is the competent authority charged with the award of a licence, and is advised by a number of consultative bodies, such as the Mining Council,[46] the State Supervision of Mines,[47] the State participant EBN,[48] TNO-ATG (former geological survey)[49] and, if so requested, the Technical Committee on Earth Movements in relation to onshore developments.[50] Depending on the area for which a licence is applied for, each of them will advise the Minister on the basis of their particular expertise. A decision to award a licence is published in the Official Gazette of the Netherlands and included in the annual report 'Oil and Gas in the Netherlands' of the Minister of Economic Affairs and Climate as well as on the website www.nlog.nl that has been developed by the Ministry and TNO.

Licences are usually applied for, and awarded to, joint ventures. The government does not intervene in the composition of the joint venture as it would like to avoid 'forced marriages'. The joint venture usually applies for a licence on the basis of a joint bidding agreement. Exploration and/or production by the joint venture will be based on a JOA, which is drafted and concluded without any government involvement or influence. Nevertheless, the entry into force of the 2003 Mining Act led to a minor change, as the Minister now

---

[43]   Art. 3 para 4 Hydrocarbons Directive.

[44]   Art. 15 Mining Act and ch 1 Mining Regulations. A notice is published in the Stc and the European Commission Official Journal. For consistency with the General Act on Administrative Law of 1992 (Art 4:13) the M-Act refers to a period of 13 weeks instead of the 90 days included in the Directive.

[45]   Art. 17 Mining Act. A decision to award a licence will be published in the Stc.

[46]   Arts. 105–12 Mining Act.

[47]   Arts. 126–30 Mining Act.

[48]   Arts. 93–97b Mining Act.

[49]   Art. 123 Mining Act.

[50]   Arts. 113–22 Mining Act.

needs to approve the company designated by the joint venture as the operator.[51] Therefore, if necessary, the Minister could reject the joint venture's choice of an operator, although this has not (yet) occurred. Similarly, Ministerial approval is required where a licensee or one of the joint venture parties in the licence wants to transfer the licence or its share in the licence to another party. The procedure for such a transfer is included in the JOA (farm in/out agreements), but the Minister needs to assess whether the new licensee meets the basic financial and technical requirements.[52] Similarly, the Minister can decide to withdraw a licence if this is justified by a change in the technical or financial capability of a licensee, the licence is awarded on the basis of incorrect data, or the activities are not carried out in conformance with the requirements set out in the licence.[53]

Normally the State participates in the production of oil and/or gas. State participation has been the general rule since the discovery of the Groningen gas field. However, State participation was initially limited to production as the State did not wish to bear any risks at the exploration stage. Therefore, there was a need for having two separate licences as discussed above. Following the award of a production licence, the State participant could decide whether or not to participate in the production activities. In practice, it has almost always made use of that possibility. This situation changed in the year 2000 following the need to stimulate offshore investments by private parties (oil companies). Upon request of the holder of an offshore exploration licence the State participant could be requested by the licensee to participate in the exploration phase.[54] The 2003 Mining Act codified this approach but also expanded the possibility for State participation to all exploration and production activities offshore as well as onshore. As a general rule, State participation shall take place in the interest of an efficient exploration or production, a systematic management and an optimal disposal of hydrocarbons in the Netherlands.[55] The company EBN is appointed as the State participant (see above section 3.1) and will be involved in exploration and/or production on the basis of a separate cooperation with the licensee on the basis of which the State participant a share of 40% in exploration and/or production. Hence, the State participant pays 40% of the costs but also receives 40% of the profits. Importantly, the State participant EBN is not a licensee, and is not part of the joint venture or the JOA.

---

[51] Art. 22 para 5 Mining Act.
[52] Art. 20 Mining Act.
[53] Art. 21 Mining Act.
[54] See TK 1999–2000, 26219, No 10, p. 77–p. 88.
[55] Art. 82 Mining Act.

4.3   Conditions Attached to the Licence

Licences are awarded with certain conditions.[56] These include standard conditions such as the type of minerals to be explored and/or produced, the area to which it applies and the duration of the licence but also some more specific conditions relating to the activity itself.

Regarding the first category of conditions, the licence will state whether it involves the exploration and/or production of oil, gas, salt, heat or any other mineral. A licensee is thus not permitted to explore or exploit any other mineral than provided for by the licence, unless a separate licence is awarded. Next, it will also state to which area it applies. This is usually done by indicating the limits of the surface area. Offshore, the Dutch continental shelf is divided into blocks of 400 square kilometers and licences are awarded for a block or part-block(s).[57] Licences thus apply to one or more blocks or part blocks. Onshore, licences are awarded for a geological unit, i.e., an area where, according to geological reports, that specific mineral can be found. These areas are usually delineated by specifying municipal or provincial borders. In practice, it is thus possible that several licences may apply to the same area as hydrocarbons reservoirs usually are situated at a greater depth than, for example, salt. Thirdly, the licence will specify for which period they apply. As a general rule the 2003 Mining Act provides that licences are awarded for the period necessary to carry out the intended activities.[58] Usually the duration of an exploration licence will vary from four to eight years and for a production licence from 20 to 25 years (except for the former concessions, which still are valid in perpetuity). If necessary, a licence can be extended if the time specified in the licence is insufficient for the completion of the licensed activities, and these activities so far have been carried out in compliance with the licence.[59] Such extensions are awarded on a regular basis. In order to promote exploration on the Dutch Continental Shelf, since 2006 the Minister commenced awarding exploration licences with a limited duration (two years) to small and inexperienced oil companies the opportunity to develop the necessary expertise, and to develop a final work programme. If successful in acquiring the necessary expertise and developing a work programme, they can apply for an extension.

---

[56]   Art. 13 Mining Act.

[57]   In certain parts of the continental shelf mining activities are restricted or excluded due to the existence of shipping routes, military training areas and environmentally sensitive areas.

[58]   Art. 11 para 2 Mining Act.

[59]   Arts. 18 paras 3 and 4 Mining Act. In such case, the subsequent licence area can be restricted at the request of the licensee or at the initiative of the Minister.

Apart from the above, the Mining Act provides for a duty of care. This means that each licensee is obliged to take all reasonable measures to prevent the licensed activity from causing damage arising from earth movement, or that will have a negative impact on health, safety, the environment, or the systematic management of the reservoir.[60] Regarding the exploration for and exploitation of hydrocarbons, since 2016 the Mining Act requires the licensee to apply a method of systematic risk management. The acceptability of risks is based on an assessment of the time, costs or efforts needed for a further reduction of risks and whether this would be disproportionate in relation to the advantages of such a reduction. When assessing these risk levels, the licensee can take into account existing best practices.[61] In order to ensure that production will not result in earth movements such as earthquakes, licensees need to perform measurements of onshore mining activities before the start of the production, during the production and for up to 30 years after cessation of the production.[62] Such a measurement plan needs Ministerial approval and has to be updated every five years.[63] Although such measurements initially were intended to control subsidence, they now play a role in measuring earthquakes that increasingly take place in the Groningen concession area.

Another condition that is attached to a licence since the entry into force of the 2003 Mining Act is the requirement of a production plan, which also needs prior approval from the Minister.[64] The Minister can withhold such approval in the interests of the planned management of the resources or in view of the risk of damage caused by possible earth movements. Since the introduction of this regulatory instrument in 1996,[65] production plans have been a matter of discussion first and foremost in relation to salt production[66] but increasingly also with regard to the production of gas from the Groningen field, especially following the earthquakes that have been taking place since 2012. The production plan is an important means to control gas production and also applies to the operators of the holders of the 'old' concessions were required to submit a draft production plan within one year after the entry into force of the 2003 Mining

---

[60] Art. 33 Mining Act.
[61] Art. 33a Mining Act. See amendment of the Mining Act, Stb 2016, no. 558.
[62] Art. 41 Mining Act.
[63] Art. 30, Mining Decree.
[64] Arts. 34–36 Mining Act.
[65] Art. 144 Mining Act provides that production plans approved in the period 1996–2004 shall be considered as production plans under Art. 34 Mining Act. Art. 145 Mining Act provides that production on the basis of a concession or licence awarded before 1996 could be continued for a specific period within which licence holders could submit a production plan.
[66] Decision RvS of 26 July 2006 (no 200406925/1) and decision Ministry of Economic Affairs of 18 January 2010 (Stc 655).

Act. This was easier said than done, especially due to major public opposition and the large number of cases and rulings by the administrative court. As a result the production plans often had to be amended but this has also led to a decision to close several production locations. Given the complexity of the gas production from the Groningen field and the decision in 2019 to close down the Groningen field in 2030 at the latest, the Mining Act was amended in July 2018 in order to include a separate chapter governing the operations of the Groningen field, which also resulted in a decision that a production plan is no longer required for the Groningen gas field as the Minister shall determine the production strategy.[67]

In addition, licensees are bound by several financial obligations. The (co-) holders of exploration and production licences are obliged to pay several levies. The Tax Authority (*Belastingdienst*) is charged with the collection of these levies, the most important being royalties ('cijns'), corporate income tax and profit sharing as well as a surface rental. For production onshore a payment also has to be made to the province(s) where the activities take place. This is a payment per square kilometer and is set annually.[68]

Last but not least, holders of a production licence are obliged to remove disused installations. For onshore installations, this obligation was initially included in the deed of concession which usually required the concessionaire to remove, after termination of the exploitation, the works made for that purpose and to bring the ground again into a state corresponding with the original use. Currently an obligation to remove disused installations is included in the Mining Act and the Mining Decree but a distinction has still to be made between the onshore and offshore removal obligations as the latter are based on provisions of International Law, i.e., UNCLOS, IMO and OSPAR.[69]

4.4   Rights Conferred

Both the exploration and the production licence provide an exclusive right to carry out the licensed activity. First, the holder of an exploration licence has the exclusive right to explore a specific area by way of exploratory drilling. In case of a discovery of an economically producible quantity of minerals, the holder of the exploration licence also has the exclusive right to apply for a production licence at any time during the term of an exploration licence.

---

[67] Stb 2018, 371.
[68] Arts. 75–80 Mining Act.
[69] See Martha Roggenkamp, 'The Netherlands' in: *The Regulation of Decommissioning, Abandonment and Re-Use Initiatives in the Oil and Gas Industry: From Obligation to Opportunities*, forthcoming Wolters Kluwer 2020.

The exploration licence remains valid at least until the time when the decision relating to the application of the production licence becomes irrevocable.[70]

A production licence obviously provides the licensee with the right to produce specific minerals such as oil and gas. In addition, the 2003 Mining Act explicitly rules that the State owns all subsoil resources located 100 meters below the surface, including on the Dutch continental shelf (DCS), and that the ownership of such minerals is transferred to the licensee upon production.[71] An exemption still applies to most onshore reservoirs where a concession initially was awarded. These licensees (former concessionaires) retain full ownership of the minerals in situ. Complications also arise if a licensee by accident strikes a different subsoil layer and starts to exploit another mineral than the one licensed.[72] The award of a gas storage licence to another party than the original concessionaire is also complicated as the concessionaire owns the subsoil resources, including those quantities of unproduced gas that might be used by the holder of the storage licence as cushion gas.

Whereas the 1810 Mining Act explicitly stated that 'mines' (specific category of minerals as discussed above in sections 2.3 and 3.1) but also equipment such as machines, shafts, galleries and even horses used for exploitation are immovable goods[73] and the materials extracted movable goods,[74] the 2003 Mining Act does not provide such a rule. Instead such qualification requires an assessment on the basis of the Civil Code, which rules in article 3:3 that 'immovable goods are the land, including the unexploited minerals, and the buildings and constructions permanently attached to the land'. Moreover, all immovable goods need to be registered in the land register (*kadaster*). Such registration is not only a prerequisite for transferring an immovable good but also to create any entitlements such as a mortgage.[75] Such registration is also a prerequisite for splitting the ownership of the installation from the ownership of the land. Under the Civil Code all installations run with the land if not otherwise provided for.[76] Obviously, this provision is of specific relevance when establishing installations for the exploration and production of oil and gas. In order to ensure that the licensee legally owns these installations, it will

---

[70]   Art. 10 Mining Act.

[71]   Art. 3 Mining Act.

[72]   Examples can be found in relation to the production of geothermal heat, which in a few instances has resulted into accidental by-catch of oil and gas. See further M.M. Roggenkamp, D.M. Hanema, 'New Uses of the Underground in the Netherlands: How to Manage a Crowded Subsoil?' in: D. Zillman et al, *Energy Underground*, OUP 2014, p. 384–p.388.

[73]   Art. 8 Mining Act 1810.

[74]   Art. 9 Mining Act 1810.

[75]   Arts. 3:10, 3: 89 Civil Code.

[76]   Art. 5:103 Civil Code.

be necessary to separate the ownership of the installation from the ownership of the land by establishing a right of superficies (*opstalrecht*), which has to be registered in the land register.[77] If necessary, these installations could be mortgaged.[78] The Civil Code, however, does not apply offshore (on the CS) and therefore offshore installations cannot be registered in the land register. Therefore, it is unclear who legally owns these offshore installations and whether these installations can be used as a security right.[79] An alternative would be to assess whether the licence could be used as a security right as according to the Civil Code all transferable assets can be encumbered with a pledge.[80] However, with regard to offshore operations this is also unclear since the Civil Code does not apply to the Continental Shelf.

5.   CONCLUSION

The above analysis has shown that a distinction needs to be made between a regime governing oil and/or gas production onshore and offshore. Although the 2003 Mining Act has been aligning both regimes, the effects of the previous concession regime are still notable. This can be illustrated by the recent developments with regard to the production of gas from the Groningen field. Following the earthquake with a magnitude of 3.6 on the Richter scale near Huizinge in 2012, and several subsequent earthquakes in the years thereafter, the situation has drastically changed as the earthquakes have led to considerable damage to properties. Consequently, approximately 100,000 claims for compensation have been filed, and severe opposition towards gas production from the Groningen field has arisen. The Dutch government therefore decided in March 2018 to cease production from the Groningen field by 2030 at the latest.[81] Initially production will be limited to 12 billion Nm3 per gas year, but under normal weather circumstances gas production could be zero in the summer of 2022.[82]

---

[77]   Art. 5:101 Civil Code.
[78]   Art. 3:227 Civil Code.
[79]   J.J.A. Waverijn, 'Navigating Legal Barriers to Mortgaging Energy Installations at Sea – the Case of the North Sea and the Netherlands', in: C. Banet, *The Law of the Seabed – Access, Uses, and Protection of Seabed Resources*, Brill, 2020, p. 503–p. 524.
[80]   Art. 3:228 Civil Code.
[81]   Letter (DGETM-EI/18057375) of 29 March 2018 from the Minister of Economic Affairs and Climate to Parliament on 'Gaswinning Groningen', www.rijksoverheid .nl/documenten/kamerstukken/2018/03/29/kamerbrief-over-gaswinning-groningen (accessed 31 Jan. 2020).
[82]   Letter (DGKE-PGG/19207029) of 10 September 2019 from the Minister of Economic Affairs and Climate to Parliament on 'Gaswinningsniveau Groningen in

The decision to cease the production from the Groningen field and ultimately to close the entire field also has financial consequences. First, it impacts the State budget, since total revenue from gas production will decrease.[83] Secondly, the State needs to invest in the Groningen region to compensate for the loss of gas income and to improve the quality of the properties to meet safety requirements. Thirdly, a decision has to be made regarding the potential compensation of the concessionaire NAM (Shell and ExxonMobil) for the natural gas *in situ*, which can no longer be produced.[84] Whilst the closure of the field can be considered as some sort of expropriation and thus would require a financial compensation, the parties involved (the State, Shell and ExxonMobil) concluded an interim agreement on 9 September 2019, where the State agrees to accept less revenues in the period until the production ceases in favour of Shell and ExxonMobil, who in turn agreed to continue to pay for the damages occurred and to invest in alternative gas supply measures such as an increase in onshore gas storage capacity.[85]

As a result of the changes to the Groningen gas field, the position of the Netherlands in the European gas market has also drastically changed. Instead of being a net exporter of gas, the Netherlands became a net importer of gas in 2018.[86] Moreover, development of other onshore fields has become nearly impossible due to public opposition and therefore the focus is now primarily on exploration and production of gas on the Dutch continental shelf.[87] Although the estimates indicate that about 200–300 BCM of gas could still be explored,[88] investments are lagging behind. This is partly due to a lack of financial incentives but also the current licensing regime as procedures relating

---

2019-2020', www.rijksoverheid.nl/documenten/kamerstukken/2019/09/10/kamerbrief ---gaswinningsniveau-groningen-in-2019-2020 (accessed 31 Jan. 2020).

[83] Whereas in 2013 the total gas revenues reached the highest level at Euro 15.4 billion, in 2016 it had decreased to Euro 2.4 billion and will decrease further in the following years. See figures Dutch statistical bureau CBS at www.cbs.nl/nl-nl/nieuws/ 2017/17/aardgasbaten-op-laagste-niveau-in-ruim-40-jaar (accessed 22 March 2020).

[84] These volumes are estimated at approximately 450 milliard cubic meters natural gas.

[85] See www.officielebekendmakingen.nl › blg-899821 (accessed 22 March 2020).

[86] See www.gasterra.nl (accessed 22 March 2020).

[87] This can be illustrated by the following numbers from www.nlog.nl: exploration licences awarded offshore in 2016 (1), 2017 (1), 2018 (1) and 2019 (4; production licences awarded offshore in 2016 (0), 2017 (4), 2018 (3) and 2019 (1). In 2019 also 2 onshore production licences have been awarded.

[88] EBN and Ministry of Economic Affairs and Climate, A Sea of Opportunity Exploration in The Netherlands, 2019, at www.ebn.nl/wp-content/uploads/2019/06/ Brochure-A-Sea-of-Opportunity-The-Netherlands.pdf (accessed 22 March 2020).

to drill new wells are generally considered too lengthy.[89] A reassessment of the Dutch licensing regime may therefore be required. This may result in a larger and/or different role of the Dutch state and thus also change the nature of the current licences.

---

[89] Applications for new exploration licences take longer than a year to be processed by the ministry. See J. van den Beukel, L. van Geuns, *The deteriorating outlook for Dutch small natural gas fields*, Hague Centre for Strategic Studies, January 2020, p. 9.

8. Legal character of petroleum licences under Norwegian law

Ernst Nordtveit

1. SUBJECT AND BACKGROUND

A petroleum production licence is an authorization or permit to "produce" or more precisely to extract petroleum from the deposits in the underground.[1] The production licence is a essential element in a complex legal arrangement between the state as the owner of the petroleum resources in the ground and as legislator and regulator on the one side and the licence holders (licensees) who usually are national or international oil companies on the other side.[2] It is the tool that grants an oil company access to this state-owned resource. In Norway, the state also, to a great extent, has had the role of participant and entrepreneur in the petroleum activity, based on contractual arrangements.

The character of the whole arrangement is a kind of "symbiotic" relationship.[3] In return for the grant of access to petroleum, the licensee undertakes to make considerable investments in exploration and production of petroleum, to make a profit for himself. The discovery and extraction of petroleum will also

---

[1]   The Norwegian term in the Act 29 November 1996 no. 11 on petroleum activities (NPA) Section 3-3, and previous legislation, is "utvinningstillatelse" which directly translated is "permit for extraction". I will use the common English term "production licence" in this chapter. In addition to the production licence, the NPA requires different forms of approvals or permits for certain activities which are based on the production licence, such as the plan for development and operation (PDO) (s4-2), to install and to operate facilities (s4-3), the production schedule, burning of petroleum above what is needed for safe production, starting of test production, s4-4 first and second paragraph and cessation of petroleum activity (chapter 5). An exploration licence gives the licensee a non-exclusive right to examination of a defined area, but does not give access to the petroleum resources. The analysis here is concentrated on the production licence.
[2]   I will use the term companies for the licensees in this chapter unless it is necessary to be more precise.
[3]   See generally on "symbiotic relationship" E Schanze, "Symbiotic Arrangements", *Journal of Institutional and Theoretical Economics (JITE) / Zeitschrift für die gesamte Staatswissenschaft*, Vol. 149, No. 4 (Dec. 1993), pp. 691–97.

benefit the state as the owner of the petroleum and more indirectly the society by taxation and creating employment in supply industry. The relationship is based on the assumption that the licensee in his interest will explore for petroleum and start production of commercially viable deposits. The state cannot, except under exceptional circumstances demand, that the licensee starts production or continues production beyond what he finds commercially exciting or acceptable.[4]

Petroleum activity will, in case of commercially viable discoveries, take place over many years. Unforeseen changes due to market fluctuations, technological changes, more general development in the society, new forms of governance, and a new understanding of economic and ecological factors will create challenges for both parties. The development might demand changes in policy and new regulation of, for instance, environmental issues. The question is how the risk for changes during the licence period can be managed in a manner that is giving both parties reasonable protection against the risk of changes and what principles and limitations for changes should be built into the system.

The purpose of classification or deciding the "character" of the arrangement between the state and the companies as an administrative decision or a "contract" has no purpose in itself. The reason for a categorization must be to decide what "background-rules" apply for issues that are not regulated or inadequately regulated in the licence or surrounding regulations. The main issue is how far the state may change the conditions in the licence or change the legal framework for the activity that is taking place on the basis of the licence, to the detriment of the companies with retroactive effect.

Classification of the production licence as an administrative decision or a contract appears to be a simplistic approach to the question of to what extent the state will be prevented from changes in the legislation. The licensing system and the surrounding regulatory system is too complex to fit into a clear dichotomy between administrative decisions and contracts. The legal arrangement between the state and the companies also transcends the distinction between private and public law in a manner that makes it difficult to penetrate

---

[4]   NPA Section 4-1 regulates the balancing between the consideration for best financial result and maximum output. The state's interest in high production will, to some extent have priority over the consideration for the best possible economic result. In cases where vital social factors are at stake, the King might decide another production profile than what was ordinarily decided or accepted, NPA 4-4 fourth paragraph. Norway has ordered companies to reduce the production as a contribution to supporting the market price for crude oil in 1985, 1986, 1998, and 2020, based on this rule. The reduction in 2020 was 250 000 barrels a day in June and 134 000 barrels a day in the last six months of 2020.

and clarify the question of the legal character of petroleum licences under Norwegian law.

The issue has to be studied on the background of the political and legal culture and traditions in Norway, and the principles and thinking behind the development of the Norwegian petroleum legislation and licensing system, in the meeting between Norwegian political and legal culture and legal principles and instruments developed by the international petroleum industry. The petroleum industry has, without doubt, influenced the Norwegian society and also its legal culture, but there are also clearly elements of Norwegian legal culture in the licence system. The influence of national and international legal tradition and culture in the design of the licensing system and the regulatory regime surrounding it is, therefore, an intriguing subject for analysis.

I will approach the issue by first presenting some central elements of the Norwegian political and legal system, with a focus on issues that will be of interest for the further discussion. Then I will present the development of the Norwegian licensing system and legal regulation of the petroleum activity, before returning to the debate on the legal character of the petroleum production licences.

2. THE NORWEGIAN LEGAL AND POLITICAL SYSTEM

The Norwegian legal system is a part of the Scandinavian legal tradition, which has developed by long-lasting unions between several of the Scandinavian states, academic influence across the borders and from legislative cooperation during the last 150 years.[5] The Scandinavian legal tradition is mainly considered a sub-category of civil law but does in many respects stand out as a separate legal tradition.

Norway does not have a civil code, but most areas of law, also private law, are regulated by statutes decided by the Parliament (the Storting). The legislation is, however, not systematically covering all possible questions and leaves considerable discretion to the courts.

---

[5]   Norway was established as an independent kingdom from 872 and adopted a consolidated legal order in 1274 when a national code was enacted based on the earlier regional laws. Around the year 1400 Norway became part of a union with Denmark and Sweden ("Kalmar-unionen"). Sweden left the union in 1523, but the union between Denmark and Norway continued, until 1814 when Denmark had to give up Norway to Sweden as a result of the Napoleonic wars. The Norwegians then adopted a new constitution and declared independence. Norway still ended up in a union with Sweden, but kept the constitution with some minor changes, securing the Storting as the legislative power. The union with Sweden broke up in 1905.

The legal method is generally flexible and pragmatic, giving weight to real considerations and the purpose of the law and regulation in question, and putting less weight on legal concepts and classification as the basis for legal reasoning. Preparatory works outlining the meaning of the legislation have considerable influence in the interpretation of the legislation.

Norway is a democratic state with a written Constitution from 1814.[6] The legislative power is with the Parliament (the Storting), which consists of 165 representatives elected for four years.

The executive power is with the Government (King in Council), which is formally appointed by the King and led by a Prime Minister. The King personally has no political power, but the Government makes the decisions in the King's name in the form of "Royal Decrees". When the Constitution or general legislation gives the King authority to make decisions or give further regulations, it means the Government (King in Council).

Norway has a parliamentary system in which the Government needs to be accepted by the majority in the Parliament. If a majority in the Parliament expresses a lack of trust in the Government, or votes down a proposal from the Government in a matter of great significance, the Government must step down. If a government loses an election it will also resign.

The Government prepares new laws, but also members of the Storting can propose new legislation. Major law reforms are usually developed by a committee of experts and representatives from different stakeholders in the matter. The Government sends its proposal to the Storting, where a Committee in the Storting scrutinizes it and sends their proposal to the Storting for decision. The Storting decides the act and sends the final bill to the King for approval (sanctioning).

The courts are independent and are organized in three levels as local courts (tingrett), regional appeal courts (lagmannsrett) and The Supreme Court (Høgsterett). The courts have the authority to evaluate whether legislation is unconstitutional or decisions from the executive branch are in accordance with the law.[7] The Supreme Court has tried a few cases related to petroleum licences.

The Constitution contains a general prohibition against legislation with retroactive effect[8] and a provision that expropriation only can take place with full compensation.[9] It is also a fundamental principle that any new duties or reduc-

---

[6]   An English version of The Norwegian Constitution available at www.stortinget .no/globalassets/pdf/english/constitutionenglish.pdf.
[7]   Grunnlova Section 89. Until 2015 this was based on customary constitutional law.
[8]   The Grunnlov Section 97.
[9]   The Grunnlov Section 105.

tion of rights of the citizens needs basis in a formal Act from the Parliament.[10] Recognition of private property and freedom of contracts are also fundamental principles in the Norwegian legal system, even if the Constitution does not mention this expressly.[11]

Norway has entered into a vast number of international treaties that limit the leeway of national authorities. The most important is the European Economic Area (EEA) Agreement that regulates the relationship to the European Union (EU). The EEA Agreement, which came into force 1 January 1994, integrates Norway and two other remaining European Free Trade Association (EFTA)-countries,[12] Iceland and Liechtenstein, into the European internal market. Central principles of the Treaty on the Functioning of the EU (TFEU), such as non-discrimination based on nationality, the free movement of goods and services, persons and capital, and the regulation of competition and state aid apply in the EEA. The EEA countries are bound by EU legal acts relevant to the area of the agreement. New EU-legislation is implemented in the EEA Agreement and Norwegian law, following a procedure laid out in the agreement.[13]

The EEA Agreement has led to substantial and, in many respects, fundamental changes in legislation and practice in Norway regarding the award of petroleum licences, and the content of such licences. It is fair to say that the EEA Agreement heralded a new era in Norwegian petroleum law and policy, although some of the changes were a result of changes in political and legal trends and would probably have been implemented without the EEA Agreement.

EU-directives directly relevant to petroleum licensing are Directive 94/22/ EC on conditions for granting and using authorizations for the prospection, exploration, and production of hydrocarbons (the hydrocarbon-directive) and Directive 2009/73/EC on the internal market for natural gas (the gas market directive). Norway has rejected Directive 2013/30/EU on the safety of offshore oil and gas operations as not geographically or substantially EEA relevant. Norway has now generally taken the position that the EEA Agreement does

---

[10] The Grunnlov Section 113, see also Sections 96, 97, and 98.

[11] Private property rights are indirectly protected in Grunnlova Section 97 and 105. The principle of freedom of contract follows from The Norwegian Code from 1687 Section 5-1-1 and 5-1-2, which are still in force.

[12] When the EEA Agreement was concluded, there were seven EFTA-members, but in 1995 Austria, Sweden and Finland became members of the EU. Switzerland decided not to join the EEA Agreement.

[13] See generally on the EEA Agreement, F Arnesen, H H Fredriksen, H P Graver, O Mestad and C Vedder, *Agreement on the European Economic Area. A Commentary*, NOMOS, 2018.

not apply on the continental shelf outside the Norwegian territory, 12 nautical miles from baseline. It is also clear that Norway sees the regulation of the directive as too much focused on minimum standards and with a "command & control"-approach that is inferior to the more functional approach developed in Norway since 1985. The Norwegian model is also based on a three-parties cooperation between authorities, the companies and the trade unions.[14] The EU has not accepted the Norwegian position and claims that Norway should implement the safety directive. It is, however, clear that Norway has taken the hydrocarbon-directive and the gas market directive also on the continental shelf.

Norway is also party to a vast number of international treaties that include minimum requirements on Norwegian law or practice even in the petroleum sector. The OSPAR-treaty regulating the dumping of waste in the North-East Atlantic will, for example, have a substantial impact on the disposal of petroleum installations that are no longer in use.[15]

To safeguard the protection of the citizens against injustice the 1967 general administrative act[16] regulates the process in administrative matters. The parties in a case that would lead to an individual decision regarding someone's rights or duties have the right to be heard, and the administration must clarify the relevant facts before the decision is made. Cases cannot be prepared or decided by people with a conflict of interest, and the administrative bodies shall make their decision based on relevant facts and considerations within the framework of the applicable legislation. Parties in the case can make a complaint and have the case tried by an agency on a higher level of the case before the decision is made. The decision must also be substantiated.[17]

---

[14] The extensive White paper St. meld. 12 (2017-2018) on safety in the Norwegian petroleum activity, does not mention Directive 2013/30/EU. See further on safety regulation in the Norwegian petroleum activity E Nordtveit, "Reguleringsmodellar for helse, miljø og tryggleik i høgrisikoverksemd", in S E Schütz, R Aarli & H S Aasen, Likestilling, barn og velferd. Rettsfelt i utvikling, Gyldendal 2020 p. 440.

[15] Convention for the protection of the marine environment of the North-East Atlantic, amended on 24 July 1998, see Annex III on the Prevention and Elimination of Pollution from Offshore Sources Article 5 on disposal of disused offshore pipelines and installations.

[16] Act 10 February 1967 on the procedure in administrative cases (the administrative law).

[17] The right to have the decision substantiated does not, however, apply in matters regarding the distribution of permissions or benefits between several parties (administrative act Section 24 second paragraph). This rule also applies in cases where the governmental body cannot substantiate the decision without revealing information that a party does not have the right to get according to Section 19 (e.g., technical or commercial information from other companies), Section 24 third paragraph. On this basis, it is not usual to substantiate decisions on the granting of petroleum licences.

A public body can overturn its decision as long as it is not to the detriment of someone who is a party to the decision before the party are informed about the decision or the decision must be considered void.[18] If the consideration for other private persons or public interests so warrants, a superior public body to the one making the decisions, can overturn the decision within three weeks from when the party was informed by the first decision.

Based on customary rules an administrative decision can also be reversed or changed to the detriment of a party out of consideration for weighty public interests which are considered more important than the interests that will suffer from the change.

The courts can, in most cases, scrutinize and overrule a decision by the administration. The courts can, however, not overrule the political discretion exercised by the authorities as far as it is within the limits of the law, in accordance with the procedural rules and no irrelevant interests have been considered. If the criteria for the decision are regulated more precisely in the law, the courts can overrule the decision if it finds that the requirements are not met.

3. DEVELOPMENT OF THE NORWEGIAN PETROLEUM REGULATION

3.1 The Factual and Political Background

Norway became a petroleum producer around 1970[19] at a stage when the country already was an industrialized welfare state with a developed legal and judicial system. The significant oil deposits that were discovered in the 1970s, seen in relation to the relatively small population, [20] made it clear that the petroleum sector would play a dominant role in the socio-economic development of the country.[21] This has led to a strong focus on petroleum policy and petroleum legislation.

During the reconstruction process after WWII, the industrial development was led by public authorities, and natural resources such as fish, forests, minerals, and hydropower played a dominant role in the industrial and economic development. The idea that the state should play an active role in natural

---

[18] The Administrative act Section 35.
[19] The first significant discovery of the Ekofisk-field towards the end of 1969. The Heimdal-field was discovered in 1968, but not considered commercial at the time.
[20] The population was 3.9 million in 1970 and is 5.36 million in 2020.
[21] In 2020 the petroleum sector represents 14 per cent of Norwegian GDP, 19 per cent of the state revenue and investments and 37 per cent of Norwegian export. The supply industry is not included in these numbers. The Sovereign Wealth Fund passed the value of 10,000 billion NOK towards the end of 2019.

resource governance and industrial development to secure welfare, employment and social and geographical balance, had broad political support. During the 1970s and early 1980s, there was stagnation in the economy, and especially shipping and shipbuilding were struggling.

The Norwegian petroleum era started towards the end of a long social-democratic hegemony in Norwegian politics. Norway was governed by a social-democratic (Labour Party) government from 1935 until 1965.[22] The economy was based on private property rights, freedom of contract and a market economy, combined with significant central planning and regulation and an active state in developing the Norwegian industry. A coalition of "non-socialist" parties took government after winning the election in 1965, but there was no substantial shift in policy in this regard.

The Labour Party again controlled the government from 1971 to 1972 and from 1973 to 1981 and came to lead the development of Norwegian petroleum policy and regulation during the first years of significant petroleum activity. Influential Labour Party members were appointed to central positions in public administration and in the State Oil Company "Statoil".

In line with many other western nations, the conservative government that took over in 1981 focused policy on deregulation and privatization and reduced the state interference in economic and industrial policy generally. This general redefinition of the relationship between state and market that has taken place in the Western World since the 1980s has also influenced the later development in Norway. The introduction of New Public Management and the general idea that politicians should focus on the prevailing principles and leave the day to day management and business decisions to professional management has also gained support in Norway. This doctrine has had some impact on the petroleum policy, especially in the reorganization of the state participation in petroleum activity in 1985, and the partial privatization of Statoil in 2003.

The Norwegian authorities saw the petroleum resources as a national resource that should be used as a basis for industrial, economic and social development in Norway. The role of the oil companies would be to help Norway achieve this. Norway had used the concession rules for the hydro-power industry as an instrument in the industrial and economic development of the country in the early 20th century and wanted to use also the newly discovered petroleum resources as an instrument for the further development of the Norwegian society.

---

[22] From 1940–45 the King and the Government was located in London. In 1963 the Labour Government was overthrown by a vote of no confidence in the Storting, but came back after three weeks.

Norway was therefore looking for a system that would give the state a basis for effective governance and control over the petroleum industry and facilitate industrial and commercial development in Norway. It would also have to make Norway attractive as a region for investment for the international companies that were needed to develop the Norwegian petroleum industry.

The principle for the development of the petroleum industry was discussed in the Storting on several occasions, and in a White Paper from the Committee for Industry in the Storting dated 14 June 1971, the committee presented ten main principles for Norwegian oil policy, which had broad political consent.[23] The essential principles in relation to the theme for this chapter were; national supervision and control of all activity on the Norwegian continental shelf, a wholly state-owned oil company to safeguard the state's commercial interests and pursue cooperation with domestic and foreign stakeholders and state involvement "at all reasonable levels" to contribute to the coordination of Norwegian interests. Other essential principles were independence from other nations in the supply of oil, development of new business activity based on the petroleum resources, necessary consideration for existing commercial activity and protection of nature and environment and landing of petroleum in Norway as the main rule.

These principles have had a substantial impact on Norwegian petroleum regulation and the development of the licence system and organization of the state participation in the petroleum activity. The main principles are also reflected in section 1-2, 2 of the *Norwegian Petroleum Activities Act* 1996 (NPA):

> Resource management of petroleum resources shall be carried out in a long-term perspective for the benefit of the Norwegian society as a whole. In this regard, the resource management shall provide revenues to the country. It shall contribute to ensuring welfare, employment, and an improved environment, as well as to the strengthening of Norwegian trade and industry and industrial development, and at the same time take due regard to regional and local policy considerations and other activities.

In the first licensing round in the 1960s, Norway had to offer better terms than the UK in order to attract foreign oil companies, since the prospects for finding petroleum on the Norwegian Continental Shelf (NCS) were not considered to be very good.[24] The discovery of the Cod field in 1968 and especially the Ekofisk field in 1969 changed this opinion and led to a more ambitious atti-

---

[23]   These principles have later been called "the 10 Oil Commandments".
[24]   Indeed in a letter in 1958 from the Norwegian Geological Survey to the Ministry of Foreign Affairs stated that "the chances of finding coal, oil or sulphur on the continental shelf off the Norwegian coast can be discounted".

tude from the Norwegian authorities. Norway also wanted an active role for the state and firm public control with the petroleum activity. In July 1972 the Storting decided to establish a wholly state-owned oil company to participate in the petroleum activity.[25]

3.2   Development of a Legal Framework and Licence System

Development of the legal framework and the petroleum licence system was a continuous process in the first two decades as Norwegian authorities gained experience with the effects of the regulations and the first licences and information of the early discoveries emerged.[26]

The basis for the later development of the legal framework and the licences was an act adopted in 1963 as a response to requests from international oil companies to do exploration for petroleum in Norwegian sea areas.[27] A declaration of sovereignty of the continental shelf was also adopted and the Continental Shelf Act Section 2 declared state ownership to natural resources on and in the continental shelf. The Act gave the King the authority to award licences for exploration of the natural resources in and on the continental shelf and to give further rules. This authority was used to develop a comprehensive and detailed regulation of the Norwegian petroleum activity in the first 20 years of the petroleum activity[28] until the Storting adopted a bill on petroleum activities in 1985.[29] The NPA repealed the 1985-Act in 1996.[30] In reality the

---

[25]   The company was called "The Oil Company of the Norwegian State", known as "Statoil". On the 15 May 2018, the company changed its name to Equinor. I will use the name Statoil in relation to historical events, but Equinor in relation to contemporary issues.

[26]   A permanent committee called "The Norwegian Petroleum Committee" (in Norwegian "Statens oljeråd" or "Oljerådet"), consisting of legal and other experts was established in 1965 and functioned until 1980, with the task to advise the authorities in the development of rules and regulations related to petroleum. The work with the development of petroleum legislation was an ongoing process until the first petroleum act was adopted in 1985.

[27]   Act 21 June 1963 no. 12 (Continental Shelf Act). Since 1985 this regulates scientific surveys and research of other natural resources than petroleum and mineral deposits, which now are regulated in NPA and in Act 22 March 2019 no. 7 on submerged minerals.

[28]   First by Royal decree 9. April 1965 (the 1965-regulation), which was repealed by a new regulation by Royal decree 8. December 1972 (the 1972-regulation).

[29]   Act 22. March 1985, no. 11.

[30]   The current legislation which is relevant for the petroleum activity consists of the NPA and around 50 regulations issued by the King or the relevant ministries. The most crucial provision concerning the issue studied in this chapter is Regulation 27. June 1997 no. 653 (the Petroleum regulation).

legislative power of this important area was delegated to the executive branch for 20 years, but the Storting discussed the principles for the petroleum policy on several occasions based on reports to the Storting from the Government ("Stortingsmelding").[31] In reality Norway needed this experience to make a permanent bill for the petroleum activity.

As the basis for the design of the Norwegian licensing system, Jens Evensen[32] was given the task to investigate how petroleum activity was organized in other countries and to provide recommendations. He delivered a report to the Ministry of Industry in 1971.[33]

In his report, he was sceptical of the concession contracts often used in petroleum activities, because they put the resource owner in a weak position. He saw it necessary to invite foreign companies with the required financial and technological capacity to develop Norwegian petroleum resources, but it was also essential to find legal arrangements that gave the state a strong position without creating tensions or conflict with the companies. He emphasized the need to balance the legitimate demand of the companies for the protection of investments and economic rights, with Norway's interests as a host state. He was attracted by the new joint venture contracts with state participation that some countries had developed. He also made positive comments about the product sharing agreements used by Indonesia.

He emphasized that Norway should not go into contracts that bind future legislation. He also saw it as imperative that in addition to legal regulation of the petroleum activity, Norway should gain control of the industrial and commercial part of the activity by participating directly in the operation (participatory intervention).[34] To achieve this, he recommended establishing

---

[31]   See from this period Stortingsmelding No 95 (1969–70), No 76 (1970–71), No 25 (1973–74), No 30 (1973–74), No 46 (1979–80), No 53 (1979–80), No 123 (1980–81), No 40 1982–83) No 73 (1983–84) and No 32 (1984–85).

[32]   Jens Evensen was at the time Director-General in the Ministry of Foreign Affairs, Legal department and head of the Norwegian Petroleum Committee. He later became Norwegian chief negotiator for the United Nations Convention on the Law of the Seas and was minister for trade and then for the law of the sea issues 1974–78. He was a judge in the International Tribunal in Haag 1985–94.

[33]   See the report "Oversikt over oljepolitiske spørsmål, bl. a. på grunnlag av utenlandsk oljelovgiving og utenlandsk konsesjonspolitikk. Betenkning utarbeidet etter oppdrag fra Industridepartementet," printed in Innstillinger og betenkninger fra kongelige og parlamentariske kommisjoner, departementale komitéer m.m., 2. del, 1971, p. 9. The organisational questions are discussed on pp. 64 ff. The report is also printed as book in English, Jens Evensen, "Report on oil policy problems viewed against the background of oil legislation and concession policies of other nations", Oslo Ministry of Industry, 1971.

[34]   As defined by Nelsen in Brent F Nelsen, *The State Offshore: Petroleum, Politics and State Intervention on the British and Norwegian Continental Shelves* (Praeger, 1990), p. 9.

a state-owned oil company that could take care of the state's commercial interests, as a participant in joint ventures with the private companies. Evensen's report did not provide a definite recommendation but pointed in the direction of the joint venture agreements that had been developed in international petroleum activity as a possible instrument to secure state participation, without giving a very detailed proposal for how this should be done.

A system with a combination of production licences and joint operating agreements with state participation was developed.[35] Licences are awarded to a group of companies composed by the ministry. This is done on the condition that the members of the group enter into a joint operating agreement formulated by the ministry and attached to the licence as a condition.[36] This system made it possible for the state to participate in the activity as one of the partners in the joint venture. In addition to give the state a part of the revenue, this opened up the opportunity for "governance from within" through participatory intervention.

Statoil was a partner in almost every licence awarded 1973–94. Its participation shares were up to 50 per cent and in some cases a "sliding scale" that made it possible for Statoil to increase its share up to 70–80 per cent after production had started, was agreed. In the first years a clause on carried interest for Statoil was usual. The other partners covered Statoil's part of the exploration costs until a discovery was declared commercial. It could be a "carried forward" interest in the meaning that the expenses later were covered by the production, but in some licences, the other partners carried the state's costs completely.[37] Statoil also was tasked with ensuring that the licensees complied with rules, regulations and Norwegian policy goals, and that the Norwegian industry got the opportunity to participate in tenders for delivery of goods and services for the petroleum industry.

From the first licensing rounds, it has been a clear policy that production licences can only be awarded to Norwegian corporations, registered under

---

[35]   See more detailed on the state participation E Nordtveit, E Nordtveit, "Regulation of the Norwegian Upstream Petroleum Sector", in T Hunter, *Regulation of the Upstream Petroleum Sector*, Edward Elgar, 2015 pp. 154–56.

[36]   Initially, these agreements were called "state participation agreements" (Norwegian "statsdeltakelsesavtaler"). From round 10B in 1981, the Norwegian term is "Samarbeidsavtale" which directly translated means "Cooperation agreement". I will use the English term "joint operating agreement" or "joint venture".

[37]   See the detailed presentation in A Frihagen, *Forelesninger i oljerett II. Statsdeltakelsesavtalene – utvikling og standardisering* Universitetsforlaget 1982 (Lectures in oil law: The state participation agreements – development and standardization. With a summary in English), pp. 51–55 and 134–35 (English summary). (The entire English summary is on pp.118 – 150).

Norwegian law and with their head office in Norway.[38] Foreign companies have to establish a subsidiary company in Norway that could be awarded the licence. The foreign company then has to make a guarantee for the fulfilment of the obligations of the Norwegian subsidiary (Morselskapsgaranti), since the subsidiary normally would not have financial capacity to cover the costs of the operation on the Norwegian shelf and possible liability as a result of the activity.[39] After the EEA Agreement, this no longer applies to companies from the EEA.[40]

The state governs petroleum activities through legislation, licence conditions and by its participation in the licence groups. Prior to the EEA Agreement this was important in promoting Norwegian industry's objectives of using contracts for the supply of goods and services to the petroleum industry to build Norwegian competence. It was mandatory to use Norwegian goods and services when they were competitive in price and quality, first as "a gentleman's agreement" between the state and the companies in 1965, and later as a direct condition in the licences (1969) and finally in legislation.[41] A special department in the Ministry of Oil and Energy, the "Office for goods and services" was established in 1978, with responsibility for the procurement policy. It was also a criterion for awarding new licences that the applicants earlier had cooperated with Norwegian industry and supported research and development in Norwegian industry. Starting with round 10B in 1986 the standard joint operating agreement has been largely the same.[42] A revision took place in

---

[38]   NPA Section 3-3.

[39]   In a recent decision by the Supreme Court (HR-2020-611-A), the court found that the standard guarantee did not cover the state's claim of repayment of tax credit that were obtained by false pretentions. The guarantee only covered claims that the licensee has undertaken in the role as such. Claims incurred outside the licence was not covered.

[40]   NPA Section 3-3 where it is said that the rule that production licences "may be granted to a body corporate established in conformity with Norwegian legislation and registered in the Norwegian Register of Business Enterprises," does not apply "insofar as other requirements are not applicable pursuant international agreements" (translation by the Petroleum Directorate). This translation might be misleading. The Norwegian text says, directly translated, that the requirement only applies insofar as other requirements does not follow from international agreements. "International agreements" in this context means the EEA Agreement.

[41]   See 1972-regulation Section 54 and the 1985 Petroleum act, Section 54.

[42]   The Norwegian term is "Samarbeidsavtalen" (directly translated "The Cooperation Agreement"). The standard licence, the Joint Operating Agreement and the Accounting agreement are available in English on the homepage of the Ministry of Oil and Energy: www.regjeringen.no/en/find-document/dep/OED/Laws-and-rules-2/ Rules/konsesjonsverk/id748087.

2007, and some changes have been made to meet new situations, such as the adaption to the Natural Gas Market Directive in 2002.[43]

In 1985 the conservative government that had taken over in 1981 reorganized the state participation by splitting Statoil's shares in two and around 50 per cent was organized as the States Direct Financial Interest (SDFI). Statoil kept the rest and was given the task to manage the SDFI-share and to market the SDFI-share of the petroleum, but the revenue went directly to the state treasury. The purpose of the reduction of Statoil shares was to reduce Statoil's political power in Norway.[44]

Due to the partial privatization of Statoil in 2003, the company could no longer manage the state's participating share in the joint ventures. A new wholly state-owned company, "Petoro AS" was established in 2001 in order to manage the state's participation interest in the joint operating agreements.[45] The special treatment of Statoil and also the other Norwegian companies (Hydro Petroleum and Saga Petroleum)[46] in granting of production licences, ended when the EEA Agreement came into force in 1994.[47] Equinor is now competing for licences on equal terms as other applicants from the EEA, and Norwegian industry competes for supply contracts on equal terms as foreign suppliers.

3.3   Award of Petroleum Licences

The procedure for award of petroleum licences might have an impact on the evaluation on whether they are seen as an administrative act or as a form

---

[43]   See more detailed E Nordtveit, "Between Market and Public Interests – Organisation and Management of the Norwegian System for Sale and Transportation of Natural Gas", in K H Søvig, S E Schütz and Ø Rasmussen, *Undring og erkjennelse*, Fagbokforlaget, 2015 p. 469–82.

[44]   See T Hunter, *Legal Regulatory Framework for the Sustainable Extraction of Australian Offshore Petroleum Resources. A Critical Functional Analysis*. Dissertation for the degree of Philosphia doctor (PhD), 2010 p. 215.

[45]   NPA chapter 11 sets some special rules for the company. The income from the sale of petroleum still goes directly into the treasury, and the Storting grants funds for Petoro's operational costs and investments as part of the state budget.

[46]   These two companies no longer exist, as Saga was dissolved in 1999 as a result of economic problems. After "political signals" from the minister of oil and energy that the authorities wanted a "Norwegian solution", the assets of Saga Petroleum was divided between Statoil and Hydro Petroleum. Statoil and Hydro Petroleum merged in 2007.

[47]   See further below on the impact of the EEA Agreement on the criteria for granting of licences.

of contract.[48] It has for example been argued that if the licensees accept the conditions by signing the licence document that is a sign of a contractual relationship or something similar to a contractual relationship.[49]

Most licences are distributed in licensing rounds, where identified areas are announced for application.[50] Since 2003 a particular round of licences for mature areas especially in the North Sea[51] has been published once a year to make it possible to obtain licences in "mature" areas with relatively well-known geology.[52]

Under the 1994 Hydrocarbon Directive, access to petroleum resources is enabled based on competition where the licence is awarded to the most competent applicant. Any preferential treatment based on nationality or ownership is not allowed.[53] The state can, however, retain a share of the licence.[54] A licence is awarded by the King in Council on the basis of a discretionary evaluation of relevant objective factors laid out in section 10 and section 11 of the Petroleum Regulations 1997. The granting of licences through the bidding process has not been seriously considered since the technological challenges arising from climate conditions have always made the applicant's ability to master the weather conditions an essential factor in the grant of a licence, along with geological competence.

Another critical element of the Norwegian licensing system has been that licences are awarded to a group of companies, composed by the ministry by

---

[48]   See more generally about the licensing procedure E Nordtveit, Regulation of the Norwegian Upstream Petroleum Sector, in T Hunter (ed.), *Regulation of the Upstream Petroleum Sector. A Comparative Study of Licensing and Concession Systems*, Edward Elgar Publishing, 2015, pp. 148–53.

[49]   S Brækhus, *Petroleum production licences on the Norwegian Part of the Continental Shelf*, 2d ed., North Sea Operators Committee, 1975. His view has been heavily critizised by other authors and must be considered a mistake, see footnote 84 below.

[50]   The published fields have to be in an area that is opened for petroleum activity in accordance with NPA Section 3-1.

[51]   Known as the Award of Predefined Area (APA) Round for areas in the North Sea that were previously subject to a production licence and then relinquished. It was under this licensing system that the Avaldes and Avalsnes fields were discovered, then unitized to become the giant Johan Sverdrup Field.

[52]   For further details see E Nordtveit, "Regulation of the Norwegian Upstream Petroleum Sector", in T Hunter, *Regulation of the Upstream Petroleum Sector*, Edward Elgar, 2015, pp. 150–51.

[53]   See more on the criteria for the award of licences in section 10 and 11 of the Petroleum Regulations 1997.

[54]   NPA Section 3-6 explicitly says that the state might participate in the activity. The state does not need a production licence, see NPA Section 1-3.

companies that have submitted individual applications.[55] The purpose is to design groups that incorporate the technology, skills, competence, and financial strength needed for each of the licence areas. This practice also strengthens the public governance and control of the activity as it makes it possible to obtain information from all the participants and to make sure different ideas for field development and other issues emerge. The oil companies generally also are interested in joint ventures to spread the economic risk, but only in a few cases has a licence been awarded to a group of applicants. The hydrocarbon directive accepts that this practice of joint venturers selected by the authorities should continue.[56] The same is the case for state participation.[57]

A licence awarded to a group of companies will be made on the condition that they enter into a standard joint venture agreement and an accounting agreement within 30 days after the award of the licence. Two alternative standard joint operating agreements are adopted, depending on whether the licence is awarded with state participation or without state participation. A separate contract regulates the participation share, voting rules, and operatorship of the licence.[58] The licence determines which of the licensees are appointed as operator for the field. The rights and duties and the liability of the operator are regulated in the joint operating agreement.

The award of a licence is based on a total evaluation of the applicant, as a discretionary administrative decision.[59] The decision to award a licence is based on relevant and objective criteria, including technical and financial capacity, the applicant's proposals for the project, any earlier lack of efficiency and responsibility displayed in operations under previous licences.[60] Such a decision is considered to be within the administrative "free discretion", and therefore cannot be overruled by the courts.

---

[55] Group applications have been accepted in a few cases. See further E Nordtveit 2015, pp. 152–53.

[56] The hydrocarbon-directive article 5, 1 para 3 states that where "the competent authorities determine the composition of an entity to which they may grant an authorization, they shall make that determination based on objective and non-discriminatory criteria".

[57] Hydrocarbon-directive article 6, 3 para 2.

[58] The standard licence documents and standard contracts used as licence conditions are found at www.norskpetroleum.no/en/framework/the-petroleum-act-and-the -licensing-system/.

[59] NPA Section 3-5, see the hydrocarbon-directive Article 5-1, 1.

[60] Hydrocarbon-directive Article 5, 1.

3.4   Conditions for Production Licences

Licences can be awarded pursuant to certain conditions.[61] The NPA and the Petroleum Regulations Section 11 give a legal basis for some of the more essential and wide-ranging conditions that routinely are connected to the licences. The general principle is that a licence condition has to be substantiated in need to secure that petroleum activity in the licence area is conducted prudently in order to safeguard relevant considerations.[62] Additional conditions such as work obligation or mother company guarantee for subsidiaries (Morselskap Provisions) are regulated separately in the NPA.[63]

A production licence is awarded for up to ten years ("initial period") and on the condition that the licensee carries out a specified work program within certain time limits, which might include drilling of wells, geological and geophysical surveys, etc.[64] A licensee who has fulfilled his work obligation and other conditions for the licence can apply for prolongation for parts of the licence area where discoveries are made, upon submission of a "plan for development and operation which has been submitted to the Ministry of Petroleum and Energy". The Ministry determines the extension of the area comprised of the extended Production Licence period in accordance with the application.[65] Special conditions can be stipulated for the individual licence, for example, to avoid vulnerable areas within the licence area, special consideration for fishing activity in the area etc., duty to report cultural heritage, shipwrecks etc.

4.   THE LEGAL CHARACTER OF THE PRODUCTION LICENCE – ADMINISTRATIVE RIGHT, CONTRACTUAL, PROPERTY RIGHT OR A HYBRID?

4.1   Introduction

The arrangement between the state and the holders of petroleum licences on the Norwegian continental shelf is, as demonstrated above, very complex and it is not made formally clear whether it is an administrative authority or a contract.

The King's right to award licences is based on legislation, not on the state's position as owner of the petroleum resource. The duties of companies are partly

---

[61]   NPA Section 3-3 first paragraph.
[62]   Petroleum regulation Section 11 first and second paragraph.
[63]   NPA Sections 3–7 (Mother company guarantee) and 3–8 (Work obligation).
[64]   Standard Licence form article 4.
[65]   Standard licence form article 4.

regulated by the licence conditions and partly in the legislation. In addition, the state influences decisions in the joint venture groups through participation, based on the joint venture agreement, which is a part of the licensing regime.

The arrangement has also changed over time, from a system with substantial public control and emphasis on national interests, to a more liberal market-based system, where participants are competing for licences based on objective criteria, although considerable participatory intervention remains. This is attributable partly to the EEA Agreement and partly to market changes.[66]

A contract, in its traditional meaning, is built on the private autonomy of the legal subjects, that gives them the ability to bind themselves towards another legal subject, while an administrative decision is based on the sovereignty of the state over the citizens and competence to give rights to or impose duties on the citizens. A licence or a concession from the state does not quite fit into this scheme. In concessions or licences for natural resource exploration and extraction, the licensee is obliged to make some "minimum" effort in order to locate and start production of petroleum.[67] Beyond that, it is up to the licensee how much he is willing to invest in a field. The fees he has to pay for the licence and for the acreage are intended to give incentives to give up areas of little interest, and cannot be seen as a payment for the licence itself, as in an auctioning system.

The company are free to decide whether a field should be developed, and the state has no authority to compel a licensee to start petroleum production.[68] Furthermore, there is no negotiation for such activities. Rather, the state sets the terms for the licence, and it is up to the applicants to accept them or not. Details in the work obligation or other issues might be discussed, but not so significant that this can be considered a contract in the usual sense.

The objective of the state is that its petroleum resources shall be discovered and produced in order to make revenue for the state. For the companies, the objective is to get access to the petroleum resources to make a profit. A rela-

---

[66]   See more generally on the development of Norwegian petroleum policy from the first phase of strong "political entrepreneurship" to a more market oriented approach as a result of lower profit margins in the mid-1980s OG Austvik, "The Norwegian Petroleum Experience as an Example?", *International Shale Gas and Oil Journal*, 2014, pp. 18–30 (esp. pp. 19–21).

[67]   NPA Section 3-8 gives the King the authority to "impose on the licensee a specific work obligation for the area covered by the production licence". Despite the wording, it seems clear that this has to be done in the licence, and cannot be done after the licence is accepted by the companies, see the Standard Licence document 4.

[68]   It is known that the discovery of the Ekofisk was made because the Norwegian state was not willing to relieve the licensee from the obligation to drill the last hole that was included in the work programme.

tionship like this could obviously have been established by contract, and many countries regulate the relationship between the state and the companies by contract. In the Norwegian system, it is, however, more appropriate to define the licence as an administrative decision. Even so, the same considerations that substantiate the binding force of contracts are also relevant for licences where the licensee is supposed to make huge investments in an activity that involves great financial risk. When the state invites companies to apply for a licence to carry out this activity and sets out the conditions and a legal framework for this, it is rather obvious that this gives the companies reasonable expectations about the framework and the conditions for the activity, that the state cannot be free to change by altering the conditions and the framework at any time, thereby imbuing contractual elements into the arrangements. It is also a question if the licence gives the companies a right that will be regarded as a kind of property right or "possession" under the EHRC Protocol 1-1. The state on the other hand needs to be able to develop the society by new regulation that might also influence the petroleum activity, like stricter environmental regulation or stronger protection of workers' rights.

The question is what legal norm can be formulated for the state's right to intervene, in the capacity of the legislator, in a manner that will negatively impact the economic return on the investments the companies have made. One needs to distinguish between different possible interventions. One situation is if the authorities make a direct change in the licence. This would have to be evaluated in relation to the customary rules on overturning administrative decisions that are mentioned in section 2 above. A change of the licence can only be envisaged in cases where the changes are minimal compared to the social interest in making the change or have such connection to the public interest that the licensee could not accept that it would be exhaustively regulated in the licence.[69]

Another situation can be if the state makes changes in the taxation system or taxation level in order to increase the total government take or changes legislation that is directly or separately relevant for petroleum activity, like the safety regulation or other issues that increases the costs for the companies.

A third situation is when new legislation of more general character also influences the situation of the companies, for example new regulation of carbon emission or general taxation to cover expenses caused by a pandemic.

---

[69]   JF Bernt, "Striden om oljeutvinningskonsesjonenes rettslige status – noen forvaltningsrettslige og statsrettslige grunnproblemer", *Lov og Rett*, 1980, pp. 323–32, see pp. 331–32.

The question of the character of the petroleum licences arose concerning the issue whether the 1972-regulation[70] also should apply to the licences awarded under the 1965-regulation.[71] This case ended before the Supreme Court in 1985.[72] The question to be determined was whether the regulation of payment deadlines for royalty from production under the 1972-regulation also could apply to licences awarded under the 1965-regulation. According to the 1965-regulation, royalty from the production should be paid for every six months of production, with a payment deadline of 30 days after the end of each six months. The 1972-regulation changed this to payment every third month and 15 days' deadline after the end of each three months. The state claimed that the new regulation should also apply to licences awarded under the 1965-regulation. This led to a loss of interest for the licensees of the Ekofisk-field (licence no 018) and they sued the state, claiming the new regulation could not apply to older licences. The companies argued that the new regulation would be a violation of their rights, even if the conditions in the licence itself were not changed. In the licence, it was said that it was awarded "on the conditions following from the [Royal] resolution,[73] at any time issued provisions according to it, and beyond this on the conditions established [in the licence]".

The Supreme Court solved the case by an interpretation of the wording of the 1972-regulation and did not take a stand on the issue whether the licence was a contract or an administrative decision. The court stated that even if it was an administrative decision, it could not be changed freely to the detriment of the licensees. The first Justice in her vote stated:

> I do not take a stand on the question if at least some provisions in production licence no. 018 is a part of a contract between the state and the licensees or if the licence in its entirety must be seen as an administrative decision where the provisions on royalties are included as a part of the conditions for the rights awarded in the licence.

---

[70]   Royal decree 9. April 1965.
[71]   Royal decree 8. December 1972.
[72]   The case is reported in Rt. 1985 p. 1355. A broader presentation and analysis of the case can be found in Krohn et al., *Norwegian Petroleum Law* 1978 part 2, O Mestad, "The Ekofisk Royalty Case: Construction of Regulations to Avoid Retroactivity", *ICSID Review – Foreign Investment Law Journal*, Volume 2, Issue 1, Spring 1987, pp. 139–51 and O Mestad, "Acquisition of Natural Resource Interests by the State: the Norwegian Ekofisk Royalty Case", *Journal of Energy & Natural Resources Law*, Volume 5 1987, pp. 82–95. See also comment on the case from A Frihagen in *4. Journal of Energy & Natural Resources Law* 203 (1986) and Dalgaard Knudsen, "Exploitation Concessions: Contracts or Permits?—Contribution from the Norwegian Phillops Ekofisk Case" in *5. Journal of Energy & Natural Resources Law*, 203, 1987, p. 165.
[73]   The 1965-regulation.

For the interpretation of the 1972-regulation, in this case, I see it as sufficient to ascertain that the production licence 018 must include limitations in the state's access to tighten some of the stipulated provisions. I then build on an overall assessment of the character of the negotiations preceding the resolution and the licences, the wording of the licence, especially the general clause that I have cited on the conditions [see previous paragraph above (author's remark)], and the opinions of both the licensees and the negotiators from the state ...[74]

The justice also said that in her opinion "the character of the negotiations and the parties' assumptions are elements that have to be taken into account in the assessment of whether the state is allowed to change the conditions".[75] In the interpretation, she put some weight on communications between the parties. It was documented that there had been a discussion between the expert committee and the ministry on to what extent the 1972 regulation should have retroactive effect. The result had been that the question of retroactivity had been left open and it was said from the Norwegian Petroleum Committee that one should be "careful" in applying the new regulation on earlier licences.[76]

The legal character of the licences was also discussed concerning the question of the introduction of a separate tax on petroleum activity in 1975. The oil embargo in 1973 led to a sharp rise in oil prices from the end of 1973, giving the oil companies super-profits that were not foreseen when the earlier petroleum licences were awarded. The Norwegian government appointed an expert committee to come up with a proposal for a taxation system that was adapted to the new situation. Based on the committee's recommendation, an act on taxation of income from submerged petroleum deposits was adopted.[77] The act introduced a separate tax on income from petroleum activity on the continental shelf of 50 per cent in addition to ordinary company tax.[78] The companies obtained a legal opinion that argued that the proposal was a violation of contractual rights established by the licences.[79] This led to a debate between other

---

[74]   Rt. 1985 p. 1355 on p. 1373 para 5. Translated by author.

[75]   Rt. 1985 p. 1355 on p. 1373 para 6. See also para 7 where she states: "I cannot agree on the state's argument that the letter ... from the Norwegian Oil Committee is irrelevant. In any case, on the basis of their request for clarification, the oil companies had to interpret the letter so that the state would not change the the conditions in the resolution unless it was positively provided for in the text of the resolution." Translated by author.

[76]   The Ministry of Industry in the reasons to the resolution, referred to in Rt. 1985 p. 1355 on p. 1376 last para.

[77]   Act 13 June 1975 no. 35.

[78]   See the proposal to the Storting in Ot. prp. nr. 26 (1974–75).

[79]   S Brækhus, *Petroleum production licences on the Norwegian Part of the Continental Shelf,* 2d ed., North Sea Operators Committee, 1975.

legal scholars on the character of petroleum licences and the limitation of the state's ability to bind its legislative power for the future in a contract.[80]

The question if the new taxation rules conflicted with the ban on legislation with retroactive effect in the Norwegian constitution,[81] was addressed in a memorandum from the Legal department in the Ministry of Justice.[82] In the memorandum, it is pointed out that many forms of activity can be carried out only with permission from the authorities. The person that has such permission can expect to be able to carry out the activity, but also that there are limitations in the right for the government to change the conditions in the permission or licence. On the other hand, the fact that a person is given the authorization to carry out a business or an activity that is otherwise forbidden, will in itself not limit the legislator to enact new general legislation which influences the activity.[83] The state has a function to develop legislation in line with the general development and a person with a licence to some activity cannot be exempted from this. The petroleum activity was a new industry with a strong influence of the Norwegian society, and the companies therefore ought to reasonably expect the need for further regulation or adaptation to unexpected or unknown circumstances.

The implementation of a new regulation had to be fair and not intervene in the company's economic expectations in a manner that is unbalanced in relation to the negotiations and preconditions and expectations that have been expressed. Also, the conditions for the concession and the risk and commitments the licensee has undertaken based on this must be taken into account. The licensee should be able to keep the gain of an increase in prices or other development as far as this was a normal development. The development in 1973–74 had created a profit far beyond anything that had been connected to

---

[80] CA Fleischer, "Statsrett, oljeskatt og juridiske mistak", *Lov og Rett*, 1976, p. 398, JF Bernt, "Striden om oljeutvinningskonsesjonenes rettslige status - noen forvaltningsrettslige og statsrettslige grunnproblemer", *Lov og Rett*, 1980, pp. 323–32, K Kaasen, "Statsdeltakelsesavtalen i norsk petroleumsvirksomhet: Kontraktsrettslig form, konsesjonsrettslig innhold – eller omvendt" in *Tidsskrift for rettsvitenskap*, 1984, s. 372–411. English language presentation of the Norwegian discussion can be found in J Rein, "The Petroleum Production Licence as Contract", *Marius*, 28, 1977 and TC Daintith, "Pacta Sund Servanda and the Licensing and Taxation of North Sea Oil Production", *Marius*, 33, 1978, pp. 8–15. A comparative study of the legal character of petroleum licences is found in T Daintith (ed.), *The Legal Character of Petroleum Licences: A Comparative Study*, University of Dundee, Centre for Petroleum and Mineral Law Studies and Energy and Natural Resources Committee of the International Bar Association, 1982. The Norwegian situation is presented by Jon A Rein l.c. pp. 185–99.
[81] Grunnlova Section 97.
[82] See Ot. prp. nr. 26 (1974–75), Attachment 1.
[83] An example could be that a permit to operate a taxi or an aquaculture plant will not in itself limit the state's right to impose new requirements in the business.

exploration for and extraction of petroleum and had nothing to do with the situation in Norway or the North Sea or traditional prospects for gain or loss attached to petroleum extraction. Given the whole situation, the department concluded it would not be a violation of the constitution to increase the taxation of the income from petroleum activity, even if it happened by the introduction of a separate tax on petroleum activity and not by changing the general taxation of commercial activity.

The case on the special tax was not tried before the court, but the legal department's evaluation of the matter seems convincing seen in the light of previous court practice. The taxation would only apply to future income. Even if the licence had been seen as a contract, it would not be able to bind the future legislative power of the Storting. The Norwegian courts have been very reluctant to accept that the authorities can restrict the future exercise of its competence by contract. No promise regarding future tax rules had been made, and such a guarantee could not be implied in the licence. An agreement could not bind the Storting without being approved by the Storting. The oil companies accepted this outcome and did not bring the case to the courts.

The royalty-case involved the question of whether the provision in the 1965-regulation[84] should be considered a part of the licence conditions, even if it was not a part of the licence conditions directly. The Supreme Court deemed the provision in the regulation as a part of the conditions for the licence, even though it was not included in the licence document. It is not clear what the result would have been if the 1972 regulation had been given reciprocal effect, but the argument of the Supreme Court indicates it might have regarded this as a violation of the section 97 of the Norwegian Constitution.

The case about the special taxation is an example of new legislation with a clear purpose to change the division of the revenue between the state and the companies. It was, on the other hand, not a change of the licence conditions, as tax issues are not regulated in the licence. The special tax could be accepted because events beyond reasonable expectation and normal market development had dramatically changed the value of the petroleum resources. The legal department, and most of the scholars that took part in the debate, were of the opinion that this had to be accepted by the companies, due to the special situation. One could argue that this situation would also constitute a change of the conditions behind an agreement, and could have led to claims of revision of the agreement about the right to exploit the natural resources owned by one of the parties.

---

[84]   Royal decree 9. April 1965.

An important issue in this relation is also the question of whether the state can bind its future legislative power by contract.[85] Norwegian courts have, as mentioned, been very reluctant to accept such binding of public authority, especially the legislative power of the Storting. The public authority shall be exercised in accordance with the law and the constitution and not be subject to bargaining. Exceptions are still possible, and it might be that the development goes in the direction of greater acceptance for such agreements. A condition will still be that it is a clear commitment, and if the Storting shall be bound by it, it also has to be accepted by the Storting. The Government cannot bind the authority of the Storting by contract.

There is not room here to go into the comprehensive discussion on when the state has the right to make changes in the legislation with retroactive effect, or what retroactive effect really is. The discussion has continued in relation to other issues than petroleum licences. It also seems that the frontlines have shifted a bit. It is difficult to formulate a more precise norm, than that the question of which changes the government can make, depends on an extensive evaluation of the public interests involved on one side, weighed against the business interests involved, the investments that are made based on the licence and the expectations the licensees reasonably could build on the negotiations and statements from the state.[86]

An indication on which criteria the courts would use is the Supreme Court Decision from 2013 in a case regarding restrictions in concessions for fishing trawlers.[87] In 2005 the then conservative government introduced so-called "structural quotas"[88] for the fishing fleet operating in the open sea.[89] There were no time limits for the quotas. In 2007, after a change of government, this was changed, so the quotas were limited to a certain number of years. The time limit was also given retroactive effect on already awarded quotas. A fishing boat owner who had his quotas limited to 25 years sued the state but lost in the Supreme Court. The case was tried by the full Supreme Court as it involved a constitutional question. The court was divided in its decision as 11 judges

---

[85] See J Andenæs and A Fliflet, *Norsk statsforfatningsrett* 11th ed., Universitetsforlaget, 2017 pp. 599–601.

[86] See the citations from Rt. 1985 p. 1355 above.

[87] HR-2013-P reported in Rt. 2013 s. 1345. The question of protection for concession rights has been discussed in several decisions by the Supreme Court in the later years, but not all of them seems relevant for petroleum licences. The general rule is that the constitutional protection of concession rights depends on the character of the right.

[88] Meaning that the purpose with the quotas was to reduce the capacity and number of vessels in the fishing fleet.

[89] Royal decree 4 March 2005 no. 193.

voted for the result and six judges found that the change was a violation of the Constitution article 97 and EHRC Protocol 1-1.

The majority found that the question was whether the interference would be considered unfair or unreasonable. The economic loss would be relatively small when tax depreciation rules were taken into account. The effects would take place in a distant future, and the new regime for structural change would also give the fish boat owner some benefits. The state should have considerable leeway to regulate the framework for the fishing fleet. The majority found that the regulation did not violate the protection for property rights in the EHRC Protocol 1-1. The minority held that the shipowner had got a position that was similar to a proprietary right and was protected and that the interference was unreasonable. The public interests in the case were not, in their view, strong enough to justify the intervention.

The general norm expressed by the majority in the case, "unfair or unreasonable",[90] might lead to a different outcome in relation to petroleum licences than in relation to the fishing quotas. The investments and the economic risk taken is of a greater magnitude in the petroleum activity and the state ownership of the petroleum might give the petroleum licence a stronger contractual character. It must be rather clear that the state could not for example change the time limit for a petroleum licence without compensation, at least not unless it was based in very urgent need for regulation. As the petroleum licences can be transferred to a new owner and also mortgaged, the argument that this is a proprietary right might be a bit stronger than for fishing quotas.

There seems to be a development also in Norwegian practice and the protection of property and established positions seems to have become stronger in Norway in the last decades than they were in the 1970s, probably as a result of international influence especially from the EHRC.

5.   DYNAMIC DEVELOPMENT OF PETROLEUM LICENCES

Norwegian authorities have seen it as essential to give the companies operating in Norway a stable framework in order to make the continental shelf attractive

---

[90]   The criteria in international bilateral or multilateral investment treaties (for example Energy Charter Treaty article 10. 1.) are generally formulated as "fair and equitable treatment" ("The FET-Standard"), see C McLachlan, L Shore and M Weininger, *International Investment Arbitration. Substantive Principles*, Oxford University Press, 2d ed. 2017 p. 31 and chapters 7 and 8. The further content of this principle has been developed by a large body of decisions from arbitration panels. The impression is maybe that these are a bit more investor friendly than the Norwegian interpretation of the Grunnlov s. 97, but it is difficult to judge based on the decisions that exists.

for investment. In situations where it has been necessary to find new solutions and change the regulation of petroleum activity like the organization of sale and transport of natural gas in 2001, this has been achieved by cooperation and negotiations.[91] In some cases, the companies have been summoned to a meeting in order to find a solution. Special discussion forums have been established to discuss new issues and find solutions by mutual consent.[92] The accounting agreement and the joint venture agreement was revised in 2007. "The Industrial Forum" was established as a meeting-place between all operators of Norwegian fields to develop good governance and improve effectiveness in the running of the fields, led by the state-owned company Petoro AS.

The petroleum industry is facing challenges, primarily due to the climate crisis and global warming, and the question of interfering in earlier petroleum licences might come to the forefront again. It is not inconceivable that the government might want to stop or reduce production or stop the development of new discoveries in the future.[93]

There is no reason to believe this would lead to a discussion on whether the production licences are a contract or not. Rather the questions that would arise include what the state can do based on the broader evaluation criteria mentioned above, the effect the interference would have at the time it took place, the strength of the public interests and considerations and whether the intervention would be a risk, and what the licensees could have reasonably expected at the time they accepted the licence. Today the petroleum industry will also have to consider the risk that climate change issues may contribute to changes in petroleum policy, or the availability of areas for licensing.[94] One case is as mentioned in footnote 95, already filed by environmental organization claiming that the 23rd licensing round violated the citizens right to a sound

---

[91]   See E Nordtveit, *Between Market and Public Interests*, 2015 p. 469–82 esp. pp. 472 and 475.

[92]   See more generally about governance by mutual consent in natural resource licences; Erich Schanze, "Regulation by Consensus", *Journal of Institutional and Theoretical Economics*, 1988, pp. 151–72, detailing investment requirements by mixes of contract and statute concerning localization and social and ecological concerns, aimed at mineral concessions and joint ventures. See also Erich Schanze, "Internationales Rohstoffrecht," in W A Kaal, M Schmidt, A Schwartze, *Recht im ökonomischen Kontext, Festschrift zu Ehren con Kristian Kirchner*, Mohr Siebeck, 2014 p.253-68.

[93]   The question what protection a licensee under a production licence has towards changing decisions not to develop a field due to climate or environmental considerations were addressed in the decision by the Borgarting appeal court 23 January 2020 (LB-2018-60499). The case was filed by environmental organizations claiming that the 23rd licensing round was a violation of the citizens' constitutional right to a sound environment (Grunnlova section 112).

[94]   Decision Borgarting Appeal Court, 23 January 2020 (LB-2018-60499).

environment, due to the climate effect. The state won the case in the Appeal Court, but the case is appealed to the Supreme Court. Internationally a vast number of climate lawsuits are filed. The state's international obligations to reduce climate emissions in the Paris agreement and as a result of EU/EEA measures[95] to reduce climate change might incur a strong pressure on the state to interfer in petroleum activity in order to reduce national emission of greenhouse gases.

---

[95]   The EU 2050 long-term strategy is aiming at climate-neutrality by 2050.

9. Russia: legal culture and character of Russian petroleum licences

Irina Fodchenko

1. INTRODUCTION

State ownership of mineral rights, and the strong hand of the state in developing those minerals has been, and continues to be, highly influential in the licensing regime pertaining to onshore and offshore petroleum resources in Russia (and the former Soviet Union). The statist approach to resource ownership and development,[1] typical of communist and former communist states, continues to dominate in Russia today, with the state (be that federal or at regional level) controlling all facets of petroleum licensing and extraction. The history of Russia, both prior to the revolution and since, and especially during the Soviet era, has established a legal culture that is unique and state-centric. Post-Soviet Russia has also seen the need to modernise, both its laws and its petroleum activities, in order to emerge as a global player with petroleum at its core. This need has led to the development and establishment of a system of licensing that confers both some typical features and rights, as well as some unique to that of the post-Soviet legal culture.

This chapter undertakes an analysis of the unique nature of the Russian petroleum licence and its legal character in relation to Russian legal culture. Firstly, it will undertake an analysis of Russian legal culture in order to establish an understanding of the context within which licences are granted. After a consideration of the legal culture of the Russian jurisdiction, this chapter will undertake an analysis of the Russian licensing system. It will then assess the rights granted to participants under the existing legal regime. Finally, an assessment of those rights conferred will be compared to other natural resource regimes in Russia to establish the context within which Russian petroleum

---

[1]   For a theoretical consideration of the statist approach see Madeline Taylor and Tina Hunter, *Agricultural Land Use and Natural Gas Extraction Conflicts: A Global Socio-Legal Perspective* (Routledge, 2018) (Chapter 4).

resources are licensed and the rights established through such licensing regimes.

2.   LEGAL CULTURE OF THE RUSSIAN JURISDICTION

The Russian legal system is not only complex and multifaceted, but also of an unprecedented nature. The Russian population, in addition to being widely dispersed over the world's largest territory, is multi-ethnic, multi-religious, and multi-cultural. It could generally be compared to a layer cake with uneven layers, wherein each layer contributes with its specific cultural properties obtained from numerous social characteristics, such as ethnic, religious and secular, urban and rural, metropolitan and peripheral.

All its manifold complexity and multi-layeredness is also built up through a series of historical legal developments, some dating back to the Byzantine Empire, some to the 250-year Mongol-Tatar occupation, some to the Europeanisation of Russian law in the 18th century, some to the revolutionary changes in 1917, and others to the collapse of the Soviet Union. As a result, Russian legal tradition has interacted with both Eastern and Western Europe throughout the existence of the Russian state. However, as a descendant from Roman law through Byzantine tradition, influenced by German, French, and other European norms in the 1700–1800s with socialist-style modification in the 1900s, and continental law influences since 1990s, it more closely resembles a civil law jurisdiction.[2]

---

[2]   For the broad historical overview of the legal science development in Russia, see several well-known fundamental monographs by Russian writers that become modern classics, for example such as O.I. Chistyakov "History of State and Law of the USSR", publishing house Yurait; Y.P. Titov "History of State and Law of Russia", publishing house Prospect; V.A. Tomsinovs' book series "Russian legal heritage", in addition to publications by such authors as L.P. Rasskazov, I.A. Isaev, M.I. Sizikov, etc. Unfortunately, much of their work is in Russian and an English translation is not available for most. For contributions on this matter in English, see several articles and books that have been written by western authors from a western perspective, for example William E. Butler, *Russian Law*, 3rd ed. (Oxford: Oxford University Press, 2009), as well as many other Butler's publications; Richard Hellie, "Early Modern Russian Law: The Ulozhenie of 1649", *Russian History* 15, no. 2/4 (1988); Gordon B. Smith, *Reforming the Russian Legal System*, vol. 11 (Cambridge University Press, 1996).

2.1   Separation of Powers

2.1.1   Rule-makers – legislature or executive?

According to Article 10 of the Russian Constitution,[3] the state power in the Russian Federation should be exercised based on its division into legislative, executive, and judicial powers, and all these branches of power should be independent.[4] The executive power in Russia is de facto split between the President and the Prime Minister.

The source (driver) of the legislative power in the Russian Federation is the Federal Assembly that is stated to be bicameral: it consists of two chambers – the Council of the Federation and the State Duma. Most of the legislation is debated and enacted through the Duma, while the Federal Assembly enacts Russian federal laws. These laws are classified either as Federal Constitutional Laws or as Federal Laws.[5] In the event of conflict, Federal Constitutional Laws take priority over all other laws. In several key areas of Russian law, the basic rules are collated into highly compressed and easy-to-follow lawbooks or codes (Russian: *kodekser*). The main purpose of this codifying technique is to avoid repeating the same principles in a long series of laws. Russian codes are published as federal laws and have a status that might be described as *primus inter pares*.

In accordance with Article 104 of the Russian Constitution, any of the following has the right to initiate legislation: the President of the Russian Federation, the Council of Federation, members of the Council of Federation, deputies of the State Duma, the Government of the Russian Federation, legislative (representative) bodies of constituent entities of the Russian Federation, and the highest courts.

A draft law must be approved first by the State Duma by a simple majority. Thereafter it must be approved by the Council of the Federation and then sent to the president for signature. If the Council of the Federation rejects

---

³   The Constitution of the Russian Federation (the Russian Constitution). The text of the Constitution was published in Rossiiskaya Gazeta, 25 December 1993, page 3, Col. 1. For the official English translation of the 1993 Russian Constitution see www .constitution.ru/en/.

⁴   The Russian Constitution was adopted by a referendum on 12 December 1993 and is the highest source of law. It establishes the principle of superiority of law in the system of legal sources.

⁵   The Russia's Federal Assembly (Russian: Federalnoe Sobranije) consists of two chambers: The Council of the Federation (Russian: Sovet Federatsii) and the State Duma (Russian: Gosudarstvennaja Duma). The State Duma consists of 450 representatives. The representatives are elected on party lists, with the threshold to win seats being set at 7 per cent of the total vote. The Council of the Federation consists of two representatives from each of the constituent entities of the Russian Federation.

the draft law, a Commission is established that includes representatives from the State Duma. If the Commission succeeds in reaching a compromise, the new draft law must be passed once again by the State Duma and then sent to the President of the Russian Federation. In the event of disagreement in the Federal Assembly, the State Duma can prevail over the Council of the Federation by voting with a two-thirds majority. In that case, the draft law is submitted to the President without the Council of the Federation's consent. In turn, the President of the Russian Federation has the right to veto the draft law. The State Duma has the power to accept amendments proposed by the president by simple majority or to overturn the presidential veto by a two-thirds majority in the Federal Assembly.

Federal laws come into force ten days after initial publication in one of the three official gazettes, *Rossijskaja Gazeta*; the *Sobranie Zakonodatelstva Rossijskoj Federatsii*; and the *Parlamentskaja Gazeta*, unless the law in question specifically provides for a different date.

2.1.2   Balance between executive and legislature

Modern Russian legal reality contributes to the establishment and maintenance of a fairer balance between all the branches of government, especially between the legislature and the executive. The system of checks and balances of the three branches occurs in accordance with Article 10 of the Russian Constitution,[6] which requires that the bodies of each branch of power assume their exclusive competence.

Among the President's exceptional powers are those related to the deterrence of the legislature arbitrariness. According to Chapter 4, Article 84 of the Russian Constitution, the President shall announce elections to the State Duma according to the Constitution of the Russian Federation and the federal law; dissolve the State Duma in cases and according to the rules fixed by the Constitution of the Russian Federation; and submit bills to the State Duma.

However, it is important to note that the Federal Assembly has exclusive jurisdiction as well. Among its powers are, for example, initiation of Presidential impeachment proceedings.[7] The State Duma may express no

---

[6]   Article 10 establishes that "The state power in the Russian Federation shall be exercised on the basis of its division into legislative, executive and judicial power. The bodies of legislative, executive and judicial power shall be independent".

[7]   See Article 93 of the Chapter 4 of the Russian Constitution. The President of the Russian Federation may be impeached by the Council of the Federation only on the basis of the charges of high treason or another grave crime, advanced by the State Duma and confirmed by the conclusion of the Supreme Court of the Russian Federation on the presence of the elements of crime in the actions of the President of the Russian

confidence to the Government of the Russian Federation.[8] It should be also mentioned that confirmation from the State Duma is necessary to appoint the Chairman of the Government of the Russian Federation, Chairman of the Central Bank of the Russian Federation or Council of the Federation, to appoint judges of the Constitution Court of the Russian Federation, the Supreme Court of the Russian Federation, the Higher Court of Arbitration of the Russian Federation, as well as a candidate for the post of the Procurator-General of the Russian Federation and appoint judges of other federal court.

2.1.3   Is legislative assent a rubber stamp?

As previously mentioned, the system of checks and balances exists to avoid the abuse of the rights by branches of power. In this case the role of Parliament is protected by the Russian Constitution, preventing it from being a body for the "rubber stamping" of laws. Even though almost all the state bodies are empowered to issue normative acts, only the Federal Assembly is authorised to make primary decisions concerning amending the Constitution and adoption of the federal laws. Moreover, as we have seen, in accordance with Article 108 of the Constitution, adoption of the federal constitution law by at least the two-thirds of the State Duma and three-quarters of the Council of the Federation.is required. The President signs the federal constitutional law within 14 days; as a result, the President may use no suspensive rights in this case.

2.2   Role of Administrative Law

Administrative law in Russia is expressed in the following normative legal acts:

a. Decrees and Orders of the President of the Russian Federation
b. Decisions and Orders of the Government of the Russian Federation
c. Normative legal acts of the Ministries

All these acts should be in accordance with the Constitution, Federal Constitutional laws, and federal laws, because administrative acts have less legal effect.

Federation and by the conclusion of the Constitution Court of the Russian Federation confirming that the rules of advancing the charges were observed.
[8]   See Article 117 of the Chapter 6 of the Russian Constitution.

2.3   Role of the Judiciary

The legal basis of the judicial power is Chapter 7 of the Russian Constitution and Federal Constitutional Law "On the Judicial System of the Russian Federation". [9] These legal sources confer that justice in Russia "shall be administered by courts alone" and "judicial power shall be exercised by means of constitutional, civil, administrative and criminal proceedings". According to Article 71 (o) of the Russian Constitution the court system is under exclusive jurisdiction of the Russian Federation. The courts therefore consider all types of case, regardless of whether they relate to federal or regional law. The competence of the Russian courts is horizontally divided between several courts with constitutional, commercial and ordinary fields of expertise, which are subsequently the following: the Constitutional Court of Russia, Arbitrazh courts, and general jurisdiction.

The Constitutional Court is responsible for deciding constitutional questions, e.g., the interpretation of the Constitution, the constitutionality of federal laws and other legal acts, and legal disputes about the allocation of authority between federal and regional bodies. The Arbitrazh courts, which are headed by the Supreme Arbitrazh Court of the Russian Federation, have the power to decide economic disputes between juridical persons. [10]

The ordinary courts have the general power to determine all types of cases that fall outside the jurisdiction of the Constitutional Court and the Arbitrazh courts. These cases are mainly administrative, criminal cases and private civil disputes in areas such as family law and inheritance law, as well as financial disputes between private individuals. The ordinary courts have a four-tiered hierarchy headed by the Supreme Court of the Russian Federation. It is the final stage of the appeals system, which begins with local courts of general jurisdiction and includes district and regional courts.

It should be mentioned that lately the role of courts in the public life has been revised profoundly, with much effort made to establish courts as an independent branch of power. The strict requirements for standing for being appointed as judges and considerable scope of rights contribute to the judges' independence and generally to the judicial branch autonomy.

An important area of law underdeveloped at present is that of judicial discretion. De jure, the Russian legal system does not recognise judicial precedent (wherein a judge is empowered to express the discretion) as a source of

---

[9]   Federal Constitutional Law "On the Judicial System of the Russian Federation" of 31.12.1996 N 1.

[10]   Also known as Russian Commercial Courts. The Arbitrazh courts should not be confused with arbitration courts and arbitration panels appointed on an ad hoc basis.

law, this means that judges should build their decision only on law. Strictly speaking, there is no doctrine of precedence in Russia. The case law is only controversially emerging as a source of law. There are several cases where the Russian courts issued diametrically opposed decisions on similar cases. The extent to which judicial precedent should be recognised as a source of law in Russia has long been a topic of heated debate among many Russian legal theorists. According to many Russian theorists, court rulings do not constitute a formal source of law. Nevertheless, de facto, judges express their discretion employing the law by utilising alternative norms. Moreover, the highest Russian courts have the power to make general recommendations on the interpretation of specific statutory provisions. Such recommendations are binding on lower courts. Practising lawyers generally take the view that a court ruling may be an important factor when interpreting the text of a law. Currently judicial discretion is being attributed more weight in practice than was the case previously. In this context, it is a more important source of law than legal theory. But, there is no doubt that Russian judicial discretion is much weaker than the same institute in the Anglo-American/Common Law legal system.[11]

3.   IMPACT OF THE NEED FOR NATIONAL SECURITY OF PETROLEUM ON THE LICENSING REGIME

Russia's self-sufficiency in oil and gas and its export capacity has for decades now placed the country as one of the leaders in the global energy market. Russia ranks third in the world in oil production, after the United States and Saudi Arabia.[12] Russia is also the second largest natural gas producer after the United States.[13] However, it is important to keep in mind, that due to excessive energy consumption, Russia is also one of the most energy-dependent countries.[14]

---

[11]   For more information about the role of judicial decisions as a source of Russian law see Hans Herman Tjønn, "Presedensrevolusjonen-En Fremstilling Av Rettspraksis Sin Rolle Som Rettskilde I Russisk Rett" (The University of Bergen, 2013) in Norwegian, not peer reviewed, not published (Master thesis under my supervision). The thesis analyses the role of judicial decisions as a source of Russian law. In addition to the historical and present situation, the possible future development of judicial decisions as a source of law is discussed. A shorter version of Hans Herman Tjønn's thesis is published: "Presedensrevolusjonen: En Fremstilling Av Rollen Til Rettspraksis Som Rettskilde I Russisk Rett", *Nordisk Østforum* 28, no. 04 (2015).

[12]   BP, BP Statistical Review of World Energy (2019), p16.

[13]   Ibid, p 32.

[14]   After China, United States and India. See ibid, p 8.

Towards the end of 2018, Russia's total proved oil reserves comprised 6.1 per cent of the world's total share. With regard to the world's remaining gas reserves, Russia has 19.8 per cent.[15] While Russia's proven gas resources are divided roughly equally between the continental shelf and land territory, only about 25 per cent of Russia's proven oil resources are on the continental shelf. Approximately 75 per cent of Russia's land reserves have been developed, and estimates suggest that approximately half of these have been exhausted. It should be mentioned, however, that large areas of Eastern Siberia are still little explored. Major finds in Western Siberia may suggest that there is a high probability of finding petroleum in unexplored areas. Western Siberia has long been an important centre for Russian petroleum activities.

With an area of 6.2 million square kilometres, the Russian continental shelf, which is divided into 16 offshore oil and gas basins, is considered the largest in the world, with 3.9 million square kilometres expected to contain oil or gas.[16] In this connection, it should also be mentioned, that the Russian continental shelf is relatively little explored, as only 9–12 per cent has been seismically surveyed. Estimates suggest that the Russian continental shelf contains almost 100 billion tonnes of oil and gas equivalent and of these approximately 66.5 per cent are in Russia's Arctic territory. The continental shelf of the Barents, Pechora and Kara Seas are considered to hold about 70 per cent of all offshore oil and gas resources in the country. Due to extensive onshore exploration and the location of offshore fields, Russia has a relatively modest offshore production portfolio to date. Today Russia is at the very beginning of developing its hydrocarbon resources on the continental shelf.[17] After a rapid start in the 1990s, Russian offshore petroleum activity has been in slow progress due to subsequent decline of oil prices worldwide, and several periods of economic challenges in the country. International sanctions, imposed against Russia in 2014, have also limited access to certain modern technology for use in oil or gas exploration of deep-sea and Arctic oil deposits. Several offshore projects that either were planned or already commenced have been put on hold, cancelled, or postponed due to economic sanctions and low oil prices. To date, there are only few ongoing offshore projects: Sakhalin I, Sakhalin II, and Sakhalin III in the Sea of Okhotsk and Prirazlomnoye oil field in the Pechora

---

[15]   The figures in this paragraph are taken from the BP, BP Statistical Review of World Energy (2019), p 14 and p 30.

[16]   See В.В. Бушуев, В.А. Крюков and В.В. Саенко, Нефтяная промышленность России-сценарии сбалансированного развития (Directmedia, 2013) p 45.

[17]   First oil and gas development commenced in the early 1990s in the Sea of Okhotsk and the Bering Sea. By 1995, over 100 exploratory wells had been drilled, including 65 wells in the Far Eastern region, and 35 in the West Arctic. First oil from Russia's continental shelf was produced in July 1999 under the Sakhalin-II project.

Sea on the Arctic shelf. Yet the continued development of petroleum reserves is vital for Russia, both to supply its national needs for petroleum, but also to maintain its position as the third largest producer of oil, and the strength and geopolitical benefits that flow from that position.

The entire Russian land territory, internal waters, the state's territorial sea, and its continental shelf are open for petroleum activities, with the proviso that certain areas or fields may be designated as national reserves and registered in a *Reserve Fund for Subsoil Resources* as per Article 22 of the Subsoil Law.[18] This Reserve Fund comprises important oil and gas fields that are not yet in production, as well as fields containing certain other critical mineral resources, including diamonds and gold. The official primary goal of Reserve Fund is to cover possible future needs for resources. One can also envisage the classification of so-called "reserve fields" being used to increase or decrease national oil production as required. Like the Russian stabilisation fund, this is one of the policies adopted by Russia in order to control the negative impacts of oil price shocks and fluctuations.[19] The Russian government has the power, subject to any contrary provisions in federal legislation, to add or remove fields from the reserve list. In contrast, the Russian Federal Assembly is not involved in the decision-making process related to the listing of reserve fields on the "Reserve Fund".

---

[18] "Law on the Subsoil of 21 February 1992 No. 2395-1 / Федеральный Закон РФ От 21.02.1992 Г. № 2395-1 'О Недрах'."

[19] Russia's Stabilization Fund was established in 2004 and was modelled on the Norwegian Petroleum Fund. In February 2008, the Russian Stabilization Fund was split into two funds: the Reserve Fund and the National Welfare Fund. Over the course of just four years, the asset value of the Russian Stabilization Fund has risen to just under 157 Billion US dollars. The strong economic growth experienced by Russia declined because of the global economic crisis followed by economic sanctions imposed by the EU Member States. As a result, the funds have already been used to fund the Bank of Russia's purchases of Russian rubles in an attempt to stabilize, or prevent the devaluation of, the currency. Moreover, on 1 February 2018 the Reserve Fund officially ceased to exist and the remaining funds were transferred to the National Welfare Fund. The National Welfare Fund's primer assignment is to co-finance voluntary pension savings of Russian citizens and to balance budget of Pension Fund. It does not finance the Russian budget per se. Since 80 per cent of Russia's exports consist of raw commodities, including oil and natural gas, the country is extremely vulnerable to fluctuations in raw commodity prices in the global market. Low oil prices will most likely mean that the Russian budget in both 2018 and 2019 will once again be in deficit. This can make it even more difficult to fund the new infrastructure that is needed to develop new oil and gas fields.

4.   ACCESSING RUSSIAN PETROLEUM RESOURCES

Despite Russia's nearly 200 years long history as an oil-producing country,[20] and several highly individual features of petroleum industry itself, the rules governing the sector have not become a specialised field in the same way as petroleum law in some young oil nations, like for example Norway.[21] In general, legal issues concerning petroleum are treated in Russian legal theory as part of natural resources law and/or mining law, with no clear distinction being made between, for example, oil, gas, gold, and other natural resources. This approach is also reflected in the relevant legislation.

There are several laws that are of key importance to the regulation of petroleum activities in Russia. In chronological order, these include the *Law on Subsoil* (the "Subsoil Law"), the *Federal Law on the Continental Shelf*[22] (the "Continental Shelf Law") and the *Federal Law on Productions-sharing Agreements*[23] (the "PSA Law").[24]

The geographical scope of the Subsoil Law encompasses the Russian continental shelf and Russian land territory, including internal maritime waters and territorial waters.

The geographical scope of the Continental Shelf Law is by definition restricted to the Russian continental shelf; see Continental Shelf Law, Article 1. Accordingly, the Continental Shelf Law does not apply to activities taking

---

[20]   A primitive oil industry, comprising approximately 80 hand-excavated oil wells, existed in Baku (at that time, a part of the Russian Empire) as early as the 1820s. A couple of decades later, in 1846, the world's first "real" oil well – a 21-metre well at Bibi-Eybat in Baku – was drilled as a scientific project. Americans claim that Edwin Drake in Titusville in the United States drilled the world's first oil well in 1859. Meanwhile, Canadians claim that drilling commenced in Canada a year earlier, in 1858, in Petrolia, Ontario.

[21]   The main source of law for the regulation of all phases of petroleum activities on the Norwegian continental shelf, including the Norwegian licensing system is the Norwegian Petroleum Activities Act (Act of 29 November 1996 no. 72 relating to petroleum activities), supplied with a number of supplementary regulations. This act reflects to a large extent the experiences of the Norwegian authorities and other relevant parties under the former regulatory system.

[22]   Federal law on the Continental Shelf of the Russian Federation of 30 November 1995 no. 187.

[23]   Federal Law on Production Sharing Agreements of 30 December 1995 no. 225. Since it was enacted, the PSA Law has been amended 10 times, most recently in April 5, 2016, and has been gradually tightened.

[24]   A number of other laws that may be relevant to petroleum activities in Russia.

place in Russian internal waters and territorial waters.[25] A separate federal law concerning the Russian Federation's internal maritime waters, territorial waters, and contiguous zone covers such activities.[26]

Both the Subsoil Law and the Continental Shelf Law apply not only to hydrocarbons, but to all types of mineral deposits, including gold, silver, and other minerals.

The scope of the PSA Law, like that of the Subsoil Law and the Continental Shelf Law, is not limited to petroleum activities. The law's provisions are applicable to exploration for and production of "mineral raw materials", see the PSA Law, Article 2, clause 1. Apart from oil and natural gas, the law also covers other natural resources such as gold, diamonds and coal. Furthermore, it applies to both offshore and onshore projects see the preamble to the PSA Law.[27]

To sum up, Russia does not have a dedicated petroleum law, despite the fact that it does have a specific law governing certain aspects of the country's gas sector: the *Federal Law on Gas Supply in the Russian Federation* (the "Gas Supply Law").[28]

4.1   Process for Granting of Petroleum Licence: Bid (Cash or Work Program) or Discretionary

The Russian state, as a resource owner, is free to determine whether and how the country's oil and gas resources should be managed and how petroleum activities should be regulated. Accordingly, the Russian state's proprietary right to petroleum resources forms the basis for the public-law regulation of petroleum activities. Currently Russian law provides for two kinds of petroleum regimes:

---

[25]   Russia has petroleum activities in areas close to the coast. For such areas, the licensing regime is somewhat different to the regime applicable to the continental shelf and is more like the regime applicable to land areas of federal importance. Areas close to the coast are usually slightly shallower. In addition, the fields that have been discovered so far in Russian internal maritime waters and territorial waters are relatively small, and accordingly are of less interest to the Russian authorities and major oil companies.

[26]   Federal Act on the internal maritime waters, territorial sea and contiguous zone of the Russian Federation of 31 July 1998 no. 155.

[27]   The regulation of onshore and offshore projects is almost identical. The main difference lies in the right of a federal subject to influence the process if the petroleum deposit lies in an area that is within the federal subject's jurisdiction.

[28]   Federal law on Gas Supply in the Russian Federation of 31 March 1999 no. 69.

4.1.1   Production sharing agreements (PSA) regime

This regime is the contractual subsoil use regime established in Russia in the 1990s. The main objective of the PSA regime was to provide foreign investors with greater stability in Russian fiscal and regulatory policies over the long term. The PSA Law (Federal Law on Productions-sharing Agreements)[29] is the main legislation governing PSAs in Russia. Potential investors are required to enter a contract with the Russian Federation that specifies the terms and conditions, including the sharing of project profits with the Russian state. Only four PSAs had been concluded, and all entered into prior to the enactment of the PSA law in 1996. The PSA regime is not a prioritised regime thus it is not considered in any greater detail. Furthermore, the PSA law requires a number of amendments to be made to become legally functional again.

4.1.2   Licensing regime

The dominant regime governing almost all exploration and production in Russia is the licensing regime. The main legislation governing the licensing regime is the Subsoil Law.[30] The licensing requirements for oil and gas development differ depending on whether it is taking place onshore, in Russia's Territorial Sea, or on the Continental Shelf. Two different legal licensing regimes for offshore oil and gas development have been established: one regime for areas located exclusively within territorial seas and another for areas either located exclusively within the continental shelf or extending from the territorial sea into the continental shelf.

If an area is located exclusively within the territorial sea, then the provisions of the Continental Shelf Law do not apply, with the result that the offshore licensing process – including the requirements for establishing who can become a "user" (licensee) of the mineral deposits – is different. In this instance, the status of the area (so-called "areas of federal importance", see

---

[29]   Federal Law on Production Sharing Agreements of 30 December 1995 no. 225. Since it was enacted, the PSA Law has been amended 10 times, most recently in April 5, 2016, and has gradually been tightened.

[30]   The Subsoil Law, Article 2.1 applies to all areas on the Russian continental shelf and to land-based oil fields that, according to the national reserves balance dated 1 January 2006, have exploitable reserves of at least 70 million tons and gas fields with reserves of at least 50 million cubic metres, together with areas in the internal maritime waters and territorial waters. The provision also applies to areas used for defence or national security, and a number of other areas that contain certain types of minerals, such as uranium, diamonds, and gold. In addition to qualifying criteria, there is a requirement for official publication of a list of areas of federal importance in an official Russian gazette, "Rossijskaja gazeta". Currently, the list of areas of federal importance includes 163 onshore areas and seven offshore areas.

Subsoil Law, Article 2.1) will form the starting point for assessing the process for granting of petroleum licence.

In accordance with the requirements of Article 13.1 (8) of the Subsoil Law, Russian oil and gas fields are typically granted for use based on the decision of the Russian Government, made according to the outcomes of an auction or without any auction, or in case of the discovery of a new field. Furthermore, it is up to the Russian Government to decide whether to hold auctions for granting right, as well as on the composition and conditions of such auctions in relation to any area or a group of areas. However, pursuant to Article 7(4) of the Continental Shelf Law, subsea areas on the Russian continental shelf from an approved and officially published list of areas of federal importance are granted without auctions. In addition, subsea gas areas are also granted without auction for commercial development or geological survey. According to Article 12 of the Gas Supply Law, such areas may be allocated to an entity that is the owner of a Unified Gas Supply System, which is at present only Gazprom.

4.2   Granting of Licences and Rights, Actors and Dominant Parties: Policy Makers, Companies, or the Regulator?

Russia is a semi-presidential republic and is fundamentally structured as a multi-party representative democracy. Russia is a federal state and consists of 85 constituent entities, including the disputed Republic of Crimea and federal city of Sevastopol. All constituent entities have equal power and representation in the Federation Council but differ in the degree of autonomy they enjoy. Petroleum resources are owned by the state and are subject to the joint jurisdiction of the federal government and the regional government where the deposit is located. So-called "areas of federal importance", including oil and gas development on the continental shelf are under the ultimate control of federal authorities, while the use of natural resources, protection of the environment, and provision for ecological safety fall under joint jurisdiction.

Until 2009, the Russian Federal Agency for Subsoil Use (Rosnedra) was responsible for granting licences on the Russian continental shelf and con-ducting auctions and tendering rounds in this connection.[31] Although Russia's federal government has ultimate authority in matters concerning the granting of licences on the Russian continental shelf, all preparatory work is still carried out by Rosnedra.

---

[31]   Rosnedra is "a federal executive authority performing the functions related to rendering State services and federal property management in the sphere of subsoil use" pursuant to Presidential Decree no. 314 of 9 March 2004.

According to Article 7, point 1 of the Continental Shelf Law, the right to develop oil and gas deposits of federal importance on the continental shelf of the Russian Federation is available only to companies that satisfy the following requirements:[32]

(1) legal entities established under the laws of the Russian Federation;
(2) have at least five years' experience in developing resources on the Russian continental shelf;
(3) the Russian state must either hold more than 50 per cent of the voting shares in the relevant entity or have the ability to, directly or indirectly, control more than 50 per cent of such voting shares.

Currently, only Gazprom, Rosneft, and Zarubezhneft fulfil these requirements.[33]

5. LEGAL FEATURES CONFERRED BY THE GRANT OF LICENCE

5.1 Actual Rights Conferred by a Licence

In Russia as in other oil producing countries, a production licence is the keystone of the licensing system. A production licence is what is of economic interest for an oil company.

A production licence gives the licensee the right to conduct "geological exploration, prospecting and production of mineral resources" in a limited area subject to specified terms, see for example Continental Shelf Law, Article 7, point 2. The Continental Shelf Law is silent in relation to defining more precisely what is covered by the above-mentioned activities. The same is true of the Subsoil Law. It is reasonable to assume, however, that a Russian production licence is equivalent to a regular production licence as concerns the scope of activities covered.

Unlike the Soviet time, the Russian Constitution does not proclaim a unified economic system based on state ownership but gives equal protection to all forms of ownership. For example, once minerals have been extracted from the ground, they can be owned by the federal, regional, or municipal government,

---

[32] Article 7, point 1 of the Continental Shelf Law provides that areas of the continental shelf may be allocated to legal entities that satisfy the criteria set forth in the Subsoil Law, article 9, point 3.
[33] For the detailed legal overview of the requirements, see Irina Fodchenko, "Legal Aspects of the Russian–Norwegian Model for Cross-Border Unitization in the Barents Sea and Arctic Ocean", *Ocean Development and International Law* 49, no. 3 (2018).

or by private persons or entities holding a subsoil use licence for such a licence area.[34]

In addition, the licence usually contains information about the subsoil block to be developed, about timelines, financial, and other mineral use condition. The basic requirements might be presented more detailed in Subsoil use terms, as for example:

- Take technological, hydro-technical, environmental, fishery, sanitary, and other measures in compliance with the Law of the Russian Federation and international standards and norms;
- Follow the relevant approved subsoil use requirements and provisions of current Russian Federation legislation to ensure rational use of natural resources, environment protection and safe operations;
- Within two years from the date of the state registration of the licence, draft and agree in due course on a program of environmental and subsoil monitoring and start the program implementation by providing the data, free of charge, to the governmental supervisory bodies;
- Prevent industrial and household waste discharge at sea;
- Comply with the levels of hydrocarbon production in accordance with the design documentation of the field development, avoid above-standard losses of recoverable reserves and selective development of the most efficient areas of the field resulting in a violation of an energy system of field accumulation as a whole;
- Keep records of hydrocarbon production, maintain geological, survey, field and other required documentation in the course of all operations within the subsoil area of federal significance and safeguard this documentation;
- Conduct all works safely and properly in accordance with applicable rules and requirements, and shall impose, using the best available technology, minimal environmental impact including but not limited to atmosphere, water basins, wildlife, and vegetation, and any other natural resources and objects of property.

5.2   The Legal Character of the Licence/Concession

The question about the legal character of the licence under the licensing regime in Russia has been debated since the 1990s with explicit reference to Article 11 of the Subsoil Law.[35] The question was if it is an administrative right, contractual, property right or a hybrid.

---

[34]   See Article 9 of the Russian Constitution.
[35]   It should be noted that also foreign legal academics participated in the debate. See, for example Giuditta Cordero Moss, "Contract or Licence? Regulation of

The wording of Article 11 does not give a simple answer to this question. Point 1 of Article 11 provides:

> The *right to use* underground resources shall be granted by a specific government permit in the form of a licence comprising a specific form with the Russian Federation state emblem, as well as text, graphic and other attachments constituting an inseparable part of the licence and setting forth basic terms and conditions for the use of underground resources.

In addition, point 4 provides that: "The licence is a document certifying the right of its holder to use a subsoil plot within specific boundaries in accordance with the purpose stated therein over an established period of time, provided its holder complies with terms and conditions agreed in advance". Accordingly, a licence is a special state permit that establishes, among other things, the main conditions attached to the extraction of petroleum. Article 11, point 5 of the Subsoil Law provides, however, that: "A concessional agreement (a contract) may be concluded between duly authorized *state bodies* and the subsoil user to lay down the terms for the use of such a plot as well as obligations of the parties under aforesaid agreements".

Thus, in accordance with this latter provision, the authorities and the potential licence holder may enter into a contract (referred to in the following discussion also as a concession agreement), which will establish the conditions upon which the licence is granted and the obligations of both parties. Otherwise, the Subsoil Law does not refer to the concept or content of a "concession agreement".

A thorough discussion of the aforementioned issues can quickly become extremely complex. For this reason, the discussion here is limited to a few key considerations. I will primarily describe how this question was resolved in Russian courts. It should be noted that there have been changes in Russian natural-resources legislation that were of course outside the scope of earlier court decisions. For the sake of order, it should be emphasised that there are no more recent equivalent discussions about this issue in legal theory or in Russian courts.

Existing judicial considerations in this area do not provide a unanimous answer. The Russian judges were divided by their opinions when clarifying how to interpret the legal nature of the licence. Some take the approach that the relationship between the company and the state is of a civil-law nature, while others assume that the relationship is governed purely by public-administrative

---

Petroleum Investment in Russia and Foreign Legal Advice", *Journal of Energy & Natural Resources Law* 16, no. 2 (1998).

law. To illustrate these approaches in more detail, the following paragraphs provide short extracts from relevant court decisions.

The Federal Arbitrazh Court for the North-West Area, in case no. A05-303/01-20/21 of 20 August 2001, held as follows: "The relationship between the parties in this contract is not based on one party subordinating itself to the other, more powerful, party but is based on legal equality between the parties ... The agreement contains *features of a transaction, as assumed in civil-law legislation*".

By way of contrast, the Federal Arbitrazh Court for the Moscow Area, in case no.KA-A40/7874-01 of 9 January 2002, held that: "... since the procedure for the issuing of licences (permits) has features of a permit-issuing situation, the disputed relationship has *no relevance in relation to civil law legislation*".

The Federal Arbitrazh Court for the Volgo-Vjatskijs Area, in case no. A29-173/02-1e of 18 July 2002 refers to a decision by a lower court: "The lower court has in its decision in the case assumed that the relationship is governed by *administrative-law*, and not civil-law, norms".

The Federal Arbitrazh Court for the West-Siberian Area, in case no. F04/2156-219/A67-2004 of 21 April 2004, held as follows: "The relationship between companies and the public authorities with regard to the re-registration of licences pursuant to the Subsoil Law is of an *administrative-law nature*, due to the fact that one party has authority, and accordingly the relationship must be regulated by special legislation".

However, just two months later, the same Federal Arbitrazh Court, in case no. F04/3406-346/A81-2004 of 23 June 2004 held that: "... the Subsoil Law *contains civil-law norms*, see Subsoil Law, Article 49, point 1 and Article 11, point 3".

The above extracts demonstrate that Russia's courts have made contra-dictory rulings regarding the legal character of the licence. This situation is obviously unfortunate from both legal and economic perspectives, since this kind of practical application of the law will reduce predictability for potential investors. It is important to emphasise once again in this context that judicial precedent is not in general recognised as a source of law in Russian jurisprudence.

Therefore, the direction of the governmental practise may, to a certain extent, be an important indicator for Russia. It is clear in this instance that Russian authorities consider licences to be administrative decisions. In 2002, the Department for Management of Natural Resources published a decision stating that concessional agreements are to be considered a potential adden-dum to the licence itself. The Parties' rights and obligations are to be construed from the licence itself. The State will through the retraction of the licence for extraction of natural resources simultaneously retract the Concessional agree-ment. The licensing regime is also closely connected with civil law regulation if we look at the reasons entailing transfer of subsoil right and the process of licence reissuing and registration.

6.   ASSESSMENT OF LICENCE RIGHTS AND THE LICENSING REGIME

6.1   Disposal, Transfer and Acquisition

The subsoil deposits themselves as well as the subsoil licence and the rights evidenced by it cannot be subject to purchase, sale, gift, inheritance, contribution or pledge under the Russian law. Subsoil rights are transferable only in a limited number of circumstances, which results in the reissuance of the subsoil use licence. Such transfer is possible when the licensee:

*   Changes its organisational form or legal status.
*   Merges with another company.
*   Undergoes a spin-off or split-off of a new company.
*   Is deemed insolvent.

A licensee can also transfer its subsoil use rights to a newly created subsidiary established to carry out operations on a particular field, provided that:

*   The new subsidiary is a Russian company.
*   The physical assets required to perform the operations are transferred to the new subsidiary.
*   The new subsidiary possesses the permits necessary to carry out the operations.
*   At the time of the transfer and reissuance of the subsoil licence, the original licensee owns at least 50% in the charter capital of the new subsidiary.

From 2006, Subsoil Law Article 17 point 1 also permits the transfer of subsoil rights from a parent company to its subsidiary and vice versa and transfer between the subsidiaries of the same parent company.

Any such transfer of subsoil rights requires a special decision of the Russian Federal Agency for Subsoil Use (Rosnedra). Because of such restrictions, the "sale" of licences is only possible through acquiring shares in Russian entities that already hold subsoil licences. Subsoil rights to strategic deposits to companies with foreign participation are not transferable unless otherwise is determined by the Russian Government for a specific deposit.

The subsoil licence will become effective and the licensee's rights and obligations will emerge from the moment of state registration of the licence in the State Register of Subsoil Areas and Licences.[36] The Russian State Agency Rosnedra performs the registration procedure issuing for each licence a unique state registration number.

6.2   Revocation of licence by the State

Violation of the material terms of licences could lead to rejection in licence extension or suspension or termination and to administrative and civil liability. The Rosnedra is permitted to restrict, suspend, or terminate the right of subsoil use.

6.3   Relationship between Licence Grantor and Licensee? Legal Relationship versus Assumed Relationship

Historically the Russian state has played an important role in the development of the national petroleum sector. The existence of close links between the Russian state and certain national companies has long been a well-established fact. Changes in the laws on licensing, whereby Gazprom and Rosneft gained dominant positions on the Russian continental shelf, are certainly proof of these close links.[37] The Russian state owns substantial shareholdings in Rosneft and Gazprom – slightly more than 50 per cent of the shares of each of these two companies. Moreover, under Russian law, the state's ownership stake in Gazprom cannot be less than 50 per cent plus one share, as specified in Article 15 of the Gas Supply Law.

---

[36]   The data from the Register is compiled into an online database open for public viewing, see https://old.rfgf.ru/licence.

[37]   These companies also have the full support of the Russian authorities in the case of projects that are not directly related to petroleum activities. In 2007, for example, a federal law was enacted that allowed Gazprom to establish its own armed forces to defend the company's pipelines. In 2008, the authorities in St. Petersburg abolished the ban on high-rise buildings in the historical centre of St. Petersburg, a World Heritage Site since 1990, which had long formed a legal obstacle to Gazprom's ambition to build a skyscraper to serve as its new headquarters. However, the World Heritage Committee opposed the construction of the 400-metre tower and the project has been moved in the outskirts of Lakhta in Saint Petersburg. The construction of the Gazprom's new head-quarters, called the Lakhta Center, was topped out in January 2018. With its 462 metres the Lakhta center is the tallest building in Europe and the 13th-tallest building in the world.

6.4   Third Parties to the Licence: Rights and Protection of Rights for Both Licence Holder and Third Parties

Under the current licensing regime, the only potential licensees for new fields on the Russian continental shelf are the state-controlled companies Gazprom and Rosneft (as well as, in theory, Zarubezneft). Foreign investors may participate in petroleum activities on the continental shelf in partnership with these companies and under state supervision. There appears to be no prospect of direct foreign participation in new offshore projects on the Russian continental shelf.

No matter how Russian petroleum activities are organised, crucial considerations for foreign investors wishing to participate will be ensuring high returns in the form of capital and competence, long-term commitments, and influence over the decision-making process. Like the Russian state, foreign investors want as little exposure as possible to financial risk when participating in petroleum projects.

Long-term investment and long-term planning characterise the petroleum industry. This means that uncertainty is likely to weaken the flow of investment. Regulatory uncertainty is a highly significant factor in relation to investment risk. Accordingly, certainty, stability, and clarity in the host country's legislation will be of key importance for foreign investors. The continual amendments to Russian natural-resources legislation reduce certainty in relation to the country's licensing regime. Other crucial factors for foreign investors are the consistent application of regulatory rules, and efficient, legally robust mechanisms for dispute resolution. Three factors that are likely to deter potential foreign investors are defective legal regulation of the sector, unclear natural-resources legislation, and a bureaucratic public administration.

Despite many unresolved issues, the Russian continental shelf nonetheless represents a very safe area for investment, compared with, for example, onshore petroleum activities. As a starting point, the new licensing system will put foreign investors in a stronger legal position, as the oil companies' rights to earnings are based directly on contracts with the licensee, for example Gazprom or Rosneft. This contrasts with the situation where foreign companies are forced to comply with a system of permits granted under a regulatory framework that is based largely on unclear, and continually amended, legislation. The strong connections between the state and Gazprom and Rosneft also reduces the risk that the licensee may lose its licence in the future. It also mean that various problems concerning relations with the Russian executive branch are easier to resolve.

6.5   Alteration of the Licensing Regime Over Time

The chosen regulatory regime is only a starting point for determining the
extent of official control over petroleum activities. In addition, the state has
the opportunity to control and manage the development of petroleum activities through its official bureaucracy, supervisory authority, and ownership.
From Russia's point of view, it is a priority that any implemented changes to
the petroleum regimes contributes to securing state revenue and control over
national petroleum resources. There is a trend in Russian natural-resources
legislation towards centralising the state's competence and control foreign
participation. Such a trend applied to not only petroleum, but also other strate-
gically important resources.

7.   CONCLUSION

As this chapter has shown, Russia has two separate petroleum regimes existing
de jure side-by-side. These regimes have always been intended to serve different purposes and have never been viewed as equivalent.

To some extent, the PSA regime was intended as a subsidised alternative,
operating almost as an exception to the general rule. This was also how the
situation developed in practice. Only one per cent of Russia's natural resources
is extracted under PSA regimes, meaning that the licensing regime is de facto
the main regime in Russia. However, neither the licensing nor the PSA regime
has remained unchanged over the years, and the state is continually introducing new elements to enhance its control. In addition, the main regimes have
undergone a process of subdivision, with various sub-regimes coming into
existence. One such example is the regime never put into operation on the
continental shelf that was based on a licensing system or a PSA regime.

Various factors may have motivated Russia's choice to implement a range
of different regimes. Firstly, we must not forget the country's enormous geographical size. Opportunities to explore for and the likelihood of discovering,
exploitable deposits will vary greatly from area to area. Secondly, the country's petroleum activities are both onshore and offshore. Here we should also
note that areas may differ in their strategic importance for Russia's defence
and national security, and regulatory rules on foreign investment will need to
be adapted accordingly. The existence of a multiplicity of different regimes
may give the Russian authorities the flexibility they need in this respect. It may
also give Russia a comparative basis for further reform of the petroleum sector.

10. The Mexican petroleum licence of 2013

Guillermo J. Garcia Sanchez

Petroleum in Mexico is not only a resource that has been used and abused by the State to finance its operations; petroleum runs in the veins of its national identity – oil rigs, barrels, and the State-owned company's eagle are present in monuments across the nation and featured on coins and circulation bills.[1] Official history books tell the story of how the Mexican revolution was fought partly to regain control of the hydrocarbons sector, which in 1910 was dominated by international oil companies. Consequently, to understand the legal nature of the Mexican petroleum licence, one needs to review the history of the constitutional treatment of hydrocarbons in Mexico. The regulation of the sector is in constant tension between a deep-rooted policy of government control over the resource motivated by nationalism, and the need to attract and maintain foreign investment to keep production flowing. The rivalry between these goals has not always been resolved successfully, and at times, two legal structures exist in parallel with each other. On one hand, according to the Constitution, the State cannot grant concessions nor transfer the property of the resources to private parties because they belong to the nation. Only the State is empowered to extract and develop hydrocarbons in Mexico. On the other hand, secondary legislation creates a contractual structure that focuses on the maximization of the recovery and allows the government to transfer the hydrocarbons to private parties at the wellhead. In the middle of this contradiction lies the ammunition for politicians that lobby for a government-controlled energy sector to amend the law and renegotiate contracts with private parties.

---

[1]   Duncan Wood and Jeremy Martin, 'Of Paradigm Shifts and Political Conflict: The History of Mexico's Second Energy Revolution' in Duncan Wood (ed), *Mexico's New Energy Reform* (Woodrow Wilson International Center for Scholars 2018) 19.

1. THE FIRST PARALLEL REGIME: PROPERTY OF THE NATION DEVELOPED BY PRIVATE PARTIES THROUGH CONCESSIONS

In the dawn of the nineteenth century, the Mexican State gave extensive concessions to American and British investors to mine and extract hydro-carbons.[2] For instance, the British-controlled Mexican Eagle Oil Company received a concession to develop almost all federal lands located around the Gulf of Mexico.[3] In practice the old concessions included a right to mineral development over extensive acreage, over long periods of time, and giving vast control of the development program to the private company.[4] The old con-cession had close similarities to the mineral rights awarded during the Spanish colonial times: individuals were granted usufruct rights to the exploitation of veins and deposits.[5] The crown reserved the right to royalties and to receive the property back after the mining development was over.[6] The holder of the concession "had full property rights, *jus utendi, fruendi* and *abutendi*, and the State retained the high dominium, that is the right to reacquire the full domin-ium after a condition was met, either because there were no regular works or because they failed to pay taxes."[7]

It is no surprise then that people identified oil development in Mexico with foreign companies and their private property. The presence of foreign com-panies was also accompanied by a sense of foreign intervention in domestic affairs. This perception was sparked in part by the occupation of American forces in the ports of Tampico and Veracruz to protect U.S. oil companies from raids and attacks by the revolutionaries in 1914.[8]

By 1917, the fervent nationalism against foreigners was at its height, and the revolutionary congress adopted Article 27 of the new Constitution declaring all the "subsoil" and its underground resources as "inalienable" and "imprescrip-tible" property of the Mexican people.[9] The revolutionary congress wanted to make sure that "as a basic, solid and unalterable principle under Mexican

---

[2]   Ernest E Smith and others (eds), *International Petroleum Transactions* (Third, Rocky Mountain Mineral Law Foundation 2010) 429–30.

[3]   ibid.

[4]   ibid.

[5]   Oscar Morineau, *Los Derechos Reales y El Subsuelo En México* (2nd edn, Fondo de Cultura Económica 1997).

[6]   ibid.

[7]   ibid 205.

[8]   Daniel Yergin, *The Prize. The Epic Quest for Oil, Money & Power* (First, Free Press 2009) 255.

[9]   ibid 254–55.

law, individual rights to property are to be subordinated to the superior rights of society as represented by the State."[10] For the revolutionaries, the absolute property of the State over minerals and substances underground was a clear example of this subordination.[11] In their minds, the regime established in 1884 had ceded the rights of the nation to develop the national treasures to landowners and private companies, violating the sovereign control over the resources that dated back to early days of the republic.[12] The new text of the Constitution ended this practice and specified that the resources belonged to the *nation* and the State could not transfer the "direct dominium" of the resources to private parties.[13] According to Article 27, paragraph 6, oil and all hydrocarbons were inalienable and not subject to limitations.[14] In a way, the Constitution recognized that even if the government in power represented the State, the nation or the people of Mexico are the "original" owners of the resources, and the government as such is precluded from ceding them to private parties.[15] When it came to national minerals, the government was a type of trustee administering the resources for the benefit of the Mexican people.[16]

However, the new Constitution did recognize the need to use private companies for the exploitation of mineral resources.[17] Article 27 stated that only through federal concessions could the State allow the exploitation of the subsoil by private actors, but the underground minerals would always remain the property of the nation.[18] The reforms presented a clear challenge to already existing concessions that, in practice, had transferred full ownership of the resources subject to taxation and relinquishment of the acreage after exploitation.[19] The British and American companies maintained that their contractual rights granted them full property rights over any hydrocarbons located in the acreage and complained against the retroactive effect of the new Constitution.[20]

---

[10] José Ovalle Favela, 'La Nacionalización de las Industrias Petrolera y Eléctrica' (2007) XL Boletin de Derecho Comparado 169, 171–72.
[11] ibid 172.
[12] ibid.
[13] ibid 177–78.
[14] José Ramón Cossio Díaz and José Ramón Cossío Barragan, 'The New Energy System in the Mexican Constitution' (Baker Institute Mexico Center at Rice University and the center for US and Mexican Law at the University of Houston Law Center 2016) 5, www.bakerinstitute.org/research/new-energy-system-mexican-constitution/, accessed 30 July 2019.
[15] Favela (n 10) 174.
[16] ibid.
[17] ibid 177–78.
[18] ibid 174.
[19] Yergin (n 8) 254–55.
[20] ibid 255.

The revolutionary government instead insisted that the State never gave up the ownership of the subsoil.[21] It was an essential right of sovereign nations.[22] Any concession, in their view, had not granted property rights in the underground resources and should not bind the newly elected government.[23]

After the approval of the Constitution of 1917, the revolutionary war entered a new violent stage, and as a consequence, the government decided not to implement the new constitutional framework.[24] By the time the war was over, in the late 1920s, the post-revolutionary government allowed the companies to operate under the previous regime, but it sustained its claims over the subsoil ownership.[25] The government could not afford to lose the oil produced by foreign investors at a time when the country was in dire need of resources for post-war reconstruction. In a way, a dual legal regime existed: one where the concessions, in practice, granted full ownership to the producers, subject only to taxation; and one where the resources belonged exclusively to the State, as drafted in the 1917 Constitution.[26]

In 1927, under President Plutarco Elias Calles, the government seemed to be willing to implement Article 27, raising tensions to the point of ordering General Lazaro Cardenas, the military commander in the oil zone, to prepare to set the oil fields on fire if the American troops threatened to invade the ports in defense of the companies.[27] The government resisted the temptation of forced renegotiation, but the industry reacted by halting new investment in the fields. In other words, since the threat was still present and taxes continued to increase, the companies suspended all new investment in the fields and stopped exploring new areas.[28] The risk and production costs in Mexico were too high.

As a consequence, in the following years, Mexico ceased to be the second largest oil producer in the world and began losing its global market share to nearby competitors.[29] In just ten years, Mexico's production fell by 80%, and by the mid-1930s, Venezuelan oil was being refined in Mexico because it was cheaper than oil produced in the Tampico wells.[30] The government blamed the loss of production and the increase in costs on the foreign-controlled companies. By the late 1930s, two foreign companies produced 95% of Mexico's

---

[21] Favela (n 10) 172.
[22] Yergin (n 8) 255.
[23] ibid.
[24] ibid.
[25] ibid.
[26] Favela (n 10) 174.
[27] Yergin (n 8) 255.
[28] ibid.
[29] ibid.
[30] ibid.

total production: 65% by the British owned, but Dutch/Shell managed, Mexican Eagle, and 35% by the American companies Standard Oil of New Jersey, Sinclair, Cities Services, and Gulf.[31]

In 1934, General Lazaro Cardenas was elected president of Mexico. He favored land reform, syndicalist trade unions, and extensive public intervention in the economy.[32] The General was a leftist-oriented revolutionary hero who was ready to enforce the unfulfilled promises made to the Mexican people during the revolution.[33] The control of the oil industry was at the center of his agenda, and the decline of production and the rising costs of oil gave him the political ammunition to move forward with his plans.[34] By 1938, the conditions in Mexico had become inhospitable to foreign investment.[35]

2. THE 1938 EXPROPRIATION: THE END OF THE OLD CONCESSION AND THE BIRTH OF THE CONTRACTUAL SIMULATION

In the late 1930s the world was dramatically changing. Nazi Germany had invaded Poland, and Japan was expanding its military grip in the Pacific islands, triggering the start of World War II. The belligerent parties need to secure energy sources for their global war efforts.[36] In the Americas, through the New Deal, President Roosevelt had successfully implemented policies that disfavored the oil barons and redefined the United States' role in Latin America as a "good neighbor."[37] Roosevelt pledged to never intervene again in domestic affairs of democratically elected governments.[38] President Cardenas read the new global environment as an opportunity to advance his social agenda in Mexico. What he needed was a political opening in the domestic sphere to implement the energy policies envisioned in Article 27 of the Constitution.

In 1937, the oil workers union went on strike for higher salaries and better working conditions.[39] President Cardenas, who had dealt with international oil companies in the past, set up a commission to review the companies' books and business practices.[40] The report argued that the companies "contributed

---

[31] ibid.
[32] ibid 256.
[33] ibid.
[34] ibid.
[35] ibid.
[36] ibid 258–60.
[37] ibid 258.
[38] ibid.
[39] ibid 257–58.
[40] ibid 257.

nothing to the country's broader development."[41] The governments of the past had allowed the companies to abuse their production plans, business models, and mistreat the oil workers.[42] The report laid out a series of recommendations which would avoid the wrongdoing of oil companies – it would keep them from extracting the national treasures without paying appropriate taxes, and would ensure they developed the fields at adequate rates and invested in exploration activities.[43] As negotiations with the union collapsed, President Cardenas used the report and a Supreme Court decision favoring the union as a pretext to nationalize the oil companies.[44] The oil barons tried to convince the British government, embedded in the European warfront, and President Roosevelt to intervene on their behalf.[45] The Mexican expropriation of 1938 was the first one of its kind around the world, and the companies feared that it would set a precedent for other leftist-oriented nations, but their hands were tied when World War II began in September 1939.[46] The response was clear: the allies could not risk blockading Mexican oil or the Cardenas administration. A blockade on Mexico could push Cardenas to partner with Japan and Germany.[47] The oil companies would have to settle for just compensation. The allied governments were not willing to fight for their property's restitution.[48]

Now, Cardenas faced a significant technical challenge. Taking over operations meant that Mexico would need to train petroleum workers, build an administrative body for the development of the oil sector, finance its operations, and arrange the efficient exploration and development of the new fields.[49] The expropriation decree not only included the assets of the companies destined to the exploitation of the concessions, but also the property connected to refining, storage, transportation, and distribution activities.[50] It was a nationalization of the entire industry value chain.[51] The solution was the creation of a national oil company, PEMEX, that would take over the nationalized companies' operations. With a state-owned company with enough resources, human capital, and infrastructure, the government, in theory, would finally be free from the need to use private actors to develop its national resources.[52] Consistent with

---

[41]   ibid.
[42]   ibid.
[43]   ibid 257–58.
[44]   ibid 258–59.
[45]   ibid 259–60.
[46]   ibid 260–61.
[47]   ibid 259–60.
[48]   ibid.
[49]   ibid 258.
[50]   Favela (n 10) 179.
[51]   ibid.
[52]   ibid 182.

this view, President Cardenas submitted a constitutional amendment to Article 27 to prohibit all concessions in the hydrocarbons industry. In the words of the text adopted by Congress, "when it comes to petroleum and hydrocarbons, there will be *no concession* and the law [secondary regulation] will determine the manner in which the nation will exploit the resources."[53] Foreign companies would lose the full mineral rights granted by the only concessions and the State would become the only player empowered to exploit them. The 1940s reform consolidated "the construction of a State petroleum sector through assigning the entirety of the goods and services necessary for its exploitation to the government."[54]

Notwithstanding Cardenas' vision of a national industry free of private foreign influence, his secondary regulation recognized the need to maintain some contractual relationship with private parties. As such, in the law that regulated the amended Article 27, President Cardenas allowed for the State to contract with private parties for "exploration and exploitation works, on behalf of the federal government."[55] Under these contracts, private companies could be paid "in cash or an equivalent percentage of the extracted production."[56] In other words, the resources belonged to the nation and the State could not grant concessions for their development, but it could contract private parties to extract them on the government's behalf. The private parties could receive in exchange the produced oil. In essence, the private companies continued extracting the national resources but now under an administrative contract on behalf of the nation and could be paid with the produced hydrocarbons.

Cardenas' successor, President Manuel Avila Camacho (1940–46), went even further with the reinstatement of a "simulation" of state independence from private companies. Less than six months after being sworn in, President Avila Camacho amended the law that regulated Article 27 to allow the State to "contract" with private parties at all stages of the hydrocarbons industry value chain. As such, the State would retain control over the sector, but it could choose between instructing the state-owned entities or contracting with private companies to complete the exploitation, exploration, transportation, storage, and distribution of hydrocarbons.[57] The textual constitutional restriction on concessions remained, and the contracts were considered to be consistent with the wording of Article 27 because they were a "way" to exploit those

---

[53] ibid (emphasis added).
[54] Cossio Díaz and Cossío Barragan (n 14) 7.
[55] 'La Amnesia de Lorenzo Meyer' (*La Razón*, 7 July 2013) www.razon.com.mx/columnas/la-amnesia-de-lorenzo-meyer/, accessed 28 January 2019.
[56] ibid.
[57] Favela (n 10) 186.

resources.[58] These contracts were not the old type of concessions, but they did allow the participation of private companies in the Mexican hydrocarbons development. Essentially, the State could grant private companies contractual rights to participate in the mineral development, but not full property rights over the underground resources. Moreover, the Law, materially, did not give a full monopoly over the industry to PEMEX, but instead, conceded a right to directly exploit the resources, with the State maintaining some regulatory and police powers over the operations.[59] Both presidents recognized that private parties were needed for the development of the industry because the State entities lacked the capacity to do it on their own. What the new regime required was tighter State control and a subordination of the industry to the national interests that included broader social and economic development through the extraction of its national resources.[60]

3.   THE PEMEX MONOPOLY (1958–2013)

It was not until 20 years after the nationalization of the oil industry that the government finally closed its door to private companies.[61] In 1958, President Adolfo Ruiz Cortines submitted to Congress an amendment to the secondary legislation of Article 27 to give PEMEX a monopoly over the industry. In his proposal, President Ruiz Cortines clearly expressed that the nation required "that the activities of such a vital industry, should not be only controlled by the government, but also *monopolized* by the State."[62] Consistent with this vision, Article 27 was amended again in 1959 to clarify that "no concessions *or contracts* shall be granted, nor those in existence shall be valid and only the nation will be in charge of the exploitation of those resources."[63] In the words of President Ruiz Cortines, "the nation has opted, as such, that the only way of exploiting petroleum is through the works of Petroleos Mexicanos [PEMEX]."[64] Finally, the secondary legislation was entirely consistent with the Mexican constitutional text and spirit.[65] The resources belonged to the

---

[58]   ibid.

[59]   Jaime Cardenas Garcia, 'Introduccion' in Marisol Angeles Hernandez, Ruth Roux and Enoc Alejandro Garcia Rivera (eds), *Reform en Materia de Hidrocarburos. Análisis Jurídicos, Sociales y Ambientales en prospectiva* (Primera, Instituto de Investigaciones Jurídicas 2017) 4.

[60]   Yergin (n 8) 260–61; 'La Amnesia de Lorenzo Meyer' (n 55).

[61]   Cossio Díaz and Cossío Barragan (n 14) 7–8.

[62]   'La Amnesia de Lorenzo Meyer' (n 55).

[63]   Favela (n 10) 187 (emphasis added).

[64]   'La Amnesia de Lorenzo Meyer' (n 55).

[65]   Favela (n 10) 184–85.

nation, the State developed the resources on the nation's behalf, and to achieve that goal, a State entity held a monopoly over the entire value chain.

Notwithstanding the intention to leave without effect the existing contracts, the then Director of PEMEX, Jesus Reyes Heroles, did not phase out the existing contracts until February 27, 1970.[66] Three years later, the Constitution was again amended to include in Article 38 a statement about the areas and activities in the national economy under which "the State has exclusive control."[67] As such, "petroleum and other hydrocarbons" and "basic petrochemical activities" fell under the exclusive and strategic State control.[68]

Coincidentally, PEMEX's full monopoly over the industry value chain coincides with a period in the industry's history where Mexico dropped from the list of great exporters.[69] After the 1938 nationalization, PEMEX's production devoted itself to supplying the domestic energy demand of a booming economy.[70] It is also during this period when PEMEX's corporate governance took the company down a road of inefficient and corrupt relationships – first with its workers and later with its suppliers.[71] The 1938 expropriation of foreign assets was unsuccessful in improving the workers' relations with the industry. Although the union was central to the nationalization process, in the early decades of the new system, the State failed to reciprocate with an adequate increase in benefits.[72] Fundamentally, the company faced increasing pressure both from the government to keep energy prices down, and from the worker's union to increase benefits.[73] The result was a policy of awarding contracts to the worker's union, mainly for midstream activities such as transportation and storage, and a reduction on exploration activities.[74] The reduced capacity of PEMEX to access finance led to development programs "guided by a conservationist ethic based on the conviction that resources should be husbanded for future generations."[75] The byproduct of such a policy was PEMEX's inability to expand its reserves at the necessary rate to maintain production in the long run. While the output of existing fields kept increasing, by not amplifying its proven reserves, the company was unable to keep up with the internal demands of Mexico's economic miracle.[76] By the late 1960s, Mexico was, in

---

[66]   ibid 187–88.
[67]   ibid 188.
[68]   ibid.
[69]   Yergin (n 8) 648.
[70]   ibid.
[71]   ibid.
[72]   ibid.
[73]   ibid.
[74]   ibid.
[75]   ibid.
[76]   ibid.

fact, a minor oil importer of Venezuelan crude.[77] The political consequences of such a reality were clear; a once major oil producer was unable to keep in business. At that point, the company launched a deep-drilling exploration plan in Tabasco and Campeche – a program that would save the monopoly of PEMEX.[78]

In early 1970s, PEMEX discovered Cantarell, a field that in its golden year produced 2.136 million barrels per day ("mbd").[79] Located in shallow waters, Cantarell allowed PEMEX to focus most of its production and investment in one field, to the point of accounting for more than 60% of Mexico's oil production.[80] President Lopez Portillo (1976–82), who had inherited a deep economic crisis from President Luis Echeverria, capitalized on the discovery and converted PEMEX's output into the primary source of foreign earnings.[81] The oil produced by Cantarell became "the engine of renewed growth."[82] Most of the investment in Cantarell came from international borrowing using production as collateral.[83] Output in Mexico moved at an impressive pace: from 500,000 barrels in 1972 to 830,000 barrels in 1976, reaching 1.9 million barrels in 1980.[84] With these production results and the price shock of OPEC's oil embargo of 1973, borrowing from abroad became the primary source of finance for State projects, not only to PEMEX but to the central government and other State-owned companies in Mexico.[85] By 1982, oil as a share of exports peaked at 77%.[86] Mexico had become a petro-dependent state.[87]

For more than 25 years, PEMEX, mostly through Cantarell, generated around 40% of the Mexican government's revenue.[88] With such an abundant field, the State did not have any need to partner with private parties, fix the corruption in the worker's union, develop new technologies, deal with the

---

[77]   ibid.
[78]   ibid.
[79]   Wood and Martin (n 1) 20.
[80]   Daniel Romo, 'The Cantarell Oil Field and the Mexican Economy' (2015) 46 Problemas del Desarrollo: Revista Latinoamerica de Economía, https://probdes.iiec .unam.mx/en/revistas/v46n183/body/v46n183a6_1.php, accessed 25 March 2019.
[81]   Yergin (n 8) 649.
[82]   ibid.
[83]   ibid.
[84]   ibid.
[85]   ibid.
[86]   Wood and Martin (n 1) 21.
[87]   Guillermo Jose Garcia Sanchez, 'A Critical Approach to International Investment Law, the Hydrocarbons Industry, and Its Relation to Domestic Institutions' (2016) 57 Harvard International Law Journal 475.
[88]   Clifford Krauss and Elisabeth Malkin, 'Mexico's Oil Politics Keeps Riches Just Out of Reach' *The New York Times* (8 March 2010) www.nytimes.com/2010/03/09/ business/global/09pemex.html, accessed 8 March 2019.

difficulties of attracting international investment to other fields, nor redress managerial and fiscal inefficiencies in PEMEX.[89] When help from the outside was needed, the law allowed PEMEX, not the State, as in the past, to contract services with private parties. In exchange, companies were to be paid in cash, never with a percentage of production.[90]

The new oil-based economy of Mexico implemented by Lopez Portillo reached its limits in 1996 when the Cantarell Field began to decline. Once more, Mexico had not invested the boom of production into expanding the reserve base, and in a desperate effort to increase production, PEMEX began to inject nitrogen into Cantarell.[91] The short-term solution allowed Cantarell to continue producing until 2003, when production in Mexico peaked to 3.4 mbd.[92] Just five years later, in 2009, Cantarell's output had dropped to 560,000 mbd. To put it bluntly, due to Cantarell's decline, Mexico lost 1.7 million bpd from its total production in just nine years.[93] At that point, "PEMEX was mired in debt, faced enormous labor and pensions liabilities and a fiscal regime that seemed to be critically weakening the company to the point of no return."[94] The end of the "goose that laid the golden egg" was near, and Mexico needed to do something about it.[95]

To expand the reserve base and production, an attempt was made in 2007 to bolster PEMEX's capacity to partner with international companies.[96] President Felipe Calderon (2006–12), who had served as Minister of Energy in 2004 when production peaked, presented a bill to Congress that would have allowed the State-owned company to sign joint ventures with international companies for exploration and production projects.[97] Moreover, the bill proposed to open the midstream and downstream sectors to private participation.[98] Calderon wanted PEMEX to focus on upstream activities and slowly allow private

---

[89]   Yergin (n 8) 648; Wood and Martin (n 1) 21.
[90]   Wood and Martin (n 1) 21; Romo (n 80).
[91]   Romo (n 80).
[92]   Eduardo Gonzalez-Canales, 'Mexican Energy Law: Industry Renaissance or Chronicle of a Death Foretold. Part 1: Upstream Ventures in Mexico' (2015) 8 Journal of World Energy Law and Business 46; Duncan Wood, 'Introduction' in Duncan Wood (ed), *Mexico's New Energy Reform* (Woodrow Wilson International Center for Scholars 2018) 1.
[93]   Wood and Martin (n 1) 20.
[94]   Wood (n 92) 2.
[95]   ibid 1.
[96]   Wood and Martin (n 1) 24.
[97]   ibid.
[98]   ibid.

companies to invest in refineries, pipelines, and storage facilities.[99] What came back from Congress was a watered-down version of the proposal.

Instead of allowing PEMEX to partner with international oil companies, the reform allowed PEMEX to sign *incentivized* service agreements for upstream activities.[100] Under the new incentivized model, PEMEX would design the contracts and the bidding system, and the companies would be paid a bonus linked to the number of barrels and a price formula if production was commercially successful.[101] The reform also modified the corporate structure of PEMEX and allowed the federal government to select independent members from industry experts to its board.[102] An agency entirely independent from the Ministry of Energy, the National Hydrocarbons Commission ("CNH"), was created to increase the oversight of the State-owned company's activities.[103] However, the central tenet of the system remained. Only the State – through PEMEX – could develop hydrocarbon resources. PEMEX, in exchange, could sign service or incentivized service agreements to achieve the goals specified in the Constitution. The new incentivized model was not attractive to the major international oil companies.[104] Only a few incentivized contracts for mature onshore fields – Magallanes, Santuario, and Carranza – were signed, but not enough to overcome the years of lack of investment in new acreage.[105] In sum, the 2008 reform fell short in halting the production decline and in dismantling the restrictions of a monopolistic oil sector.

4.   THE 2013 ENERGY REFORM: OLD CONCESSION WINE IN A NEW LICENCE BOTTLE

As mentioned above, in 2004 Mexico's oil production began to plunge dramatically.[106] In that year, Cantarell accounted for 63% of Mexico's 3.4 mbd, dropping to 400,000 mbd in 2013.[107] Cantarell was phasing out, and PEMEX had not invested enough in new exploration.[108] Production was in decline and, at the existing rate, Mexico's crude oil production would fall below two mbd

---

[99]   ibid 25.
[100] ibid 24.
[101] ibid.
[102] ibid 25.
[103] ibid.
[104] ibid.
[105] ibid.
[106] Krauss and Malkin (n 88).
[107] Tim R Samples, 'A New Era for Energy in Mexico: The 2013-14 Energy Reform' (2015) 50 Texas International Law Journal 603, 612.
[108] ibid.

by 2017.[109] The alternative was clear: if Mexico wanted to increase output to continue financing most of the social programs supported by oil revenues, the government needed to access finance and partner with international actors fast to bring new fields into production. Once again, a reform of the existing model was necessary to keep public finances afloat.[110]

In 2012, Enrique Peña Nieto was elected president of Mexico, and within his ranks, he had a group of technocrats who believed in liberalized markets and the need to open the energy sector.[111] The result was the Energy Reform of 2013 that focused on allowing private parties to compete with PEMEX over the contracts that the government was constitutionally authorized to sign. According to the Peña Nieto Administration, Mexico could, with the help of private partners, stop the decline in production. By their assessment, the reform would allow Mexico to uptick its oil output to an additional 500,000 bpd by the end of the Peña Nieto Administration in 2018.[112]

Now, for the government of Peña Nieto to pass legislation allowing for private parties to develop the resources, Peña Nieto's advisors needed to convince the population that the reform would not be giving away the national treasures to private parties, and that the average Mexican would benefit from the new energy model. Since the memory of Lazaro Cardenas was regularly invoked by the opposition to exclude private participation in the sector, President Peña Nieto decided to use the text of the Constitution as amended by Lazaro Cardenas back in 1938.[113] It was a political maneuver to silence the left-leaning opposition. If Cardenas was the example to follow, then the reform would "copy/paste" the constitutional amendment implemented by Cardenas.[114] But the devil is in the details.

As explained above, the Cardenas reform textually prohibited the government from signing "concessions" with private parties, but it left open the possibility for the State to develop its resources by "contracting" companies.[115] As such, it was constitutionally permissible to exploit the national treasures

---

[109]   ibid.

[110]   ibid 606.

[111]   Wood and Martin (n 1) 25–26.

[112]   ibid 20.

[113]   Constitutional Reform (n 83).

[114]   Guillermo Jose Garcia Sanchez, 'The Fine Print of the Mexican Energy Reform', *Mexico's New Energy Model* (Woodrow Wilson International Center for Scholars 2018) 37.

[115]   "Palabras del Presidente Enrique Peña Nieto, durante la Presentación de la Iniciativa de Reforma Energética" [Speech of President Peña Nieto introducing the energy reform initiative], August 12, 2013, www.gob.mx/presidencia/prensa/ palabras-del-presidente-enrique-pena-nieto-durante-la-presentacion-de-la-iniciativa-de -reforma-energetica.

through private parties, as long as the term "concession" was not employed in the process. It is not without irony that the President who promised to bring the energy sector into the twenty-first century had to put to use the wording of a nationalist post-revolutionary reform of the early twentieth century.[116] It took a step to the past to bring Mexico's oil production into the future.

In order to be consistent with the Cardenas' text, the government did not include in the amendment the type of contracts that could be signed by the State with private parties. Instead, different contractual arrangements were specified in the transitory articles of the reform. Article 4 Transitory determined that the contracts to extract hydrocarbons on behalf of the nation "should be, among others: service agreements, profit or production sharing, or licenses."[117] The transitory articles also regulated the government considerations of these contracts:

I) cash for the service contracts; II) a percentage of the profit, for the profit-sharing agreements; III) a percentage of the production, for the production-sharing agreements; IV) with the onerous transfer of hydrocarbons after being extracted from the underground, in the case of licenses, or V) any combination of the above.[118]

The use of transitory articles to specify the contracts was not without risk.

Under the Mexican legal system, the transitory articles serve as guidelines to help the constitutional norm to transition.[119] That is, they set the timeline for the new rules to take effect, and specify the steps that Congress must take to execute the new constitutional arrangement.[120] Thus, they are temporary in nature and are supposed to expire after the specified timeline, or when Congress enacts the secondary legislation that gives life to the reform.[121] None of these characteristics are fully respected in the case of the 2013 Energy Reform.

The transitory articles of the Energy Reform, far from being temporary norms that should expire at some point in time, serve instead as atypical sec-

---

[116]   Garcia Sanchez (n 114) 37.

[117]   "Decreto por el que se reforman y adicionan diversas disposiciones de la Constitución Política de los Estados Unidos Mexicanos, en Materia de Energía, DOF (Edición Vespertina), 2 (20 de diciembre de 2013)," December 20, 2013, http://dof.gob .mx/nota_detalle.php?codigo=5327463&fecha=20/12/2013 (hereafter, Constitutional Reform, Transitory Article 4).

[118]   ibid.

[119]   Carla Huerta Ochoa, 'Artículos Transitorios y Derogación' (2001) 102 Boletín Mexicano de Derecho Comparado 102.

[120]   Sergio Nudelstejer, 'Artículo Transitorio', *Enciclopedia Legal* <https://mexico .leyderecho.org/articulo-transitorio/#Recursos>; Huerta Ochoa (n 119).

[121]   Nudelstejer (n 120); Huerta Ochoa (n 119).

ondary legislation of the Constitution. They set up the rules that the secondary legislation should follow, but also awarded rights to private parties, such as the right to book the reserves, and specified the types of contracts that the government could sign with private actors for exploration and production ("E&P") activities.[122] Hence, these "transitory" articles can be interpreted as hierarchically and normatively below the Constitution, but above the federal legislation that regulates Article 27.[123] They serve as "endnotes" or the "fine print" of the constitutional reform.[124] They were used to "mislead and conceal" the actual intention of the amendment.[125]

If federal law contradicts the transitory articles, these, in theory, would be upheld. The trickier question is whether the transitory law contradicts the text of the Constitution. According to the Supreme Court of Justice of Mexico's jurisprudence, these temporary articles are part of the reform and cannot be interpreted as challenging constitutional text. They are jurisprudentially an appendix of the Constitution.[126] However, the existing Supreme Court's jurisprudence dealt with cases of traditional transitory articles involving timelines, steps, and different legislative stages to appoint judges and regulators or enact secondary regulation; not the granting of rights to private parties.[127]

The open possibility of a contradiction between the transitory articles and the Constitution leaves the Energy Reform in a weak position.[128] The spirit of

---

[122]   Constitutional Reform, Transitory Articles (n 110).

[123]   "Artículos Transitorios. Formas Parte del ordenamiento Jurídico Respectivo y su Observancia es Obligatoria", Segundo Tribunal Colegiado en Materia Administrativa del Sexto Circuito, Tesis Aislada, VI.2o.A.1 K, Num. De Registro: 188686, Novena Época, Semanario Judicial de la Federación y su gaceta, Tomo XIV, Octubre de 2001.

[124]   Garcia Sanchez (n 114).

[125]   Diego Valadés, "La Constitución desfigurada" [The disfigured constitution], Reforma, December 12, 2013.

[126]   Amparo en Revisión 1106/2015, resuelto 02/03/2016, Segunda Sala de la Suprema Corte de Justicia de la Nacional; see also Acción de Inconstitucionalidad 99/2016 y acumulada 104/2016 (regarding electoral judges); Acción de Inconstitucionalidad 58/2016 (anticorruption law in Chihuahua); Acción de Inconstitucionalidad 56/2006 (anticorruption law in Veracruz).

[127]   Ron Snipeliski Nischli calls the transitory articles "a new modality" of the constitutional legislator to "detail certain aspects of the constitutional text" in the "transitory" articles "which are not transitory at all, because they share the same nature and characteristics of other constitutional provisions" Ron Snipeliski Nischli, "Artículo 27," Constitución Política de los Estados Unidos Mexicanos Comentada, Vol. 1, edited by Jose Ramón Cossio Días (Mexico: Tirant lo Blanch, 2017), 558.

[128]   See comments from José Antonio Prado of Holland and Knight in Alejandra López, "Confunden términos licencia y concesión" [They confuse the terms licence and concession], Reforma, June 8, 2015, www.reforma.com/aplicacioneslibre/articulo/default.aspx?id=560100&md5=8651197a2972748724fcac21ebf63411&ta=0dfdbac11765226904c16cb9ad1b2efe&po=4; and Alejandro Guzmán Rodríguez,

not granting any concessions to private parties could be interpreted as hindered by the transitory articles that allow the State to sign "licenses" or "production sharing agreements," paid with the hydrocarbons extracted from the underground.[129] The only difference between these contractual arrangements and a traditional concession from the late nineteenth century is the granting of a property right to the underground minerals, in large extensions of land and without a relinquishment formula – a type of contract that is rarely available in any jurisdiction around the world.[130] Today, around the globe the terms "concession," "permit," "license," and "E&P agreements" are used to refer to the same type of contractual arrangement where private parties extract the resource at their own risk and expense, and in exchange, pay royalties, bonuses, and different tax arrangements.[131] Depending on the jurisdiction, this type of contract has different levels of government control, terms of operation, minimum work requirements, and terms for the relinquishment of the area.[132] But the spirit remains – the State owns the resource in the subsoil and the property of the mineral is transferred to the private parties at the wellhead.[133] As explained above, if the spirit of Article 27 of the Constitution and the 1938 nationalization was to prevent private parties from extracting the national treasures and handing them a full property right at the moment they are extracted, then both the secondary legislation in 1938 and the Energy Reform of 2013 violate that spirit.

Now, if the government decides that the best option for a particular field is for PEMEX to develop it, then the Ministry of Energy can "assign" the field directly to the State-owned company.[134] In this way, the block is omitted from the public bidding process of the rest of the contracts.[135] The Ministry of

---

"¿Contratos o Concesiones?" [Contracts or concessions?], Energía a Debate, n.d.,www .energiaadebate.com/¿contratos-o-concesiones/.

[129]   ibid.

[130]   Smith and others (n 2) 442-443.

[131]   ibid 447-453; Gordon Barrows, 'A Survey on Incentives in Recent Petroleum Contracts' in Nicky Bredjick and Thomas W Walde (eds), *Petroleum Investment Policies in Developing Countries* (Graham & Trotman 1998) 226; Carmen Otero García-Castrillón, 'Reflections on the Law Applicable to International Oil Contracts' (2013) 6 Journal of World Energy, Law & Business 129, 133.

[132]   Smith and others (n 2) 447-53; Carol Nakhale, 'Petroleum Fiscal Regimes: Evolution and Challenges' in Philip Daniel, Michael Keen and Charles McPherson (eds), *Taxation of Petroleum and Minerals: Principles, Problems and Practice* (Routledge 2010) 89–95.

[133]   Smith and others (n 2) 447–53.

[134]   Decreto por el que se expide la Ley de Hidrocarburos y se reforman diversas disposiciones de la Ley de Inversión Extranjera, Ley Minera, y Ley de Asociaciones Público Privadas, DOF: 11/08/2014 (hereafter, Hydrocarbons Law), Article 6.

[135]   ibid.

Energy only needs to justify its decision "as the most adequate mechanism for the interest of the State in terms of production and that guarantees the supply of hydrocarbons and that the recipient of the assignment had the technical, financial and execution capacity to extract the hydrocarbons in the most efficient and competitive way."[136]

Regarding the existing fields operated by PEMEX and that were deemed as appropriate for its operation, the State-owned company is authorized to sign farm-outs with private companies.[137] However, the farm-out process requires PEMEX to receive approval from the Ministry of Energy and to conduct an open bidding process designed and supervised by the National Hydrocarbons Commission.[138] In other words, PEMEX can only set up the requirements, but CNH chooses the partner.

5.   NEW "INDEPENDENT" AUTHORITIES AND THE NEW AUCTION PROCESS

The Energy Reform of 2013 also had the goal of decentralizing the decision-making process of the energy policies in Mexico. To achieve decentralization, the reform gave additional powers and levels of independence to the energy regulatory agencies: the National Hydrocarbons Commission for upstream activities, and the Energy Regulatory Commission ("CRE") for the remaining value chain (midstream and upstream).[139] As opposed to administrative agencies wholly dependent on the Ministry of Energy, the reform transformed them into "coordinated regulatory agencies" with budgetary autonomy and with a two-thirds Senate majority approval process to select their members.[140] The reform, however, was unable to abandon the old ways of Mexican presidential centralism entirely.[141]

---

[136]   ibid.

[137]   Adrián Lajous, Mexican Oil Reform: The First Two Bidding Rounds, Farmouts and Contractual Conversions in a Lower Oil Price Environment (New York: Center on Global Energy Policy, School of Public and International Affairs, Columbia University, October 2015), http://energypolicy.columbia.edu/sites/default/files/Mexian%20Oil %20Reform_October%202015.pdf.

[138]   Jeremy Martin, 'The Politics of Oil in Mexico: Consolidating the Reforms' in Duncan Wood (ed), *Mexico's New Energy Reform* (Woodrow Wilson International Center for Scholars 2018) 61.

[139]   Miriam Grunstein, 'Coordinated Regulatory Agencies: New Governance for Mexico's Energy Sector' (Rice University's Baker Institute for Public Policy 2014) Issue Brief 06.10.14 1.

[140]   Garcia Sanchez (n 114) 48–49; Grunstein (n 139) 1.

[141]   Garcia Sanchez (n 114) 42.

Just as before the reform, the Constitution recognized that the Ministry of Energy sits at the head of the national industry. Transitory Article 10 states that the Minister of Energy, who is solely appointed by the President, will "establish, conduct and coordinate the energy policy."[142] The constitutional reform also emphasized the fact that all hydrocarbons activities and the distribution of power are "strategic" activities "of social interest and public order, and as a consequence will have preference over any other activity that benefits from the development of the surface or underground."[143] Consistent with its central role, the Minister of Energy is the authority who decides which areas of the national territory will be developed by the State, and most importantly, whether the State will do so by contracting private parties or assigning them to State production entities, such as PEMEX.[144] The Ministry of Energy is also in charge of designing and drafting the terms of the contracts to be signed with the private parties if the government decides to use any of the E&P authorized contracts.[145] The only elements of the agreement that cannot be designed by the Ministry are the economic and fiscal terms, which are delegated to the Ministry of Finance.[146] According to Transitory Article 10, the Minister of Finance will establish the economic conditions for the bids and contracts in connection with the fiscal regime that will allow the nation to obtain, in time, the profits that will contribute to long-term development.[147] These include determining the standard royalties, corporate tax and costs deduction, and adjustable rates for windfall profits.[148] Consistent with this view, the Hydrocarbons Income Law sets up a sliding-scale royalty adjustable by the Minister of Finance with varying rates depending on the fields, production rates, and the global price of the hydrocarbons.[149] Thus, for projects with narrower profits, the Ministry can authorize a royalty discount.[150]

In the process of selecting which areas will be open to development, the independent upstream agency, CNH, has an advisory role.[151] The CNH can

---

[142] Constitutional Reform, Transitory Article 10 (n 110).
[143] Constitutional Reform, Transitory Article 18 (n 110).
[144] Hydrocarbons Law, Article 29 (n 134).
[145] ibid.
[146] Constitutional Reform, Transitory Article 10 (n 110).
[147] ibid; Hydrocarbons Law, Article 30 (n 134).
[148] Garcia Sanchez (n 114) 44–45; Hydrocarbons Law, Article 30 (n 134).
[149] Decreto por el que se expide la Ley de Ingresos sobre Hidrocarburos, se reforman, adicionan y derogan diversas disposiciones de la Ley Federal de Derechos y de la Ley de Coordinación Fiscal y se expide la Ley del Fondo Mexicano del Petróleo para la Estabilización y el Desarrollo, DOF:11/08/2014. (Hereafter, Hydrocarbons Income Law.)
[150] ibid.
[151] Hydrocarbons Law, Article 6 and 29 (n 134).

only provide an "opinion" to the selected areas by the Ministry of Energy and comment on the terms of the contracts.[152] Ultimately, however, it is up to the Minister of Energy to decide whether the most attractive fields will be exploited with the help of private parties or through the State-owned company.[153] It is also up to the Minister to decide whether a licence, a production sharing agreement, a profit-sharing agreement, or a service contract will be employed to develop the fields with private parties. Once the decision is made, the CNH cannot modify the government's choice.

The real CNH independence only kicks in once the Ministry selects the field and the type of contracts.[154] At that point, the CNH must design, supervise, and execute the auction process.[155] It is then when the CNH is at its full independent powers. The Ministry cannot intervene nor can it select a winner of the auction.[156]

The CNH also has the responsibility of processing all the hydrocarbons information that PEMEX used to monopolize the industry and establishing the National Center of Hydrocarbon Information so that the competing companies can prepare their bids.[157] There is a pre-selection stage in which the CNH filters those companies that have the capacity and technical expertise for the particular fields, but everything else is done at an opening ceremony live-streamed with the representatives of the companies present.[158] The pre-classification rules and bidding processes are set to maximize transparency and ensure that the State collects the most revenue out of the bids.[159] It is an economically-driven process where the winner is the party that bids a higher added economic benefit to the State. In the case of licences, the companies can include in their bid a signing bonus, additional initial investment contributions, and an additional royalty percentage to the State. In the case of production and profit-sharing agreements, the companies can include in their bid an additional signing bonus and a higher additional percentage of production or profit to be awarded to the State. In all of the cases, the Ministry of Finance establishes a minimum signing bonus, royalty rate, and exploratory phase fees. In other

---

[152] Hydrocarbons Law, Article 31 (n 134).
[153] Hydrocarbons Law, Article 6 and 29 (n 134).
[154] Constitutional Reform, Transitory Article 10.b (n 110).
[155] Hydrocarbons Law, Article 23 (n 134).
[156] ibid.
[157] Grunstein (n 139) 3.
[158] Hydrocarbons Law, Article 23 and 24 (n 134).
[159] ibid.

words, under the Energy Reform, the predominant principle for selecting the winner is to maximize the nation's revenue.[160]

Once the winner of the block is announced, the CNH continues exercising its independence by transforming into the supervisory entity of the company's activities and must ensure that the projects maximize recovery. As such, the contracts in the energy reform are not only contracts for extraction, but imbue a constitutional requirement to maximize recovery for the benefit of the State. The CNH is the body in charge of rescinding the contract in case the company or PEMEX does not follow the agreed terms.[161] Moreover, it is this independent agency that would have to defend the agreement before tribunals if a private party were to challenge its terms or the decision from the CNH to rescind it.[162] The CNH is also tasked with promoting reserve restitution, using suitable technology in the upstream activities of the companies, and issuing regulations in matters respective to its authority.[163]

6.   IN 2018, ANOTHER JUMP TO THE PAST: MAKING PEMEX GREAT AGAIN AND THE GROUNDS FOR THE RESCISSION OF EXISTING CONTRACTS WITH PRIVATE PARTIES

In the summer of 2018, by a margin of 53%, the Mexican people elected Andres Manuel Lopez Obrador as their 58th president.[164] Lopez Obrador is a social justice fighter who started his political career in the 1990s by running as governor against the establishment and by leading a protest against PEMEX's drilling plans in indigenous lands in his home state of Tabasco. He has always expressed admiration for President Cardenas and his vision of relying on State oil production to boost Mexico's development. Once again, the old tension between nationalism and the need to increase output emerges. With production in Mexico at 1.763 mbd in 2018, the continuing decline was blamed on the 2013 Energy Reform and on private companies.[165] The reality

---

[160]   Constitutional Reform, Transitory Article 4 (n 110); Hydrocarbons Law, Articles 29.III (n 134).

[161]   Hydrocarbons Law, Article 20 (n 134).

[162]   Hydrocarbons Law, Article 21 (n 134).

[163]   Grunstein (n 139) 3.

[164]   'Mexico's AMLO Takes Office With Attack on Energy Overhaul' (1 December 2018)   www.bloomberg.com/news/articles/2018-12-01/lopez-obrador-takes-the-reins -in-mexico-vowing-a-transformation, accessed 22 March 2019.

[165]   'Vowing to Transform Mexico, AMLO Takes Aim at Energy Reform in Inaugural Speech', at www.naturalgasintel.com/articles/116657-vowing-to-transform -mexico-amlo-takes-aim-at-energy-reform-in-inaugural-speech?v=preview, accessed 22 March 2019.

is that most of the 107 contracts signed with private parties as part of the 2013 Energy Reform are not even close to reaching full production.[166] The first bidding round took place in July 2015, and out of the 14 blocks that involved production sharing agreements with the State, only two received offers.[167] Although the E&P contracts represent a total future investment value of more than $160 billion, the defenders of the reform have little to offer in terms of overall output to defend the claims of Lopez Obrador.[168] To his base, the Energy Reform has not delivered Peña Nieto's promises of a massive increase in production.[169]

It is no surprise then that one of the first things Lopez Obrador announced as president was the halting of any new bidding rounds with private parties until 2021.[170] His administration's goal is to "make PEMEX great again."[171] In Lopez Obrador's view, the previous administrations "surrendered some of the [S]tate's functions to private national and foreign interests."[172] Consequently, they are exercising the powers awarded to the Ministry of Energy to rely on assignments to PEMEX, strengthening its finances, and ensuring that the significant midstream and downstream projects in Mexico, including building a new refinery, benefit the State-owned company first.

The question then becomes: will Lopez Obrador force a renegotiation of the 107 contracts signed with private parties as part of the energy reform? He already canceled, against all advice, a $13 billion project for Mexico City's new airport using similar nationalist views against foreign investors and arguing the abuse of former government officials.[173] Lopez Obrador has proved to be consistent when it comes to fulfilling promises that affect foreign investors, even if the State has to pay billions of dollars in compensation, like

---

[166] David Blackmon, 'AMLO Impacts Energy Markets Even Before Taking Office' (*Forbes*) www.forbes.com/sites/davidblackmon/2018/08/27/amlo-impacts-energy-markets-even-before-taking-office/, accessed 22 March 2019.
[167] 'CNH-R01-L04-A1.CPP-2016 - Rondas Mexico - Rondas Mexico - Rondas Mexico' https://rondasmexico.gob.mx/CNH-R01-L04-A1.CPP-2016/, accessed 30 August 2018.
[168] Wood (n 92) 2.
[169] ibid.
[170] 'Mexico's AMLO Takes Office With Attack on Energy Overhaul' (n 164).
[171] 'Event - Energy Policy in Mexico Under President López Obrador' (8 November 2018) </events/1958/> accessed 25 March 2019; 'Mexico Should Leave IEA, Eye OPEC: Pemex Adviser' (19 September 2018) www.argusmedia.com/en/news/1757437-mexico-should-leave-iea-eye-opec-pemex-adviser, accessed 25 March 2019.
[172] 'Vowing to Transform Mexico, AMLO Takes Aim at Energy Reform in Inaugural Speech' (n 165).
[173] 'AMLO's Mexico City Airport Plan Baffles Airlines Seeking Answers - Bloomberg' www.bloomberg.com/news/articles/2019-03-01/airlines-question-amlo-s-three-airport-plan-for-mexico-city, accessed 22 March 2019.

the $6.6 billion cost of the new airport's cancellation.[174] When it comes to the 107 upstream contracts, so far, Lopez Obrador has pledged to "review" them but not cancel them unless his administration finds signs of corruption.[175] If Lopez Obrador finds reasons to renegotiate the contracts, he will have to face the fact that only CNH can cancel the agreements on behalf of the government. As mentioned above CNH is the signing authority of each E&P contract on behalf of the Mexican State. The grounds to cancel the contract are set by the Hydrocarbons Law.[176]

According to Article 6, CNH can rescind a contract if the company does not start operations under the pre-established timeline; if it discontinues activities for no just cause; if it fails to comply with the approved exploration or extraction development plan; if it neglects to comply with a final judicial resolution; if it declines to invest the agreed amounts in the contract; if it transfers interests without authorization; if the operator has an accident due to negligence or fraudulent conduct; if the companies are unsuccessful in reporting adequate information and data on production rates and costs to the CNH; and finally, if the companies fail to produce payment in accordance with the terms of the law or the contract.[177] The Hydrocarbons Law is textually explicit in that these are the *only* (*"únicamente"*) grounds for which the CNH can rescind a contract.[178] If the CNH cancels the contract, then the area is relinquished "without any charge, payment, or compensation."[179] There is nothing in the law or the existing E&P contracts that would allow the new government to legally rescind the contract for suspicion of corruption or because the government decides that PEMEX is in a better position to develop the field as opposed to the winning private consortium. In other words, "making PEMEX great again" is not a legally recognized ground to rescind the contract.[180] The rescission of the agreement is subject to judicial review under the federal administrative tribunals in Mexico.[181] The private party cannot bring an international claim if the government decides to cancel the contract under the terms established by the law.[182] However, if the company wins the case in federal administrative

---

[174] 'Cancelling New Mexico Airport Would Cost $6.6 Billion: Company CEO | Reuters' www.reuters.com/article/us-mexico-election-airport/cancelling-new-mexico -airport-would-cost-6-6-billion-company-ceo-idUSKBN1H22VQ, accessed 22 March 2019.

[175] Blackmon (n 166).

[176] Garcia Sanchez (n 114) 43.

[177] Hydrocarbons Law, Article 20 (n 134).

[178] ibid.

[179] ibid.

[180] ibid.

[181] Garcia Sanchez (n 114) 45–46.

[182] ibid.

tribunals, and the rescission is found to have been groundless, the investor can bring a claim to international arbitral tribunals for the quantification of compensatory damages and loss of profit.[183]

If the government decides to relinquish the area under different grounds not pre-established in the Hydrocarbons Law, then the private party can bring a claim under any of the international treaties that award rights to private investors in Mexico.[184] These include 29 Bilateral Investment Treaties and 16 Trade Agreements with Investment Protection Provisions in force with arbitration provisions that provide jurisdiction to international tribunals.[185] The E&P contracts include a clause specifying that, notwithstanding the domestic administrative remedial proceedings, the companies "will enjoy all of the rights recognized in international treaties signed by the State."[186] Classic examples of claims that might arise out of violations of investment treaties include: a forced renegotiation of the contract terms; a modification of the tax regime that affects the profitability of the project; the repeal of the hydrocarbons law that affects the structure of the project; the discrimination of foreign companies in terms of policy and contractual changes; and the nationalization of the assets without just, prompt, and adequate compensation.[187]

7.   CONCLUSION: WHAT LIES AHEAD FOR THE MEXICAN CONTRACTS

The arrival to Los Pinos of a new leftist-oriented government reignites the old discussion in Mexico of whether the secondary laws violate the spirit of the Constitution. As the first subsections in this chapter explained, this debate is as old as the 1917 revolutionary constitutional convention. The old concession regime inherited from colonial times awarded a usufruct on the mineral rights to the producers only subject to taxation and relinquishment by the state once the extraction was over. The 1917 revolutionaries wanted to create a system where the nation was the primary owner of the resources in the subsoil, and the State had to develop them in the way that maximized the benefits to the Mexican people. The Constitution affirmed the sovereignty of the resource

---

[183]   ibid.

[184]   Garcia Sanchez (n 114) 46.

[185]   'Mexico | Bilateral Investment Treaties (BITs)' https://investmentpolicyhub .unctad.org/IIA/CountryBits/136, accessed 22 March 2019.

[186]   See, for example, Contract No. CNH-R01-L04-A1.CPP/2016 with China Offshore Oil Corporation E&P Mexico, S.A.P.I. de C.V., Section 26.9, www.gob.mx/ cms/uploads/attachment/file/198308/Contrato_Area_1_Cinturon_Plegado_Perdido .pdf.

[187]   Garcia Sanchez (n 87).

by making them inalienable and imprescriptible. However, they recognized that in order to extract the resource the government could award concessions to private parties to exploit it on behalf of the nation. Hence, from a usufruct, the regime moved to an administrative contract awarded by the State. Lazaro Cardenas, who nationalized the industry in 1938, believed that State-owned companies were the dominant vehicle to achieve the constitutional mandate, even if for particular projects the government could contract private actors and pay them with the produced hydrocarbon. Hence, in essence the Cardenas regime created a system of partnership with private parties to extract the resource. Under Cardenas, even if the constitutional mandate recognized that the hydrocarbons in the subsoil belonged to the State, once they were extracted, they could be transferred to the private operator as payment. It wasn't until the 1970s when the government decided to close the door to the possibility of associating with private companies to develop the nation's resources. At that point the State could only develop the resources through PEMEX, but the state-owned company could sign service contracts with private companies and pay them in cash.

The Energy Reform of 2013 brought back private participation as an instrument for the State to achieve its constitutional mandate. As explained above, the 2013 Energy Reform reinstated the power of contracting with private parties to arguably maximize recovery.[188] The reform allows the government to sign licences, production and profit-sharing agreements, and service contracts. The new production and profit-sharing contracts are nothing more than a revival of a contractual association between the State and private parties to jointly develop the resources. Moreover, the 2013 Mexican licence looks, in essence, similar to the old concessions of the early twentieth century, in that it gives *erga omnes* rights to the private parties operating "on behalf of the nation" to exploit the riches of the national underground.[189] Under the Mexican licence the moment the resources are extracted, they now entirely belong to the private party, who in exchange, pays a royalty fee and additional fiscal contributions.[190] And just like in 1940, the State only reserves the right to regulate activities, police, and sanction the companies, but the resources at the wellhead belong to the licensee. The main difference between the two legal figures is that the 2013 licence limits the period of extraction, establishes minimum working requirements, and constraints the operations to smaller blocks.

In this modern version of the State associations, PEMEX is treated as another competing party. As a state-owned entity it can associate with private

---

[188] Garcia Sanchez (n 114).
[189] Cardenas Garcia (n 59) 4.
[190] ibid.

parties to present bids, it can farm-out its existing fields, and it can hire private parties for services related to its acreage. But it no longer remains the single operators with a monopoly over the industry. The Peña Nieto Administration could have amended the Constitution and clarified how public-private partnerships are not contradictory with the principle of maximizing the government's revenues. However, they decided to use the text of Lazaro Cardenas to bypass the opposition and left open a flank for future litigation.

The transmission of property to private parties is even consistent with the transitory articles. They allow the companies to book the reserves for purposes of accessing international financing.[191] The booking of reserves is permitted under the Energy Reform as long as a statement is added specifying that the hydrocarbons contained in the subsoil belong to the State, even if at the well-head the property is transferred to the companies.[192]

It is clear that Lopez Obrador will not continue with the implementation of the 2013 Energy Reform as designed by the previous administration. He is already taking significant steps to recentralize the government's energy policies. His new Minister of Energy announced that the goal of the administration will be to strengthen PEMEX's participation in the sector and that they do not expect to sign any new contracts with private parties for upstream activities in the short run. Moreover, during the transition period, they forced the Peña Nieto Administration to negotiate the inclusion in the United States-Mexico-Canada Agreement ("USMCA") of a new chapter entitled "Recognition of the Mexican State's Direct, Inalienable, and Imprescriptible Ownership of Hydrocarbons."[193] Chapter 8 states that Canada and the U.S. recognize and fully respect the sovereignty of Mexico's right to regulate the development of hydrocarbon resources.[194] Moreover, they recognize that Mexico reserves the right to modify its Constitution and laws to reflect the fact that "the Mexican State has the direct, inalienable and imprescriptible ownership of all hydrocarbons in the subsoil of the national territory."[195]

---

[191] Constitutional Reform, Transitory Article 5 (n 110); Hydrocarbons Law, Article 45 (n 134).

[192] Cardenas Garcia (n 59) 4; Francisco Javier Dorantes Díaz, '¿Existen Los Derechos Reales Administrativos En México? Un Planteamineto a Partir de La Dogmática y de La Reciente Reforma Constitucional En Materia Energética' in Marisol Angeles Hernandez, Ruth Roux and Enoc Alejandro Garcia Rivera (eds), *Reforma en Materia de Hidrocarburos. Análisis Jurídicos, Sociales y Ambientales en Prospectiva* (Primera, Instituto de Investigaciones Jurídicas 2017).

[193] 'Agreement between the United States of America, the United Mexican States, and Canada Text', at /trade-agreements/free-trade-agreements/united-states-mexico-canada-agreement/agreement-between, accessed 27 March 2019.

[194] ibid.

[195] ibid.

The USMCA was negotiated to replace the 1994 North American Free Trade Agreement ("NAFTA"). One of the leading expectations of the USMCA negotiators was to "modernize" the old trade agreement that did not contemplate changes in technology, the services market, new global trade adversaries – such as China – and the new realities in Mexico's energy and telecommunication sectors.[196] In other words, one of the goals was to finally bring into agreement the energy sector that was left out of the 1994 deal, since back then the State-owned companies held a monopoly over the industry.[197] Lopez Obrador's request to modify the negotiated text shows clear signs that the new administration does not want to signal Mexico's openness to private investment, but rather reinforce the idea that the State and its companies will remain at the helm of development in the sector. As opposed to bringing the trade deal into modernity, the agreement, when it comes to the energy sector in Mexico, is a reinforcement of the 1938 nationalistic views of Lazaro Cardenas and the revolutionaries. Canada and the U.S. signed side letters addressing the integration of the energy markets by facilitating the flow of products and commodities.[198] However, under Lopez Obrador's instructions, Mexico did not participate in those letters.

Will the contracts with private parties of the energy reform, and particularly the licence model, survive the political change in Mexico? It will all depend on whether PEMEX can overturn the continuous depletion of its reserves and a push for rapid increase in existing production. The government does not need to modify the law or the Constitution again to assign all new fields to PEMEX. They could easily ignore the sections that allow participation of private parties and focus on the powers that the reform left to the government to centralize the activities of State-owned companies. Regarding the 107 signed contracts, from a political standpoint, Lopez Obrador would need to offer an alternative before forcing a renegotiation. Perhaps it is better for his administration to wait for the fields to start producing before compelling any changes in legislation that could affect the contracts and bring international litigation. From a legal standpoint, there are reasons to believe that they could fight off in courts the contradiction between the transitory articles and the constitutional text. As explained above, there are solid arguments that the spirit of the 1938 nation-

---

[196] Jacob M Schlesinger and Bob Davis, 'U.S., Mexico and Canada Sign Pact to Replace Nafta' *Wall Street Journal* (30 November 2018) www.wsj.com/articles/u-s -mexico-and-canada-sign-pact-to-replace-nafta-1543581929, accessed 27 March 2019.

[197] Bradly J Condon, 'Mexican Energy Reform and NAFTA Chapter 11: Articles 20 and 21 of the Hydrocarbons Law and Access to Investment Arbitration' (2016) 9 The Journal of World Energy Law & Business 203.

[198] 'Agreement between the United States of America, the United Mexican States, and Canada Text' (n 193).

alization could be disregarded by the contractual models offered by the 2013 Energy Reform.

The ball is up in the air, and one more time, Mexico must debate whether nationalism will prevail over efficiency and production. The Mexican political class must decide whether they believe in making PEMEX great again, or in a practical approach that allows the government to keep the property of the resource but use private or State entities to develop the resource on behalf of the nation. The choice between State monopolies and private participation for the development of oil is not a new debate; and just as in the days of the revolution, it sparks heated deliberations over sovereignty, foreign intervention, and the use of resources for government programs in a country desperate for solutions to reduce massive poverty and inequality. The unparalleled overexploitation of Cantarell was insufficient to bring Mexico into modernity. Will new governments learn the lesson or will they fall into the trap of the petro-dependent curse? Will they try to maximize short-term goals but sacrifice the future of generations to come?

11. The legal character of petroleum licences in the People's Republic of China

Yong Li

1. INTRODUCTION

The granting of licences for petroleum in the People's Republic of China is required across the entire petroleum chain. These licences either grant the administrative right to access petroleum (an 'access licence'), or to sanction an activity such as the construction of infrastructure, the movement of oil and gas, and the refinement and sale of petroleum products ('operational licences').

The regulatory approach to petroleum in China is unique, with strong state involvement (participatory intervention) and control through all aspects of the petroleum value chain, both onshore and offshore, where administrative rights to search for, take, move, process and sell petroleum are granted. Therefore, it is necessary to consider both access and operational licences throughout the entire petroleum value chain to gain a sense of the legal character of petroleum licences, the role of the state in the licensing as well as the legal character of those rights granted. Given the state's involvement and control, there will also be a consideration of foreign investment in licences and its impact on legal character.

2. OVERVIEW OF THE ADMINISTRATIVE SYSTEM OF CHINA'S PETROLEUM INDUSTRY

2.1 Property Rights System and Status of the Policy of China's Petroleum Industry

Classified as a mineral resource, petroleum resources are concealed, non-reproducible, and have dynamic value. Given the complexity of property rights related to these resources, regulation of their boundaries and planning warrants clarification. According to Article 9 of the *Constitution of the*

People's Republic of China and Article 11 of the *Mineral Resources Law of the People's Republic of China*, the following stipulations apply: mineral resources belong to the State; petroleum resources are owned by the State; and the competent department of Mineral Resources of the State Council shall carry out unified management of its exploration, exploitation, and operation. China's petroleum resources and mining rights can be divided into exploration rights, mining rights, management rights, and other specific rights. Applications for the exploration and exploitation of oil and natural gas must be approved by the State Council and registered with the Land and Resources Department in accordance with the law.

2.2   Evolution of the Management Institutions in China's Petroleum Industry

Upon the founding of the People's Republic of China under the traditional planned economic system, management institutions of the Chinese petroleum industry implemented a policy of public ownership. The policy also incorporated public utilities and public management of petroleum resources to manage China's petroleum and petrochemical industry via militarization and administration. Following China's economic reform and opening up, management institutions in the country's petroleum industry have fallen under the purview of first the Ministry of the Fuel Industry, followed by the Ministry of the Petrochemical Industry, Ministry of Energy, the State Petroleum Corporation with some state functions, and finally the State Petroleum and Chemical Industry Bureau, where it remains today.

The role of the Chinese government in the petroleum industry has also shifted from an operational to supervisory capacity as the industry has developed. Prior to 1998, the centralized and unified management of the Central Petroleum Industry Ministry and Oil Field Administration Bureau dominated China's petroleum industry. Conversely, administration of the petrochemical industry was managed on multiple administrative levels: by the central government; local governments (e.g., provincial and city level); and in some cases even on the county level, which occupies the lowest level in China's administrative hierarchy. Government management of the petroleum industry changed after 1998, ushering in a new managerial approach rooted in government supervision and macro-control.

The current management system of China's petroleum industry was implemented in early 2008. Various management functions were spread among the State Development and Reform Commission, the Ministry of Land and Resources, the Ministry of Commerce, the State-owned Assets Supervision and Administration Commission, the Ministry of Science and Technology, and other ministries or agencies dispatched by the State Council.

These agencies cover resource protection, resource development and utilization, industry access, investment approval, and price transfer along with macro-decision-making, administrative licensing, inspection and supervision, and other functions.

2.3   Formation and Roles of the Three Major State-Owned Companies

China's three major national oil companies, often referred to as the 'Three Barrels of Oil' and referred to here as the Three Barrels Consortium, consist of China National Petroleum Corporation (CNPC), China Petrochemical Corporation (Sinopec), and China National Offshore Oil Corporation (CNOOC). At present, these companies largely monopolize China's oil and gas sector. With the exception of Shaanxi Yanchang Oil Mine, which the State Council approves, the exploration and exploitation rights of oil resources are almost exclusively granted to the Three Barrels Consortium and their subsidiaries; the same goes for mining rights. The state has also authorized the Three Barrels Consortium to monopolize external oil and gas cooperation.

Prior to restructuring of the Three Barrels Consortium, many enforcement and supervision functions in the oil industry were performed by the head offices of CNPC, Sinopec, and CNOOC. In other words, the same government departments formulated policies and implemented supervision. After restructuring, the government's industry management functions in the petroleum industry were partially separated from the Three Barrels Consortium and concentrated in the comprehensive management department of the government. The original professional management force mostly remained within these companies. Under the currently imperfect government supervision mechanism, CNPC and Sinopec still assume several government functions that should not be under enterprise control: the leaders of the Three Barrels Consortium are still appointed by the government, and the government's administrative instructions remain relatively strong.

2.4   Licensing in the Chinese Petroleum Industry – Access Conditions

2.4.1   Overview of Sino–foreign joint venture and cooperative oil exploration and development licences

According to the *Rules for Implementation of the Mineral Resources Law of the People's Republic of China*, the unified management, grading examination, and approval systems shall be implemented for Chinese laws concerning the exploration and exploitation of petroleum resources. The permit system is the foundation for the exploration and exploitation of petroleum resources in

China. Foreigners who wish to obtain a petroleum exploration and development licence must first possess an exploration and mining licence.

Enterprises participating in Sino–foreign joint ventures and the cooperative exploration and development of petroleum must satisfy several criteria. First, foreign enterprises must register with the State Administration for Industry and Commerce to obtain a business licence from the People's Republic of China. No entity may engage in production or business operations without approval from the appropriate body and registration authority. When a foreign enterprise applies for a licence, it must submit the application to the State Administration for Industry and Commerce, and the application must be signed by the chairman of the Board of Directors or the general manager of the enterprise. In addition, the enterprise must submit the approval certificate for foreign-invested enterprises issued by the Ministry of Commerce, a capital credit certificate of the foreign enterprise, a letter of authorization from the person in charge, and identity certificates and other relevant documents.

For cooperation with foreign companies, Chinese petroleum companies (e.g., CNPC, CPC, or CNOOC) must submit the foreign cooperative exploitation contract to the Ministry of Commerce for examination and approval. After the petroleum contract is approved, the Ministry of Commerce issues the approval certificate. In addition to the above oil contracts, other geophysical exploration agreements and joint research agreements must be submitted to the Ministry for approval, but an approval certificate is not required.

The Ministry of National Resources (formerly known as the Ministry of Land and Resources) examines and approves exploration and mining licences. An enterprise must participate in the bidding process organized by the Ministry of Land and Resources to obtain an exploration licence. Petroleum exploration norms require necessary geophysical (e.g., two- and three-dimensional earthquake) and drilling studies to identify underground oil resources. Then, according to reserve specifications, the enterprise must submit the reserves for review and recording.

Lastly, an application is submitted to the National Development and Reform Commission for approval. When applying, the enterprise is required to submit the following materials: the foreign cooperation request document, an overall project development plan and project application report, a statement of the competent provincial government's energy/industry department, and site selection issued by the Department of Urban and Rural Planning and the Ministry of Land and Resources. The application shall also include pre-examined statements by the competent administrative department for land or sea, an oil and gas resources reserve certificate, and a project social stability risk assessment report.

2.4.2   Licensing system for offshore oil exploration in cooperation with foreign countries

In 1982, the State Council promulgated the *Regulations of the People's Republic of China Concerning the Exploitation of Offshore Petroleum Resources in Cooperation with Foreign Enterprises*, providing a legal guarantee for Sino–foreign cooperative exploitation of offshore oil. The regulation underwent four revisions between 2001 and 2013, and the system has become increasingly standardized.

China's foreign cooperation in offshore oil exploitation adheres to the following principles. First, ownership of oil under China's jurisdiction belongs to China. Second, the Chinese government protects mining activities and the legitimate interests of foreign enterprises according to law. In terms of a specific system structure, China's foreign cooperation in offshore oil exploitation possesses several unique features.

2.4.2.1   The role of the CNOOC

The CNOOC has the exclusive right to exploit offshore oil. Therefore, within the sea area intended for cooperation between Chinese enterprises and foreign companies, the CNOOC is entitled to the licence of exploitation, development, production, and sale. Once a Chinese company enters into a contract with a foreign counterpart in relation to exploitation and development, the contract shall be reported to the Ministry of Commerce.

As the CNOOC is a large state-owned enterprise directly under the State-owned Assets Supervision and Administration Commission of the State Council, the organization assumes managerial responsibilities. When implementing a contract, a foreign contractor must supply complete and accurate data, records, samples, vouchers, and other original materials of various petroleum operations along with information about and samples of technology, economics, accounting, and administrative measures to the CNOOC on a regular basis. Original materials obtained during implementation of the oil contract belong to the CNOOC.

2.4.2.2   Rights and obligations of foreign contractors

A foreign contractor must use a base within Chinese territory for operations. A foreign contractor shall be responsible for exploration operations and bear all exploration risks. The foreign contractor is also responsible for development and production operations until the CNOOC takes over production operations as agreed upon in the contract. China does not impose taxes on foreign contractors' investments and earnings; however, under certain circumstances and in accordance with public interests, part or all of the oil to which a foreign enterprise is entitled may be expropriated in accordance with legal procedures. In this case, the foreign contractor will be compensated accordingly.

2.4.3 Licensing system for onshore oil exploration in cooperation with foreign countries

In 1993, the *Regulations of the People's Republic of China on Sino–foreign Cooperation in the Development of Continental Petroleum Resources* were officially promulgated and implemented. Since then, the document has undergone four amendments from 2001 to 2013. At present, the CNPC and Sinopec enjoy exclusive rights to cooperate with foreign enterprises in onshore oil exploration, development, and production. Once a block has been publicized for use in cooperation with a foreign company, it can only be exploited by a Chinese petroleum company and foreign company jointly; other companies cannot become involved in any activities related to that block.

Enterprises that entered blocks for oil exploration before an announcement must withdraw when a Chinese oil company signs a contract with a foreign enterprise. The Chinese petroleum company shall be responsible for the sale of exploration data obtained by the enterprise to properly compensate for its investment. Following discovery of an oil field of commercial value in the block, enterprises withdrawing from the block can participate in the development through investment.

2.4.4 Foreign investors indirectly control mining rights through mergers and acquisition or contractual cooperation

This arrangement can only be implemented in a transaction between equal parties. The entity holding the mining rights or licence will remain unchanged, but shares of such an entity may be transferred or the shareholder of such an entity may be merged with another entity. Commercial departments at different levels will be responsible for briefly reviewing relevant transactions, and these transactions will be subject to the Regulations for Merger with and Acquisition of Domestic Enterprises by Foreign Investors.

In accordance with law, administrative statutes, and by-laws related to foreign investment, in the event that foreign investors take over the shares of a domestic company foreign investors are required to submit documentation that addresses shareholder agreements, contracts and articles of association, merger agreement, financial reports, and requisite licences.

In the case of an asset deal merger and acquisition by a foreign investor, the investor shall submit the following documents to the competent examination and approval authority regarding the type of enterprise and industry in which the investor is engaged. These materials must align with the provisions, laws, and administrative regulations and rules of foreign-invested enterprises in accordance with the total investments of the foreign-invested enterprise to be established.

3.   REGULATORY FRAMEWORK FOR PETROLEUM LICENSING IN CHINA

3.1   Classification of China's Petroleum Value Chain

China's petroleum value chain is divided into upstream, midstream, and downstream. Upstream includes exploration, exploitation, rolling exploration, and development as well as oil and gas trial production. Midstream links include oil and gas transfers and transportation, whereas downstream links include the operation and sale of crude oil and refined oil.

Due to the scarcity and uneven distribution of upstream petroleum resources, in addition to the great risks involved and high demand for capital support, resource exploration and exploitation occur on a multinational scale. Exploration includes mineral exploration; seismic exploration; gravity, magnetic, and electrical exploration; and geological exploration among other types. Production links include primary oil recovery, secondary oil recovery, drilling development, and construction of oil recovery engineering. Linking exploration and management, the midstream component of the value chain includes petroleum transportation and storage. The downstream component covers petroleum operations, management, and sales, including refining links and refining crude oil or other oils into kerosene, gasoline, diesel, heavy oil, and other fuels. In terms of chemical links, further processing of secondary petroleum products results in various petrochemical products (e.g., sales of processed petroleum products through retail outlets). The following sections introduce relevant licensing systems across all parts of the petroleum industry chain.

4.   LICENSING SYSTEM OF PETROLEUM INDUSTRY ACCESS CONDITIONS

4.1   Petroleum Exploration Licence

The Petroleum Exploration Licence grants the holder access to China's petroleum resources, and confers a right to undertake activities such as seismic survey, drilling, and other necessary and sanctioned activities. The licence is a certificate enabling the relevant subject to engage in oil exploration activities.

It is approved and granted by the Ministry of Natural Resources.[1] Applicants for the licence must meet the following requirements:

1. The applicant shall obtain an approval document from the State Council to establish an oil company or agree to perform oil and gas exploration (except for coal bed methane and shale gas exploration);
2. The applicant (or prospecting unit entrusted by the applicant) shall have the corresponding qualifications for oil and gas mineral exploration:
   (1) The application scope shall not exceed 2500 basic unit blocks;
   (2) The application scope shall not overlap with existing oil and gas exploration rights and/or mining rights;
   (3) The applicant shall have an exploration and implementation plan conforming to legal provisions and shall have a financial guarantee for implementation.

In essence, a licence holder is granted an administrative right to perform the activities outlined in the certificate. In addition to the rights granted, there are a number of administrative obligations that attach to a Licence of Exploration.

A holder of a Licence of Exploration will delay exploration activities, instead seeking funding by establishing a joint venture or cooperative exploration. To meet market demand, China has established a reservation system for oil exploration licensing.

In accordance with the provisions of *Regulation for Registering to Explore For Mineral Resources Using the Block System* (2014 Revision), the licence holder is entitled to delay the minimum expenditure for a certain block without compromising the validity of the licence, given that resources have been discovered and the licence holder has obtained approval from a competent agency.[2] The period of suspension should not exceed two years and can only be applied twice during that period. Once the suspension period has expired, if the licence-holder does not pursue exploitation, the licence will be withdrawn.[3]

4.2   Oil Mining Licences

An Oil Mining Licence is an administrative certificate denoting the right to engage in oil production activities, as approved and issued by the Ministry

[1]   Art. 3 of *Administrative Measures for Registration of the Mining of Mineral Resources* (amended in 2014).
[2]   Art. 21 (1) *Regulation for Registering to Explore For Mineral Resources Using the Block System* (amended in 2014).
[3]   Art. 21 (2), (4) ibid.

of Natural Resources. An applicant for an Oil Mining Licence must meet the
following conditions:

1. The applicant presents either a document from the State Council approv-
    ing the establishment of a petroleum company, or a document permitting
    exploration of petroleum and/or gas as well as the Legal Person Certificate
    for the exploration unit;
2. The applicant provides an application for the registration of mining rights
    within the period specified in the scope of the mining area or within the
    limit stipulated in the mining rights contract;
3. The applicant possesses the necessary qualifications of mining right
    applicants;
4. Except under certain circumstances, the scope of the mining area for which
    registration is applied will not overlap with the vertical projection scope of
    the established mining rights, and will conform to mineral resource plan-
    ning and national industrial policy;
5. The plan for exploitation and utilization of mineral resources, the plan for
    protection of the mine geological environment, and the plan for land rec-
    lamation must have been evaluated and approved, and the environmental
    impact assessment report approved by the relevant regulatory authority
    (Environmental Protection Department);
6. The grant of mining rights must conform to all relevant provisions, and
    the paid disposal of mining rights must be completed according to the
    provisions;
7. The exploration right-holder has submitted relevant geological data in
    accordance with the provisions;
8. In cases where an exploration right has been transferred to a mining right,
    the original exploration right has been cancelled.

4.2.1   Rolling exploration and petroleum development

Oil rolling exploration and development comprise a rapid exploration method
involving simplified evaluation and exploration of complex oil and gas fields,
and is utilized to accelerate the construction of new oil field production capacity and realize simultaneous exploration. Rolling exploration and the development of oil are outlined in the general rules of petroleum exploration and
development, but the application conditions for this permit and licence period
differ from a common mineral resources exploration licence. Conditions
required for approval include a rolling exploration and development of petro-
leum/natural gas reserves report, rolling exploration and development of material and rolling exploration and development and utilization plan, and other
information demonstrating the necessity and feasibility of rolling exploration
and development.

4.3   Oil and Gas Trial Production Licence

Before proven reserves of petroleum resources can be formally exploited, a small-scale trial production may be required. Oil and gas trial production licences shall be obtained in accordance with the law for oil and gas trial production activities in China. Applicants for the Oil and Gas Trial Production Licence must meet the following conditions:

1. The exploration entity possesses a qualification certificate from the exploration unit issued by the competent department of Geology and Mineral Resources;
2. Trial production is only undertaken by the trial production licence holder;
3. The applied trial production area must be within established oil and gas exploration rights, and the longitudinal and latitudinal coordinates of the applied trial production well must be accurate and detailed;
4. The applicant shall conform to national mineral resource plans and national industrial policies;
5. The applicant shall comply with other relevant laws and regulations regarding exploration of oil and gas resources.

5.   LEGAL CHARACTER OF UPSTREAM PETROLEUM ACCESS LICENCES

Either the *Administrative Licensing Act* or *Mining Resource Act* and its *Implementation Rules* dictate that the exploration of natural resources should be granted or approved by the administrative authorities.[4] Thus, in terms of legal character, the rights granted for upstream petroleum licences can be considered administrative licensing rights.

Under the petroleum licensing system, the grant or the formation of the licence will confer a property right that is able to be transferred with a negotiated price. The *Mining Resources Law* provides the given circumstances under which the transfer of the licensing is feasible, if (i) the person who possesses the right of exploitation has accomplished a minimal investment in the given the exploitation area can transfer the right of exploitation to a third party with the approval from the competent authority(ies); or (ii) the companies which pursue the mining industry, if merged, split, establishing a joint venture with others, selling assets, or other form of change to the ownership, which leads to the modification of the subject company, they can transfer the mining right to

---

[4]   See Art. 12 of *Administrative Licensing Law*, Art. 3 of the *Mineral Resources Law* and Art. 5 of the *Implementation Rules of the Mineral Resources Law*.

others with permission from the authority(ies).[5] The parties that participate in the process of petroleum licensing include the administrative authority and the licence holder or the licence applicant. In China, the relationship between the authority and licence holder can be viewed as a legal relation administrated by administrative laws or rules rather than a contractual relationship protected by the contract law or other civil codes.

As described above, despite the licence arising from the administrative authority's grant or permission it can also be characterized as a private right. As such, any effort to nationalize or expropriate the private property must adhere to existing laws and rules[6] and compensates the person or entity which holds the licence with a consideration, usually calculated with a criterion set under administrative rules enacted by state or provincial agencies. The *Law of the Protection to the Mining Resources* provides that the state protects the right of exploitation and right of mining from being infringed as well as the production order and work order beyond being disrupted or demolished.[7]

5.1   Rules for Bidding, Auction, and Listing of Exploration and Mining Rights

According to Article 13 of *Measures for The Regulation for Registering to Explore Mineral Resources Using the Block System* (amended in 2014), 'If anyone applies for exploration rights to any blocks containing mineral deposits discovered by the State, and at the State's expense, the applicant shall pay a reimbursement fee for [the] exploration right based on the State's prior investment, in addition to the exploration fee.' After the exploration and exploitation rights of oil resources are defined, government departments will transfer oil exploitation rights to the three major state-owned oil companies (i.e., the Three Barrels of Oil). These companies are responsible for specific mining, transportation, and operational matters, whereas mining rights are mostly obtained through government bidding, auctions, and listings.

5.1.1   Bidder
A bidder must be a qualified subject who holds an Oil Exploration Licence and Oil Mining Licence. The bidder must also 'be able to meet the comprehensive evaluation criteria specified in the bidding documents to the greatest extent.'[8]

---

[5]   See Art. 6 of *Mining Resources Law*.
[6]   See Art. 21 of *Promulgation to Trials to the Cases Relating to Administrative Agreements*, issued by the People's Republic of China's Supreme People's Court.
[7]   See the *Law of the Protection to the Mineral Resources*.
[8]   Art. 33 of *Regulations for the Administration of Tendering, Auction and Listing of Prospecting and Mining Rights*.

In addition, there should be more than three bidders at any time; if there are fewer than three bidders, the competent authorities should either reorganize or cease bidding in accordance with these measures.

5.1.2   Competent authorities

The bidding, auction, and listing of exploration and mining rights shall be organized and implemented by the Land and Resources administrative departments of the Chinese government at or above the county level in accordance with the statutory limits of authority for issuing exploration and mining licences.

5.1.3   Bidding process

Before the formal bidding auction process begins, the competent authorities shall formulate a bidding and auction plan in accordance with local mineral resource plans, national industrial policies, and market supply. These authorities should also entrust an evaluation agency with adopting inquiries, analogies, and other factors to determine the lowest price for bidding, auctioning, and listing; this information must then be reported to higher-level competent authorities for registration.

Then, the competent authorities shall make a public announcement according to law to publicize the conditions. The announcement of bidding, auction, and listing must include the following in part: name and address of the competent department; summaries of the exploration blocks and mining areas to be listed in the bidding, auction, and listing; qualifications for applying for exploration and mining rights; and requirements for obtaining bidders' qualifications.[9]

After bidding, auction, and listing activities have been completed, the competent authorities shall publish the results, including the winning bid, to the designated places and media within ten working days. If the winning bidder provided false documents to conceal facts or otherwise used malicious collusion, bribery, and other means to win, the results of bidding will be invalid, and deposits paid toward bidding will not be refunded.

5.2   Petroleum Industry Operation and Management Licence System

5.2.1   Crude Oil Business Licence system

In order for a production licence holder to sell the crude oil produced it is required to obtain a Qualifications for the Crude Oil Business Licence, which incorporates a Crude Oil Sales Licence and Crude Oil Storage Licence. These

---

[9]   Art. 17 ibid.

administrative licences are reviewed and issued by the Ministry of Commerce. An enterprise applying for the qualification to sell crude oil must meet the following conditions:

1. The applicant shall hold legal person status of a Chinese enterprise with registered capital of no less than 100 million yuan;
2. The enterprise shall have a long-term and stable crude oil supply channel:
   (1) crude oil mining enterprises that have obtained an Oil Mining Licence with the approval of the State Council and have actual production, or
   (2) an import enterprise qualified to import crude oil that imports more than 500,000 tons of crude oil annually, or
   (3) entrance into a crude oil supply agreement with an enterprise that meets the above requirements (1) and (2) for more than one year consecutively in line with its business scale;
3. The enterprise shall have long-term, stable, and legal crude oil sales channels;
4. The enterprise shall have a crude oil depot with a storage capacity of no less than 200,000 cubic meters, and the oil depot construction must conform to local urban and rural planning and oil depot layout planning. The enterprise must also conform to required conditions for land and resources, planning and construction, safety supervision, public security fire control, environmental protection, meteorology, and quality inspection and other inspections.[10]

Enterprises applying for crude oil storage qualifications must meet the following conditions:

1. The applicant shall hold legal person status of a Chinese enterprise with registered capital of no less than 50 million yuan;
2. The enterprise shall have a crude oil depot with a storage capacity of no less than 500,000 cubic meters, and the construction of the oil depot must conform to local urban and rural planning as well as oil depot layout planning. The enterprise must also conform to required conditions for land and resources, planning and construction, safety supervision, public security fire control, environmental protection, meteorology, and quality inspection and other inspections;
3. The enterprise shall be equipped with transportation pipelines or dedicated railway lines for receiving and discharging crude oil or water transportation terminals with a capacity of no less than 50,000 tons.

---

[10]	Art. 6 of *Rules of Regulation to Crude Oil Market* (2015 Revision).

5.2.2 Refined Oil Business Licence system

The term *'refined oil'* refers to gasoline, kerosene, diesel oil, and other alternative fuels that meet national quality standards and satisfy the same purposes as ethanol, gasoline, and bio-diesel. An application for the Refined Oil Business Licence includes a Certificate of Approval for the Wholesale of Refined Oil, Certificates of Approval for the Retail of Refined Oil, and a Certificate of Approval for the Storage of Refined Oil.

An enterprise that applies for the qualification to engage in wholesale business of refined oil must meet the conditions set out in Rules of Regulation to Refined Oil Market.[11]

Demonstrating the administrative nature of the downstream operations licences, a refined oil retailing enterprise must purchase refined oil from enterprises qualified to engage in the wholesale business of refined oil. No refined oil retailing enterprise may sell refined oil on a commission basis for any enterprise without the qualification to engage in the wholesale business of refined oil. If an approved enterprise violates the above requirements, or its licence is obtained by circumventing legal authority or other illegal means such as fraud.

5.2.3 Oil transportation licensing system

In accordance with the Provisions on the Administration of Road Transport of Dangerous Goods, *dangerous goods* refers to explosive, inflammable, toxic, infectious, or corrosive goods which can cause injuries or casualties during production, operation, transportation, storage, use, or disposal; as well as substances and articles that require special care to prevent property damage or environmental pollution. As refined oil is categorized as a flammable and explosive dangerous good, a Road Transportation Business Permit or a Road Licence for Dangerous Goods is required to transport refined oil. An enterprise engaging in the road transportation of dangerous goods shall obtain the Road Transportation Business Permit, whereas the Road Licence for Dangerous Goods shall be obtained by a non-operating transport entity.

5.2.4 Other relevant operational licences

5.2.4.1 Administration of offshore oil work safety

Non-coal mining enterprises such as metal and non-metal mining enterprises and their tailing ponds, geological prospecting entities, excavation engineering enterprises, and oil and natural gas enterprises shall obtain work safety licences before engaging in production activities.

---

[11] See Art. 7 of *Rules of Regulation to Refined Oil Market*.

5.2.4.2   Licence to operate hazardous chemicals
As petroleum is regarded as a hazardous chemical per the Catalogue of Hazardous Chemicals within China, an enterprise engaging in this business must obtain a permit to operate hazardous chemicals.

5.2.4.3   Licence for oil pipeline construction and operation
An oil pipeline enterprise must establish a pipeline construction plan according to the National Plan on the Development of Pipelines and submit its pipeline construction plan to the Department of Urban and Rural Planning at or above the county level in the location where pipelines are to be constructed. If the area where a new pipeline will pass is restricted by geographical conditions and therefore cannot meet the requirements for pipeline protection, the pipeline enterprise must propose a protection plan. The enterprise must not initiate pipeline construction until pipeline protection experts have reviewed the protection plan and administrative approval is granted.

    If construction operations involve 'passing through or crossing over the pipeline', the construction entity must file an application with the pipeline protection administrative department at the county level where the pipeline is located. After the pipeline protection administrative department receives the application, it shall arrange for the construction entity and pipeline enterprise to determine a construction operation scheme through negotiations and sign a safety protection agreement.

6.   FOREIGN INVESTMENT AND PETROLEUM INDUSTRY LICENSING

6.1   Overview of Foreign Investment in China's Oil Exploration and Exploitation Industry

6.1.1   Importance of Chinese and foreign petroleum cooperation
In recent years China's oil production has declined whilst importation of oil products continues to rise. In 2017, China's foreign oil dependency was 67.4%,[12] exceeding the internationally recognized 50% security threshold. This high dependency on foreign oil imports arises from China possessing only one kind of mineral oil coupled with a lack of innovation. Accordingly, China's long-term energy security is not assured, posing a direct threat to the achievement of China's sustainable development goals. It was therefore inevi-

---

[12]   Data from: China Petroleum Group Economic and Technological Research Institute, 'Report on the Development of Oil and Gas Industry at Home and Abroad 2017' 215.

Table 11.1   Petroleum external cooperation from 2015 to 2017

Year	Newly proved geological reserves of oil (tons)	Issued Foreign Cooperative Exploration Licences	Issued Foreign Cooperation Mining Licences
2015	11.8	36	39
2016	9.14	32	37
2017	8.77	33	38

Source: National Oil and Gas Exploration and Exploitation Bulletin.

table for China to introduce foreign investment into the petroleum industry to constantly strengthen Sino–foreign petroleum cooperation.

President Xi Jinping gave an elaborate presentation on the importance of Chinese cooperation with foreign businesses at the 16th meeting of the Central Financial and Economic Affairs Commission on July 17, 2017. In his speech, Xi noted that

> One of the important motivations behind establishing an open economy is to accelerate our own institutional and regulatory development, improve our business and innovation environment, reduce market operating costs, improve operational efficiency and enhance international competitiveness. Foreign investment has promoted the rational allocation of resources, promoted market-oriented reform and played an important role in China's economic development. We will continue to promote structural reforms on the supply-side, achieve higher economic growth and keep up with the pace of global scientific and technological progress.

6.1.2   Means for foreign capital to enter China's petroleum exploration and mining industry

Article 7 of the *Rules for the Implementation of the Mineral Resources Law of the People's Republic of China* stipulates that the state allows foreign companies, enterprises, other economic organizations, and individuals to invest in the exploration and exploitation of mineral resources on Chinese territory and other sea areas under its jurisdiction in accordance with relevant laws and regulations. Foreign ordinary civil subjects can invest in the exploration and mining industry in China; however, Article 2 of the *Special Management Measures (Negative List) for the Access of Foreign Investment (2018)* limits the exploration and development of oil and natural gas to joint ventures and corporations.

At present, the circulation of mining rights in China can be classified into two levels: the primary market and secondary market. The primary market, with the government as the main body, can be further divided into the approval application method, agreement transfer method, and bidding and listing auction method. The secondary market is composed of equal subjects, including cooperation, joint ventures, and mergers and acquisitions.[13]

7.   OTHER RELEVANT ISSUES PERTAINING TO THE LEGAL CHARACTER OF CHINA'S PETROLEUM LICENCES

7.1   Sino–Foreign Petroleum Cooperation under the Belt and Road Initiative (OBOR)

The Belt and Road Initiative (OBOR) refers to 'the Silk Road Economic Belt and the 21st-century Maritime Silk Road.' The aim of OBOR is to use China as a starting point to link Central Asia, the Trans-Caucasian region, the Middle East, and West Asia. OBOR is also intended to expand to the south, with Africa, Europe, and Latin America as the three major endpoints. In the following years, China has established long-term, stable cooperation and exchange with countries along the Belt and Road, and several partnerships have been established in the upstream, middle, and downstream parts of the oil and gas industry. The Blue Paper on the Development Analysis and Prospect Report of China's Oil and Gas Industry in 2017, released by the China Petroleum Enterprises Association, pointed out that the 'one belt and one way' area has become the most important oil and gas cooperation zone for Chinese oil and gas enterprises; its oil and gas investment and output account for more than 50% of total overseas investment and total output of China's oil and gas enterprises.

Today, China has launched a series of joint oil-related projects with countries along the Silk Road Economic Belt (e.g., the Sino–Kazakhstani pipeline developments). Many Chinese enterprises have also cooperated with Kazakhstan in oil and gas exploration and development, such as through important collaborative projects such as the Aktobe, Kashagan, and Karazhambas projects. Energy cooperation between China and Uzbekistan mainly includes cooperation projects in the Brack oil field and petroleum exploration projects in salt water. China and the United Arab Emirates have cooperated in the exploration and development of oil and gas resources, construction of storage and transportation facilities, petroleum refining, and chemical industries along with other fields. China and Singapore have launched technical cooperation around the development and construction of oil and gas infrastructure; additionally, China

---

[13]   Huo Jinhui, 'Study on the Legal Regulation of Foreign Investment in China's Mineral Resources Exploration and Mining Industry: From the Perspective of National Security', [2012] Dissertation of Hebei Univ. 7.

has always been a prime petroleum market for Singapore. China and Russia have cooperated on the construction of the Eastern Siberia–Pacific Ocean oil pipeline. China has also opened its downstream industries to Russia appropriately. As the two countries share interests, the level of cooperation has grown.

The Belt and Oil initiative is inclusive and innovative, meaning that China's oil cooperation with other countries along the route should introduce new modes of cooperation on the basis of existing projects to realize mutual benefits and development. Among existing projects, oil and gas exploration projects in salt water fall under the product-sharing mode, the China–Kazakhstan oil pipeline project falls under the technical service mode, and the Aktubin project falls under the joint operation mode.[14] The joint operation mode includes joint investment, benefit sharing, and risk sharing between the partners and is consistent with the goal of sustainable development in the Belt and Oil initiative. It is possible that new forms of licences may be issued or decided for such new projects, although this remains to be seen.

7.2   China's Emerging Legal System

It is important to note that China's petroleum regulatory laws and regulations have tended to lag behind those of other countries. Most such regulations originated in the 1980s and 1990s and do not meet current needs for petroleum management. Although China is not a resource-rich country with abundant petroleum resources, it is nevertheless a major player in petroleum production and consumption. Therefore, it is necessary to learn from foreign legal systems while considering China's national conditions. Then, the country can gradually build and improve a legal system that holds energy law at its core but also includes basic laws, administrative regulations, local regulations, departmental regulations, and local government regulations. It is also important to gradually abolish laws and regulations of 'combining government with enterprise' and 'replacing government with enterprise' (e.g., monopolized rights to land and ocean foreign cooperation)[15] to improve legislation around foreign cooperation and pipeline supervision, to fulfil World Trade Organization commitments, and encourage foreign investment. Such reforms would bring advanced technology, promote industrial innovation, and accelerate oil supply-side reform. This stocktake of China's petroleum licences provides a much-needed insight

---

[14]   Gao Jinrui, 'Research on Energy Cooperation between China and the Countries along the Belt and Road', [2016] Hebei Univ. 19.

[15]   Pan Jiping, Wang Yue, Shen Yanping, Yang Lili, 'Norway, Brazil and Britain's Oil and Gas Resource Management System and Its Enlightenment to China', [2019] Land Resource Information 7.

into the legal character of those licences, upon which such reforms can take place.

12. Afterword: Licence rights – what's left?

Terence Daintith

It is not often that one gets the chance to revisit work done 40 years ago and to relate it to current scholarship on the same subject, and I am most grateful to Professor Tina Soliman Hunter for offering me this opportunity for reflection on the changes in petroleum licensing evidenced by this exciting new collection of essays. In 1981 I set myself, and my collaborators from Australia, Canada, Denmark, and Norway – along with the distinguished international lawyer Professor (later Judge) Rosalyn Higgins – the same task of comparative analysis of legal issues related to petroleum licensing.[1] This volume offers a more varied and contextualised discussion than we achieved, but there are still useful comparisons to be drawn between the findings of the foregoing chapters and those that resulted from our earlier work.

In 1981 we were in the midst of rapid expansion of oil and gas production, both offshore and onshore, with the offshore being the key province in the countries we selected. While these were all 'first world' countries, their oil politics to some degree reflected the turbulence of the world oil scene generally. Over the previous decade or so, the Organization of the Petroleum Exporting Countries (OPEC) production cartel had succeeded in overturning the regime of long-term concession agreements enjoyed by the large international oil companies, successfully making new demands for control of prices and high levels of participation in assets, by way of renegotiation of agreements or, if push came to shove, expropriations. Some of our subject countries were likewise led, by the appearance of unexpectedly high production profits, both to modify their fiscal regimes and, in certain cases, to apply OPEC-like pressure for new exploration and production terms more favourable to the

---

[1] Terence Daintith ed., *The Legal Character of Petroleum Licences* (Dundee, 1981) (cited below as '1981 volume'). The contributors were Rosalyn Higgins (international law, pp. 35–59); Michael Crommelin (Australia, pp. 60–100); Rowland Harrison (Canada, pp. 101–62); Uggi Engel (Denmark, pp. 163–77); Asger Thylstrup (Greenland and the Faeroe Islands, pp. 178–84); John Rein (Norway, pp. 185–99); Terence Daintith (Introduction, pp. 1–34, and United Kingdom, pp. 200–26).

state than those originally offered. It was therefore not surprising that the main preoccupation of those writing in 1981 was with the stability of the licensing arrangements that represented the common basis of the regimes we examined. Could a licence be unilaterally amended? Could it be revoked, with or without compensation? And to what extent did the answers to these questions depend upon the legal character of the licence?

A comparison of contributions to this volume with 1981 papers covering the same countries (Australia, Canada, Norway, and the United Kingdom) shows that some of the answers to these questions are today different from those we recorded or anticipated, notably by reason of intervening case-law, as in Australia and Norway, or through the strengthening of international protection of property rights and investments, as applied in Canada and the United Kingdom. At the same time, it appears that some of the puzzles we encountered – such as the extent to which licences were or should be treated as contractual in character – continue to be puzzles today, not only in some of our 1981 jurisdictions but also in others. The overriding conclusion I draw from this volume as a whole, however, is that the three questions I mention above are today much less central to the general issue of the stability of a petroleum regime and the strength of the economic guarantees it offers investors in explo- ration and production activities. Of course they continue to be of considerable interest and difficulty, as the Australian chapter demonstrates;[2] but judging a regime simply by the responses it returns to these questions may result in misjudgement of the legal risks presented by its operation. Several different factors lead me to this conclusion.

1.   ALTERNATIVE LEGAL VEHICLES DISPLACING OR QUALIFYING LICENCES

The first, obvious, point to make is that the licence itself is no longer the dominant form of legal instrument through which companies hold their exploration and production rights. I regard today's 'licence' as a concession in modern form. In many ways it differs remarkably from the traditional petroleum concession, as used in the Middle East and in Latin America from the late-nineteenth to the mid-twentieth century. Those concessions covered vast areas, sometimes entire countries, and imposed little control on the activities of concessionaires. In contrast licences – which have also drawn on other precedents, such as the private petroleum lease developed in the United States or the mining lease, influential in Australia – cover quite small areas

---

[2]   Soliman Hunter, this volume.

of land and are awarded competitively.[3] They share with such concessions, however, the key characteristic of guaranteeing to the licensee, in return for its assumption of all risks and costs, the property in petroleum once recovered (though not necessarily prior to that point). It is this that distinguishes them from other forms of title, such as the production sharing agreement (PSA) and the risk service contract, whose use spread rapidly in the later decades of the twentieth century, especially in developing countries. Such agreements differ from the concession in that the contractor does not obtain title to produced oil or gas at the wellhead, but only at a defined delivery point and by way of acquisition from the State, whose property it remains up to that point. They were also designed to secure for the state a much greater degree of control over the continuing operations of the contractor than was afforded by the traditional concession. While in 1981 the concession – in traditional form or modernised as the licence – was probably still the dominant form of title, today it represents a minority choice. In an unpublished worldwide study of exploration and production agreements I undertook in 2016, covering 37 countries, only 17 of the 60 agreements examined were of the concession type. The remainder were PSAs or other kinds of risk service contract.

None of the countries represented in this volume, it would appear, has wholly abandoned the licence in favour of these other forms of legal instrument. Indeed, a slender majority – Australia, Canada, Norway, the United Kingdom, the United States – have been faithful to the licence as the sole means of admitting non-state actors to the business of exploring for and exploiting petroleum resources under state ownership or control. But in China, Mexico, Russia, and Uganda the licence now appears alongside other forms of title, in a fascinating variety of configurations. In Russia it was displaced, for a relatively brief period, by the PSA, but appears now to be once more the only form of title.[4] In Mexico, however, after a long period in which licensing was ruled out by the operation of PEMEX's monopoly, the licence reappeared over the period 2013–18, but as only one of several alternative kinds of agreement, alongside service agreements and PSAs,[5] that might be concluded by the Ministry of Energy. Elsewhere the situation is more complex. It would appear that in China and in the Russian offshore, what we might regard as

---

[3]   Denmark was an exception: at the time we wrote, the whole Danish offshore had been awarded as a single concession to A P Moeller and Co. See Engel, 1981 volume, 163–75.

[4]   Fodchenko, this volume, section 4.1.

[5]   Sanchez, this volume, pp. 219–221. It would appear that all the contracts concluded under this regime by the Ministry of Energy (see Sanchez, pp. 223–226) have taken the form of licences, though PEMEX has also concluded some service agreements with private companies in this period under the pre-existing regime.

a licence can only be held by state-owned or state-controlled companies: CNOOC, Sinopec or CNPC for China[6] and Gazprom and Rosneft for Russia.[7] In these cases, we may encounter a two-level system, in which the national oil company holds the petroleum licence but co-opts private or foreign capital through PSAs. From the standpoint of the oil company, however, the situation remains straightforward: its rights and obligations will be comprehensively set out in the PSA or service agreement, and it should not need to concern itself with the terms of the licence.

Not all countries that prefer PSAs or service agreements, however, have established a national oil company or choose to use it as a monopoly licence-holder. Uganda provides an example. Its legislation envisages the grant of licences accompanied by the conclusion of a PSA or some other form of agreement. In fact the PSA is negotiated first and the licence granted in accordance with its terms.[8] India also has a regime that combines a licensing system, broadly on the British model, with PSAs,[9] and there are certainly others. The result of the combination may be that the key feature of a licensing system as an expression of the concession approach – the acquisition by the licensee of property in petroleum at the wellhead – is nullified or substantially modified by an associated contract framed on the contrasting approach of the service agreement. Conditioning the award of a licence on acceptance of an associated agreement is certainly not new. State participation agreements – of which there are several examples in the contributions here[10] – come to mind, but while these may increase the constraints on licensees they do not change the underlying legal nature of those licensees' relationship with the state. Grafting PSAs or other service agreements onto an established licence system – as opposed to displacing it entirely – may however have the effect of reducing the licence to a mere formality or of creating awkward problems of reconciling licence rights and obligations with those contained in the associated agreement.

---

[6]   Li, this volume, pp. 235–239, referring to a virtual monopoly of these companies in the holding of licence rights.

[7]   Fodchenko, section 6.4.

[8]   Kasimbazi, this volume, pp. 116–118.

[9]   See the Petroleum and Natural Gas (Amendment) Rules, 2003, r. 7, and Model Production Sharing Contract (5th offer of blocks) (2005), at http://petroleum.nic.in/sites/default/files/MPSC%20NELP-V.pdf (accessed 4 April 2020).

[10]   See Roggenkamp, this volume, p. 149, p. 156; Nordveit, this volume, pp. 165–171. The nature of the 'concessional' agreements that may be attached to onshore licences in Russia (Fodchenko, section 5.2) is not clear.

2.   LICENCE FORM AND CONTENT

Countries that remain faithful to the idea of a 'pure' licensing regime may nonetheless design them in remarkably different ways. The most obvious contrast to be observed in 1981 was between the United Kingdom and Danish licences, on the one hand, and the Canadian, Norwegian, and Australian licences on the other. In the first group the regime stayed close to the style of the traditional petroleum concession – which in countries without industrial development might be the only law of any relevance to petroleum operations – by incorporating in the licence itself, alongside the rights granted to the licensee, the great majority of the specialised rules, both economic and operational, applicable to upstream petroleum activities. In the second, the licence was more skeletal in form, containing only the location and terms of the grant and the financial provisions and work obligations specific to the licence area. In Canada and Norway licence obligations were filled out by the making of regulations, which were then deemed to operate as part of the licence relationship. In Australia (in the Commonwealth's offshore jurisdiction) all the operational rules were contained in the primary legislation, the Petroleum (Submerged Lands) Act 1967, or in 'directions' issued to licence holders under it. By these means the content of the licence could, within limits, be modified by governmental decisions for which the consent of the licensee was not required, whereas in the United Kingdom and Denmark the licence did not make provision for its own modification. This contrast is likewise visible among the countries added by this study: the Mexican licence of 2013–18 contains a comprehensive ordering of the licencor-licensee relationship,[11] while as John Lowe reminds us, US federal licences, both onshore and offshore, are short, but 'incorporate by reference other statutes and regulations, often including future changes.'[12]

We noticed in 1981, and should remind ourselves now, that this contrast does not correspond to a choice between contractual and administrative bases for licensing. The United Kingdom licence was (and remains) a contract, like those in Canada, Norway, Mexico, and the United States; the Danish licence was an administrative authorisation, like the very different Australian offshore licence. And while we might assume that the strongest form of licensee protection is offered by a detailed contractual licence of the United Kingdom type,

---

[11]   For an example see Contrato para la Extracción de Hidrocarburos bajo la modalidad de Licencia entre Comision Nacional de Hidrocarburos y Canamex Energy Holdings, S.A.P.I. De C.V. (10 May 2016) at www.resourcecontracts.org/contract/ocds -591adf-7768716171/view#/pdf (accessed 2 April 2020).
[12]   Lowe, this volume, at p. 64.

with no provision for its own modification, we have only to look at the United Kingdom's Petroleum and Submarine Pipe-lines Act 1975, which unilaterally changed the terms of all existing licences,[13] to see that stability and protection need to be measured by reference to the overall environment of the licence relationship, including the constitutional framework and the degree of assurance offered by past governmental behaviour.

3.   REGULATION FROM OUTSIDE THE LICENCE

The second important development is the ever-increasing part played in the determination of the viability of the licence bargain by the operation of controls that may be superimposed upon that bargain from the outside: that is to say, controls that have their source in other legislative or regulatory powers and are then made applicable to the behaviour of licensees.

The United Kingdom offers a recent and striking example. As Gordon and Paterson demonstrate,[14] its licence today remains a quite comprehensive document that still contains detailed economic controls and general rules directed at the avoidance of waste and pollution (though obligations to protect the health and safety of workers were removed in 1992 in favour of the application of general health and safety law); but there is now superimposed upon it a second set of statutory obligations imposed under the Energy Act 2016 in the interest of securing the maximum economic recovery (MER) of the United Kingdom's offshore petroleum resources.[15] These obligations may well conflict with choices about development and operations that licensees might be empowered by the terms of their licence to make. Gordon and Paterson comment that

> the significance of the licence is thereby diminished, with the action taking place at the level of the MER UK Strategy. It is still important to have a licence – and to understand how one maximises one's chances of obtaining one – but, once held, the state's ability to regulate depends to a lesser extent on the terms and conditions of the licence and much more on the Strategy and its statutory foundation.[16]

It is easy to see the parallel here between the diminution produced by the Strategy and that effected by making licence rights subordinate to an annexed PSA.

Other contributions to this volume make reference to different types of additional control that may also have significant impacts on the viability of

---

[13] See Daintith, 1981 volume, 213–15.
[14] This volume, at pp. 128–129.
[15] At pp. 132–137.
[16] At p. 137.

the licence. The Australian chapter refers to the public opposition, on environmental grounds, to operations under licences granted in the Great Australian Bight.[17] It envisages a scenario in which licence revocation results; but development might in any event be rendered impossible if the title-holder's environmental plan for the project fails to satisfy the National Offshore Petroleum Safety and Environmental Management Authority (NOPSEMA) that its environmental impacts and risks will not only be reduced to the lowest practicable level but will also 'be of an acceptable level'[18] – a standard which, it has been acknowledged, means that some projects might be unable to take place at all.[19] The Canadian chapter highlights the economic impact of Guidelines of the joint Canada-Newfoundland and Labrador Board determining the minimum sums that licensees must devote to research and development expenditure – regardless, apparently, of whether this was necessary for the achievement of their general licence obligations. As Bankes notes, the Guidelines were made compulsory in relation to existing licences 'by making them a condition of the operator's Production Operations Authorization (POA), which is renewed annually.'[20]

These two cases are specific expressions of two major changes to petroleum licensing regimes that, over the last 40 years, have been taking place across the globe. The first is the ever-increasing stringency of environmental regulation, which has moved from being the concern of vague and hard-to-enforce standards in the licence itself to an all-encompassing discipline for every stage of operations, a discipline whose demands have meant that some licensees have simply been unable to exercise their granted rights to 'search, bore for, and get' the petroleum in their licensed area: notably, if this exercise requires fracking. Those demands are surely set to increase still further as we advance into the transition to a post-carbon world.

The second change is the arrival of the idea that development and production should be conditioned not just on the possession of a production licence but also on a range of additional consents, such as the Canadian POA referred to by Bankes. This notion was already gaining traction in 1981: the United Kingdom had introduced such a requirement by way of its unilaterally

---

[17] Soliman Hunter, this volume, at pp. 18–20.
[18] Offshore Petroleum and Greenhouse Gas Storage (Environment) Regulations 2009 (as amended to 2019), reg. 10A(a), (b).
[19] It is worth noting that in its first few months of operation in 2012, NOPSEMA initially rejected (though not necessarily on this ground) 60 of the 77 environment plans that came before it for approval: John Chandler and Terence Daintith, 'Offshore petroleum regulation after Montara: the new regulatory style,' (2015) 34 *Australian Resources and Energy Law Journal* 34, at 45–46.
[20] Bankes, this volume, at p. 89.

imposed licence changes in 1975. Today, however, the most far-reaching of these controls, the requirement that, once a commercial discovery is made, an exploiting company must obtain approval for a multi-year development plan in order to proceed further, is all but universal across all kinds of petroleum contracts, including licences.[21] Where a country adopts a multi-stage approach to licensing, with separate titles for exploration and production (and perhaps for a 'holding' stage as in Australia's retention lease and Canada's significant discovery licence), such an approval may fit naturally into the procedure for the award of the production title, but countries whose licence or contract covers all stages of exploration and production insert the same kind of approval procedure as a barrier between the exploration and development stages, often stipulating required development plan contents in considerable detail.[22] A company that cannot get approval for a development plan that it considers economically viable will have to walk away from the contract and write off its exploration expenditure.

4.   CONCLUSION

When we take these different developments together – the reservation of licence access to national or other privileged petroleum companies; the subordination of licences to PSAs or other risk service contracts; the appearance of parallel control systems like the United Kingdom's MER strategy; the potential freezing of licence activity by ever-stricter environmental standards; and the interposition into the development process of additional control mechanisms – the conclusion must surely be that the practical significance of holding a licence has changed dramatically since our 1981 analysis was offered. Alternative methods of offering acreage, such as the PSA, were introduced, and gained in popularity, largely because they offered the state the opportunity to exercise much closer control over all stages of petroleum exploration and production than was afforded by the traditional concession. But between then and now, the control opportunities provided by the licence regime changes I have analysed have moved such regimes further and further away from the concession relationship on which they were based, and have made it all but

---

[21]   Onshore US federal leases may provide an exception, but offshore lease arrangements now incorporate the requirement of a plan of development: Lowe, this volume, at pp. 63–66. Roggenkamp's chapter on the Netherlands offers an interesting example of a specific exception in the light of equivalent control arrangements: this volume, at p. 145.

[22]   See for example the list of minimum contents of a development plan contained in Annex 9 to the Mexican licence referred to at note 11 above, which extends to four pages.

impossible to distinguish the level of state control under most licence regimes from that available under most other regimes.

It is of course true that the licence may still possess certain legal character-istics that a PSA or other service contract may not – notably the proprietary character adverted to in several contributions to this volume – and that these may have some relevance, depending on the general constitutional and legal environment, to the protection of the licensee in extreme circumstances like revocation. Short of this, however, it is today difficult to see that the special promise offered by the licence, of property in petroleum once recovered, provides any greater assurance of ultimate reward than does the right to take petroleum at the delivery point, or to receive a cash payment, offered under a risk service contract. The same obstacles have to be surmounted on the way.

As for the future, we should not rule out the possibility of further changes in the licence relationship. The most radical innovation introduced by the United Kingdom's 2016 Energy Act and the MER strategy promulgated under it has been the obligation on licensees and others to direct their efforts to securing maximum economic recovery not just from their licence area, but from the United Kingdom's offshore territory as a whole, if necessary through collab-oration with other licensees. While not changing the legal appearance of the licence, this strikes at its nature as a purely bilateral contract between the licen-see and the government. Offshore licensees are now effectively conscripted as participants in a collective enterprise for the maximisation of United Kingdom offshore petroleum recovery, under the guidance, and if necessary direction, of the licensing authority. If we revisit this topic again, several decades hence, it will be interesting to see whether the challenge of exploiting dwindling hydrocarbon resources, or of facilitating the shift from carbon by producing only the most attractive petroleum deposits (whether judged by economic or environmental criteria), leads other countries down this path of collectivisation of the licence regime.

Index

access and operational licences 3–4
anti-trust/competition law 61, 130, 163
arbitration 88, 90–92, 94, 135, 229
Armour Group 105
Australia 1, 2, 16–50, 254, 255, 257
   Constitution 21, 31
      Commonwealth Parliament 23
      High Court of Australia 21–2
      judicial system 21
      rule of law 22
      s 51(xxix): external affairs
         power 24, 27, 29
      s 51(xxxi): just terms 19, 20,
         26, 33, 35, 38–9, 40,
         46, 47
      separation of powers 22
   environmental protection 19, 24–5,
      259
   federation 10, 21–2
      co-operative 23, 31
      powers of Commonwealth 23,
         24–5, 27–32
      powers of states 23–4, 25–6,
         27–32
      territorial sea 27–32
   High Court of Australia (HCA)
      21–3, 36, 50
      acquisition of property without
         just terms 26–7, 37–41,
         42–7, 49, 50
      continental shelf 29, 30
      exploration permit 37–41, 42–3,
         44–5, 46–7, 49
      leave to appeal 22
      retention licence 48, 260
      territorial sea 29–30
   legal character of petroleum titles
      49–50
   legal history and culture 9–10, 14,
      20–24
   offshore petroleum licences 257

continental shelf 29, 32, 39, 44,
   45–6, 47, 50
   development of 27–32
   exclusive economic zone 32, 44
   exploration permit 33, 36–41,
      42–3, 44–5, 46–7, 49
   personal property 35
   production licences 33, 39,
      41–7, 49–50
   property capable of acquisition:
      Commonwealth 33–49
   registration 44
   retention licences 33, 47–8, 50,
      260
   substance over form 36
   territorial sea 27–32, 44, 49, 50
onshore petroleum titles 24–7
   common law and statutory
      mineral lease 26–7
   environmental protection:
      EPBCA 24–5
   OPGGSA 28, 31, 32, 33, 35, 36, 41,
      44, 48
   s 780: acquisition of property
      not on just terms 33,
      48–9, 50
   public interest 22
Avila Camacho, Manuel 213–14

Bell, J 9
bilateral investment treaties 131, 135,
   229
BP/British Petroleum 11, 18, 19
Brexit 119–20, 122, 130

Calderon, Felipe 217–18
Calles, Plutarco Elias 210
Canada 1, 17, 72–94, 254, 255, 257
   boundaries of coastal provinces/
      territories 73
   continental shelf, extended 78–9

federalism 72–3, 75, 94
    intergovernmental agreements/
        accords 73–4, 87–8
    judicial review 74–5, 89–90, 93, 94
    legal system and character 9–10,
        72–6
    offshore area of Newfoundland and
        Labrador 76, 77, 87–8, 94
        calls for nominations and calls
            for bids 77–9
        exploration licence (EL) 77,
            79–81, 87, 93–4
        production licence (PL) 77,
            83, 94
        research and development
            88–92, 259
        significant discovery licence
            (SDL) 77, 80, 82–3,
            93–4, 260
    ownership of petroleum resources
        73, 75–6, 80
    petroleum licence 75–6, 92–4
        cancellation 84–7
        changes to regime over time
            87–92
        general rules 84
        legal character 92–4
        process for obtaining 76–84
    privately owned minerals 75–7
    Production Operations Authorization
        (POA) 89–90, 259
    profit à prendre 76, 92, 93–4
    research and development 88–92,
        259
    rule of capture 77
    rule of law 74
    United States-Mexico-Canada
        Agreement 53, 231–2
Canon law 6, 8
capture, rule of 54, 63, 64, 77
Cardenas, Lazaro 210, 211–13, 214,
    219–20, 226, 230, 231, 232
character, concept of legal 4–5
China 3, 11, 13–14, 15, 232, 234–52,
    255–6
    administrative system 234–9
        licensing: access conditions
            236–9
        management institutions 235–6
        property rights system 234–5

State-owned companies 236,
    255–6
    Belt and Road Initiative (OBOR)
        250–251
    foreign enterprises/investment
        236–9, 248–50, 251
    legal character of licences 243–8
        Belt and Road Initiative
            (OBOR) 250–251
        bidding, auction and listing
            244–5
        crude oil business licence
            system 245–6
        emerging legal system 251–2
        oil transportation licensing
            system 247
        other relevant operational
            licences 247–8
        refined oil business licence
            system 247
    licensing: regulatory framework 230
    licensing Sino-foreign joint venture:
        access conditions 236–9
        contractual cooperation 239
        exploration and mining licence
            237
        foreign investors: indirect
            control 239
        mergers and acquisitions 239
        offshore oil exploration 238
        onshore oil exploration 239
        overview 236–7
    oil and gas trial production licences
        243
    oil mining licences 241–2, 244
        rolling exploration and
            petroleum development
            242
    ownership of oil resources 238
    petroleum exploration licences
        240–241, 244
    state: participatory intervention 234
    time limits 241
China National Offshore Oil Corporation
    (CNOOC) 236, 244, 256
    cooperation with foreign companies
        237, 238
Uganda 95
China National Petroleum Corporation
    (CNPC) 236, 244, 246

cooperation with foreign companies
    237, 239
China Petrochemical Corporation
    (Sinopec) 236, 244, 256
    cooperation with foreign companies
        237, 239
climate change 184–5
colonialism 3, 208
competition/anti-trust law 61, 130, 163
concept of legal character 4–5
contract 5, 9–10, 11, 13, 254, 255, 256,
    257, 260, 261
    Australia 14, 16, 35
    Canada 10, 12, 92, 93, 257
    China 237, 238, 239, 242, 244
    economic balancing arrangements
        135
    Mexico 207, 209, 213–15, 217, 218,
        219, 220–222, 224–9, 230,
        231, 232–3, 257
    Netherlands 11, 12, 147, 148
    Norway 159, 160, 163, 166, 169,
        171, 172–3, 174, 175–83,
        184, 257
    Russia 197, 200–202, 205
    Uganda 12, 107, 114, 115, 117–18
    United Kingdom 11, 12, 132–6, 137,
        257–8, 261
    United States 10, 12, 61, 62, 64, 65,
        257
Convention on the Continental Shelf 29,
    142
Convention on the Law of the Sea 44, 47,
    142, 154
    continental shelf 78–9
    United States 53
Convention on the Prevention of Marine
    Pollution by Dumping of Wastes
    and Other Matter 142–3
Convention for the Protection of the
    Marine Environment of the
    North-East Atlantic (OSPAR
    Convention) 142, 154, 164
Convention on the Territorial Sea and
    Contiguous Zone 28–9, 142
corruption 215, 216, 228
Crommelin, M 17, 18, 26, 33–5, 36–7,
    39, 47, 49–50

Deepwater Horizon blow out and oil spill
    10, 60
Denmark 1, 257
dualism 124

earthquakes 153, 156–7
Energy Charter Treaty 131, 135
environmental protection 259, 260
    Australia 19, 24–5, 259
    Canada 80–81, 93
    China 242, 246, 247
    environmental impact assessments
        130, 242
    Netherlands 142–3, 148, 153, 154
    Norway 160, 164, 167, 177, 184–5
    Russia 198, 200
    strategic environmental assessments
        (SEAs) 80–81, 130
    Uganda 102, 110, 112–13, 115, 117
    United Kingdom 127, 129, 130, 258
    United States 52, 58, 60
Equinor (formerly Statoil) 2, 13, 19, 166,
    168, 170, 172
European Convention on Human Rights
    (ECHR) 122, 123, 143
    property rights 124, 143, 177, 183
European Economic Area (EEA) 163–4,
    171, 172, 176, 185
European Union 122, 141–2
    climate change 185
    competition law 130, 163
    Gas Market Directive 142, 163, 164,
        172
    Hydrocarbons Licensing Directive
        6, 11, 130–131, 142, 147,
        149, 150, 163, 164, 173, 174
    Offshore Safety Directive 163–4
    state aid 130, 163
Evensen, Jens 169–70
ExxonMobil 157

fair and equitable treatment standard 90
fracking 70, 259
France 7, 141
Friedman, L M 8

Gazprom 198, 199, 204, 205, 256
Grotius, Hugo 142

health and safety 58, 84, 87, 129, 142, 258
human rights
European Convention on (ECHR) 122, 123, 143
property rights 124, 143, 177, 183
hybridity 93, 132, 135, 148
Hydro Petroleum 172

Iceland 163
India 256
Indonesia 169
international investment arbitration 88, 90–92, 94, 135, 229
Isidor of Sevilla 7–8, 15

Kazakhstan 250, 251

legal character, concept of 4–5
legal culture approach 5–7
legal culture and petroleum licensing regimes 7–15
Lenin, V I 14
LetterOne 136
Liechtenstein 163
Lopez Obrador, Andres Manuel 226–8, 231, 232
Lopez Portillo, Jose 216, 217

maximum economic recovery (MER): UK strategy 2, 130, 131, 133–6, 137–8, 258, 260, 261
Mexico 3, 11, 13–14, 15, 207–33, 255, 257
first parallel regime: concessions 208–11, 229–30
1938 expropriation 211–14, 230, 232–3
1958–2013: PEMEX monopoly 214–18, 230
2013 Energy Reform 218–23, 230–231, 233
2018: 'make PEMEX great again' 226–9, 231
Cardenas 210, 211–13, 214, 219–20, 226, 230, 231, 232
decentralization 223
international arbitral tribunals 229

judicial review 228
Ministry of Energy 218, 222–5, 227, 231, 255
National Hydrocarbons Commission (CNH) 218, 223, 224–6, 228
rescind/cancel contracts 226, 228
nationalism 207, 208, 226, 227, 232, 233
ownership of resources 208–10, 213, 214–15, 222, 229–30, 231
PEMEX 212, 214–18, 219, 222–3, 224, 225, 226–9, 230–231, 232, 233, 255
profit-sharing agreements 220, 225, 230
United States-Mexico-Canada Agreement 53, 231–2
minimal intervention 6, 9–10, 14
monism 124
Montesquieu, Charles 8

NAFTA (North American Free Trade Agreement) 53, 90–92, 232
nationalization 211–18, 229, 230, 232–3, 244
Netherlands 3, 139–58
continental shelf 142, 143, 146–7, 148, 152, 155, 156, 157–8
earthquakes 153, 156–7
from concessions to licences 143–8
concessions 144–6, 147, 156
licences 146–8
immovable goods 155
joint ventures 150–151
joint operating agreement (JOA) 148, 150, 151
transfers 151
legal character of licence 147–8
legal culture of 10–11, 139–43
EU law 6, 141–2, 147, 149, 150
French legal tradition 7, 141
international law 142–3, 154
licensing regime
2003 Mining Act 141, 143–4, 147, 148–9, 150–151, 153–4, 155, 156
award of licence 149–51
conditions attached to licence 152–4

disused installations 154
duty of care 153
exploration licences 147, 148,
    149–50, 152, 154–5, 158
financial obligations 154
geothermal heat licences 148–9
Minister of Economic Affairs
    and Climate 150–151,
    152
pipelines 149
production licences 147, 148,
    149–50, 151, 152, 154,
    155
production plans 153–4
rights conferred 154–6
storage licences 148–9
time limits 150, 152, 153
non-discrimination 149
ownership
    of installation and land 155–6
    of subsoil resources 144–5,
        147, 155
Parliament sovereignty 11
State participation 14, 145–6, 151
    agreement of cooperation 145,
        148
New Public Management 166
non-discrimination 131, 149, 163, 172,
    173
North American Free Trade Agreement
    (NAFTA) 53, 90–92, 232
Northern Ireland 120, 121–2, 124, 125
Norway 1, 6, 7, 159–85, 195, 254, 255,
    257
    award of licences 172–4
        accounting agreement 174, 184
        discretionary administrative
            decision 174
        groups of companies 173–4
        joint venture agreement 174,
            176, 184
    continental shelf 164, 167, 168, 179,
        183–4
    development of petroleum
        regulation
        award of licences 172–4
        background 165–8
        conditions for production
            licences 175

foreign companies: subsidiary
    in Norway 171
joint operating agreements 170,
    171–2, 172, 174
legal framework and licence
    system 168–72
productions licences 170–171,
    172, 175
report by Jens Evensen (1971)
    169–70
research and development 171
White Paper 1971: principles
    for oil policy 167
dynamic development of licences
    183–4
legal character of production licence
    160–161, 175–83, 184
    fishing quotas and time limits
        182–3
    taxation 177, 179–81
legal and political system 11, 13, 14,
    15, 161–5
    administrative cases 164–5
    EEA Agreement 163–4, 171,
        172, 176
    international law 164
non-discrimination 163, 172, 173
public interest 177, 182, 183
research and development 171
retroactivity 178–9, 182–3
state participation 13, 171, 173, 174,
    176
    participatory intervention 170
    Petoro AS 13, 172, 184
    Statoil (later Equinor) 2, 13, 19,
        166, 168, 170, 172
taxation 177, 179–81
time limits 174, 175, 178–9, 182–3

OPEC (Organization of the Petroleum
    Exporting Countries) 216, 253
operational and access licences 3–4
Oranto 105
overview of petroleum licensing regimes
    12

participatory intervention 6, 9, 11,
    13–14, 15

PEMEX 212, 214–18, 219, 222–3, 224, 225, 226–9, 230–231, 232, 233, 255
Peña Nieto, Enrique 219–20, 227, 231
Petoro AS 13, 172, 184
precedent/*stare decisis* 10, 11, 13
    Australia 10, 21
    Russia 191–2, 202
privatization 13, 166, 172
production sharing agreements (PSAs) 169, 255–6, 258, 260, 261
    China 256
    India 256
    Mexico 220, 222, 225, 230, 255
    Russia 195, 196, 197, 206, 255, 256
    Uganda 95, 101, 117, 256
profit à prendre 17, 41, 63–4, 76, 92, 93–4, 108
profit-sharing agreements 220, 225, 230

regulatory intervention 6, 9, 10–11, 14
research and development
    Canada 88–92, 259
    Norway 171
risk management, systematic 153
risk service contracts 255, 260, 261
Roosevelt, Franklin D 211, 212
Rosneft 199, 204, 205, 256
Ruiz Cortines, Adolfo 214
rule of capture 54, 63, 64, 77
Russia 3, 186–206, 255–6
    accessing petroleum resources 195–9
        company requirements 199
        licensing regime 197–8, 206
        process for granting licence 196–8
        production sharing agreements regime 195, 196, 197, 206, 256
    assessment of licence rights and licensing regime 206
    alteration of licensing regime over time 206
    disposal, transfer and acquisition 203–4
    licence grantor and licensee 204
    revocation of licence by State 204
    third parties to licence 205

China 251
continental shelf 193–4, 195–6, 197, 198, 199, 204, 206
Federal Agency for Subsoil Use (Rosnedra) 198, 203, 204
federal state 186, 198
foreign investors 205
Gazprom 198, 199, 204, 205, 256
judicial precedent 191–2, 202
legal character of licence/concession 200–203
legal culture 11, 13–14, 15, 187–92
    administrative law 190
    judiciary 191–2
    separation of powers 188–90
national security and licensing regime 192–4, 206
Reserve Fund 194
rights conferred by production licence 199–200
Rosneft 199, 204, 205, 256
sanctions 193
territorial sea 194, 195–6, 197
time limits 200
Zarubezhneft 199, 205

Saga Petroleum 172
Scotland 120–123, 124, 125, 128
shale gas 125, 128, 132, 241
Shell 11, 18, 157, 211
Singapore 250–251
stare decisis/precedent 10, 11, 13
    Australia 10, 21
    Russia 191–2, 202
state aid 130, 163
state participation agreements 256
    Netherlands 145, 148
    Norway 170
state sovereignty over natural resources: UN Resolution 1803 24
Statoil (later Equinor) 2, 13, 19, 166, 168, 170, 172
strategic environmental assessments (SEAs) 80–81, 130

taxation 2, 222, 229
    China 238
    Mexico 15, 209, 210, 212, 224, 229
    Norway 177, 179–81

terra nullius 20
Total 95
trade agreements
    investment protection provisions
        229
trade unions 164, 211, 212, 215, 216
transplants, legal 6–7
Tullow Oil 95

Uganda 3, 95–118, 255, 256
    downstream sector 103, 115–17
        time limits 116
    legal character
        compulsory acquisition of land
            100–101
        of jurisdiction 11, 96–8
        ownership of petroleum
            resources 99–100
        of petroleum industry 99–103
        rule of law 98
        separation of powers 97
    midstream sector 103, 114–15
        time limits 115
    petroleum licences, process for
        obtaining 103–17
        downstream sector 103, 115–17
        midstream sector 103, 114–15
        upstream sector 103, 104–14
    upstream sector 104–14
        annual production permit 108,
            109–10
        cancellation of licence 111–12
        dealings with licences 110–114
        decommissioning and
            rehabilitation 110, 112
        exploration licence 95, 103,
            105–7, 108–9, 111, 113,
            118
        facility licence 107–8
        force majeure 113–14
        permit to drill 107
        petroleum production licence
            95, 102, 103, 106,
            108–9, 111, 113
        reconnaissance permit 104
        security for fulfilment of
            obligations 113
        strict liability 112
        time limits 104, 106, 108–9,
            111

    transfer of licences 110–111
United Arab Emirates 250
United Kingdom 1, 6, 14, 119–38, 167,
        254, 255, 257–8, 259–60
    Brexit 119–20, 122, 130
    continental shelf 124, 133
    Department for Business Energy and
        Industrial Strategy or BEIS
        125–6
    England 120, 121, 124, 128
    grant of licences
        allocation method 127
        Crown Estate 127–8
        exploration licence 126
        offshore 125–8
        onshore 126, 128
        production licence 126–7, 128
        special conditions 128–30
        supranational laws 130–131
        term structure 129
    Innovate Licence 137–8
    judicial review 123, 132
    legal character of licence 132–6
    legal culture of 10, 11, 119–25
        dualism 124
        judicial review 123
        rule of law 123
        separation of powers 123
        uncodified constitution 124
    maximum economic recovery
        (MER) 2, 130, 131, 133–6,
        137–8, 258, 260, 261
    Mexico 212
    national security 131
    non-discrimination 131
    Northern Ireland 120, 121–2, 124,
        125
    Oil and Gas Authority (OGA)
        125–6, 128, 131, 132, 133,
        137
        decommissioning 133–6
        enforcement 134–6
        licence data 136
        transfer of licences 136
    Parliament sovereignty 10, 11
    Petroleum and Submarine Pipe-lines
        Act 1975 258
    renewables 124, 125
    rights conferred by licence 136
    Scotland 120–122, 124, 125

licensing within onshore area
122–3, 128
Sewell Convention 122
shale gas 125, 128
Wales 120, 121–2, 128
United Nations
state sovereignty over natural
resources 24
United States 3, 15, 17, 37, 51–71, 255
aliens 59
anti-trust law 61
citizenship 59
coastal states: submerged lands 55,
57
Constitution 51
powers of federal government
and states 51–2
property rights 51
Supremacy Clause 52
continental shelf, outer 57, 68
environment 52, 58, 60
impact statement 60
exclusive economic zone 53, 57
federalism 51–2
co-operative 52
environmental laws 52
fiduciary relationship 56
government leases 67–8, 69, 71
federal 56–61, 64–7, 68–9,
70–71, 257
Indian 56, 64–5, 66–7, 68, 70,
71
lease term 64, 65, 66, 68, 69
offshore federal 59–61, 66,
68–9, 70, 257
onshore federal 57–9, 64, 65,
68–9, 70, 257
penalties 67
rights created by 64–7
royalties 64, 65, 66–9, 70–71

rule of capture 64
state 55–6, 64–5
legal character
of jurisdiction 9–10, 51–3
of lease rights and leasing
regime 67–71
Mexico 208, 211, 212
petroleum licence
process for obtaining 53–61
rights created by 61–7
privately owned mineral rights 53–5,
67, 68, 69–70, 71, 254
fractionalization of mineral
rights 54, 55
implied covenants 62
inchoate right 63
lease term 62, 69
litigation 63, 68
marketable-product rule 63
real property ownership 63,
65, 68
rights created by leases 61–4
royalties 62–3, 70
rule of capture 54, 63
public interest 67–8
rule of capture 54, 63, 64
rule of law 51
separation of powers 52
United States-Mexico-Canada
Agreement (USMCA) 53, 231–2
universal law 6
Uzbekistan 250

World Trade Organization (WTO) 251
World War II 212

Xi Jinping 249

Zarubezhneft 199, 205